THAT WHICH I FEAR

THAT WHICH I FEAR

*Understanding the truth about fear
and its detriments to the life of a Christian*

THE COMPROMISED CHRISTIAN SERIES

PRESTON NOTON

XULON PRESS

Xulon Press
2301 Lucien Way #415
Maitland, FL 32751
407.339.4217
www.xulonpress.com

Unless otherwise indicated, Scripture quotations taken from the King
James Version (KJV) – *public domain.*

Paperback ISBN-13: 978-1-6628-0516-5

Ebook ISBN-13: 978-1-6628-0517-2

FROM YOUR DAD'S HEART

THIS BOOK I DEDICATE TO MY PRECIOUS DAUGHTER Sky and her wonderful husband Jared.

May you both be richly blessed as you read this book and hold dear the works of our Lord in your life.

Passing our scriptural understanding and God given knowledge down to our children is of such great importance and a responsibility that cannot be neglected.

I believe that the content of this book is one such topic that we as Christians should be strongly grounded in especially in the turbulent times we are now facing.

You have now begun your own family and the children that you produce will face even worse times as prophetically presented in scripture and it is your task to ensure they are great in faith.

The Word of God reveals to us that as parents, pursuing the knowledge of God's treasures will result in our children being remembered by the Lord and blessed in His ways.

Be mindful of this, hold fast the faith and be mightily encouraged.

Psalm 128

Hosea 4:6

Love

Dad

TABLE OF CONTENTS

NOTICE

THIS BOOK IS NOT FOR THOSE WHO WANT THEIR itching ears tickled, or for those who are happy to have their sin justified by todays many apostate teachers and preachers. This book is for the Christian who appreciates truth regardless of how uncomfortable it might be to read and accept.

preach the word; be instant in season, out of season;
reprove, rebuke, exhort with all longsuffering and doctrine.
For the time will come when they will not endure sound doctrine;
but after their own lusts shall they heap to themselves teachers,
having itching ears;
and they shall turn away *their* ears from the truth,
and shall be turned unto fables.
(2 Timothy 4:2-4)

What I have written is based upon the experiences that I have had and the scriptures which have backed up my experiences over these many years in service to our Lord.

How to use this book as a study guide

You will find at the end of each chapter a "Key Statement" which is important to consider. At the end of the book the "Key Statements" are combined to form the summary of the entire topic of this book.

If studying in a group setting then each Key Statement can be considered for open discussion.

CHAPTER 1

THE TRUTH ABOUT FEAR

SUBTLE LIES

I SUPPOSE THE TIPPING POINT FOR ME ON DECIDING to write a book on this specific topic "that which I fear" was instigated one morning in the form of an email. The email was a daily devotional which I had signed up for online. As I read, the content seemed pretty sound and as with all scripture related teachings which I seek for as "my daily bread" I was in anticipation of the reward of revelatory wisdom which I was hoping to glean for the day ahead, and there it was. Instead of celebrating the words I found myself as deflated as a fisherman who had just experienced the rush and excitement of hooking into a whopper only to lose the fish before landing it, or at least even seeing it.

I was angered, it sparked a thought for me in that moment, "How do I protect my children from falling victim to the false and deceptive teachings offered by so many in this dark age of Christian compromise and apostasy"? I thought, if it is this bad now then what on earth will it be like in twenty years from now?

How do I help protect them from the terrible watered-down compromising Christianity that abounds so freely today? The emergent church is happening right before our very eyes and oh so many have already been swallowed up by its devilish and deceptive darkness.

When receiving this email, I decided that I must write and I must not stop writing until I have penned enough to help protect not only my children from falling away into the soup of this end-times apathy and apostasy but to leave to my Grandchildren and even their children something which might in a time of desperation pull them back to the supernatural reality of a pure faith in our Lord Jesus Christ.

So, what was it that had me so riled up about the content of this email? It was five simple words – "fear is not a sin", this was supported by a wishy, washy reasoning as to why fear in a believer's life is no big deal and went on to say – "is actually healthy".

I could not believe what I was reading. Being that this email was one of those daily devotional types sent out by a well-known American ministry to hundreds of thousands across North America and whose leader is the author of several books aimed towards the spiritual well-being of men.

After pondering this over for a few days, I thought it crucial to set the record straight on the power and devastation of fear in the believer's life and that of the church in general, and if my writings are never read by another soul outside of my family then at least for the sake of my children I have not kept silent.

I believe this topic is of such great importance at this time, and as far as having earned the right to teach on this subject I will state that I am in no way a stranger to the sickness of anxiety, stress and fear, as this is an evil of which I have past endured and suffered with for the greater part of my life.

Furthermore, from my experience over the many years of biblically counseling others I have found that so many of us Christians have yet to receive a firm understanding and revelation of the spiritual defilement, physical repercussions and eternal judgement of not dealing with and defeating the sickness of fear which so often manages to raise its ugly head to overwhelm us during our times of weakness.

One of the problems that we are facing in the church today is a very troubling one indeed in that for the most part, the books that we do come across on this topic are more often than not only emphasising that "not struggling with fear" is a "nice to have" instead of outlining the issue in all of its ugliness in the light of it being an abominable sin and as Jesus describes it, "a perverseness".

Only recently since the outbreak of the worldwide Coronavirus pandemic are we witnessing an abundance of these books and commentaries coming out of the woodwork, this book however has been in the making for the past five years and is not something that was just suddenly whipped together in a moment to capitalize on the Christian community.

I have found that instead of these books truly warning Christians of the seriousness of fear and how grieving it is to God, the majority of them offer an un-God-fearing approach to the issues of fear in a believer's life, this is not the God ordained approach to dealing with such sin.

Hopefully this book will open the eyes of the reader on this subject and expose the truth about fear once and for all.

This book will:

1. Expose fear for what it really is.
2. Expose that it is alien to the design of mankind.
3. Expose its diabolical intentions on mankind.
4. Highlight the repercussions of the individual acting out in fear.
5. Highlight the repercussions of the individual speaking out in fear.
6. Provide an everyday and long-term strategy for destroying it in the family line.

But first, to bring home the reality of the sin of fear I must first go to where the revelation of this evil first became a spiritual reality of understanding to me personally.

SPIRITUAL REALITY

When I first invited Christ into my life, I came across the scriptures in 1 Corinthians 12 which presents the gifts of the Holy Spirit to "all who believe". I was drawn to the gift of "discerning of spirits" and thought to myself, wow, if one could discern spirits then one would have the upper hand on the enemy. This I believed would be very beneficial to me as a husband and father of three small children.

I became even more excited when coming across the verse penned by Paul which states that we are to covet the gifts.

> But covet earnestly the best gifts
> (1 Corinthians 12:31)

And so, I prayed and prayed for the gift of the discerning of spirits. Once I had received this gift the Lord started opening the doors for me to minister into the lives of others. God had set me free from so much demonic bondage in the first two years of knowing Him. He then pointed me to a scripture in the book of Matthew.

> Freely ye have received, freely give.
> (Matthew 10:8)

This scripture immediately inspired me in a ministry to others. This was when we still lived in South Africa before immigrating to Canada in 2000. God threw me into the deep end even though I had only been a Christian for three years; it was such an exciting time.

One incident of which is related to our topic happened on a typical South African summer's morning when I paid Piet and his family a planned visit back in the summer of 1999.

At that time, we lived in the Gauteng province (previously known as the Transvaal province) in the town of Vereeniging which is just an hour's drive south of Johannesburg.

Vereeniging is one of three large towns in what is known as the Vaal triangle, three towns which form a triangle in which the Vaal River runs through.

It was Friday morning on the 15th January when I arrived at Piet's house on that lovely summer morning, I was warmly welcomed by Piet at the front door. Piet invited me in and I entered the living room where I was then greeted by the smiling faces of his three teenage sons and his wife.

As Piet took his seat to the left of me, I stood conversing with his wife who was seated across the room and their sons sat on the couch to the right of me. After the pleasantries of greetings, I turned and looked at Piet and immediately saw a spirit of fear which had a hold of Piet's heart. I had not experienced such a thing before, but I knew I had to speak up.

I said, "Piet, you have a spirit of fear which has a tight hold of your heart and the Holy Spirit is showing me that it is going to result in a heart attack if you don't get rid of it".

Piet then replied, "Preston, I've had two heart attacks already".

This I did not know about Piet but replied to him that I am seeing the next heart attack is going to end his life.

> And there shall be signs in the sun, and in the moon,
> and in the stars;
> and upon the earth distress of nations, with perplexity;
> the sea and the waves roaring;
> men's hearts failing them for fear,
> and for looking after those things
> which are coming on the earth:
> (Luke 21: 25-26)

Now obviously not all heart attacks are caused by fear, however an endless number of clinical and psychological studies over the past decades have proven the link between fear, anxiety, stress and heart disease and heart attack.

The American Institute of stress has this to say about this relationship.

> *"The relationship between stress, heart disease and sudden death has been recognized since antiquity. The incidence of heart attacks and sudden death have been shown to increase significantly following the acute stress of natural disasters like hurricanes, earthquakes and tsunamis and as a consequence of any severe stressor that evokes "fight or flight' responses. Coronary heart disease is also much more common in individuals subjected to chronic stress and recent research has focused on how to identify and prevent this growing problem, particularly with respect to job stress".* [1]

It is pretty clear from this public statement that stress is a killer, we also know that stress has its root in fear. It is also now public knowledge that heart disease is the worlds leading cause of death today and has been for at least the last fifteen years.

According to the World Health Organization a whopping 15 million deaths due to heart disease alone were realized in 2016 which was more than double that of any other cause of death on the planet besides stroke which was the second leading cause of death worldwide. [2]

Anxiety disorders are now more than double than that of subsequent years in many countries across the globe and in some countries more than triple in the last decade alone.

In an in-depth study conducted by leading scientists in China in June of 2016 called "Meta-analysis of the prevalence of anxiety disorders in mainland China from 2000 to 2015", the introduction opens: [3]

> *"The 21st century is the age of anxiety. Anxiety disorders (ADs, equivalent to 'any AD'), as severe mental disorders with a high prevalence and inheritance, are characterized by feelings of anxiety (worries about the future) and fear (worries about the present) that can simultaneously cause physical symptoms such as increased blood pressure, quickened respiration and tightness of the chest".*

The trends in this research reveal that anxiety amongst the overall populace has more than tripled since 2011 and the interesting thing about this trend in China is that the analysis confirmed a 'similar rate in urban versus rural areas, one would think that the peace of the countryside would show a far lower trend even in a poor economy, but China has been thriving for a number of years now.

In the USA anxiety levels have skyrocketed. The Anxiety and Depression Association of America states that *"Anxiety disorders are the most common mental illness in the US today, affecting 40 million adults in the United States age 18 and older, or 18.1% of the population every year".*[4]

Another alarming trend can be found in the U.S Military. On Monday 4th November back in 2013 the Pentagon confirmed the rate of reported anxiety disorders among U.S. troops to have jumped 327% between 2000 and 2012.[5]

An article posted in the "World Economic Forum" in January 2019 stated the following:

> *"The early years of the 21st century have witnessed a worldwide epidemic of poor mental health and related illnesses. But while depression is the condition most will associate with mental health issues, and the leading cause of disability worldwide, it is not the number one mental health concern people face. That unwanted accolade goes to anxiety".*

The article further states that by 2030, the cost to the global economy of all mental health problems could amount to $16 trillion. [6]

And back in my own home country of South Africa, fear and dread is just a normal part of everyday life as one navigates the ongoing common place brutal murders and rape, moral decline and the horrendous governmental corruption which has plagued the nation for the past twenty plus years.

In relation to fear, we are in the most turbulent times of our existence and the kingdom of darkness is not wavering in capitalizing in the misery of mankind. However, we might think that things are really bad in the world at present, but we have seen nothing yet, the worst is still to come.

> For then there will be great tribulation,
> such as has not been since the beginning of the world until this time,
> no, nor ever shall be.
> (Matthew 24:21)

And if the world population is manifesting such fear as is revealed in all these studies then what will it look like when it really gets bad.

Up from the Rabbit hole and getting back to Piet, I went on to inform him that if he was willing to repent of the sin of fear then God would set him free from that evil spirit immediately. Piet agreed and humbly submitted himself to God.

I took Piet through a simple prayer of repentance and then commanded the unclean spirit to depart from him. What happened next had his family all amazed. Piet turned as red as a tomato and started shaking violently and sweating at the same time. After about a minute with what seemed like a great release Piet suddenly gave a dramatic short, sharp groan and the spirit came out of him. His colour immediately returned to normal and he felt great.

Piet went on to explain to me afterwards that he could actually feel the physical sensation of something loosening from around what felt like his heart.

The family needed no convincing that what dad had just been set free from was a demonic spirit, this was due partly to the fact that I had spent some time with the family working with their eighteen-year-old son who had been caught up in a satanic coven whilst living away from home in the city of Pretoria.

On the son's return home, the family was suddenly plunged into some very scary paranormal activity on a nightly occurrence. They were all so deeply afraid of what was taking place in their home and they knew that somehow it was related to their son as he had become a very different person to the one they had known before he left home.

He eventually owned up to his parents as to what he had been involved in and that the paranormal or rather demonic activities now harassing the entire family was related to his satanic ritualistic involvement back in Pretoria. At this point Piet had no choice but to seek for some help.

Piet reached out to some friends, one of which having heard of my "deliverance ministry" and help in the community thought that I could be of some assistance.

Before we move on any further however, I would like to bring a little clarity to the use of the term "deliverance ministry" (in the Catholic world the word used is exorcism). In protestant churches the term deliverance is used to describe the administering of freedom from the demonic, however I do not believe that this terminology is correct when describing it as a ministry for as the Word of God clearly shows us everyone who believes should be walking in this authority or ministry over evil spirits and not just a select few, but I will continue to use this term throughout the remainder of this book for the sake of those unfamiliar with the spiritual authority that every believer possesses.

I'm not going to elaborate on the deliverance of his son now although I will say that the demonic manifestations witnessed by his family when I challenged the evil spirits which had entered him through his satanic ritual involvements shook their religious world to the core. For parents to witness their child's facial skin instantaneously manifest multiple blotches, facial contortion and eyes glazing over and then to hear a gruff voice speaking a demonic language from his mouth in a stance of challenging me made the hair stand up on the back of their necks.

By this witness they had no problem understanding that one can be spiritually defiled by an unclean spirit through sin. Today this family are free from all religiosity and gratefully serving Jesus in the Spirit of liberty and truth as born-again believers, praise God.

For many Christians reading what has been written here would cause concern, disbelief, and in some cases, downright shock.

The sentences regarding fear being a demonic spirit living on the inside of a Christian's flesh and being the cause of a heart attack might be hard to wrap one's thinking around. However, the Word of God is more than proficient to bring clarity to these issues and in a later chapter I will present the Biblical evidence of the fact that a Christian can indeed suffer the indwelling of an unclean spirit.

A person's heart can fail, can permanently stop, can die, it is a heart attack caused by a fear attack.

> men's hearts failing them for fear,
> (Luke 21: 26)

Dr. John Burnet of "Discover the book ministries" when expounding on this scripture quotes it like this', he reveals the word for the heart "failing" as quite descriptive in the Greek, it is the word *"apopsucho"* which means *"to breathe out life"* which is from the root words *"apo"* and *"psyxo"* meaning "separate from", "the vital breath", "the human soul". He states– *"it speaks of the nonmaterial part of us, the spirit leaves the person, they die of fright, they die from fear".* [7]

A spirit of fear is the culprit, it is an intelligent "being" which has the ability to afflict.

> For God hath not given us the spirit of fear;
> but of power, and of love, and of a sound mind.
> (2 Timothy 1:7)

What is kind of crazy is that the Christians who do not believe that unclean spirits can influence a believer's life and who will use and even twist scriptures to prove otherwise are the very same Christians who cannot explain how a believer can get ill or deathly sick even though

Christ took our infirmities upon Himself (Matt 8:17), such believers will often quote 2 Corinthians 5:17 which states:

> Therefore if any man *be* in Christ, *he is* a new creature:
> old things are passed away; behold, all things are become new.

Yet, throughout the New Testament we find so many examples of unclean spirits being directly related to sickness and disease.

So, what now? Do Christians only contract sicknesses and diseases that are not related to unclean spirits, most certainly not in my experience?

I have met many Christians who love to misquote this scripture above, they will state that the moment a person becomes a Christian, he or she is absolutely perfect (a new creature) and can sit back and relax, they are on their way to heaven. These Christians will twist this scripture to justify their perfection and are the most outspoken against the deliverance ministry, even though we Christians are commanded to cleanse ourselves from all filthiness of the flesh and of the "spirit" (2 Corinthians 7:1), now why on earth would we be commanded to cleanse ourselves if we are already perfect, it doesn't make any sense at all.

They also have no reason to believe that we as Christians are to confess our sins one to another (James 5:16), or any reason to believe the Apostle Paul's sorrow at the plague of sin abounding amongst the Corinthian Christians.

The Word expressly highlights and warns Christians repeatedly that satan and his demonic forces will try and afflict us in every way possible.

> Be sober, be vigilant; because your adversary the devil, as a roaring
> lion, walketh about, seeking whom he may devour:
> (1 Peter 5:8)

For we wrestle not against flesh and blood, but against principalities, against powers, against the rulers of the darkness of this world,

against spiritual wickedness in high places.
(Ephesians 6:12)

And here we as Christians are commanded to submit ourselves to God and resist the devil, why? So that he will flee from you and I the Christian. How can a devil flee from a Christian if a devil is not on, against, in or oppressing the Christian in the first place?

Submit yourselves therefore to God.
Resist the devil, and he will flee from you.
(James 4:7)

Please read these scriptures carefully, they are warning instructions to Christians not to sinners. I recently watched a gentleman on tv who has a ministry in Texas, USA with quite the anointing to heal, he has stated on a number of occasions that Christians cannot have an unclean spirit working on the inside of them, however you will see him praying for non believers and Christians alike for pains or sicknesses within their bodies and rebuke a spirit of infirmity. I would ask such a minister, which is it, make up your mind?

and the diseases departed from them,
and the evil spirits went out of them.
(Acts 19:12)

Such false statements would completely negate the whole lifelong ministry of teachers like Derek Prince and Lester Sumrall who have been used of God to set free many hundreds of thousands of Christians who have fallen captive to the devil and who this particular gentleman cannot even come close to comparing himself too.

I remember on one occasion when living in South Africa, I was teaching a group of work colleagues who were all Christians regarding the demonic infiltration into a particular stream of churches in the USA. The churches manifest a phenomenon whereby an uncontrollable stupor comes over the entire congregation, pastor and leaders during the services. The flicking of the tongue like a snake manifests in the minister along with a hissing and many others slide down from off their seats in a serpentine like manner.

I told my friends that I have some video footage of these events to which they all urged me to see and so we set up a time and gathered one lunch time at work. Now one of the group members was an avid follower of this ministry in question and he would not stop defending it and wanted to see the footage to further rebuke our concern toward it.

So, there we all sat watching the content when suddenly this brother "in the Lord" started to manifest a spirit. His eyes glazed over, and he went into the same foolish state as those manifesting on the television. He could not talk properly, and his face was contorted with a sickening smirk; he was so out of sorts and we were just not able to connect with him. We stopped playing the footage and began to minister to him, but he was having none of it. Today this spirit has swept across the USA in a troubling manner and multitudes have invited it into their lives because of a lack of discernment.

We must always be aware that satan is well set up to guide the believer away from his existence, presence or residence in our lives and it comes as no big surprise that such facts would be difficult to digest by the general Christian populace when considering the terrible apathetic and compromising state that the modern-day church is in.

It is also not surprizing then that the subject of fear in the life of a believer would be looked upon as no big deal as well, and in so many churches not even a consideration.

The Supernatural faith of a believer cannot grow without that faith being tested in action and it is fear which destroys the action part of our walk with Christ. It is for this reason we see that Supernatural faith in the believer's life either diminishes over a period of time or never even launches to begin with. Its like having a powerful race car but the owner is too afraid to get in and drive it.

The late Reverend David Wilkerson best known for his authorship of the *"Cross and the switchblade"* stated he believed that fear is one of the most powerful weapons against God's children. [8]

In his sermon "Overcoming the spirit of fear" he speaks about the coming flood of satan's onslaught against the remnant of God's children in these last days.

He quotes prophetic scripture with regards to the end times, the book of Isaiah stating:

> When the enemy shall come in like a flood,
> the Spirit of the Lord
> shall lift up a standard against him.
> (Isaiah 59:19)

The enemy of our souls shall come in like a terrible flood in the end times. This flood is a flood of evil with its intent being the destruction of God's people and disarming them of faith and of all Supernatural power.

This flood of evil against the church will result in the apostasy and the result of the apostasy is the falling away from the faith.

> Now the Spirit speaketh expressly,
> that in the latter times some shall depart from the faith,
> giving heed to seducing spirits, and doctrines of devils.
> (1 Timothy 4:1)

The object is faith, or rather a departing from true Biblical faith. The scripture further reveals that seducing spirits will accomplish this through divisive devilish doctrines that have somehow infiltrated the mainstream church.

This scripture is a warning to all Christians, for it is not possible to fall away from something you do not have. In order to fall away from something, one has to be a part of it in the first place. This scripture speaks of

Christians who fall away from pure Biblical Christianity, Christians who "depart from the faith".

It is when true Biblical faith is so watered down or even absent for so many Christians that the spirit of fear will have its heyday.

David Wilkerson goes on to explain:

> Fear, and the pit, and the snare, are upon thee,
> O inhabitant of the earth.
> And it shall come to pass,
> that he who fleeth from the noise of the fear shall fall into the pit;
> and he that cometh up out of the midst of the pit shall be taken in
> the snare:
> (Isaiah 24:17-18)

To flea from something means you have to first be intimidated by it to begin with, intimidation then opens the door to fear.

David Wilkinson explains the Hebrew meanings of these words in this above scripture as follows:

Fear – finding oneself in a prison of fear.
Pit – finding oneself in the pit of despair.
Snare – feeling of being trapped.

He highlights that this scripture is saying that those who's faith is weak will succumb to fear; they will become imprisoned by this fear. The prison is a pit of despair and even if they escape the pit, they will be taken in the snare of feeling trapped simply because they have not completely dealt with the fear.

It will become a vicious cycle, one of which can only be broken by a revelation of trust and faith in God our Almighty Father through our Lord, Saviour and friend Jesus Christ.

Now I ask you reader to carefully think about this for a moment, for satan to even think that he stands a chance against God's children by using the weapon of fear would mean that he has gained his confidence somehow to believe that this weapon would even work, otherwise why waste his time and effort.

I offer that his great confidence will be found in the fact that he has by this time done such a remarkable job of destroying the faith levels within the modern-day church to have any chance of accomplishing this fete.

Jesus himself stated this concern.

> Nevertheless when the Son of man cometh,
> shall he find faith on the earth?
> (Luke 18:8)

Not being firmly grounded in one's faith is obviously a big problem. It means that when fear comes along it seems more intimidating than it should be, it then has more influence over the believer than it should have, fear wins over faith in the believer who in such a moment becomes an unbeliever.

The problem with the manifestation of fear is that it is not even a reaction of the flesh or even a normal trait of mankind which we will discover in the coming chapters.

Scripture has enlightened us to the fact that fear is a spirit, and it is not a heavenly and or holy spirit. It is a real entity, an intelligent being, a demonic spirit which is assigned by satan against Christians to destroy their faith and render them useless for God's kingdom work in the Spirit.

Simply put, fear is in direct opposition to faith; it is an opposing spirit to the Holy Spirit of Power, the Holy Spirit of Love, and the Holy Spirit of complete soundness of mind and God did not give it to us.

> For God hath not given us the spirit of fear;
> (2 Timothy 1:7)

In Conclusion, the Bible clearly shows us that not only is fear a demonic spirit assigned by satan to destroy our faith but according to the word of God, as we shall discover in the following chapter, is absolute wickedness worthy of Hell with no exceptions and over the next few pages we will discover in a little more detail as to why God places fear in the same sentence of judgement alongside the abominable and why we are to wage an all-out war on it.

KEY STATEMENT 1: Scripture has enlightened us to the fact that fear is a spirit, and it is not a heavenly and holy spirit. It is a real entity, an intelligent being, a demonic spirit which is assigned by satan against Christians to destroy their faith and render them useless for God's kingdom work in the Supernatural.

THE ABOMINATION OF FEAR

But the fearful, and unbelieving,
and the abominable, and murderers, and whoremongers,
and sorcerers, and idolaters, and all liars,
shall have their part in the lake which burneth with fire and brimstone:
which is the second death.
(Revelation 21:8)

Most Christians never think of general or common fear as being much of a sin but here it is in all its glory on God's list of abominations.

An even bigger eye opener is that the fearful are mentioned first and foremost before all the other dregs of humanity. Wow, if this does not bring it home and into perspective then nothing will.

You would think that based upon this scripture alone, we would be hearing so much more teaching on this subject, especially with the fact that fear is in direct opposition to the building of a believer's faith.

Please notice that this scripture of judgement does not end with the exclusion or exemption of Christians that manifest fear and unbelief of whom there are oh so very many.

Being that fear and anxiety was so personal to me, when I discovered this scripture, I wasted no time in entering into a study of the word fearful, and here's what I found.

The word fearful in this verse is the Greek word "deilos" from the root "deos", meaning 'dread, timid, faithless and fearful. Jesus uses this same word when rebuking his disciples in Matthew 8:26 and Mark 4:40 with regards to their storm buffeted boat journey in which they thought they were going to die.

In other words, in that moment their true colours were manifested, and they fell into the category of those found in the judgement alongside the abominable, the liars, whoremongers and sorcerers. Jesus was saying to them "you timid and faithless disciples".

For God hath not given us the spirit of fear;

In this scripture the Greek word for fear is *"deilía" (from deilos) which means* timidity, fearfulness and cowardice and/or a lack of courage. It is never used in a good sense anywhere in the Bible. The context of this scripture is Paul encouraging Timothy to press on and forward in the Gospel.

Now when we combine the Greek words *"deilía and deilós"* we now have a picture of timidity, fearfulness, cowardice and faithlessness.

In other words, Fear and faithlessness are completely related; they are one of a kind and they walk hand in hand. A faithless person is a fearful person, and a fearful person is a faithless person. Jesus equates faithlessness to perversity in Matthew 17:17

Then Jesus answered and said,
O faithless and perverse generation,

Again, is it not the case then that if a long-standing professing Christian lives in fear then according to scripture such a person is classed as faithless, which then qualifies such a person as an unbelieving person, which would also in turn mean that the person is not actually a Christian, and is spiritually perverse?

These professing Christians are everywhere.

I know of one lady who manifests fear in every single conversation that I have ever had with her and to date I have never heard a single proclamation of faith come from her mouth in any way shape or form yet she truly believes that she is a Christian, how can this type of contradiction take place?

Faith is an opposite, or an Antonym of fear and God's Word declares:

for whatsoever is not of faith is sin.
(Romans 14:23)

When a believer fails to deal with the strongholds of fear then such a person will never have the boldness or courage to step out in supernatural faith in the public eye to proclaim the gospel or minister to people in the workplace.

> And he said unto them,
> Why are ye so fearful?
> how is it that ye have no faith?
> (Mark 4:40)

No faith, just fearfulness, one or the other, we cannot continue to walk in both. We are either at one end of the scale or at the other end.

At the time that these words were spoken by Jesus to His disciples they had already decided to follow Him, they had seen Him cast out a multitude of devils, witnessed the healing of Simon's mother-in-law, witnessed Him heal all types of sicknesses and diseases including leprosy, they had listened to devils declare Him to be the Christ and the Son of God and were even ordained by Him as His 12 Apostles to perform the same miracles and yet...they only had a wavering faith.

Now I don't know about you, but I have met many, many Christians who just like the Apostles in that boat have seen and witnessed more than a few miracles of God and yet still walk in fear just as they did.

I would also add that I speak from personal experience myself having walked for several years experiencing incredible and miraculous moments with God only to find myself having a great fear in my life that I just could not trust God for.

In the closing of this chapter, we can safely conclude that the spirit of fear is unholy. So, the next question is, what does God think about unholiness in the believer's life if the believer suffers with fear.

KEY STATEMENT 2: The fear which God is displeased with, is simple, down to earth, common fear, this is the same fear that we are all very used to in our daily lives.

HOW SERIOUS IS IT TO BE UNHOLY?

We have clearly established that walking with or agreeing with common fear in any shape or form means that one is standing in agreement with an unholy spirit which equates to sin and not just any sin but that which shares itself with the abominable who are destined for the lake of fire.

To understand the seriousness of this defilement we must consider the whole Bible and not just that of the new covenant.

I have met many, many Christians over the years who do not understand the importance of the Old Testament and how absolutely crucial it is for us as New Testament believers to refer to it in light of what we read in the New Testament.

God put these two books together for a reason, we cannot truly understand one without the other.

An example of this is that of over three hundred separate, specific and unique prophecies captured in the Old Testament over a two-thousand-year period, all penned by different authors, none of which copied another and all pertaining to the specifics of the arrival of Jesus on the earth, His life, His death and the reason for it all.

Jesus then arrives and everything from His conception to His death is captured in the New Testament by multiple authors outside of Orthodox Judaism which fulfilled every single one of these three hundred plus prophecies right down to the very details.

This is something that not even the most powerful of all modern-day computers could replicate in this day. Both books coming together more precisely than that of the greatest jigsaw puzzle of all time. The two books together are an absolute miracle of which only God Himself could create and manifest.

The prophecies of Jesus and the fulfillment of those prophecies are only a small part of the overall miracle of how these two books both dance together in the most perfect of spiritual harmonies resembling that of the first dance between a new husband and wife before God on

21

the most magical day of marriage, one cannot be without the other. No other book on the planet could boast of such a miraculous weaving.

Furthermore, Paul reminds us of this collaboration between the two books in that all of the Word, both Old and New Testaments are required to bring the believer to a place of wholesome understanding, wisdom and truth.

> and that from a child
> thou hast known the holy scriptures
> (OLD TESTAMENT),
> which are able to make thee wise unto salvation
> through faith which is in Christ Jesus.
> All scripture *is* given by inspiration of God,
> and *is* profitable for doctrine, for reproof,
> for correction, for instruction in righteousness:
> (2 Timothy 3:15-16)

In order for us to understand the issue of a Christian being subject to the indwelling of an unclean spirit, such as the spirit of fear, we must visit both the New and Old testament for a clear understanding. Many have argued the point using the New Testament only but as identified above it is the entirety of God's Word which reveals the truth to us.

Many a Theologian will agree that the Old Testament is a shadow of the New testament.

Whatever we read in the New Testament will have its explanation and details found in the Old Testament. Another example of this would be with regards as to why God would bring such harsh judgements on Christians of the New Testament who tolerate the spirit of Jezebel, we cannot understand the reason unless we go to the Old Testament and read details of such a defiled state and how such a spirit is in absolute opposition to the Kingdom of God.

Likewise, we know because of both books that when Jesus died for us there was a transformation of God's temple. The temple transformed from a stone-built temple of the Old Testament to the new human temple of the New Testament.

The pattern of the temple never changed in the Old Testament even though the first temple was made of cloth in the desert to the final temple of stone in Jerusalem, there remained an outer court, a Holy place and then the Holy of Holy's in which God's spirit resided.

When the transformation from the stone-built Temple to the Temple of man occurred, it remained in the same pattern.

The outer court now the flesh, the Holy place now the soul of man and the Holy of Holy's now being the spirit of man indwelt by the Holy Spirit upon the rebirth or decision for Christ.

Just as much as the Old temple suffered demonic defilement within the outer court (see Ezekiel 8) so to the born-again believer through the same compromise can suffer defilement in the flesh and just as much as God's Temple in the Old Testament could not be possessed, so too the born-again believer cannot be possessed.

God called all the sin of idolatry which was committed in His Temple "abomination", which eventually resulted in God abandoning the Temple because there was no repentance.

Today it is a well-known fact that adultery, pornography, and idolatry is practiced by many Christians and Church leaders alike.

So, do we now not believe that these abominable sins so many are committing in today's church is anything less? Are such Christians not committing abomination in the temple of God, the Christian?

What does the new testament say about the new Temple, you and I?

What? know ye not that your body is the temple of the Holy Ghost
which is in you, which ye have of God, and ye are not your own?
For ye are bought with a price:
therefore glorify God in your body,
and in your spirit, which are God's.
(1 Corinthians 6:19-20)

The story of the defiled Temple in the Old Testament resulted in the destruction of the Temple.

And likewise, the New Testament Temple, you and I, are warned:

If any man defile the temple of God, him shall God destroy;
for the temple of God is holy, which *temple* ye are.
(1 Corinthians 6:19-20)

Is it not a strange thing how we do not hear these scriptures being preached to us in this Apostate era? So then, what are we to do with such defilement if it is evident in our own lives? God shows us in his Word what we are to do with it.

Having therefore these promises, dearly beloved,
let us cleanse ourselves from all filthiness of the flesh and spirit,
perfecting holiness in the fear of God.
(2 Corinthians 7:1)

Now this is so eternally important to understand. We are commanded by God Almighty to cleanse ourselves not only from all filthiness of the flesh but also "of the spirit". This scripture reveals to us that unless we cleanse ourselves there can be no perfecting of holiness.

What is the repercussion for negating holiness?

Follow peace with all *men,*
and holiness,
without which no man shall see the Lord
(Hebrews 12:14)

Who is God speaking to?
Answer: Again, He is speaking to the New Testament Christian.

God commands us that in order to perfect holiness "without which no one shall see the Lord", we are to cleanse ourselves from all filthiness of the flesh and the spirit, which would include the spirit of fear.

24

The only way we can accomplish this is in the "fear of the Lord".

The fear of the Lord is the "ONLY PERMISSABLE" fear in which a born-again spirit filled Christian is allowed to walk in.

God not only expects us to receive, embrace and own this fear but this fear is absolutely essential and something we cannot be without, this fear is crucial in order for our foundation to be strong, for us to experience growth and abundant life as strong Christians.

Please carefully note that the following statement is one of the most important statements in this book:

This "fear of the Lord" is the central key to our eternal salvation and without it we are completely robbed of God's wisdom, God's knowledge, any ability whatsoever to depart from sin and evil or any ability to perfect ourselves in holiness.

- *The fear of the Lord is the beginning of knowledge (Proverbs 1:7).*
- *The fear of the Lord is the beginning of wisdom (Proverbs 9:10).*
- *By the fear of the Lord men depart from evil (Proverbs 16:6).*
- *By the fear of God, we perfect ourselves in holiness (2 Corinthians 7:1).*
- *Without holiness no man shall see the Lord (Hebrews 12:14).*

Wow, to think that we cannot even have the beginning of true Godly wisdom and Godly knowledge without first having the fear of the Lord in our lives. One can be a Christian for many, many years and still have no fear of the Lord.

Furthermore, we can now see this to be the root cause of why so many Christians and church leaders today have such an inability to truly depart from evil and sin and I speak of those who so easily entangle themselves in the affairs of adultery, pornography and the like and other perversions for the world to laugh at, all which are filthiness of the flesh and spirit, all of which are in opposition of holiness.

The "fear of the Lord" is one of the most positive, powerful, and desirably essential attributes to run after as a believer.

In short, "the fear of the Lord" is reverence for the Almighty which produces nothing less than pure holiness, blessing and protection in a believer's life and without the fear of the Lord a Christian does not have a foundation by which to build a true relationship with God upon. We are commanded not to fear man but to fear God only.

> And fear not them which kill the body, but are not able to
> kill the soul: but rather fear him which is able to destroy
> both soul and body in hell.
> (Matthew 10:28)

Again, this is a commandment to Christians, we are to fear God and God alone. We are to work out our own salvation with fear and trembling, lest we neglect such a great salvation and not escape hell.

> how shall we escape, if we neglect so great salvation;
> (Hebrews 2:3)

> work out your own salvation with fear and trembling.
> (Philippians 2:12)

A Christian, no matter what age, is to ponder on life in the light of eternity. This means that every day is to be approached with Godly fear and trembling with a focus on working out one's own salvation, these are not my words; they are the words of Almighty God.

God says be ye holy for I am holy, not once a month, not when we feel like it or when it suits us, it means every waking moment of every day. Jesus said, take up your cross daily and follow me.

All these scriptures and commandments are active and in the present tense.

In the 1999 film adaption of "Snow Falling on Cedars", actor Max Von Sydow when making his appeal to the jury in his closing argument as a defending Lawyer stated: [9]

"I'm an old man, I don't walk so well anymore, one of my eyes is close to useless, and my life is drawing to a close. Why do I say this? I say this because, well it means that I ponder matters in the light of death, in a way that most of you do not". – (Max was referring to the average age of the jury being a lot younger).

Max's character had a wise understanding of his final years and as for myself, well after living as many years as I have on this planet, I have been a witness to death taking the old and the young alike and I would make some emphases here on the young for I have witnessed much more the young being taken than the old.

With this said, I tend to feel that the pondering on life as Max puts it *"in the light of death"* can be and is a security against the reckless living that has been the root cause of death for so many who never made it beyond the prime of life.

Many young people will never understand this concept of thinking and for most, they either never will or will only when they are very old in years, or some life threating calamity comes their way.

More importantly, my point is this, that for the Christian to adopt this pondering of life in the light of death is a very good thing to cultivate at any age and especially in this age when just about anything and everything can, might and will happen.

A good example of this is of the many, many children in the United States who have faced a gun barrel in all the school shootings over the past two decades. Who would have ever imagined such a thing?

This pondering is too difficult for the world in any age group, however for a Christian this type of pondering is supposed to be a normal part of everyday life.

Even stated, there are vast numbers of Christians who have yet to adopt any such thought life even after supposedly knowing Christ for many years. The rampant sin plaguing today's church is clear evidence of this.

We must fear God; we must cultivate an attitude towards thinking correctly. We must ponder on the things of our lives in the light of death and eternity.

If this is acceptable to you and I, then let us ponder in such a manner whilst reading the rest of this book and let us ponder this one fact regarding fear. We know that common fear is sin and therefore it is evil and unholy.

And so, in closing out of this chapter and in accordance with Proverbs 16:6 which states *"by the fear of the Lord men depart from evil"* we can conclude this:

- Only those Christians who walk in the "fear of the Lord" will depart from evil.
- Fear is sin, which is evil.
- Therefore, those Christians who do not depart from the sin of fear are not walking in the fear of the Lord".
- Such Christians either do not understand the abomination of common fear and unholiness or don't believe that they should be "working out their own salvation" in the "fear of the Lord and trembling" (Philippians 2:12).

We have been commanded to fear God and give glory to Him.

And I saw another angel fly in the midst of heaven,
having the everlasting gospel to preach unto them that dwell
on the earth, and to every nation, and kindred, and tongue, and
people, saying with a loud voice, Fear God, and give glory to him;
for the hour of his judgment is come: (Revelation 14:6)

KEY STATEMENT 3: Without the fear of the Lord which is "good fear" we cannot overcome the evil sin of common fear, for ONLY by the fear of the Lord can we depart from any and all sin, fear included.

CHAPTER 2

THE ORIGIN OF COMMON FEAR

DEMONIC INFILTRATION IN THE GARDEN

FEAR IN ONE'S LIFE IS A TERRIBLE BONDAGE TO LIVE with, I have such a passion to see people set free from this most wicked, evil and filthy thing. It has destroyed God's planned purpose for millions of individuals throughout history.

Having knowledge and understanding about our enemy is halfway to defeating it, and to assist us in defeating this diabolical spirit of fear in our lives it is helpful to know and understand where it came from to begin with.

Originally, fear was as foreign to man as a snow blizzard in the desert, it just did not belong.

If this is so, then where did it come from? Well to answer this question, we must consider the core common traits of mankind today?

The first manifestations of the sinful nature after Adam's fall were the traits of Shame, fear and control which are all linked, one leading to the other and none of which were found in the lives of Adam and Eve before their fall.

> And the LORD God called unto Adam, and said unto him,
> Where *art* thou?
> And he said, I heard thy voice in the garden, and I was afraid,

because I *was* naked; and I hid myself.
And he said, who told thee that thou *wast* naked?
Hast thou eaten of the tree, whereof I commanded thee
that thou shouldest not eat?
(Genesis 3:9-11)

Look at the unfolding process as the mind of Adam was awakened to another dimension. First, he realized that he was naked before God (shame). Then he was afraid to be seen by God (fear) and he found himself trying to control the situation by hiding.

Adam had stepped from an existence of a God focussed nature to a self-focussed nature, from faithfulness to faithlessness, from complete security to fear, and from clothed in God's glory to naked and ashamed before God.

I will say it like this—Adam was awakened to darkness and to share in satan's nature and his world, if you will – Adam now resided under satan's fatherhood, nature and social culture. All of mankind who have not accepted Christ's atonement for their sin remain in the adamic nature with blinded minds and with no hope.

In whom the god of this world hath blinded the minds
of them which believe not.
(2 Corinthians 4:4)

He that committeth sin is of the devil;
(1 John 3:8)

Ye are of *your* father the devil, and the lusts of your father ye will do.
(John 8:44)

After the forbidden fruit had been bitten into, fear along with every other form of evil flooded into and dominated Adam and Eve's lives and this we know was achieved by demonic deceit and subtlety, satan had achieved his goal.

> the whole world lieth in wickedness.
> (1 John 5:19)

The Word reveals to us that they were both naked with NO shame before that dreadful day, before their fall from God's glory.

> And they were both naked, the man and his wife, and were not ashamed.
> (Genesis 2:25)

And so, let us clearly state that shame, fear and control are ABNORMAL to mankind. We were originally made in the image and likeness of God Almighty whose attributes are the exact opposite of these dark and sin rooted attributes which are not the original and normal state of mankind.

Adam and his wife were covered with the Glory of God. God's absolute divine and complete covering and protection over and around them was like that of a child in the womb of its mother – they had no awareness whatsoever that anything dark or sinful even existed beyond the glory of God. That is until the fateful bite which changed things for man on earth forever.

In this fall, satan had obtained a legal hold or "right" if you will, over mankind through the new sin nature. The sin nature being void of faith now gives access to the spirit of fear as man has no choice but to walk in agreement with it. Mankind now knows nothing but fear as a common trait because mankind is now resident in satan's kingdom and lives under satan's dominion, his lordship and fatherhood.

The Word of God is very clear, the father of everyone who does not love Jesus is satan himself.

Jesus said unto them, If God were your Father, ye would love me:
(John 8:42)

As Christians, we manifest that we do not love Jesus when we walk in opposition of his commandments and in opposition of His holiness.

If ye love me, keep my commandments.
(John 14:15)

KEY STATEMENT 4: Adam and Eve changed from the normal God designed state of mankind into an abnormal condition.

- From the God thinking state to the satanic thinking state.
- From a heart and mind of faith to a heart and mind of fear.

THE ETERNAL TRANSITION

Jesus won the ultimate victory for us over that which satan had accomplished in the garden.

Jesus became the one and only gateway for man to return back to the original undefiled state of that which God created – in His image.

> because strait *is* the gate, and narrow *is* the way,
> which leadeth unto life, and few there be that find it.
> (Matthew 7:14)

> Jesus saith unto him, I am the way, the truth, and the life:
> no man cometh unto the Father, but by me.
> (John 14:6)

Simply put, this means that when a sinner repents and accepts Jesus the living Christ to be their personal LORD and SAVIOUR, that person has stepped back into everything that is of Supernatural faith as before the fall.

At this point, such a person is supposed to return to NORMALITY. That means a clean transition:

- ✓ From satan's kingdom back to God's kingdom.
- ✓ From satan's nature back to God's nature.
- ✓ From satan's characteristics to Godly character.
- ✓ From infected design, back to perfect design.
- ✓ From unnatural paranormal fear, back to the original condition of Supernatural faith.

Jesus won the victory; He has made a way for us to return to normality.

Ultimately, we must understand that the very moment a person accepts the Lord into their lives – such a person is now free to return from the un-natural realm of sin and fear and back into the original, intended and normal realm of faith, the person has now become a new creature and is one hundred percent free from the slavery of sin and can now live in the eternal realm of freedom in faith in Christ Jesus.

Therefore, if anyone *is* in Christ, *he is* a new creation;
old things have passed away; behold, all things have become new.
(2 Corinthians 5:17)

Having one foot in one realm and another foot in the other just does not work.

When God said, let us create man in our image and likeness that image and likeness did not include fear in any way shape or form. If fear is not in the likeness of God then how can it be in our makeup as believers if we were only created in the likeness of God Almighty, it cannot, its impossible.

Again, the problem is that our minds are so used to thinking in the old corrupted fallen nature that until the believer embarks on an all-out effort to clean the mind then their will always be a struggle in one area of thinking or another.

I look at it like this: If you were to take twin brothers who both accept Jesus at the same time and one hits the scriptures like the German Blitzkrieg in the second world war and the other just slothfully dawdles along in spiritual laziness and hardly ever picks up his Bible to meditate on the truth then it is obvious which one would see the greatest freedom first. There is no other way around this, the personal effort is absolutely critical.

A well-known evangelistic minister while being interviewed on television puts it like this.

> "a person's spirit is in 100% contact with God if you are born again, however the problem that we face is in our soulish realm, for example, if the average Christian were to enter the shopping mall and see someone in a wheelchair, and the Holy Spirit said "go over there, grab him out of his wheelchair and declare with boldness arise and walk in the name of Jesus", your spirit would say "YES", but your mind would say, "control yourself you fool, are you crazy".

This is the intellectual activity of the mind which from childhood has been conditioned by the sinful nature which in turn is inspired by the kingdom of darkness alone.

This is what every new believer is up against. The mind must be completely renewed and transformed with no more conformity to the old unnatural way of thinking, or unholy thinking.

> And be not conformed to this world:
> but be ye transformed by the renewing of your mind,
> (Romans 12:2)

As previously stated, this means a complete one-eighty, a total disagreement with, cut off, discarded, ignored, warred against, and resisted at all costs on an ongoing basis until biblical Supernatural faith has become the norm and reality. (We will look at the transformational process in a later chapter "False vs True identity").

In other words – for the Christian, fear should no longer be the norm in any way, shape or form. Fear is sin and 1 John 5:18 clearly states:

> We know that whosoever is born of God sinneth not;
> but he that is begotten of God keepeth himself,
> and that wicked one toucheth him not.

When God tells us "He did not give us the spirit of fear", He is telling us that the fear we suffer with is not of Him or from Him. He gave us the Holy Spirit of love and of power and of a sound mind.

A person cannot walk in the freedom of love, the power of God and a clean and sound mind while fear is allowed occupancy, the mind would obviously not be sound then would it? Such a state of mind is just not compatible and is classed as double mindedness.

> But let him ask in faith, nothing wavering. For he that wavereth is like
> a wave of the sea driven with the wind and tossed.
> For let not that man think that he shall receive any thing of the Lord.
> A double minded man *is* unstable in all his ways.
> (James 1:6-8)

Bottom line is that a person's unity with a spirit of fear is a person's unity with satan and his kingdom, therefore it falls into the arena of the sin which eventually carries a person to Hell (Revelation 21:8) with the rest of the abominable.

Walking in unity with this spirit is evidence of a believer not yet receiving the fullness of God's love which encompasses everything He has for us.

Forasmuch then as the children are partakers of flesh and blood,
he also himself likewise took part of the same;
that through death he might destroy him that had the power of death,
that is, the devil; and deliver them who through fear of death
were all their lifetime subject to bondage.
(Hebrews 2:14-15)

And again:

There is no fear in love;
but perfect love casteth out fear:
because fear hath torment.
He that feareth is not made perfect in love.
(1 John 4:18)

I cannot emphasise enough that the kingdom of darkness is the origin of all our unwarranted common fear, it did not exist before the fall of man, it came along with satan and again—according to the Word of God—it is a spirit.

God speaks ill of it repeatedly and expects all of us as believers to overcome and utterly destroy it in our lives.

The spirit of Fear opposes faith in every possible way and at every turn, it is one of satan's foot soldiers sent by him to destroy the faith of the Christian thus rendering such a Christian unfaithful.

But without faith *it is* impossible to please *him:*

for he that cometh to God must believe that he is,
and *that* he is a rewarder of them that diligently seek him.
(Hebrews 11:6)

- Faith is the force that operates the hand of God – life.
- Fear is the force that operates the hand of satan – death.

More aptly put, fear is faith in satan.

We must trust and believe regardless of how circumstances appear to the eye. This is God's expectation of the professing Christian and nothing less is acceptable.

We must also know our enemy.

Knowing our adversary is halfway to defeating our adversary. The old life has past and with it our old mentally and faithless belief system must be dealt with and completely destroyed as we are no longer captives of satans kingdom.

KEY STATEMENT 5: We must understand that when a person becomes a believer – that person has stepped from the un-natural realm of fear and into the original and normal realm of faith.

- Fear must be left behind.
- Fear must be discarded.
- Fear and faith CANNOT coexist in harmony.
- A fearful Christian is a faithless Christian, unpleasing to God.

THE MANY FACES OF FEAR

There are a number of acronyms for fear floating around, one of which many are familiar with, it is "False Evidence Appearing Real".

This description of fear is also very much a description of paranoia which is evidence of a spirit of fear having a strong foothold in one's life. I know this condition firsthand as it was an affliction I suffered with for many years. In fact, my condition was much worse than this in that I suffered with bi-polar disorder, schizophrenia and often heard voices in my head to the point that I would have conversations with them. Paranoia allowed such dread to enter my life in certain moments and to this day I can clearly remember its paralyzing effects.

The older I got the darker my condition became, and this is only a small part of my story. It was only by inviting Jesus into my life that I now live today in complete freedom.

In the first two and a half years of my new life in Jesus I was directed to submit to the ministry of deliverance. Never would I have believed for a moment that I had the demonic living on the inside of me controlling my thought life. The more deliverance counselling and prayer I went through the more freedom I experienced.

On one particular occasion I was at a church service one South African Sunday morning and as the service began, I started to feel as though my mind had become somewhat darkened, I didn't feel well at all.

The worship band was now playing and all around me the congregation sung their jubilant songs to our Great God. I too stood to my feet and raised my arms in worship but as I did it felt as though I was being pulled to my seat.

I fought hard to keep standing but it felt as though something inside of my body was trying to control my muscles in pulling me downward to my seat. I was up and down like a yo-yo as I tried to fight it.

I eventually gave in and sat down spending the rest of the service in torment. I sat there with my eyes closed and said to the Lord that I knew that He was greater than all of this and that He was capable of setting me free from whatever it was that was causing me such an issue. I also stated that I was not going to leave church that morning until I was free.

I had read many things in the Bible over the past few weeks and the one thing stood out to me was God's desire to set the captives free and right now my mind was in captivity. As the service came to an end, I could hear the people leaving the auditorium as they shuffled out of their seats; I refused to open my eyes or move from my seat until God had set me free.

As the auditorium became quieter, I suddenly heard a voice in front of me, "are you ok Preston"? "You don't look too well"? It was the voice of one of the ladies from our weekly home group meetings.

Sheila began praying for me and then I heard the voice of our home group leader Dr. Gys behind me. Gys was a local medical doctor well known in the community and a wonderful man, he put one arm around my shoulders and another hand upon my head and then started praying.

As the first few words of prayer flowed from his mouth I suddenly and forcefully began rocking hard back and forth, it was all I remembered from that moment and only recovered my consciousness when standing in the adjacent isle. I saw the path that I had taken through all the chairs which were now scattered.

The next thing I remember is being back in the Isle next to where I was sitting but now in a wrestling match with three men. After managing to wrestle me to the ground I remember staring up at them and my vision became tunnel-like, my lips felt huge and swollen. Suddenly the tunnel seemed to be longer and then I could see only the Pastor.

He commanded "come out you evil spirit" to which I experienced a violent shaking within my body, then a loud roar came out of my mouth and I felt something come up out of my body and out of my head. I experienced a complete release all over and within my body. I then lay there exhausted and began sobbing for what had just taken place as I know that Jesus had just answered my prayer and delivered me from something which had been controlling me all of my life.

Well, this was the first of a number of such events but the only one inside the walls of the church. The Pastor suggested I pay some folk a visit who deal specifically with these issues and so I did. After each of my visits to a deliverance ministry team I would feel lighter and clearer in my mind, sicknesses also began to leave my body and the voices that I once clearly heard ceased, the depression that I had suffered with for so many years completely stopped and the extreme bipolar swings also came to an end.

This was the beginning of my renewal and little did I know that I was headed towards receiving the desires of my heart, namely, to become the Husband and Dad that I had always desired to be.

I tell this story because as these issues were dealt with on a spiritual level in the form of confronting evil spirits, I was set free from the spirit of fear and paranoia and many other spirits which have their link to fear of which traits I suffered.

I must add here that the biggest consolation that I experienced was that of seeing my middle child set free who was only two years of age at the time. Every time I was set free from something, my wife and I would see a noticeable change in him for the better. I won't go into detail here but will write about it in another book later on. He suffered from a number of issues of which we were very concerned about but during this time, God, by His most wonderful mercy blessed my wife and I with Deuteronomy chapter 7 which declares that "if you destroy the enemy in your land then the fruit of your womb will be blessed".

Now all the high-minded theologians and desperately religiously prideful pastors can say what they want but it will not change the fact that I am a walking testimony of being set free from demonic spirits post conversion. Today I and my family live in Christ's freedom, He first secured me in His kingdom and then performed His surgery for which my family and I are forever so very, very grateful.

For a clear understanding on this subject, I would encourage the reader to read "*They shall expel demons*" by the late Derek Prince. [10]

The spirit of fear is a "strongman spirit" or chief spirit which when having a foothold in one's life will then open the door for its subservient spirit companions to come in. In my own personal life experience and also from that of counselling many others I believe that this foothold for most people is obtained in early childhood.

The subservient spirits of the strongman fear are a vast array of evil companions which are highly active throughout the earth.

The spirit of fear and its subservient spirits will manifest as:

- Agitation
- All kinds of hysteria
- All kinds of phobias
- Anxiety (Philippians 4:6)
- Apprehension
- Dread (Exodus 15:16)
- Faithless (Matt 8:26; Revelation 21:8)
- Fear of man (Prov 29:25; Ps 118:5-9; Matt 10:28; Luke 12:4-15; John 4:18; Rom 14:23; Heb 13:6)

- Fear of death (Heb 2:14,15; Ps 55:4)
- Fright & horror (Ps 55:5)
- Heart-attacks (Luke 21:26)
- Worry (Matt 6:25-34)
- Timidity (2 Tim 1:7)
- Torment (1John 4:18)
- Trembling (Job 4:14-15)

Other symptoms of fear are: Shyness, uselessness, worthlessness, hopelessness, despair, withdrawal, escape, hyper-sensitiveness, perfectionism/striving, loneliness, depression, fear of starvation, fear of losing everything (monetary), tension and stress and last but certainly not the least – Superstition.

A spirit of fear is cunning as it hides itself and then professes from the lips of leaders in the church, sayings such as "fear is not sin", or "fear is healthy", or everyone has a little fear, don't worry about it". But we now know very well that this is not true.

As faith is the foundation of our belief in God and His kingdom – so too is fear discovered in the foundation of evil and the kingdom of darkness.

The spirit of fear feeds off unbelief and holds captive those who will unite with it.

Fear will rob one's mind of peace as it magnifies our problems and distorts our understanding of situations.

The spirit of fear will also break our relationships, ruin our health. Fear will goad us into foolish, impulsive and sometimes violent actions as it aims to paralyse our thinking, our trusting and our loving. Fear is a deceiver and again, it is the opposite of faith, it is dark, and it is evil.

Jesus rebuked His disciples repeatedly for their fears and lack of faith.

> And he said unto them, Why are ye so fearful?
> how is it that ye have no faith?
> (Mark 4:40)

In a nutshell, fear is anxiety caused by the approaching of danger or of the unknown, in other words—it has an object.

Fear is obsessive because it holds a person back from life and faith. It distorts reality and imprisons the emotional wellbeing.

When a person is born on this earth they are automatically born as slaves to sin and the devil, they are in essence under a spirit of bondage and remain as such until the moment of accepting Jesus into their lives. It is this spirit of bondage (slavery) which makes it possible for a human being which God has created in His image to be infiltrated by a spirit of fear.

> For ye have not received the spirit of bondage again to fear;
> but ye have received the Spirit of adoption,
> whereby we cry, Abba, Father.
> (Romans 8:15)

The Word says that we did not receive the spirit of bondage (slavery) AGAIN.

A believer's lack of faith, lack of wisdom and lack of knowledge coupled with unresolved issues, coupled with a lukewarm approach to their walk in the Lord will open the door to slavery once again. It's all downhill from there, I've seen this with my own eyes in the lives of Christians and it's not pretty.

> Stand fast therefore in the liberty wherewith Christ hath made us free, and be not entangled again with the yoke of bondage.
> (Galatians 5:1)

God's Word directs us to "stand fast" and not to be "entangled again", this would obviously only be stated if in fact we could let our guard down and be entangled again to the slavery of our enemy. This is God's warning to us, and God does not warn if there is no need for it.

The spirit of fear is an isolating spirit and people suffering from fears will build a protective shell around themselves where nothing and nobody can touch them.

One has only to look at the multitude of given Antonyms of faith, that is—the words descriptive of the opposite of faith which marries itself with fear to know that this is not Godly or Holy ground.

- Agnosticism
- denial
- disbelief
- dishonesty
- disloyalty
- distrust
- doubt
- faithlessness
- inconstancy
- lying
- misgiving
- rejection
- skepticism
- suspicion
- treachery
- unbelief
- uncertainty
- unsteadiness

It is God's intention that a believer walk in complete freedom in the mind, and that of a sound mind, not a distorted mind plagued by fears.

Fear creates these distortions in a three-fold manner:

1. By giving one a false perception of themself,
2. By distorting the nature of the danger facing them, and
3. By distorting the picture that one should have of God as their Father.

God gives us a clear picture of our struggles which are contrary to the freedom we should be walking with in Him.

If it is not of the Spirit of love and of power and of a sound mind according to 2 Timothy 1:7, then it is not of God.

> For we wrestle not against flesh and blood,
> but against principalities, against powers, against the rulers of the
> darkness of this world, against spiritual wickedness in high *places*.
> (Ephesians 6:12)

I am quite amazed of how many times when I have brought up the topic of our enemy the devil or demonization or demonic oppression to other Christians how so very many of them immediately manifest fear.

Ignorance of our fight, ignorance of the war that we are engaged in, and ignorance of our enemy will not let us off the hook. We are supposed to be bold, courageous and powerful spiritual soldiers in Christ's army and soldiers go to war, they do not hide away in fear and intimidation.

> Thou therefore endure hardness, as a good soldier of Jesus Christ.
> No man that warreth entangleth himself with the affairs of *this* life;
> that he may please him who hath chosen him to be a soldier.
> (2 Timothy 2:3-4)

Clear Biblical evidence shows that we are at war with the Kingdom of darkness to save souls. The power of faith combined with the Word of God is the power of God to save these souls.

As I have previously stated, by now we should have no doubt that the source of all fear is purely demonic, which means that it is paranormal not supernatural. With this being fact, it would also then be reasonable to state that a Christian who is walking in common fear must be a prisoner of this paranormal army instead of a free and effective soldier in Christ's army, would it not?

To help us destroy this evil in our lives it would be advantageous to thoroughly understand what Jesus accomplished for us on the cross and in His resurrection, and to what end we play in taking a hold for ourselves the victory in which He won for us. In the following chapter we will discover the role we play in working out our own salvation as individuals, that is, taking what He accomplished for us and applying it to our lives.

We will also discover the very important role that words play in either our demise to fear through bad verbal habits or our victory over it through Supernatural declaration.

KEY STATEMENT 6: It is God's intention that a believer walk in complete freedom in the mind, and that of a sound mind, not a distorted mind plagued by fears. Fear is not the natural or the original state of man.

LEGAL GROUND

Now that we understand what fear is, where it originates from and more importantly, what God thinks of it, we can now move through a couple of additional topics which will help us to understand the relationship between the sin of fear and its repercussions.

It is one thing to know what fear is, where it comes from and what God thinks of it, but it is another thing to understand why on earth it remains in a Christian's life when such a person has tried everything to overcome it only to see it return at every opportunity to torment the individual.

It is important to understand that the crime of the sin of fear can be carried out in different ways, which are:

Believing in fear
Acting in fear
Speaking in fear

We must understand that God's kingdom is a kingdom of justice.

The highest form of justice was played out on the cross whereby God made a way for the redemption of mankind through a legal process. God wanted to give eternal life to mankind, and He did it on legal grounds. It was a legal act.

When Jesus died on the cross, He paid the penalty for man's transgression and it was through this act that God could legitimately and justly give eternal life to man. God had obtained the right to give eternal life to us because He purchased it with His Son's blood.

And for this cause he is the mediator of the new testament,
that by means of death,
for the redemption of the transgressions that were under
the first testament,
they which are called might receive the promise of eternal inheritance.
For where a testament is,

> there must also of necessity be the death of the testator.
> For a testament is of force after men are dead:
> otherwise it is of no strength at all while the testator liveth.
> (Hebrews 9:15-17)

We might wonder why God is subject to legalities if He is God. Simply put, He is a just God and lives by the rules that He has set up in His Kingdom. He does not chop and change the rule book as He pleases; He is completely and utterly just in all His ways.

Therefore, we can understand that satan will always be playing a legal game against us in every possible way and he will not falter at taking every chance that he gets to lead us down the garden path.

When the Word states that the "wages of sin is death" this legality does not distinguish between the non-believer and the believer. The penalty and consequences for Adultery is the same for both parties. Furthermore, the Bible is the Christian's user manual for life, God is not warning the sinner in Proverbs 6:32, He is warning the believer.

> But whoso committeth adultery with a woman lacketh understanding:
> he that doeth it destroyeth his own soul.

Therefore, we must guard our hearts, our actions, our attitudes and most importantly our tongues. It is a scriptural fact that Christians can give satan opportunity or a foothold in their lives.

> Be ye angry, and sin not:
> let not the sun go down upon your wrath:
> neither give place to the devil.
> (Ephesians 4:26-27)

We have a hedge of God's protection around us (Job 1:10) but when we create a breach or hole in that hedge through sin, which includes the sin of fear, then satan the serpent is ready and waiting to afflict us with his poison.

He that diggeth a pit shall fall into it; and whoso breaketh an hedge,
a serpent shall bite him.
(Ecclesiastes 10:8)

Likewise, the tongue can also create such a breech.

A wholesome tongue *is* a tree of life:
but perverseness therein *is* a breach in the spirit.
(Proverbs 15:4)

Perverseness of the tongue would mean "anything spoken in an unfaithful manner", speaking in fear would be counted as such.

So, based upon the legal grounds and these two above scriptures, we should ask ourselves what the outcome is, of when "a serpent bites", or a "breach in the spirit" takes place and over the next few chapters we will delve into this for some enlightening revelation in the light of the sin of fear.

KEY STATEMENT 7: It is important to understand that the crime of the sin of fear can be carried out in different ways, which are:

Believing in fear
Acting in fear
Speaking in fear

CHAPTER 3

THE WORD & WORDS

BLESSINGS OR CURSES

Why is it that the average New Testament Christian has absolutely no problem in believing that all the blessings and goodness of God as described throughout the entire Old Testament are still completely relevant for us today but when it comes to the wrath of God, His judgement and all the curses as set out in the very same book are somehow irrelevant and ignored.

Many will say when it comes to the blessings, "God is the same yesterday, today and forever, quoting Hebrews 13:8:

> Jesus Christ the same yesterday, and today, and for ever.
> (Hebrews 13:8)

But when it comes to the curses the very same people will forget this scripture by somehow pushing it off the page as though it doesn't exist. They somehow believe that Jesus who is the "eternally established Word" and who declared and set into motion the spiritual laws by which we have always been governed by has somehow changed His words. In so doing they have formed their own God, which is idolatry.

I call heaven and earth to record this day against you,
that I have set before you life and death, blessing and cursing:
therefore choose life, that both thou and thy seed may live:
(Deuteronomy 30:19)

We would not dream of believing that the physical laws of which we are so accustomed to would change, it would be like saying that bathing in the refreshing water of a swimming pool on a super hot day is ok but the repercussions of falling into boiling water are no longer relevant or real just because we do not want to believe such unpleasantness exists.

God has not changed and just as much as His children of the Old Testament were given the choice between blessings and curses, so too His Children of the New Testament are offered the same choice.

One day back in 2018 I was in conversation regarding sin at a home group of a church which I was attending. During this conversation I mentioned the possibility of a Christian receiving a self-imposed curse and I said this as I had discerned a curse resting upon one of the attendees of the group and simply wanted to see where the group stood on this issue. The home group leader (let's call him Rod) did not seem too enthusiastic but then again, he did not seem to be on board with much when it came to the Supernatural or faith.

A few days later I received a phone call from Rod who informed me that he was not happy with what I had said and that I should not mention such things again in our weekly gathering. He said that he had studied the Word and concluded that Jesus had taken all our curses upon the cross and therefore there is no way a Christian can suffer a curse.

Was Rod's statement true?

We can answer Rod's belief by analysing what Jesus accomplished in His death.

1. He took our sin (2 Cor 5:21).
2. He took our sicknesses and diseases (Matt 8:17).
3. He took our curses (Gal 3:13).

If Rod's statement was true, then that would mean that the same would apply to everything else that Jesus took to the Cross with Him would it not?

He took our curses therefore no curse whatsoever would affect us; He took our sin therefore it is impossible that we could walk in any sin. He took our sicknesses and diseases therefore we can never again walk in sicknesses and diseases.

Obviously, Rod's statement was not true. Yes, Jesus took our sin; therefore, through Him sin no longer holds dominion over us. By His shed blood we can now have victory through true repentance, this involves action on our part to fulfill the requirements of the sanctification process.

Likewise, Jesus took our sickness and infirmities, therefore when we suffer such affliction, we now have access by faith to His healing power, again this involves action on our part to fulfill the requirements of the process.

And again, Jesus took our curses, and no differently we can have freedom from all curses by wielding our God given authority (Hosea 4:6) and/or deal with our own sin and self defilement, which can lead to certain curses, by the guidance of the Holy Spirit as we pray, He reveals such issues to us.

And yet again, this involves action on our part to fulfill the requirements of the process.

Let us break this down into a little more detail and iron it out in truth across the entire Word of God, Old and New Testament.

A CHRISTIAN AND SIN

Firstly,–if we were completely free from all sin then we would not be commanded in the word "as Christians" to confess our sins one to another, we would also not be warned repeatedly to keep ourselves from sin and to stop sinning (James 5:16; Hebrews 10:26).

In 1 John 1-8:10 "speaking to Christians" it states:

> If we say that we have no sin, we deceive ourselves,
> and the truth is not in us.
> If we confess our sins, he is faithful and just to forgive us *our* sins,
> and to cleanse us from all unrighteousness.
> If we say that we have not sinned,
> we make him a liar, and his word is not in us.

Yes, Christians do sin, but as we progress (1 Corinthians 9:25) in our walk with Jesus we are supposed to grow, mature and get sin under control so that we move on into perfection and sin no more.

> For sin shall not have dominion over you:
> for ye are not under the law, but under grace.
> (Romans 6:14)

We progress to the point of not sinning:

> Whosoever is born of God doth not commit sin;
> for his seed remaineth in him: and he cannot sin,
> because he is born of God.
> (1 John 3:9)

And:

> We know that whosoever is born of God sinneth not;
> but he that is begotten of God keepeth himself,
> and that wicked one toucheth him not.
> (1 John 5:18)

CONCLUSION

Jesus destroyed the power of sin in our lives – Romans 8:3

For what the law could not do, in that it was weak through the flesh, God sending his own Son in the likeness of sinful flesh, and for sin, condemned sin in the flesh:

Jesus obtained victory over sin for us, He did not eliminate it magically for us.

Yes, He took it to the cross no differently than that of curses, but it still exists in our lives, however it no longer holds power over us. Under the Adamic or fallen nature we had no power over sin, sin dominated our lives, and we could not escape its clutches. In Jesus however, we now have power over sin because Jesus lives on the inside of us (Col 1:27).

This means that through the name of Jesus we can now conquer sin. This takes time, and it is a process. In other words, it is up to each Christian to take what Jesus obtained for us and apply it to our lives.

We have to play our part; we can choose to "work out our own salvation" (which is what we are commanded to do) by recognizing the sin in our lives, repenting of that sin, having mastery over the sin, living holy and moving on into perfection with no sin in our lives, whilst readying ourselves to be a bride without spot or blemish as the wise virgins or we can stay in a state of foolishness and remain with our defilement of spots and blemishes. (Phil 2:12); (Heb 5:14); (1 John 1:9); (Rom 6:16); (Heb 6:1); (1 John 3:9); (Eph 5:27)

A CHRISTIAN AND SICKNESS

The exact same rules and principles apply when speaking of sickness and disease.

Jesus most definitely obtained the victory for us: Matt 8:17 – "that it might be fulfilled which was spoken by Esaias the prophet, saying, Himself took our infirmities, and bare *our* sicknesses".

(A note for all Christians who discard the Old Testament, the above New Testament verse is quoting Old Testament).

As explained above with regards to sin, if we likewise were magically and completely set free from sickness and disease the moment that we accepted Christ into our lives then Christians would never be sick, but we know that this is also not the case.

Again, He obtained the victory for us, but we again have a part to play. James 5:14 is a typical example of this:

Is any sick among you?
let him call for the elders of the church; and let them pray over him,
anointing him with oil in the name of the Lord:

Jesus destroyed the power of the devil who will stop at nothing to bring infirmities into the believer's life (Luke 13:11; John 10:10).

On the spiritual level this can happen when a believer commits sin, walks in apathy, takes offense or defiles themselves by evil words spoken. Please take note of this.

Obviously, there is also sickness which is brought on by a Christian who fails to look after their own body through neglect or bad habits, however this is not our focus.

This next scripture shows a relation between sin and sickness.

Behold, thou art made whole: sin no more,
lest a worse thing come unto thee.
(John 5:14)

This scripture reveals that the person's sickness of 38 years was a result of sin. Jesus warns, do not go and sin again otherwise you will receive a worse sickness than the one I just healed you from.

I would like to drop a nugget here of which I was thankful to come across in a book on the life of the healing evangelist John G. Lake. It is said and documented that his wife Jenny walked in the gift of discernment. She would often receive a word of knowledge from

God concerning those who did not receive healing when prayed for by her husband. [11]

In what was called their healing rooms in Spokane, Washington, John would lay his hands on the sick and those who were instantly healed would be sent on their way. Those who received no healing were sent to sit in another room until John had seen everybody.

John and his wife Jenny would then attend to those who had not received healing and Jenny would personally reveal to each person the hindrance of sin and the secrets of their hearts through a "word of knowledge" (1 Corinthians 12:8).

Those who repented and asked God for forgiveness would receive a healing once prayed for again and those who refused to repent even after acknowledging the truth of what Jenny had told them went on their way without a healing.

CONCLUSION

Regardless of the above statement regarding John Lake, Jesus took our infirmities to the cross, "Himself taking our infirmities, and baring our sicknesses"; However, this did not eliminate infirmities in a believer's life. Instead, we now have power over infirmities through and by the power of His name.

A CHRISTIAN AND CURSES

Once again, the exact same rules and principles apply when speaking of curses.

According to Galatians 3:13, Jesus accomplished two things regarding curses.

1. Christ hath redeemed us from the curse of the law,
2. being made a curse for us: for it is written, cursed *is* everyone that hangeth on a tree:

Firstly, He redeemed us from the curse of the law. So, what does this mean? Well to explain it in simplicity it means that before Christ came to set us free and as previously stated, sin had dominion over us and it was impossible to escape it, so God's written Law was put in place for the Hebrews which comprised of do's, don'ts and rituals for them to follow in order to gain pardon from God. In this the blood of lambs, calves, doves, etc. was a requirement made by God to cover their sin.

For those who have now accepted Christ, both Jew and gentile, this requirement is no longer valid, for as stated we now have power over sin through Christ. We are no longer under the curse of the law of sin and death, but by faith we are now under "the law of life in Christ Jesus" (Romans 8:2).

We are free from the curse of the law of sin and death. However, that does not mean that "curses" no longer exist or that we cannot find ourselves once again under the "curse of the law" by our own doing. The Galatians fell into this error of receiving Christ but then continued walking under the law and by its rituals to gain God's acceptance.

For as many as are of the works of the law are under the curse:
for it is written, Cursed *is* every one that continueth not
in all things which are written in the book of the law to do them.
(Galatians 3:10)

For example, the law states that the male is to be circumcised on the eight day after birth to fulfill the law. In Christ we are no longer required (if one is Jewish) to be circumcised. We as born-again believers now undergo a circumcision of the heart by walking in faith in Christ.

Being set free from the curse of the law of sin and death (singular) and being set free from a curse from a pool of curses (Plural) is two totally different things.

Curses have not disappeared or become obsolete, they still exist, all of them. Nowhere in scripture does it say that curses came to an end when Jesus died and was raised. Curses do not cease to exist until we are in Heaven as God declares in Rev 22:3 –

And there shall be no more curse.

The spiritual laws or dynamics in the spiritual realm stay the same. Until then certain sin will always result in curses, this is why we as Christians are urged to stop sinning.

It would be a benefit for every believer to memorize this very important verse.

sin no more, lest a worse thing come unto thee.
(John 5:14)

Once again, we have a part to play. There is no different rule or process with regards to curses than dealing with sin, sickness or disease in our lives.

Curses do not fall under a different set of rules.

In Deuteronomy 28, God asks us to choose between "Blessing and Curses", walk righteously and holy and the reward is the blessings of God, do what is considered as evil and you will reap the curses as stipulated, it is that simple. God makes it easy for us through the power of what Jesus accomplished.

FINAL CONCLUSION
1. **SIN** – Jesus took our sin to the cross – THIS DID NOT ELIMINATE SIN. Instead, we now have power over sin through Him.
2. **SICKNESS** – Jesus took our infirmities to the cross – THIS DID NOT ELIMINATE INFIRMITIES. Instead, we now have power over infirmities through Him.

3. **CURSES** – Jesus took our curses to the cross – THIS DID NOT ELIMINATE CURSES. Instead, we now have the choice not to sin which in some cases will result in a curse and the power to break curses through Him by repentance.

We can clearly see that with fear being a sin in a believer's life, it is not something that magically just disappears when we become born again, or something that we should just accept as the norm, no, it is our duty no differently than every other sin under the sun for us to deal with.

KEY STATEMENT 8: We are responsible for appropriating what Jesus accomplished for us on the cross. This means action on our part, not mindless apathy, and convenient false belief.

BIBLICAL CURSES

As mentioned on the previous page, a curse is described as the opposite of blessing. A curse is in the negative and we suffer curses by committing sin either by our actions, attitudes or spoken words.

In the modern-day mainstream church, it is as though demons no longer exist, and even more so, that one can even be plagued by them. Through a combination of Hollywood movies and frightened Pastors even the thought of demonization or demonic possession immediately provokes the thought of something dark, horrific and extremely harmful yet if truth were to be understood then we would realize that a demon is nothing worth worrying about at all and the demonization of people the world over is more common than one would realize.

I would have no problem whatsoever on betting that there are demonized Christians in every church on the planet.

The same, can be said for curses, the moment we hear the word "curse" we immediately think of a witch or a witch doctor conjuring up a spell to place on someone.

However, and once again if truth were to be understood then we would know that curses are a very common part of everyday life and we can walk into cursing ourselves or others very easily.

But no man can tame the tongue. *It is* an unruly evil,
full of deadly poison.
With it we bless our God and Father, and with it we curse men,
who have been made in the similitude of God.
Out of the same mouth proceed blessing and cursing.
My brethren, these things ought not to be so.
(James 3:8-10)

The words "curse men" in this scripture does not mean to use foul language concerning the person or person one is speaking of, this is the Greek word "*kataraomai*" which means to doom, to curse and this scripture is again a warning to Christians, not sinners.

When the word of God tells us to choose between life and death, blessing or curse, God is not saying that it is harder to be cursed than it is to be blessed. He places them both on equal terms. When He tells us to choose, He is saying, by your beliefs, actions and words you will either operate in blessing or a curse, so choose with great wisdom.

We are fools if we believe that there is every chance of provoking a blessing and no chance at all in provoking a curse into our lives.

In the book of Genesis Chapter nine we read of Ham's son Canaan who received a curse because his father Ham looked upon the nakedness of his father Noah, he suffered a curse upon his family for his irreverence of his father.

For just simply looking at his father's nakedness, a curse was birthed into Canaan's life.

So, what now? God is not the same, yesterday, today, and forever!

To note, I have personally brought a curse upon myself through the despising and cursing of my biological father. I did this out of deep frustration and a lifetime of disappointment amongst many other reasons, which is no excuse, just like Ham did, I too looked upon his nakedness (his faults, his sin) with disregard and truly despised him in my heart, and this brought a curse upon me (Ephesians 6:1-3).

Honor your father and mother," which is the
first commandment with promise:
"that it may be well with you and you may live long on the earth."

In other words, if you do not honor your father and mother then it will not go well with you, question: blessing or curse?

Whoso curseth his father or his mother,
his lamp shall be put out in obscure darkness.
(Proverbs 20:20)

Cursed be he that treats with contempt his father or his mother.
(Deuteronomy 27:16)

Within the next few days, I lost my job (I was the sole source of income in my home), we then lost our home and were only a few weeks away from being homeless. I was not restored until I repented (appropriated what Jesus did for me) before God and then asked my un-believing father to forgive me. The very next day I got a job after being out of work for 18 months.

Some would say that this was not a curse that I suffered; they would say that this was the chastisement of my Heavenly Father, but one only has to read Deuteronomy 28 to understand that God describes the fruits of a curse as lack, loss, physical sickness and disease and all are in line with chastisement as seen on the nation of Israel throughout the Old testament.

Here are just a few types of curses we find in the scriptures.

A Written curse

According to the book of Numbers, chapter 5 verse 11 to 31, if a husband suspected his wife of adultery, she was taken to the high priest who invoked a curse over her and mixed holy water with the dirt of the floor to make it bitter. The Priest would then write a specific curse in a book and then pour bitter water over the words causing the ink to run with the water into a vessel.

The ink tainted bitter water was then given to the wife to drink. If she was in the sin of Adultery her thigh would then rot and her belly would swell. This was not a fairy tale; it was a real curse invoked by the writing of words.

Cursed by Actions and Attitudes

The unspoken attitude and the open irreverence of King David's wife Michal brought an instantaneous curse of barrenness upon herself. She would never experience the joy of having children just because of an evil thought in her mind and open irreverence toward her husband (2 Samuel 6:14-23; Eph 5:33).

Some theologians have argued that her baroness had nothing to do with her irreverential thoughts toward her husband however it is clear from scripture that a wife is commanded to reverence her husband, not simply respect but reverence' as some new Bible versions offer, and violating this commandment is again, sin.

This reminds me of a time when the Lord led me to pray for a Christian woman with breast cancer. We had been invited for dinner by a small group of Baptists one summer evening. The group consisted of half a dozen couples all of who we had never met before.

After the meal, the Holy Spirit led me to ask this lady if she had ever belittled her husband or contended with him in front of her children to which she answered yes. I explained to her the seriousness of the sin she had committed based upon a number of scriptures and stated that if she was willing to repent, I believe that God would heal her.

The lady agreed with heartfelt tears of conviction, I then asked her to turn to her husband and ask for his forgiveness to which she did. My wife and I then anointed her with oil, placed our hands on her and prayed for a healing. We left for home soon afterwards and heard nothing for a few weeks until one morning when I received an email from her.

She explained how wonderful she had felt the very next day and had not experienced having so much energy in quite some time. She also stated that she had been for a checkup and the test results came back negative for cancer, she was completely healed of breast cancer.

Spoken curses

In the book of Acts Chapter 13, Paul cursed Elymas the sorcerer with blindness for his opposing ways against the works of God. Yes, this is a Christian placing a curse on a non-believer in the New Testament, boy oh boy, if we could only find such bold Christians today.

In Acts 23 verse 12 the Jews who were determined to kill Paul bound themselves under a curse of death if they failed to kill him.

Judas one of Jesus's very own disciples and a commissioned Apostle was cursed with eternal separation from God due to his actions.

It is obvious that satan will stop at nothing to ambush a believer in receiving a curse upon their lives, he achieves this by the Christian's lack of knowledge of scriptures around this subject, a subject which is hardly ever preached in our modern-day lukewarm churches.

So many believers are ignorant of satan's strategies and tactics in goading a person to receive the fate by which he seeks to bind them up with and destroy their faith. God is not pleased with this and His judgement upon the apathetic father is stern and serious as presented in Hosea 4:6 which reads:

> My people are destroyed for lack of knowledge:
> because thou hast rejected knowledge,
> I will also reject thee, that thou shalt be no priest to me:
> seeing thou hast forgotten the law of thy God,
> I will also forget thy children.

This is hair raising to say the least, that God would reject the man who rejects spiritual knowledge and would also forget the children of such a spiritually passive man and father, this too is a curse, it is most certainly not a blessing is it?

Is this maybe the reason why so many children of Christian parents are walking away from the faith in these times. I have counselled many such parents and most often found that the dad is clueless and has very little depth of understanding on spiritual matters.

You can weigh this up however you want but it sure does not sound like such a man has chosen blessing, all he had to do was pick up his Bible and discover this warning from God.

KEY STATEMENT 9: When the word of God tells us to choose between life and death, blessing or curse, God is not saying that it is harder to be cursed than it is to be blessed. He places them both on equal terms. When He tells us to choose, He is saying, by your beliefs, actions and words you will either operate in blessing or a curse, so choose with great wisdom.

THE SPIRITUAL DYNAMICS OF THE TONGUE

In the light of God's Word, we cannot fail to understand the role that words play in orchestrating either blessings or curses in our lives.

Words are the very power of what has shaped human existence as we know it today. Without words we would never have seen the advances in every area of our lives as we have, such advancements without the communication of speech would have been impossible.

In the same light we can also state that if it were not for words, we would never have witnessed all the evils that have plagued mankind throughout the ages. Hitler spoke the perfect string of words on an ongoing basis to sway the masses into destroying the lives of millions across the planet.

Each of us are a vault of words if you like we are walking words.

As previously stated earlier in this book, scripture reveals that Jesus made man in the image of God.

All things were made by him;
and without him was not any thing made that was made.
(John 1:3)

So, if we are made in the image of Jesus then what is that image?

And the Word was made flesh, and dwelt among us,
(John 1:14)

Jesus is the Word, and we are made in His image; therefore, we are also "word".

Now think about this for a moment, every single word that came out of the mouth of Jesus was absolutely perfect in wholeness, purity, order and timing.

Each and every sentence that He stringed together was perfect and powerful and reached its mark. His words are the highest words ever spoken on this planet throughout the entirety of mankind.

Jesus who is "the Word" is the Universal highest of high, His words created and set into motion everything that we can see and everything we cannot see.

I personally cannot find enough of the right words to magnify the absolute greatness of Jesus the living Word because my being is so constricted, limited and earthbound but what I can understand is this one thing, it is that if we are made in the image of Him "the Word" then should we not as transitioned born-again beings having now entered back into our original state and design also be releasing our words in a manner fitting of the image we are created in and in the light of eternal conversation at all times?

Is this perhaps why we are warned that as Christians we will be judged by our words in the day of judgement.

For by thy words thou shalt be justified,
and by thy words thou shalt be condemned.
(Matthew 12:37)

Some will say that this is a warning to the unbelieving sinners, but I would disagree because unbelieving sinners are already condemned.

As Christians we are representatives of the image and likeness of Jesus the living Word, so we too are to be walking as living, pure and holy Words, with words that breath blessing and life to our fellow man.

Just as much as fear is no longer a part of our new nature so too is to curse or speak ill of someone no longer part or parcel of our new nature. This includes speaking negative things over ourselves.

This topic of the power of words is a lot deeper than we realize, especially when it comes to cursing and curses and when we understand the magnitude of our words and the power that they hold, then and only then will we also understand the highly impactful revelation of the implications and the power that our words hold especially in the spiritual realm and with regards to the topic of fear.

If the revelation is truly gleaned then the impact should be like that of a bucket of ice water being dumped on the unsuspecting victim laying on the beach sun tanning and if is not so, then the reader should ask God for more clarity if I have failed to bring it.

In order to help our understanding of this impactful revelation we must approach it in the settled understanding that we are in the image of Jesus and should not be misrepresenting Him in any way whatsoever especially in the words we speak.

For the next few chapters, we will focus on this topic as it is necessary to bring home the main topic of this book "that which I fear" and its powerful relation to the words we speak.

Unclean spirits (demons) are nothing more than spiritual parasites and just as much as the human body is susceptible to physical parasites in the natural, so too are they susceptible to spiritual parasites.

In the physical a person can eat or drink something contaminated and the body becomes sick. In the spirit the opposite rule applies whereby spiritual parasites gain access by what comes out of the mouth and not what is put into it.

The following scripture describes spiritual defilement of a person, Christian and non-Christian alike.

> But those things which proceed out of the mouth
> come forth from the heart;
> and they defile the man.
> (Matthew 15:18)

The confession of our mouth is our amen (so be it). As Christians, we have power and authority over the kingdom of darkness and so it is of no surprise that satan and his hordes listen to what comes forth from the mouths of Christians.

Remember it is not what goes into the mouth that defiles a man but what comes out of his mouth that defiles. The defilement is not physical, it is spiritual. God is speaking of spiritual defilement.

Because we have been uttering such words our entire lifetime, we seem to think nothing of it, but in reality, it is no different than any other evil and sinful habit that we have formed as sinners. This is just one of the more serious issues that the majority of Pastor's rarely highlight or confront.

Our walk with God is a delicate one indeed when we consider that each word that we speak holds power. Consider this that one only has to call another person a fool to be in danger of hell.

> but I say unto you,
> That whosoever is angry with his brother without a cause
> shall be in danger of the judgment:
> and whosoever shall say to his brother, Raca,
> shall be in danger of the council:
> but whosoever shall say, Thou fool,
> shall be in danger of hell fire.
> (Matthew 5:22)

Again, this verse is written as a warning to Christians, not to sinners. This is Jesus speaking to His disciples, His followers' His believers, warning them that they can be in danger of the fire of hell by simply calling someone a fool. This cannot be a warning to non-believers as their fate is Hell anyway.

Here are a few more examples of self-imposed curses that I would like to mention. These are personal to me as they both resulted in the death of my friends before I met Christ.

Gerry's Binding Words

Back in 1994 I had a friend who was quite the character. Gerry (not his real name) was a single dad with children who were just coming into their teens. Unfortunately, Gerry was divorced due to his wife being involved in sexual relationships with his cousins.

When Gerry discovered this, he was devasted. I have no doubt that Gerry became very bitter because from there on he would not trust women and for many years had no concrete relationships. Furthermore, Gerry began to prey on married woman and caused many to fall into adultery with him.

Without knowing the Lord at that time, I obviously did not understand the spiritual dynamics of his sin but when I look back, I realize that I was witnessing Gerry's impending death as described in Proverbs 6:32 and Proverbs 9:18 relating to the union with an adulterous and foolish woman, which states:

~ he *that* doeth it (commits adultery) destroyeth his own soul.
~ her guests (the adulteress) *are* in the depths of hell.

Having committed this ongoing and vile sin, without repentance before God, Gerry's fate was sealed. Satan now having the legal right over Gerry's soul executed his plan for Gerry's demise. This came in the form of utterances into Gerry's mind convincing him that he would one day be shot dead.

Living in South Africa in the 1990's was difficult. For a country that had little crime before the takeover of black government to becoming one of the highest crime rates in the world was just devastating for all. It was a regular occurrence for people to be shot dead whilst driving their car, shopping or simply residing at home minding their own business.

Gerry was in the gambling slot machine business which took him into the local black townships south of Johannesburg. Everyone knew Gerry in these locations and he never had any issues when visiting these places. Even though there was never any threat to his life he would constantly tell everyone that there was a bullet with his name on it. When people would ask Gerry why he would say such a thing he would reply

"I just know it", he would say. Gerry made this statement and confession over and over again.

Well, it just so happened that on one fateful afternoon the very thing that Gerry had confessed repeatedly soon became a reality. Driving out of the location known as Orange Farms, he pulled into a gas station when three African youths walked over and shot him dead to steal his vehicle.

> Death and life *are* in the power of the tongue:
> and they that love it shall eat the fruit thereof.
> (Proverbs 18:21)

This verse shows us that words from the tongue hold power and the words we speak will bear fruit and the fruit will either produce life or death. This is not describing the results of orders such as an order to a firing squad to shoot or a declaration from a judge that the guilty person will not face the death penalty. This power of the tongue is describing spiritual power, life and death as in the spirit, blessings and curses.

The Word of God states that our words reach into and have an effect in the spirit realm and as established in an earlier chapter we know that everything that is not of faith is sin; this means every single word we speak, every word which opposes the promises of God's Word for one's life.

> But I say unto you, That every idle word that men shall speak,
> they shall give account thereof in the day of judgment.
> (Matthew 12:36)

Again, this scripture is given to Christians. The wise Christian will heed and repent, but the foolish Christian will see no fault and continue on his way.

Again, such words create a breach in the spirit realm, our hedge of protection is breached when we sin with our words.

A wholesome tongue *is* a tree of life:
but perverseness therein *is* a breach in the spirit.
(Proverbs 15:4)

Kevin's Binding Words

I first met Kevin back in the mid 1980's during my days of night-clubbing and debauchery.

Kevin became "one of the gang" and a good friend. We would meet on most weekends to party and drug it up and this went on for several years.

Kevin was known as a constant abuser of every drug or medication that he could possibly get his hands on, he would stop at nothing to get high no matter what the detriment to his health.

Kevin's sexual exploits were often perverse, and he was in no way shy to express his actions to those of us who were just as debased as himself.

One thing that sticks out for me about Kevin is the fact that he would regularly claim his belief that he would be dead before his thirtieth birthday.

When confronting him about his words he would simply reply, I have no desire to die but I just know it's going to happen.

One week before Kevin's thirtieth birthday he was found dead on his bed. Kevin had been experimenting with a fire extinguisher by releasing into a plastic bag and then breathing in the carbon monoxide which he thought might give him a buzz.

The power of Kevin's words were realized and once again the power and fruits of the tongue were manifested. We were obviously saddened by Kevin's death as one is with the death of any friend.

Both Gerry and Kevin's negative confessions are just two powerful examples of the tongue and the fruits that such evil speaking produces.

My Binding Words

I remember once watching a movie, I cannot remember exactly how old I was but I'm guessing around my early teenage years. The movie was about a man who was wrongly convicted of murder and who was then sentenced to death by electrocution on the chair.

I remember that such fear came upon me in realizing that this terrible tragedy could happen to anyone, I then thought what if it happened to me. I also remember voicing to my younger brother how I also feared the possibility of being falsely accused of murder and facing the same terrible consequence.

I would have to conclude that this was by far my greatest fear in life but I managed not to dwell on it and just secretly tucked it away hoping never to think about it again.

Lo and behold in my early twenties during military service my younger brother and I got into some serious trouble and yes you guessed it, we were both charged with the murder of one of our friends. I will not go into any detail about this but will state that it bought me to my knees in prayer for the first time in my life.

I obviously did not get convicted and go to the electric chair or I would not be here to tell the story but I can admit that it was one of the scariest moments of my life and it was only by the grace of God that the charges were dropped after five agonizing months.

To conclude this matter of the tongue and the power of words spoken, the Bible is pretty clear on the spiritual implications and because so many Christians do not understand the seriousness of this topic the church and the individuals of a church struggle to see, receive and realize the blessings of God in their lives.

Here follows what I call the rule book of the tongue:

1. The tongue holds the power of Life and death spiritually which then manifests physically.
2. Words of a confessing nature ride on only two waves – either Faith or Fear.
3. Words are spoken either from the "heart pool" of foolishness or wisdom.

4. Words are the most powerful spiritual force/weapon in the heavens.

KEY STATEMENT 10: satan plays a legal game and the confession of our mouth is our amen (so be it). This is reality. Remember this, that every negative confession is sin. The Word of God states that everything that is not of faith is sin. Therefore, every negative confession is in fact an act of calling God a liar in His promises toward us.

For us as believers God gives clear warning as to the final detriments of a loose and foolish tongue.

> But I say unto you, That every idle word that men shall speak,
> they shall give account thereof in the day of judgment.
> (Matthew 12:36)

CHAPTER 4

THAT WHICH I FEAR

How many times have you heard the words coming from a person's mouth "my greatest fear is"?

We know and understand that fear is demonic, we know that fear is sin, we know that perverse speaking is a breach in the spirit and we know that curses travel on words spoken, therefore with all this understanding, should Christians ever utter the words "my biggest fear is"?

Ask the next ten Christians you meet what their biggest fear is? Chances are you will get an answer from almost every one of them.

The moment one utters what they fear is the moment satan has just gained legal ground in which to bring that which the person fears upon them.

So, what then are we guilty of when speaking such words:

1. We sin because they are not words of faith—Hebrews 11:6
2. Fear is sin, therefore saying that I fear is sin—Romans 14:23
3. We are breaking our hedge of protection—Ecclesiastes 10:8
4. We are causing a breach in the spirit realm—Proverbs 15:4
5. We are agreeing with a demonic spirit—2 Timothy 1:7
6. We walk in satan's realm and not God's—1 Samual 28:5-20

For a Christian who is in the image of Christ, "the Word", to state "my greatest fear is", is to agree in unity with that which satan has managed to establish either as a stronghold in the believer's life or the believer is agreeing with the prompting in the mind by an unclean spirit so that the legal battle might be won against such a Christian.

Again, professing fear is professing sin, it cannot be argued.

for whatsoever is not of faith is sin.
(Romans 14:23)

Marlene's Great Fear

Marlene walked over to me at the end of the church service and asked if we could talk, she needed some prayer and had heard that I might be able to assist her. Marlene explained to me the struggle that she was going through with the fear of having a car accident. I asked her if she had ever been in a car accident, yes, she replied, I have been in three.

I asked her about her first accident, she went on to explain that when she was six years of age, she and her dad was in a fatal car accident in which her father died. It was a terribly traumatic experience for her as a little girl.

I went on to explain to Marlene that this would have been the point where a spirit of fear would have entered her life. In her mind, even the protection of a father was not enough to save her from this event especially with the fact that her dad was in control of the vehicle. In her soul, not even her heavenly father could now protect her from another car accident. I explained that walking in fear of this happening only gives satan the legal right to cause such an event again. She experienced the second accident as an adult, the two adults in the other vehicle were killed.

Marlene also stated that she seems to be struggling with more and more fear as she is getting older. This I explained is because the enemy already had a foothold due to her sin of fear and simply grows in strength by inviting more spirits (Matt 12:45; Luke 11:26) to come and harass her thereby robbing her of all peace. Marlene was terrified of having another car accident and was even too afraid to go home to her house in the night time.

After our talk, I asked Marlene if she would be willing to repent of her sin of fear to which she agreed. I lead her in a prayer of repentance and then commanded the spirit of fear to let her go and leave (Matt 16:19; Matt 18:18).

Marlene was instantly set free and a look of liberty and restoration of spirit manifested in her face. She seemed overjoyed and stated that she could even feel the difference within herself. Well after a couple of weeks I saw Marlene again and she was like a different person altogether—praise God.

Some might ask the question, is there any scriptural evidence of this idea of that which a person fears will come upon them?

The answer is yes.

> For the thing which I greatly feared is come upon me,
> and that which I was afraid of is come unto me.
> (Job 3:25)

This is taken straight from the book of Job, and alarmingly from the very heart of Job himself.

> A good man out of the good treasure of his heart
> bringeth forth that which is good;
> and an evil man out of the evil treasure of his heart
> bringeth forth that which is evil:
> for of the abundance of the heart
> his mouth speaketh.
> (Luke 6:45)

Now wooooah, just hold on a cotton-picking minute, how is this possible, Job was such a great man of God, so righteous and upright. How is it even possible that he had evil treasure in his heart?

Well, let us take an in-depth look at Job and maybe we'll find some reason for this evil sin of fear in his life.

THE REAL JOB

The book of Job must be one of my most favorite books in the Bible. The problem with this book is that it is misunderstood and so terribly misinterpreted by so many modern-day Pastors and Teachers and thus the teaching of it has become completely powerless in setting the captives free. This leaves the followers of Christ clueless as to why they face so many issues that they seem unable to overcome them, including the sin and bondage of fear.

As a new Christian back in the 90's I had a dilemma on my hands. The spirit of pride was so entrenched in my life and that of my wife that the arguments were brutal and common. I did not know why we argued so much until God revealed the truth of His Word. Proverbs 13:10 states:

Only by pride cometh contention.

This scripture clearly states that contention (in all forms) comes by no other means than by pride. We know from scripture that pride is demonic in nature and results in loss and destruction in one's life and might I point out that Christians are not exempt from its outcome.

The fall of satan was due to this deadly sin. Proverbs 16:18 states:

pride *goeth* before destruction,
and an haughty spirit before a fall.

In our case the pride of my wife and I was so well entrenched in our lives that gaining a clear revelation of its severity was of the highest importance even though we did not see, know or clearly understand it.

God states in His Word that Leviathan is the King over all the children of Pride (Job 41:34). This is the first clue as to what Leviathan is. The second clue is that he has more than one head as stated in Psalm 74:14. I have heard many ill-informed Pastors and teachers state that Leviathan is a crocodile; some will say he is a prehistoric animal;

however, this is all nonsense as there is no animal on planet earth that has been designed and created by God that has more than one head. Secondly, no animal on earth has any power or authority to be a King over prideful human beings throughout the entire planet.

In short, Leviathan is a powerful demonic principality that is a King over all who are walking in the sin of pride the planet over with no exceptions and this includes Christians.

My personal encounter with Leviathan operating in my life was quite the thing. I had suffered under a gloomy state of melancholy and severe depression for many years of my life which is one of the manifestations of this spirit. After I had invited Jesus into my life as my Lord and Savior, He began the cleanup of my soul along with the relevant teachings of each issue that I was facing and being set free from.

Well, I can tell you that when I met Jesus, I was ecstatic with joy and excitement that I had entered the realm of God's kingdom and that the veils of blindness had been removed from my mind. I sought Him with all my heart. I knew without a shadow of a doubt that there were spiritual bondages in my life that just had to be broken and I was unwaveringly determined to seek his gracious deliverance.

On one Sunday morning my wife and I did not attend church as I was suffering somewhat with another bout of this melancholy, so we decided to visit her parents in the town of Vanderbijlpark.

After being there for a while I decided to go and visit another Christian friend who lived close by who would be able to pray with me but on arrival at his home, I was informed by his wife that he was out for the morning.

The melancholy was getting worse by the hour and eventually to the point of despair. I decided to phone our home group leader Gys who lived back in our hometown of Vereeniging which was about a fifteen-minute drive.

Gys answered the call but stated that he was at church and said that he would meet me at his home in a while, so I headed straight for his house.

I pulled up into his driveway. The waiting seemed like forever and the darkness in my mind was so intense that I took off my wristwatch, hung it over the steering wheel and decided that if he did not arrive by 1:30pm that I was going to drive home and shoot myself. I was in such a terrible state of gloom and doom and was deadly serious and totally committed to my decision.

I watched the seconds tick by and as 1:30 struck I turned the ignition key, put my vehicle into reverse and looked over my shoulder to exit the driveway. At that very moment Gys arrived and pulled up behind me. My exit was blocked and so I shut off the engine. I explained to Gys what was going on and he invited me into his house. He ushered me into a quiet room and informed me that he was going to make a phone call to the Pastor for some help.

I remember sitting there on my own for some time and while doing so I was experiencing the strangest feelings in my body. It felt like my legs and arms were twisting around, yet they were not physically moving. I had never experienced such a thing before. Gys returned into the room and said that the pastor's wife is on her way over. Gys then asked if he could pray for me to which I agreed.

As he began to pray the sensation of my body twisting suddenly increased and then it was as though a great release took place. The whole room seemed brighter and the gloom within my mind instantly disappeared. Joy returned into my being accompanied with a great big smile. Well, I felt like a bit of a fool as I was now sitting there as though there was absolutely nothing wrong with me. I couldn't understand it and little did I know at that moment that one of a number of battles had just been won against the spirit of Leviathan.

The revelation only unfolded later as God started to open my understanding through a deliverance minister called Sally who I visited down in KwaZulu Natal which was some six hours from where we lived.

While I was there receiving ministry, Sally's words to me were "I hope we are not dealing with Leviathan here". Well up to that time I had never even heard of Leviathan and with this spirit being so entwined within my mind it blocked me from enquiring of Sally what she was talking about.

Her words however stuck with me for some time after and it was only when God so graciously began to help me see the pride in my life that He directed me to another deliverance ministry closer to home in Johannesburg who were no strangers to dealing with this particular spirit.

Upon receiving freedom from Leviathan, I found that I was hearing God's voice easier and with much more clarity. I had more peace than ever, and my thinking was different. This was not so with my wife who was still in bondage to this spirit and was still looking for argumentative opportunities on a regular basis.

After praying for her for a number of weeks with no breakthrough I awoke one morning and immediately heard the Holy Spirit say that I must read the back of the book of Job starting with the last few chapters which is where I found Job repenting to God for his wickedness or as Job put it—his vileness.

This made no sense to me as like many Christians I had already read the beginning of Job which kind of describes him as being one heck of a guy. The Holy Spirit then instructed me to read everything in between the great guy and the repentant guy. It was only after studying these chapters that the light bulb went on.

In short, the book of Job is about a man who fears God and shuns evil from a religious bent (this will be clearly proven), a man who by his very own profession had never seen God (Job 42:5) and who unknowingly walked with Leviathan as his King. Job's hedge of protection is removed thus no longer being under the protection of Psalm 91, he experiences his fall and destruction which is the judgement of pride, God then humbles Job and draws Leviathan out of him. Job is transformed from a religious person to a humble spirit. We will prove this without any doubt by the end of this chapter.

The book of Job unfolds as follows:

1. Chapter 1 – Job is introduced as an upright man and perfect.
2. Chapter 1 – God tricks satan into sifting Job.
3. Chapter 1 – Destruction comes upon Job and his entire family.
4. Chapter 1 – Job lays no foolish charge against God.
5. Chapter 3 – Job changes his tune and manifests self-pity.
6. Chapter 4 to 31 – Job's three friends highlight the sin of Job in a condemning manner; they have no breakthrough with this strategy and then ceased their dialogue with Job.
7. Chapter 32 to 37 – Elihu the young Spirit filled, humble of heart, mighty man of God takes over and uses a strategy of exalting God in the highest degree. This strategy disarms Job's pride and self-righteousness.
8. Chapter 38 to 41 – God takes over from Elihu and vehemently challenges Job (Can you do what I do, and can you do what I am doing to you?) Job's pride and self-righteous religiosity is exposed.
9. Chapter 42 – Job humbles himself and repents. God restores Job. God has rescued Job from the bondage of pride (Leviathan) from the clutches of satan.

Now I really do not want to go into a lengthy teaching of Job which is necessary to bring about the full revelation of Leviathan in a believer's life, this I aim to do in a separate book but due to the great deception of this evil spirit I must at least try to bring the minimum clarity in order to take us to the connection between pride and fear, this will then bring further understanding as to why so many Christians are unable to escape the spirit of fear.

So, let's analyze this for a moment. The standard idea of Job that most Christians follow is that he was some great guy that suffered a great injustice allowed by God in order to test his loyalty. The result of this misaligned thinking in the minds of so many is oh "poor, poor, Job", however, Job is "vile" and this was concluded by he himself, his own words, out of his own mouth (Job 40:4).

Do you think that it is fitting that we in our apostate thinking would believe that we know this man Job better than he knows himself? If he himself concluded that he is vile then who are the modern-day Christians to declare otherwise, such Christians make Job's heart felt confession and God's Word to be a complete lie.

As convincing as this idea of "poor, poor Job" might seem it does not align with the rest of God's Word concerning God's nature. The evidence against Job is overwhelming. In fact, and this is where it gets quite interesting because we never ever hear our modern-day Pastors and Teachers quote the following things that this great guy Job actually said and did.

Let's see, he stole from his own brother, robbed the widows, stripped the naked of any clothing they owned and ignored the needs of widows (Job 22 verses 6, 7 & 9), he surrounded himself with workers of iniquity and wicked men and justified this by stating that there is no profit in delighting in God (Job 34:7-9), he multiplied his words against God in the spirit of rebellion (Job 34:37).

Let's take a breath,

He accused Almighty God of bullying him and persecuting him (Job 16 and 19:22).

Job is on a role, way to go Job...

He darkened Almighty God's council toward him (Job 38:2) he disannulled God's judgement and condemned the God of the universe (Job 40:8), wow, he just doesn't give up, off with the gloves Job.

He contended with, instructed and reproved the God who created the Heavens and the earth (Job 40:2-4).

And guess what..., the God who created Job was not happy with any of it.

But hold on just a minute, we're not done with Job just yet, and continuing-on we find the darkness of Job's pride and self-righteousness is also revealed:

Job stated that he is clean and without transgression (PRIDE), innocent and without iniquity (PRIDE), Job was righteous in his own eyes

(PRIDE), he also stated that his righteousness was more than God's (PRIDE). (Job 32:1; 33:9; 35:2)

Wow, I mean 'gulp', God's aim with a lightning bolt is pretty darn accurate Job, I would be quiet now.

Is it not amazing how deceptive we are until the pressure of tribulation squeezes the ugliness out of us? How true the scripture is which states:

> The heart *is* deceitful above all *things*,
> and desperately wicked: who can know it?
> (Jeremiah 17:9)

Job went from "laying no foolish charge against God" in chapter one to this great deluge of rebellion as the pressure mounted and as time rolled on without any relief. Funny how the religious facade is so easily torn down under pressure.

Boy, I can understand why God was so angry with Job as is exposed in these following verses:

> (God speaking)
> Who is this who would darken my council
> with words without knowledge.
> (Job 38:2)

> (God speaking)
> Wilt thou also disannul my judgment?
> wilt thou condemn me, that thou mayest be righteous?
> (Job 40:8)

> Moreover, the LORD answered Job, and said,
> Shall he that contendeth with the Almighty instruct *him*?
> he that reproveth God, let him answer it.
> (Job 40:2-4)

I think it safe to say that God never got so angry and said such things to the likes of King David, Solomon, Elijah, Moses, Noah or anyone else in the Bible for that matter, I think the closest we get to this is the record of Jesus confronting the religious and bigoted Pharisees.

Well, many Christians and even Pastors who have read the verses in Chapter 1 will only see the description of Job as favorable and they stop there either due to laziness, a lack of spiritual discernment of the book as a whole or because Leviathan is present in their own lives, which in my experience of the many leaders I have met over the years is more so the case.

So, in order to dismantle the absurdity of the "great Job" phenomenon as created by the modern-day apostate teachers we have to answer the question "what is it then that is really being described of Job in the first chapter?

I offer to you that these verses are descriptive of a religious man of which we will discover as we take a dive into the Hebrew words behind the English translation.

The Pharisees and Sadducees were upright, perfect, feared God and shunned evil just like Job, but they were not upright in their hearts. They had all the good God-fearing qualities of religiosity but lacked the one thing that God was looking for and that was true agape love and a humble spirit – an upright heart.

The Pharisees were without any doubt full of pride and self-righteous, in other words, an upright man is an unfinished man, a religious man.

On the other hand, Elihu, the young man who God used to reach Job after the exhausting and failed attempt of Job's three friends was described as such a man as this, that is, with an upright heart (Job 33:3) and this is why God was able to use him.

There is a big, big difference between an upright man and an upright heart.

Elihu states:

My words *shall be of* the uprightness of my heart:

and my lips shall utter knowledge clearly.
(Job 33:3)

God is in the business of holiness and He demands purity, and we all know that He hates sin. Job on the other hand sees no profit for a man to be cleansed of his sin, he obviously knows better than God.

Elihu spake moreover, and said,
Thinkest thou this to be right, *that* thou saidst,
My righteousness *is* more than God's?
For thou saidst, What advantage will it be unto thee?
and, What profit shall I have, *if I be cleansed* from my sin?
(Job 35:1-3)

My desire *is that* Job may be tried unto the end
because of *his* answers for wicked men.
For he addeth rebellion unto his sin,
he clappeth *his hands* among us, and multiplieth his
words against God.
(Job 35:36-37)

The Word of God reveals that Job had plenty of un-repented sin in his life, BIG TIME. The scriptures reveal that he had dealt with very little of his sin as he believed that his religiosity was good enough.

The verses which trip up the general masses today regarding the story of Job is found in the initial description of Job in Chapter one, whereby he is described in the English language as perfect and upright.

There was a man in the land of Uz, whose name *was* Job;
and that man was perfect and upright,
and one that feared God, and eschewed evil.

Because of the difficulty in translating to the English language with the clarity of the Hebrew meaning it would appear that Job is truly a humble and godly man but when we take a close look at these words in the original Hebrew it says something quite different. The Hebrew word for perfect in this verse is the word "*tam*" which means "pious", the word pious meaning religious, and the Hebrew word here for "upright" is the word "*yashar*" which means "convenient".

Presented correctly in English we find that Job was a conveniently religious man, in other words he was religious when it suited him.

Furthermore, Job is described here as one that "feared God" which most would equate to aligning to the "beginning of wisdom" and/or the "beginning of Knowledge" as possessed by those who "fear the Lord" as given in the book of Proverbs and elsewhere, however the "Fear of God" as found in the description of Job and the "fear of the Lord" as found in proverbs and elsewhere are not the same.

The "fear of God" as displayed here as one of Job's traits is described with the Hebrew word "*yir,ah*" which is a lesser form of fear as opposed to the Hebrew word describing the "fear of the Lord" in Proverbs which is the word "*yare*" which is a higher fear, an infinite fear, a dreadful and exceeding fearfulness which is the makeup of true God fearing reverence on a personal level.

If I may describe it like this, it is the difference between that of true Godly fear leading to God's wisdom, knowledge and the departing from sin and that of a common fear of God as given in Job's case being a religious, un-intimate stance, such a person only "knows of God" but has not truly "seen Him" in the reality of everyday intimate life. This revelation manifests in Job's understanding only after God in His mercy had revealed Himself to Job one on one.

I have heard of thee by the hearing of the ear:
but now mine eye seeth thee.
(Job 42:5)

When we weigh Job up against Elihu we see two very different levels of spirituality.

- With Job we see an unfinished conveniently religious man.
- With Elihu we see a finished humble product walking in the Spirit of God.

Do we need more evidence of Job's condition, well maybe, for I know that a person reading this who might be in such a state of pride and self-righteousness and under the influence of Leviathan as Job was will struggle immensely to receive this revelation?

> *His* scales *are his* pride,
> shut up together *as with* a close seal.
> One is so near to another, that no air can come between them.
> They are joined one to another,
> they stick together, that they cannot be sundered.
> (Job 41:15-17)

I have met many Pastor's and even entire congregations which are so bound up by Leviathan. This spirit is so cunning and powerful in the mind of those enslaved to it that you just cannot get through to them.

We once met an elderly couple who much like Job, had lost everything. They had invested all their life's savings in the biggest pyramid scheme in South Africa history. It crippled a small city, and a number of people took their own lives after losing everything.

They honestly believed that their continued losses and struggles over the years were simply just due to some stupid mistakes. The husband had so much pride that he just could not take ownership of their situation being any fault of his own. We listened to him on several occasions blame his wife for where they had now ended up in their old age. "When I thought we should do this or that, I listened to my wife who did not agree, and we ended up doing the opposite", he would state. Even in this he was manifesting sin in going with his wife's will instead of God's will for their lives without realizing it.

Because thou hast hearkened unto the voice of thy wife,
(Gen 3:17)

In all thy ways acknowledge him, and he shall direct thy paths.
(Proverbs 3:6)

No matter how much we carefully tried to minister to him and his wife they were having none of it. He and his wife had supposedly at some stage many years back invited Christ into their lives, been baptized, read the Bible, but had never dealt with their pride which was so obviously evident. With my own ears I heard this man confess the same as Job, that he had no sin, iniquity or transgression in his life.

Neither of them could see the pride in themselves, and they could not relate their own story of continual loss to the story of Job. To this day they still have no breakthrough of God's blessings in their lives, their journey of sanctification is at a complete standstill, for the most part it never even started. They will blame everyone else for their misfortunes but themselves, their story is like that of so many other professing Christians who are so wrapped up in pride that out of desperation they run to the prosperity gospel teachings for a solution and in so doing go even deeper into error.

Can we bring any more evidence to the forefront of Job's condition? Let's take a closer look and break down Jobs trial against other scriptures outside of the book of Job.

To start with, Psalm 91 is God's promise to those who live in "the secret place" of the "most high God". Such a person shall abide under his shadow and under His protection. He promises that no disaster will come near such a person's dwelling (home).

He promises that they will not even dash their foot against a stone, in fact verse 10 promises that "there shall no evil befall thee", yet Job's property was destroyed, his servants were slain, his livestock stolen, and his children killed.

Wow, I guess God must be lying in Psalm 91 if Job was such a great guy then, um...I think not.

One only has to read the blessings and curses of Deuteronomy 28 to realize that Job was most definitely not the recipient of the blessings, it was the manifestation of the curses given in this chapter that came upon him, and came upon him swiftly.

So why did God do this and when we answer why' we can then clearly see the tactical "how"?

The Word of God obviously aligns with Job's calamity in many ways, one of which is that pride comes before a fall and a haughty spirit before destruction (Proverbs 16:18). Did Job have a fall, he most assuredly did and a mighty one at that. Did he suffer destruction, he sure did, he was wiped out and then some, and left hanging on by a thread of God's goodness?

We all know that one cannot enter into God's Holy Heaven being full of pride and self-righteousness, it is impossible, no matter how much one believes in Jesus, or the evil doctrine of "once saved, always saved", a false doctrine inspired by a false king called Leviathan will not save you. God is only coming back for those who are without spot and blemish. Without holiness, no person shall see the Lord (Hebrews 12:14).

We must remember that satan and all of his unholy followers (who were Angels before the fall) knew Jesus better than every believer on this planet. Yet, PRIDE CAME BEFORE THEIR FALL. Who are you and I to think that we can enter heaven with such evil in our hearts? Pride keeps one hell bound.

God loved Job so much, He saw such great potential in him that he blessed him with destruction and loss to reach him, to cleanse him, to save him and God achieved it. He in His great wisdom tricked and used satan against himself and saved Job. What a great and magnificent God we serve, praise his name.

If satan knew for one moment what the outcome would be he never would have accepted the challenge.

So, how did God accomplish this amazing feat?

1. He set up satan to accomplish his plan.
2. He allowed the three friends to address Job in order to show us how not to try and reach someone with Pride in their lives.
3. He made sure Elihu was on hand to disarm Job.
4. Elihu did not use the strategy of Job's three friends, instead, he used the strategy of highly exalting God – He then kept on asking Job, can you do what God does?
5. This strategy disarmed Job of his greatness which caused him to enter into a humble enough state to hear God's voice.
6. God then takes over from Elihu and begins His rebuke of Job and demands to know–Can you do and accomplish that which I do? (Job 38 to 41)
7. God further challenges and enquires–Can you do what I am doing to you? (Job 40:6-24).

Cast abroad the rage of thy wrath:
and behold every one *that is* proud, and abase him.
(Job 40:11)

8. God speaks and says, Job, can you draw out Leviathan (Pride) like I am doing to you (Job 41)?

Canst thou draw out leviathan with an hook?
or his tongue with a cord *which* thou lettest down?
(Job 41:1)

Now there is much more to say on this topic, and I have kind of rushed through it in order to get back onto the topic of fear.

However, I am sure that if the above does not convince you of the pride in Job's life then nothing will. God is a faithful and just God and if we lack insight and are humble enough to ask God to open our eyes to the marvelous revelation of Job, He will do it.

JOB'S BINDING WORDS

So, to move on, we find that when a person walks in pride they also walk in fear. Why is this, well the soul of man knows that under the spirit of pride there is no eternal security even if the person does not realize or understand this dilemma, the soul of the person surely does.

It is for this reason that the conveniently religious Job could verbalize such a vile and self exposing evil in his life.

> For the thing which I greatly feared is come upon me,
> and that which I was afraid of is come unto me.
> (Job 3:25)

Job by his very own confession was not a man of true faith; he operated in satan's kingdom because Leviathan was his King. He walked in unity with a spirit of fear, and fear is sin, and the fearful are bound for the lake of fire (Revelation 21:8).

I have to say it again, wow, what a great thing God did for Job, praise Him, praise Him, and praise Him.

Job had no idea that he had such pride in his life and simply because pride is so very blinding. The only thing that Job really had going for him is that he hung in there, had patience, and God's pity and mercy on his side.

> Behold, we count them happy which endure.
> Ye have heard of the patience of Job, and have seen the end
> of the Lord;
> that the Lord is very pitiful, and of tender mercy.
> (James 5:11)

A cursed man cannot enter heaven with the sin of pride, it must be purged which is part and parcel of the sanctification process in Christ.

I have met many a prideful Christian man and woman over the years, and many such Pastors included. These Christians resist the purge of pride for so long and for many they resist until it is too late. Such prideful Christians are under a curse of which they themselves are responsible for negating through repentance.

Thou hast rebuked the proud *that are* cursed,
which do err from thy commandments.
(Psalm 119:21)

Look at this verse very carefully, this is not talking about sinners for sinners will never follow the commandments of God, these are those who have followed God's commandments but have fallen into compromise or apathy, they are back-sliders who have erred from the path, from the commandments of God and it is pride which caused it.

People seem dumbfounded as I have heard many say, "why do bad things happen to good people" as though they know what is in the heart of a man, how arrogant. We cannot know if a person is good by the outward appearance, only God knows what is in the heart of man. Jesus Himself stated the following:

Jesus answered. "No one is good–except God alone.
(Luke 18:19)

This reminds me of an interview we listened to on a radio station in 2005. My wife and I had returned from Canada and were living back in South Africa for a year in the province of Kwazulu Natal (KZN) in a town called Bothas Hill.

The interview was with a Christian man who was giving his testimony, however he spent most of the interview boasting about how great he was.

He had achieved in all forms of athletics and business. As he spoke of his amazing and mind-blowing achievements, he went on to explain how one day he had jumped headfirst into a river and broke his neck. He now sat paraplegic in a wheelchair. He went on to explain how he had invited Christ into his life as his Lord and Savior after this tragic event.

He further went on to explain how long he had laid in his hospital bed and how the doctors were so dumbfounded at the strange odour that came from his scalp and the sores and scabs that started to form and even though he was now discharged from hospital this condition just would not clear up.

The accident and his paraplegic condition had not humbled him one bit and further clues surfaced as to his condition by his continuing words of how great and wonderful a Christian he was, and that God had great plans for him even though he was crippled. His pride oozed out of him through all of his boasting and self-grandeur.

I turned to my wife and asked if she was listening to this, she too knew what was manifesting. Leviathan was still his King and in such a way that the crown of Leviathan (which is a heavy crown of pride) was resting so heavily on his head in the spirit that it was manifesting in the physical in the rotting of his scalp with the vile aroma of stink.

After I myself was set free from the enslavement to this principality the Lord took me into the lives of others suffering with the same. It was such a great learning experience.

In all the cases the recipients were suffering with financial hardships and loss and after ministering to each of them and conducting deliverance their prosperity always followed and almost immediately, just like Job. Praise God. You won't hear this preached in the prosperity gospel churches!

And let me add this one very important note before we go any further. In my dealings in ministry to others when encountering Leviathan over the years I have observed this one common occurrence; it is that Christian businessmen and Pastors are so prone to be ensnared by this spirit. I have seen this all too often, and just like job their businesses or ministries struggle and fail because of their pride, Leviathan frolics in the sea of mankind amongst the merchant ships and pride comes before a fall and the merchant ship is sunk, and God will not rescue the ship because he is more concerned about the soul of man than his business.

> There go the ships:
> there is that leviathan, whom thou hast made to play therein.
> (Psalm 104:26)

This I believe is why the Word of God states:

> And again I say unto you,
> It is easier for a camel to go through the eye of a needle,
> than for a rich man to enter into the kingdom of God.
> (Matthew 19:24)

I can give several more examples of these encounters, but I will save it for another time. Annihilating fear so that faith will have its rightful place is what this book is about.

So, let us continue and take a moment here to analyze Job's evil confession of his lips in stating the "thing which he greatly feared had come upon him".

Job's fearful summary exposes:

1. The condition of Job's heart is revealed by words (Luke 6:45).
2. That which a man speaks defiles him (Matthew 15:11).
3. Fear is sin (Romans 14:23).
4. Fear is a demonic spirit (2 Timothy 1:7).
5. The fearfull and abominable are cut from the same cloth (Revelation 21:8).

Again:

> A good man out of the good treasure of his heart
> bringeth forth that which is good;
> and an evil man out of the evil treasure of his heart
> bringeth forth that which is evil:
> for of the abundance of the heart his mouth speaketh.
> (Luke 6:45)

Job did not just simply fear, he confessed that he "greatly feared", which meant that he was void of any trust in God. Job was saying "I am confessing by my mouth the true condition of my heart and stating that I am in unity with the abomination of satan's spirit of fear. I have therefore given satan legal right over me to enter in and destroy me in this area of my life, I believe satan over God."

Unfortunately, Job is not alone in such a confession and as I have stated previously, I often ask brothers and sisters in Christ the question "What is your greatest fear" and I only ask out of curiosity to know where they stand on the subject.

I do this to get a feel for how educated the modern Christian is on this subject, a kind of survey you might say.

The results are troubling to say the least, it is surprising how many confess their greatest fears and yet why should this be so surprising in this Apostate watered-down era of teaching even though the Word of God commands us to "Fear not" and "Be not afraid" over one hundred times.

KEY STATEMENT 11: We find that when a person walks in pride they also walk in fear. Why is this, well the soul of man knows that under the spirit of pride there is no security even if the individual does not understand this the soul surely does.

JOB'S IDOLATRY

If Job's walking in fear was not bad enough it was compounded by the fact that it was rooted in idolatry.

> For the thing which I greatly feared is come upon me,
> and that which I was afraid of is come unto me.
> (Job 3:25)

Job's fear had an object and in order to understand the idolatry we must first find the object and we find this object in what came upon him.

Job lost all his five hundred yoke of oxen which equals one thousand oxen, he lost all five hundred of his donkeys, he lost all seven thousand sheep and all three thousand camels, not to mention all his servants but four who escaped as messengers – (Job 1:14-19)

This adds up to a whopping 11500 livestock in total which would have been such great wealth back in Job's day.

So, Job's declaration of what he feared was loss of his wealth because that is exactly that which "came upon him". Job's object of his fear was losing his wealth and comforts which in turn was his idolatry. He feared the loss of mammon instead of having a fear of the Lord.

Does the Word of God not say?

> The fear of the LORD leads to life,
> So that one may sleep satisfied, untouched by evil.
> (Proverbs 19:23)

> The reward of humility and the fear of the LORD
> Are riches, honor and life.
> (Proverbs 22:4)

We must remember that the religious can have a form of the fear of God, but it is a religious form and nothing more, Muslims have this form but do not have Jesus in their lives, therefore their fear of God is meaningless.

Again, God does not lie. Notice these scriptures – untouched by evil which aligns with Psalm 91 and then the receipt of riches, honour and life. God does not lie, and God will not take second place in one's life and God will not be equal to another god or idol in one's life, ever.

Furthermore, when we look at the word in Matthew 6:24 and Luke 16:13 we are warned by God that we cannot serve two masters.

> No man can serve two masters:
> for either he will hate the one, and love the other;
> or else he will hold to the one, and despise the other.
> Ye cannot serve God and mammon.

Might I also add that one cannot truly fear God and also fear mammon simultaneously and equally at the same time. When one has a fear of something other than God then one is stating that something is higher and more powerful in their life than God.

This is, in essence stating that God is weaker than the situation. Mammon therefore becomes another god, a higher god, we are only to fear Almighty God and Him alone.

> Now therefore fear the Lord,
> and serve him in sincerity and in truth:
> and put away the gods which your fathers served
> on the other side of the flood, and in Egypt; and serve ye the Lord.
> (Joshua 24:14)

Again, as I have previously stated, not only is the fear of something else other than God an idolatry but when one is walking in fear then such a one is obviously void of faith which is faithlessness.

And as we can recall in the beginning of this book, in reaction to the faithlessness of His disciples in Matthew 17:17 Jesus rebuking them called them "perverse".

> Then Jesus answered and said,
> O faithless and perverse generation,
> how long shall I be with you?
> how long shall I suffer you?

And so, in summary when we bring the story of Job together with all of its evidence and not just the first few scriptures of Job, we can state that Job was a conveniently pious, prideful, fearful, faithless, perverse, idolater whom God loved so very much as to allow such great calamity to come upon him to sift him of his sin so that he would make it into heaven. And again, I state "wow", what a great God and Father we have. Praise His Holy name, hip, hip, hurray.

In my own life as mentioned in the beginning of this chapter, I was a full-blown Job and suffered and lost and had such a hard time trying to figure it all out.

Although God had revealed to me the pride and the revelation of Leviathan in my life in the early days of my walk with Him it was only twenty plus years later that I received the revelation of unfinished business in my life and here is how it all happened.

To explain the story clearly, I have to go back to before I accepted Christ into my life.

I was a young man suffering with emptiness and much low self-worth. Little did I realize that I was so desperately running away from the extremely poor self-image I had of myself and one day I thought that maybe being a successful businessman would solve this issue. And so, I entered the business world and started a business in Air-conditioning and refrigeration, both of which I knew absolutely nothing about, but my arrogance drove me to believe I could do anything.

I borrowed some money from the bank and secured a contract and by the tenth month of business a million in revenue with significant profit was realized. By the fourth year of business, I had a team of fifty workers, a fleet of vehicles and by this time had turned fourteen million.

The success was recognized by the Small Business Development Corporation of South Africa and an award presented by the Mayor of the town where the business was operating from which was then followed by an interview on National TV.

Well, I became a legend in my own mind, my arrogance and pride reflected this clearly, however...I still felt so very empty and worthless and pride became the breastplate to cover the truth in my heart and after a while I lost complete interest in the business and suffered with bouts of sickness and spiralled once again into depression with the only form of relief being found in alcohol and drugs. I did not care anymore, and the business began to suffer for it.

Well, to cut a long story short, it was during this time through a miraculous chain of events that Jesus reached me and then as described earlier, He revealed Leviathan in my life. I then vowed to God that I would never run after business and money again unless He opened the doors. I knew that it was good and humbling for me to work under a boss so that God could work out His character in me and with that said I have continued in the Oil and Gas and Petrochemical Construction Industry till this very day.

The problem with this Industry is that you never know where your next job is coming from. One project might last three years and the next one three months. In between the projects you have to make your money last until the next job comes along. Also, when a recession hits the construction workers are usually the first to be laid off and the last to be rehired when the economy picks up again. It can become a hard life, especially after losing two homes over a 12-year span as I have and that with a young family.

Although my wife and I had witnessed so many of God's miracles in our lives we did not realize that our experiences of loss had over time conditioned us. Here we were twenty-two years in the Lord and suffering with fear, in fact I would say it was more like dread which is an enhanced form of fear.

We would both dread having to look at our bank account. We just did not want to see what was in the account when we knew the funds were getting low. We both knew that looking at it would send us into a downward spiral of faithlessness and despair; it was so overwhelming at times.

Even though we would repent and ask God to forgive us of our fear it would happen over and over again until one day God revealed the revelation of the root of idolatry. God was using the ups and downs of the Construction Industry to reveal to us the fear and idolatry of mammon.

We had always proclaimed faith in God and had always revered Him, and were diligent in His ways and His kingdom, we served Him, sowed thousands and thousands of dollars into the kingdom in helping the less fortunate and yet we could not understand this horrible cycle of lack.

There was another thing that was reoccurring like a pattern for many years as well. It was a dream that I would often have with different scenarios but always the same storyline. In the dream I was being pursued by people, soldiers or animals.

They were out to catch me, and I was running for my life. In the dream I would have the same sense of fear, dread and despair and every single time the dream would end the same way, without any conclusion, I was neither caught nor did I escape. There was no ending to the story.

It was only when God started revealing the root cause of our financial issue that I then remembered the dream and realized how it was connected. God was showing me that there was a reoccurring cycle in my life with dread, fear and despair as its fruits and it was only in financial matters that I and my wife ever suffered these emotions.

For God speaketh once, yea twice, *yet man* perceiveth it not.
In a dream, in a vision of the night,
when deep sleep falleth upon men, in slumberings upon the bed;

then he openeth the ears of men,
and sealeth their instruction,
(Job 33:14-16)

Now let me state that I made a lot of money doing what I did but no matter how much I made it was never enough. Now think about it for a moment, no matter how much money I made, I was responsible for never having enough because I feared not having enough, in short this is nothing less than a self-imposed curse.

For me, this book has been a journey that I did not know would transpire into freedom for my wife and I, for as I am finishing up these final words for this particular chapter (September 2018), I am in a place that I have not stood before.

Even though my wife and I stand once again facing this test that our Heavenly has challenged us to face and pass on so many occasions, this time it is different, for I dare say I believe my wife and I have made it, we have overcome because we now understand.

Since the recession hit us in 2015, I had only worked for 13 months out of 43 which has left us in quite some debt. Even as I was writing this book, we had only enough money in our account to pay a few more mortgage payments, some bills and food and there was no definite prospect of a job until next year (in 2019), another 3 months.

By this point of our financial crisis, we would usually be in a state of fear leading to dread, yes, a state of sin in fear and idolatry. But this time nothing, just a deep sense of great peace and contentment.

Our breakthrough came when we decided to kneel before God in our bedroom and repent for our fear of mammon and our idolatry of fear. We decided that this prayer was to be as deep and as serious a thing as it could possibly be in the light of the sin that we were guilty of.

We laid the burden at the cross in that room and as we exited the bedroom doorway I said to my wife "stop". When we cross over the threshold of this doorway, we have completely and utterly left that burden behind never to pick it up again, do you agree with me wife? To which my little lady agreed, and we took that step, and we took it in complete faith knowing that we had now stepped into a life never to see that burden–the "fear and the idolatry" ever again.

The very next day my wife and I put our new-found peace to the test and even though we had no money to spare we decided to sow financially into a ministry to help free enslaved children, and the peace remained upon us, praise the living God.

Within the next couple of weeks, a job unfolded to me that would not only destroy the mountain of debt that had almost but buried us alive in a very short period of time, but it would be a job that would catapult me into something that I would never have believed.

> For the wages of sin *is* death;
> (Rom 6:23)

Idolatry and fear are both terrible sins and the wages of sin is death. This sin of fear of mammon was death to our finances, we had cursed our finances by our sin.

I think it is also important to mention outside of the fear of financial lack that I have also met a number of Christians over the years who fear disease or sickness coming upon them because it afflicted their father or mother and their Grandfather or Grandmother before them, a generational curse if you will, inflicted by a familiar spirit who has gained legal ground in the family line.

I believe according to scripture that many types of revisiting generational diseases are caused by familiar spirits travelling down the family line and have seen much evidence to prove this and might I add that it is usually the fear of the individual worried about the same disease coming upon them that creates the open legal doorway.

Again, this is a self-imposed curse through the sin of fear.

"That which I greatly feared has come upon me".

Before closing out this chapter I would like to add one more nugget to the mix. Remember we looked at the Blessings and curses of Deuteronomy 28 when deciphering the story of Job, well in this we find God's judgement and chastisement for the sin of idolatry in the form of a curse:

and thy life shall hang in doubt before thee;
and thou shalt fear day and night,
and shalt have none assurance of thy life:
in the morning thou shalt say, Would God it were even!
and at even thou shalt say, Would God it were morning!
for the fear of thine heart wherewith thou shalt fear,
and for the sight of thine eyes which thou shalt see.
(Deut 28:66-67)

We must remember these two very clear realties, they are:

1. God will hand us over to that which we idolize if we are unwilling to turn away from such idolatry (Ezekiel 23).
2. God warns us to fear Him ONLY, His warning is to the Christian, not to the ungodly, the ungodly are already destined for hell.

And fear not them which kill the body,
but are not able to kill the soul:
but rather fear him which is able to destroy both soul and body in hell.
(Matth 10:28)

So now that we have gone through all of the mechanics of the origin of fear, the unnatural state of fear in the human life, how fear operates to pervert pure truth, the sin and idolatry of fear and what God thinks of it, let us move on to completely defeating this evil in our lives once and for all.

KEY STATEMENT 12: Fear is idolatry and God states:

Thou shalt have no other gods before me.
(Exodus 20:3)

And:

a blessing,
if ye obey the commandments of the LORD your God,
which I command you this day:
and a curse,
if ye will not obey the commandments of the LORD your God,
but turn aside out of the way which I command you this day,
to go after other gods, which ye have not known.
(Deuteronomy 11:27-28)

CHAPTER 5

PUTTING FEAR TO DEATH

FROM STUDYING FEAR OVER THE PAST TWENTY years and from my own life's experiences and ministry to others I have concluded that the evil of fear and the workings of this spirit can be overcome and defeated as the Christian follows these steps:

1. Destroying our old identity and receiving a clear understanding and revelation of our new identity in Christ.
2. Recognition of sin and repentance.
3. Complete TRUST in our Heavenly Father.
4. Understanding purpose, destiny, equipping and authority.

We will address each of these on the following pages, however a more detailed understanding is presented in the second book of this series called "3 levels of faith".

FALSE VS TRUE IDENTITY

Over the years I have had the opportunity and privilege of ministering to many people. I have found that so many men in particular who struggle with pride and arrogance all seem to have certain background commonalities, either they suffered abusive father's or absent fathers, and by the way when I say absent fathers that also includes the fathers that are physically present but emotionally absent.

I remember one young man in particular; we'll call him Glen.

Glen conveyed his story to me in that when he looked back on his life, he had wondered why he had struggled so much with pride and fear. He realized that he could trace it all the way back to child abuse. He recalls that up until the age of five he was horribly beaten by his biological father. Everyone who knew him from his childhood and into his twenties and thirties had no idea of what he had suffered.

The abuse stopped at the age of five when his mother divorced his dad, she then remarried.

The damage was done, imprinted, sown into his soul and he grew up hating male authority and bullies. He stated that as skinny and short as he was, he would never be bullied again, and no one would ever get away with bullying his younger brother either, he vowed. He recalled remembering when at the age of twelve he managed to buy a pair of army hobnail boots which he would wear if he knew he was going to end up in a fight.

All the kids his age were taller than he and his brother and so they would both get picked on plenty by the other kids, even those in the lower school grades would take their chance. At age twelve he developed a fighting style which involved getting his assailant to the ground as quickly as possible, then grab a hold of his hair and kick him in the face until the blood started flowing, he was so determined to give the bullies what they deserved, and it got him into a lot of trouble.

At such a young age the fear of being physically beaten by someone bigger than him was the motivating factor behind his brutality, he was absolutely terrified of physical confrontation and of being overpowered.

110

Beating the bigger kids helped his confidence level to grow over the years which then fed his pride and in certain other talents he possessed he thought he was the best thing since sliced bread, and went on to becoming a perfectionist, which eventually tired him out in his later life.

Fear was his driver, which led to self confidence, which led to perfectionism, which led to pride and arrogance.

Glen went on to explain how his soul was crying out for recognition, having never received it from his biological father or from his stepdad.

Although he only had vague memories of the abuse, it was his soul which remembered it all. The verbal abuse and beatings as a child from his biological dad, and then the ongoing putdowns for the rest of his youth and into his thirties and forties by his stepdad. When he did achieve anything, he so desperately wanted to hear the opposite, he wanted to hear praise–"well done, I'm so proud of you Son" but it never happened, not one single time, ever.

Eventually he learnt to praise himself which along with speaking ill of others became common practice. Self promotion, boasting, self grandeur and pride became a big part of his identity.

We all know that when we meet such people, the last thing we want to do is feed their ego, so it becomes a catch twenty-two. He so desperately desired to hear affirmation but no one would offer it to him.

Eventually Glen hated the world and would rather see a person in pain than a dog suffering. He suffered the worst depression, and the suicidal thoughts went on for years, he truly hated a loathed himself extremely.

There is so much more to Glen's story, but I hope you are getting the point. When you meet one of these boastful, prideful, arrogant types you can rest assured that their self-worth is near zero, and this is where the grace of God should be shown by all confessing Christians.

These prideful people are the type that state "I fear nothing" just like Glen professed, but deep down inside under all the armor of self-protection there are fears that even they are not aware of and the armour of pride and arrogance hides this weakness at all cost. It is only Jesus who can bring these things to the surface for them.

It is healing from the past wounds such people need and only Jesus can do this, and today Glen is living proof of this.

However, this takes a little work on the believer's part and Glen for one did not receive renewal or deliverance overnight from his issues; it took some years before he started to get his final breakthrough.

He had to submit himself to God's process and yield to His counsel regarding his new identity in Christ and the revelation of his Heavenly Father's love for him.

Identifying these ungodly traits in oneself through self examination will bring about the revelation of the fruits that manifest in one's life. The fruits come from roots which come from seeds past sown. These are lies which are to be destroyed by the renewing of the mind and the healing of the heart.

I would encourage the reader to consider Craig Hill's book, "*The Ancient Paths*" for further understanding on the issue of roots and fruits, [12]

Our Heavenly Father has made this renewal possible for each and every one of us through His Son's sacrifice, and this is His perfect love for us, and in this perfect love is the highest of Heavenly security for the soul of a child of the living God.

I hope I have explained this clearly enough for it to be a revelation, this is the key for those who find themselves as bound up as Glen was.

Again, I repeat this following scripture:

> There is no fear in love;
> but perfect love casteth out fear:
> because fear hath torment.
> He that feareth is not made perfect in love.
> (1 John 4:18)

This is the eternal key to being set free, when the light truly goes on regarding this scripture it holds all the power in the universe to liberate the abused soul.

God loves each and every one of us with a love which is so very much far above the love that can be experienced here on earth.

The closest we can come to this pure love here on earth is through our own biological fathers.

When a child is born it is God's intention that everything that a child needs to absolutely flourish is given first and foremost by its father. The father is accountable for making sure that these things happen, he is responsible for the strength and security of the family unit.

I like to give the analogy for the upbringing of a child like that of a chicken egg whereby the shell represents the father; the white represents the mother [nurture) and the yoke represents the child.

When the shell is broken and not intact as it should be, the family gets fried. The Bible defines the father as the strongman of the house and satan's plan is to bind up the strongman and plunder his household.

The father's responsibility to his children before God is to provide:

1. Security
2. Blessing
3. Identity
4. Encouragement and confidence

Now in Glen's case and in the case of millions of children the world over and especially with today's divorce rate as it is, we are seeing an unprecedented number of broken eggs.

The one human being on this planet that a child relies on for its identity and purpose is now no longer in the picture or is abusing them. Now if that child grows up without experiencing everything that encompasses true love from their earthly father as God intended it then how on earth will that child ever grow up thinking there is a father in heaven that loves them.

Glen for one was in Christ for over twenty years before he even started to get a glimpse of the reality of his Heavenly Father's true and pure love for him. Such understanding was so foreign to him and when he heard sermons and read scriptures on this subject, he just could not receive the revelation.

God the Father has the most perfect plan, purpose, and destiny for our lives. He is the most perfectly balanced Father that has ever existed. He means each and every one of us absolutely no harm, and His intention toward us all is to bring us into heaven as purely loved sons and daughters.

He desires to provide for you and I in every possible way down to the smallest of concerns and He wants us to come to a place of complete and utter trust in Him, so much so that fear, anxiety and stress would have absolutely no way of infiltrating our daily existence.

His perfect love received and fully understood will cast every ounce of fear into the wind of the past, never again to be experienced in any way shape or form.

We must be re-made if you will, to receive, understand and embrace His perfect love.

He that feareth is not made perfect in love.
(1 John 4:18)

In order for us as Christians to thrive in our faith, it is of the utmost importance that we thoroughly cast of our old identity and embrace the new identity in Christ; this however takes some work on our part. It means studying the scriptures diligently and faithfully on a daily basis.

One must pursue the sanctification of the heart and the renewal of the mind, again I state, this means action on the part of the Christian.

Sanctify them through thy truth: thy word is truth.
(John 17:17)

and be renewed in the spirit of your mind;
and that ye put on the new man,
which after God is created in righteousness and true holiness.
(Eph 4:23-24)

Without this transition becoming complete we will either have an endless struggle with not knowing who we truly are, be in danger of continued defeatism or worse still end up falling away from our faith and salvation because there is no firm grounding.

> And these are they likewise which are sown on stony ground;
> who, when they have heard the word, immediately receive it
> with gladness;
> and have no root in themselves, and so endure but for a time:
> (Mark 4:16-17)

In Chapter two we looked at the eternal transition of the human being from being in the Glory of Almighty God, not knowing any of the emotional attributes of the fallen state of sin to moving into an enslaved state.

In this state man's identity is defined by the nature of sin and evil and in this state, man is enslaved to fear and every other darkened reaction and emotion.

As previously stated, once in Christ we now begin a journey to complete freedom from everything which enslaved us, from the unnatural to the natural, from the defiled state back to the glorious state and from all fear to a powerful, complete and pure faith. There is no greater state of security for the human soul.

> Therefore if any man *be* in Christ, *he is* a new creature:
> old things are passed away; behold, all things are become new.
> (2 Corinthians 5:17)

We have now become the children of the living God and the Father above all fathers.

> Ye are of God, little children, and have overcome them:
> because greater is he that is in you, than he that is in the world.
> (1 John 4:4)

We can no longer look at ourselves in the natural because the moment we accepted Jesus into our lives we became completely new creatures... supernatural creatures once again.

Now the struggle is this: You have spent a lifetime being you. Life, upbringing, situations bad and good, education and the list goes on, this is what has defined you.

The habits you have formed, the traits you have acquired, your moral stance and convictions and everything else that has rubbed up against your life and into your life is what has made you who you are. Good and bad.

You are who you are and there is no escaping this reality, which is... until Christ entered your being.

Christ in you, the hope of glory
(Colossians 1:27)

Notice the Word "hope" in this scripture, it implies that it "might be". It is a word that describes something in the future.

Christ in the human being is two becoming one, a partnership of renewal and the covenantal agreement of a unity of the whole person with and in Christ, His Spirit and our spirit as one, His mind and our mind becoming one. The "hope" is the journey in this scriptural marriage to be.

In other words, a complete sanctification from the old man into a new man with a completely renewed mind free from all the baggage of the old mindset. This is achieved by the believer meditating on the Word of God and by absolutely no other means. Again, Paul states:

Sanctify them through thy truth: thy word is truth.
(John 17:17)

Sanctification is spiritual cleansing; it is a process which takes time. Look at this scripture carefully; we are sanctified by the truth of the Word. So, Christian's who do not emerge themselves in God's Word regularly will find very little sanctification taking place in their lives, little or no renewing of the mind, their salvation is not being "worked out", they fail to deal with the spots and blemishes, they fail to make themselves ready for the Lord.

For those who are diligent, the cleansing by His Word will rid the believer of all the negative attributes of the old personality and character.

Jesus takes over and we become the new person defined in Him, and all those nasty things which defined us, and distorted our self-image then lose their grasp, strength and power in our lives.

Many know that Christ is in them, but few come to understand they and Christ are now truly one.

> But he that is joined unto the Lord is one spirit.
> (1 Corinthians 6:17)

The two must become one, with the greater rising above the lesser, Jesus being the head and we the body. We must say more of Him and less of me.

> He must increase, but I *must* decrease.
> (John 3:30)

However, the length of this transitional process is up to the individual and is dependent firstly, as I have previously stated, on the amount of time spent in the Word of God followed by our sincere self-examination, prayer and repentance.

> And be not conformed to this world:
> but be ye transformed by the renewing of your mind,
> that ye may prove what *is* that good,
> and acceptable, and perfect, will of God.
> (Romans 12:2)

His Word must become the new measure of what defines us as children of God. This is so vitally important.

An analogy of this would be like taking an old computer which has picked up a bunch of viruses and cannot run efficiently.

Without the anti-virus program installed it will always run with problems. However, download the anti-virus program and run it then the cleanup takes place, and the computer will run as it was initially intended to do so, back to the original state.

The key however is not just to install the program but to run it too. Christians can read all the scriptures they want but unless one walks in the scriptures then it only just becomes a headful of knowledge, the heart must change.

As with the computer, the hard drive must be debugged, so too the heart of man must be sanctified.

I have counselled many Christians over the years who have come to me with basic issues and who have been Christians for over twenty years but cannot even quote half a dozen short scriptures.

Does God's Word not state that the person who meditates on the Word day and night shall be blessed (Psalm 1)? Well then, the opposite must also be true.

Does the Word also not state that we are to talk of the scriptures daily to each other? (Deut 6:6-8 and 11:18-20)?

Does not the Word command that the Word is to dwell within us richly?

Let the word of Christ dwell in you richly.
(Colossians 3:16)

We each have a choice. Your image depends upon which mirror you look into on a daily basis, is it going to be the image from the world's mirror which has been created and tainted by satan or the mirror of God's Word?

Which reflection do you see, do you see your old self, new self or something in between?

The more you look at the image of Christ and His glory, the more you begin to reflect Jesus in you. Remember, what you behold you become.

Know the Truth and the Truth will set you free. Truth liberates us from the image of death for in Christ we will live forever.

> and ye shall know the truth, and the truth shall make you free.
> (John 8:32)

The partnership that we have with Christ who dwells within each one of us must be a unity of the spirit soul and body. Jesus is not a fornicator or a drunkard, therefore if I am in the sin of fornication or drunkenness then I am not in unity with Him for He is without sin and if He and I are one then how can darkness and light dwell in unity and in the same body, it is impossible.

> Then spake Jesus again unto them, saying,
> I am the light of the world:
> he that followeth me shall not walk in darkness,
> but shall have the light of life.
> (John 8:12)

> Doth a fountain send forth at the same place sweet *water* and bitter?
> (James 3:11)

> whosoever believeth on me should not abide in darkness.
> (John 12:46)

Sin is darkness and every trait that abides in a person such as pride, arrogance, jealousy and fear, etc. has no place in the Christian.

All sin inspired characteristics and emotions are not to be part of our identity. Our image is to be that of Christ and Christ alone.

There are hundreds of scriptures declaring our new identity, here are just a few:

In John–I am a child of God (1:12); I am part of the true vine, a channel of Christ's life (15:1, 5); I am Christ's friend (15:15); I am chosen and appointed by Christ to bear His fruit (15:16).

In Romans–I am free from sin and I am a servant of righteousness (6:18); I am a servant to God (6:22); I am a son/daughter of God and adopted by God the Father (8:14, 15); I am joint-heir with Christ, sharing His inheritance with Him (8:17).

In 1 Corinthians–I am a temple, a dwelling place of God. His Spirit and His life dwell in me (3:16, 6:19); I am united to the Lord and am one spirit with Him (6:17).

When we truly meditate on these scriptures and truly receive them for ourselves then the sanctification takes place. The truth completely overrides the entrenched lie in our soul.

The light eliminates the darkness, but we must embrace that light of the truth and hold onto it with everything we have and believe it, and then rejoice in it. Remember – "you shall know the TRUTH and the TRUTH shall set you FREE (John 8:32).

As discussed in Chapter 3 under the "blessings or curses", in this new identity, we now live under a new law.

For the law of the Spirit of life in Christ Jesus hath made me free
from the law of sin and death.
(Romans 8:2)

Two opposite laws exist in this life and only two.

The one is "the law of sin and death" and the other is "the law of life in Christ Jesus". There is nothing else in between or on either side; it is either one or the other.

In one you will find fear and in the other you will find faith.

- **In death** – we find fear, sin, sickness, death and suffering, worry and anxiety.

- **In Life** – we find faith, righteousness, healing and God given health, peace and love, a completely new identity.

Before becoming a Christian, most people have a fear of death and those who have a fear of death usually do not know it until it faces them square on in the moment.

When we are "born again" most Christians will have an inward witness that we need not fear death. I say most because there are still those that fear even lesser things than death.

Forasmuch then as the children are partakers of flesh and blood,
he also himself likewise took part of the same;
that through death he might destroy him that had the power of death,
that is, the devil;
and deliver them who through fear of death
were all their lifetime subject to bondage.
(Hebrews 2:14-15)

As believers, we must decide not to fear, it is up to the believer to choose which spiritual law will operate in his or her life.

The LORD *is* on my side; I will not fear:
what can man do unto me?
(Psalm 118:6)

As stated before, a believer cannot live with one foot in the kingdom of darkness and the other foot in the kingdom of light.

When a human being is conceived in the womb the spiritual curse of the fall which is death is passed on from the parents to the child.

Because Jesus did not have a human father, he did not receive hereditary sin or the curse or the fear of death.

Jesus had no manifestation of sin because God could not accept a sacrifice blemished with sin. Jesus who knew no sin came to rescue us from sin and the law of sin and death.

The next day John seeth Jesus coming unto him, and saith,
Behold the Lamb of God, which taketh away the sin of the world.
(John 1:29)

So, you and I not only have partnership and unity with a Holy God, but He actually lives on the inside of us.

This oneness with Christ can be so difficult to comprehend for many, however it is important to strive towards grasping this as a clear and firm understanding, it must become a revelation, it must become "Rhema" (received in deep faith) to our souls and for the following reasons:

- ✓ So that we can do His good works.
- ✓ So that we can bring Him glory.

For we are his workmanship, created in Christ Jesus unto good works,
which God hath before ordained that we should walk in them.
(Ephesians 2:10)

even every one that is called by my name:
for I have created him for my glory,
I have formed him; yea, I have made him.
(Isaiah 43:7)

Remember, our identity is no longer an identity that fears. It is an identity which is as bold as a Lion.

the righteous are bold as a lion.
(Proverbs 28:1)

All that God intends and wants is not dependent on us but on Christ in us. God's motive is pure grace so that we can do all things through Christ who strengthens us. (Philippians 4:13)

His Love is our Security

But Fear is torment

Once we have a true revelation of our identity as God sees us then we can be equipped with Authority and Boldness to do the work of the Lord, in this state of identity we are ready to receive the faith of a servant, as the Word states – to bring Him glory.

KEY STATEMENT 13: We have a new identity in Christ, but it takes work on our part to renew our minds by the sanctification process through the studying and meditating on the word of God regularly.

THE POWER OF TRUST

So here are two men in the middle of Africa, the driver and his friend are volunteer doctors who are hundreds of miles from the nearest town and sitting in a pickup truck at the edge of a wide, fast flowing, and deep river. Before them is an old wooden bridge which has no safety rails, it is the middle of the night, pitch dark and the wind is howling. The rain is coming down in buckets and the bridge seems to be moving eerily.

This bridge is very old and dilapidated and due to its severely poor and unsafe condition it has become renowned for taking a number of vehicles and their occupants over the years to a watery grave.

They must cross it to get to the other side because there is nowhere else to cross, the supplies they are transporting include some critical vaccines and life saving medicines which are desperately needed at their destination.

The friend says he will walk ahead of the vehicle and in the light of the headlamps will attempt to guide the vehicle around the rottenest parts of timber.

They know that there are only two outcomes, either they will make it, or they will not. They both have the courage to face the challenge but at the same time they are plagued by uncertainty. If they decide to go for it then their decision will be based solely on the confidence and trust they have in themselves as they both suffer a very limited trust in the bridge.

When you or I take this situation into our Christian walk as an analogy it goes something like this.

Every single situation and trouble we find ourselves facing is like a river we have to cross. Yet, no matter how hard the wind is blowing, no matter how foreboding the crossings seems to be, we have complete confidence and complete trust that the bridge will ensure a safe crossing and this is because the bridge is our Heavenly Father, the comfort that we sense is the Holy Spirit and the one guiding us across is Jesus.

We know that whatever the outcome, it has been planned for our good even if at the time the outcome seems bad.

And we know that all things work together for good
to them that love God,
to them who are the called according to *his* purpose.
(Romans 8:28)

Unlike the scenario given in the analogy, the roles are switched, and the greater confidence and trust is in the bridge and not in ourselves. The bridge is totally sound and built perfectly and will never fail for all eternity. In each and every situation of our Christian lives there is one factor that remains solid, it's the bridge.

If I find that my trusting is not absolutely one hundred percent, then I have not yet arrived in the completeness of my identity as a "believer". Believing and trusting go hand in hand. I must unwaveringly trust the bridge in order to believe that I will arrive on the other side.

If I fail to completely trust the bridge then likewise, I have failed to believe God's word for the issues at hand and if I do not fully believe then I must proclaim God's word to be a lie and that I am not truly a believer.

I cannot do justice to God on this topic any more than which these two following verses do so powerfully establish.

Read them carefully, meditate on them over and over again, never let them fade away but have them at the forefront of your thinking every single day of your life, in so doing we will establish the perfect trust that God is looking for.

Do what you must do to remember them and to place them on the mantle of your existence. The first of these two verses provide the answer to the obtaining of "perfect peace". This is the highest form of peace in existence with absolutely no conditions attached other than the absolute complete and unwavering trust in our Heavenly Father.

Thou wilt keep him in perfect peace,
whose mind is stayed on thee:
because he trusteth in thee.
(Isaiah 26:3)

Trust in the Lord with all thine heart;
and lean not unto thine own understanding.
In all thy ways acknowledge him,
and he shall direct thy paths.
(Proverbs 3:5-6)

Hundreds of thousands of ungodly people the world over have placed their absolute trust in an elastic rope, a harness and some aluminum clips when jumping off a bridge bungee jumping even though any one part of all the equipment mentioned has the potential to fail through the smallest of manufacture flaw.

Millions and millions of people will place their trust in a pilot that they have never met when boarding a plane which will take them to thirty thousand feet in the air and without the supply of a parachute, and billions of folk will put their trust in false gods to protect them, yet, so many Christians find it difficult to place one hundred percent, absolute trust in their Heavenly Father.

The trust that our Heavenly Father desires for us to walk in toward Him is the trust that Daniel had when having to face the lions. What a moment that must have been, what Christian would have such trust today if faced with the exact same predicament.

The trust that our Heavenly Father desires for us to walk in toward Him is the trust that Shadrach, Meshach, and Abed-nego had when stepping toward the burning fiery furnace. Again, "what a moment", imagine facing such a thing. Yet, these three men of God did not even flinch, they manifested not even the smallest amount of fear.

In both of the above cases the outcome was that of a terrifyingly painful death, yet it bothered them not in the slightest.

It is this level of trust that every Christian is to cultivate within their lives. Recognizing the hindrances and barriers in one's own life to cultivating such trust is of paramount importance. Only with this trust can God move us along the path of His perfect plan for our lives. In my book titled 3 levels of faith I give a detailed account of my own personal experience with being tested in a higher trust, although my experience does not have me facing death it most assuredly was a test of which effected my entire family.

We start in belief which builds into trust, the greater the trust the greater the faith, and in this the sin and spirit of fear will be defeated forever.

RECOGNITION OF SIN AND REPENTANCE

So often we fail to deal with the defiling things of our spiritual walk with our Lord simply because we fail to recognize the characteristics of the sin itself.

For example, alcoholics and addicts never start on the road to recovery until he or she recognizes and receives the revelation of their sickness. These people are usually under such self-deception and/or denial that no matter how hard one tries to convince them that they need help it is just not going to happen, they simply do not see it or want to see it. To rise above the denial is always the first step to freedom.

There are other types of sin that have the same delusional effect such as pride, vanity, control, fear and covetousness just to name a few and these are so very difficult to see in oneself.

However, I have found over the years of ministering to others that it is not until I breakdown the fruits and characteristics of the sin that the person begins to get a breakthrough of seeing the sin in its ugly wholeness for the first time in their lives.

I once asked an elderly man if he recognized any sin in his life to which he replied "I have no sin", and he was so totally convinced of it. I knew otherwise for I had witnessed him committing much sin in such a short time frame.

His sin ranged in extreme pride, boasting, filthy talk, swearing, course jesting, hatred, racism, lying, self-righteousness, selfishness, self-grandeur, controlling and hypocrisy just to mention a few things, yet he stated he had no sin and believed he was a Christian. After a while I managed to talk to him about what God classifies as sin to which he replied he had never seen those things as sin before. Remember, Job stated the same thing, "I am clean, neither is there iniquity in me" (Job 33:8-9).

You see like most Christians who do not know the Bible this elderly man thought that sin was all the big stuff like adultery, murder, theft and the like. Unfortunately, he had given his heart to the Lord some thirty years back but never bothered picking up a Bible to read it and so he adds the sin of apathy and spiritual slothfulness to his un-repented baggage and probably wonders why things have gone so very wrong for him for so many years.

> He who conceals his transgressions will not prosper,
> But he who confesses and forsakes them will find compassion.
> (Proverbs 28:13)

When we read this scripture, we tend to immediately think towards financial prosperity but that is not what it is saying, this scripture covers the prosperity of the Christian in every area of their life, prosperity in health, wealth, the soul, the mind, one's intellect, knowledge, wisdom and the list goes on. We have to come clean with God, nothing can be hidden from Him, He sees everything. If we come clean and repent and look to Him for deliverance from all fear, He will do it.

> I sought the Lord, and He heard me,
> And delivered me from all my fears.
> (Psalm 34:4)

As we have discovered in the beginning of this book, there are many fruits that the tree of fear bears and it helps to know what they are so that we can look at our daily lives and the reactions that we have in situations to determine if any of these fruits are present.

If you recognize any forms of fear in your life then it is as simple as owning it as sin, it cannot be sugarcoated. One must be remorseful about the sin, and then ask your Heavenly Father to forgive you and to set you free of its hold in your life. This is the first step to real freedom in the realm of fear. See it, own it, REPENT, it's that simple.

Analyse it. What are you afraid of? Where did it begin? Were your actions controlled by fear? Confess the bad and unacceptable reactions fueled by fear as sin, and this goes for all sin (Psalm 38:18).

Work out a plan of responsible behaviour. Sometimes doing the thing that you fear the most (within reason) will ascertain the death of that fear. (Psalm 91:5,9-10)

Determine beforehand what your response to a fear should be (in the Lord) and then carry it out. Respond verbally to resist the attack of fear by using the sword of the Spirit and the Name of Jesus. (Matt 10:25-27, 1 John 5:18-20)

I must state that God has given to us a clear process for repentance and it is this:

Confess *your* faults one to another,
and pray one for another, that ye may be healed.
(James 5:16)

This means sitting with a brother or sister in Christ that you can earnestly trust and ask that person to pray for you as you openly confess your sins. Why would God have it done this way, well for a couple of reasons?

1. Confessing your sin to another can only bring about humility which is what God wants to see.
2. Confessing your sin to another creates accountability.
3. Confessing your sin to another means there is a witness to your humility, honesty, sincerity and commitment to holiness, this is powerful in the spirit realm.
4. And last but not least you are fulfilling God's requirement as the above scripture commands. We so often like to do it our way and not Gods way, but our way does not work or yield the fruits that God's given process will yield.

KEY STATEMENT 14: So often we fail to deal with the defiling things of our spiritual walk with our Lord simply because we fail to recognize the characteristics of the sin itself.

PURPOSE, DESTINY, EQUIPPING AND AUTHORITY

Moses had a calling on his life and what a mighty calling it was. He would go down in history being known not only by those who read the story in the Bible but by many non-believers the world over. Ask the average person if they have ever heard of Moses and chances are, they know who you are talking about.

Do you think that Moses ever thought that he would be remembered in such a way during the first forty years of his life as an Egyptian, or how about the second forty years of his life tending sheep in Midian? I am pretty sure he did not. Even if Moses were resolute within his heart that he had a calling on his life when he discovered that he was actually a Hebrew and not Egyptian, such a resolution would have faded across the expanse of forty years tending sheep in the middle of nowhere.

What about Joseph, do you think that he saw much of a calling on his life after being sold into slavery, being falsely accused by Potiphar's wife, and then sitting in a dungeon for a number of years? I don't think so.

These however are both typical examples of God's preparation period of one's character. Once accomplished, God will then birth the refined person into their purpose and destiny.

Consider this, that God is not in the business of birthing even one single human being onto this planet that he has not already designed a purpose and destiny for.

To fulfill one's God ordained purpose and destiny can only come about by first acknowledging God's will for one's life is perfect and that our own will for our lives' is imperfect,–our will, our mess.

Secondly, complete surrender to God's will for our lives is without any reservation whatsoever, which means seeking Him out daily for the road ahead.

And last but not least, accepting the pains of preparation no matter how isolating, lonely and dark that preparation period might be or last, it's all for a reason and no different than everything Moses or Joseph had to endure.

When I look back on my own life, I can confess that I have hated my job for the best part of forty years. I always felt that there had to be more to life than putting metal together. I would look at these oil refineries that we were building or repairing and see nothing but meaningless in the light of eternal value. Fear was ever present in all of my jobs, "have I done enough, am I doing well, can I do the job", I hated it but knew there was nothing I could do about it, I had to work to earn money to provide for my family just like everyone else.

Little did I realize that every challenge I faced, every problem to solve and every mistake that I made was a steppingstone to the next level of knowledge, understanding and wisdom.

Had I not gone through everything I did, had I not faced my fears and overcome them then I would not be who I am today, and I would not be of any use to God.

None of us who are walking in God's will for our lives is allowed or permitted to skip a steppingstone, Moses had to tend sheep for forty years and Joseph had to visit prison. We might not understand God's reasoning, but He knows perfectly well how He needs to equip us for the Authority that He is planning to give us for the task at hand.

You and I might not be a Moses or a Joseph but that by no means eliminates or disqualifies us from God's personal and devoted attention on us as an average everyday person.

The Word gives us proof of this in James 5:17 with regards to a man who we would consider just as big a deal as Moses and Joseph however God states that he was a man with a nature like any other man.

Now if Elijah was no different than any other man then it would do us good to know what that means on a spiritual note.

In 1 Kings, chapter 17:1 the Word reveals that Elijah was a Tishbite, who was of the inhabitants of Gilead

Tishbite – (Heb)–"recourse"–adopt as helper or advisor.
Gilead – (Heb) – "Heap of Testimony"

This is the beauty of God's Word insomuch as every single name of a place or a person has a meaning behind it that God wants us to discover.

Plainly put, Elijah was a man with a "heap of testimony" for he was from Gilead, he like many a man had a long past of useful experiences that had helped to shape his character. Being a Tishbite (recourse–adopt as a helper or advisor) was by no small coincidence pointing towards the call of God in his life, God could now use him as a useful yet mature helper and mouthpiece and that He did, He made him a Prophet to the people.

We can therefore summarize the scripture without altering it's meaning as such:

Elijah, appointed of God, was a helper and advisor (Tishbite) from among those who had a heap of testimony (Gilead).

Each and every one of us are no different than Elijah, we all have our own heap of testimony from our life experience, if you will, we are all from Gilead in the calling of God.

Every single one of us has been called to be a mouthpiece for the good news of Christ, if you will, we are all Tishbites,–mouthpieces for God.

And they overcame him by the blood of the Lamb
and by the word of their testimony,
(Revelation 12:11)

Preach the word! Be ready in season *and* out of season.
(2 Timothy 4:2)

The Kingdom of darkness does not want for you or I to enter in to our calling of God. If Moses had remained in any bondage to fear then such courage to confront Pharaoh and eventually lead God's people from Egypt would never have taken place, Moses did his job.

If Joseph had remained in any bondage to fear, then such courage to run the Egyptian empire through a seven-year famine would never have taken place, Joseph did his job.

If Elijah had remained in any bondage to fear, then such courage to challenge the prophets of Baal on Mount Carmel would never have taken place, Elijah did his job.

God's ultimate goal during the refinement process of preparation is to purge each and every one of us from the bondage of fear to the end that our complete and unrestrained trust is in Him and Him alone.

Once accomplished God can then move the individual into his or her calling, to do their job.

Being in bondage to anything that would either rob us of our pure identity in Christ, rob us of our individual calling and purpose, rob us of His most good and perfect will for our lives would mean to rob us of becoming the "overcomer" which is our right, our being and our inheritance.

He that overcometh, the same shall be clothed in white raiment;
and I will not blot out his name out of the book of life,
but I will confess his name before my Father,
and before his angels.
(Revelation 3:5)

how shall we escape, if we neglect so great salvation;
(Hebrews 2:3)

work out your own salvation with fear and trembling.
(Philippians 2:12)

YOU CAN DO IT
Be encouraged,
And be transformed.

Notes:

For further reading on this topic please go to the second book in this two-part message called "3 levels of faith".

For prayers concerning fear please see the next section of this book.

AUTHORITIVE PRAYERS

REPENTANCE OF FEAR

Dear Heavenly Father

I come before you now in the precious and all-powerful name of Jesus Christ, your beloved Son and my Lord and Savior.

I ask you Father, to forgive me for the sin of fear in my life.

I repent of every form of fear and everything related to this evil spirit that has been robbing me of boldness, courage and bravery in certain areas of my life and which has held me back from fully developing in the Supernatural faith of your Kingdom that I am supposed to be walking in.

I take authority over that spirit now and as I have been given the authority over all the power of the enemy in accordance with Luke 10:19, I wield that authority now in your name Lord Jesus and I command the spirit of fear to loose my life and be gone from me right now. The Lord Jesus Christ rebuke you.

Father, bless me with understanding, guide me into knowledge and equip me to do your work.

I now commit myself to your good and perfect will for my life. Reveal to me the plans, purpose and destiny that you have for me and I will commit myself, body, soul and spirit to your refining process and the building up of my faith to proclaim you to the world.

Thank you, Heavenly Father, in Jesus name.
AMEN

DESTROYING FEAR IN MY CHILDREN

Dear Heavenly Father

I come before you now in the precious and all-powerful name of Jesus Christ, your beloved Son and my Lord.

I ask you Father, to forgive me for allowing the sin of fear to rule my child/children.

I take up the authority over all the power of the enemy in accordance with Luke 10:19, and I wield that authority now in your name Lord Jesus and I command the spirit of fear to loose my child/children and be gone from them right now. The Lord Jesus Christ rebukes you.

Father, please help me to find practical ways of installing boldness, courage, bravery and Supernatural faith into the lives of my child/children in a well-balanced manner along with teaching them the power of your written Word for this life ahead of them.

I thank you for the responsibility that you have blessed me with in raising these young Christians soldiers for your kingdom.

I pray a hedge of protect around them. I cancel the works, the plans and the schemes of the kingdom of darkness against them and I pray according to your Word in Hosea 4:6 that no weapon that is EVER forged against the shall prevail. I thank you for hearing my heart and my prayer.

In Jesus name.
AMEN

REPENTANCE FOR DECEPTION

Dear Heavenly Father

I come before you now in the precious and all-powerful name of Jesus Christ, your beloved Son and my Lord.

Father, please forgive me for all and any error or deception that I might be walking in or have walked in due to my beliefs, false teachings that I have accepted or denominational error.

I sincerely repent and distance myself now from a powerless faith, please guide me in your truth of the whole Word and counsel of God no matter how uncomfortable it might be for me.

From here forward I will submit myself to the guidance and teaching of your Holy Spirit and I will be diligent in questioning that which I listen to without fearing man.

I take up the authority over all the power of the enemy in accordance with Luke 10:19, I wield that authority now in your name Lord Jesus and I command you spirit of error and deception to be gone from my life forever. I sever all ties and unity with you and the Lord Jesus Christ rebuke you.

Father I pray in accordance with your Word in Isaiah 11:2-3 that the spirit of the LORD would rest upon me, and that I would receive without reserve the spirit of wisdom and understanding, the spirit of counsel and might, the spirit of knowledge and of the fear of the LORD;

So that I would receive quick understanding in the fear of the LORD. May your name be praised from my whole being from this day forward and may I bring Glory to your NAME in everything I do.

In Jesus precious name I pray.
AMEN

KEY STATEMENT SUMMARY

KEY STATEMENT 1: Scripture has enlightened us to the fact that fear is a spirit, and it is not a heavenly and holy spirit. It is a real entity, an intelligent being, a demonic spirit which is assigned by satan against Christians to destroy their faith and render them useless for God's kingdom work in the Spirit.

KEY STATEMENT 2: The fear which God is displeased with, is simple, down to earth, common fear, this is the same fear that we are all very used to in our daily lives.

KEY STATEMENT 3: Without the fear of the Lord which is "good fear" we cannot overcome the evil sin of common fear, for ONLY by the fear of God can we depart from any and all sin, fear included.

KEY STATEMENT 4: Adam and Eve changed from the normal God designed state of man into an abnormal condition.

- From the God thinking state to the satanic thinking state.
- From a heart and mind of faith to a heart and mind of fear.

KEY STATEMENT 5: We must understand that when a person becomes a believer – that person has stepped from the un-natural realm of fear and into the original and normal realm of faith.

- Fear must be left behind.
- Fear must be discarded.
- Fear and faith CANNOT coexist.

KEY STATEMENT 6: It is God's intention that a believer walk in complete freedom in the mind, and that of a sound mind, not a distorted mind plagued by fears.

KEY STATEMENT 7: It is important to understand that the crime of the sin of fear can be carried out in different ways, which are:

- Believing in fear,
- Acting in fear,
- Speaking in fear.

KEY STATEMENT 8: We are responsible for appropriating what Jesus accomplished for us on the cross. This means action on our part, not mindless apathy, and convenient false belief.

KEY STATEMENT 9: When the word of God tells us to choose between life and death, blessing or curse, God is not saying that it is harder to be cursed than it is to be blessed. He places them both on equal terms. When He tells us to choose, He is saying, by your beliefs, actions and words you will either operate in blessing or a curse, so choose with great wisdom.

KEY STATEMENT 10: satan plays a legal game and the confession of our mouth is our amen (so be it). This is reality.

Remember this, that every negative confession is sin. The Word of God states that everything that is not of faith is sin. Therefore, every negative confession is in fact an act of calling God a liar in His promises toward us.

For us as believers, God gives clear warning as to the final detriments of a loose and foolish tongue.

> But I say unto you, That every idle word that men shall speak,
> they shall give account thereof in the day of judgment.
> (Matthew 12:36)

KEY STATEMENT 11: We find that when a person walks in pride they also walk in fear. Why is this, well the soul of man knows that under the spirit of pride there is no security even if the individual does not understand this the soul surely does.

KEY STATEMENT 12: Fear is idolatry and God states:

> Thou shalt have no other gods before me.
> (Exodus 20:3)

And:

> a blessing,
> if ye obey the commandments of the LORD your God,
> which I command you this day:
> and a curse, if ye will not obey the commandments of the
> LORD your God,
> but turn aside out of the way which I command you this day,
> to go after other gods, which ye have not known.
> (Deuteronomy 11:27-28)

KEY STATEMENT 13: We have a new identity in Christ, but it takes work on our part to renew our minds by the sanctification process by studying and meditating on the word of God regularly.

KEY STATEMENT 14: So often we fail to deal with the defiling things of our spiritual walk with our Lord simply because we fail to recognize the characteristics of the sin itself.

KEY STATEMENT 15: Consider this, that God is not in the business of birthing even one single human being onto this planet that he has not already designed a purpose and destiny for.

To fulfill one's God ordained purpose and destiny can only come about by first acknowledging God's will for one's life is perfect and that our own will for our lives' is imperfect,–our will, our mess.

ENDNOTES

1   The American Institute of Stress, *Stress and Heart Disease*, (https://www.stress.org/stress-and-heart-disease/).

2   The World Health Organization, The top 10 causes of death, (https://www.who.int/news-room/fact-sheets/detail/the-top-10-causes-of-death), 24th May 2014.

3   Xiaojing Guo, Zhen Meng and Guifeng Huang, *Meta-analysis of the prevalence of anxiety disorders in mainland China from 2000 to 2015,* (School of Public Health of Guangxi Medical University, Nanning, Guangxi, China, 2016), https://www.nature.com/articles/srep28033

4   Anxiety and Depression Association of America, *Anxiety disorders are the most common mental illness in the US today,* https://adaa.org/about-adaa/press-room/facts-statistics

5   Anxiety Disorders on the Rise in the Ranks, https://swampland.time.com/2013/11/05/anxiety-disorders-on-the-rise-in-the-ranks/

6   Anxiety Disorders on the Rise in the Ranks, https://swampland.time.com/2013/11/05/anxiety-disorders-on-the-rise-in-the-ranks/

7   Dr. John Burnet https://discoverthebook.org/

8   Reverend David Wilkerson, https://en.wikipedia.org/wiki/David_Wilkerson

9   Max von Sydow, https://en.wikipedia.org/wiki/Max_von_Sydow

10   Derek Prince, They Shall Expel DEMONS, ISBN 10:0-8007-9260-2, Published by Chosen books.

11   John G. Lake, https://web.archive.org/web/20110131113853/http://johnglake.org/#main

12   Craig Hill, *The Ancient Paths*, (Harvest books, 1992, ISBN: 1-881189-01-5)

Lightning Source UK Ltd.
Milton Keynes UK
UKHW021339270123
416064UK00015B/1072

SANDRAKER

HEIDE GOODY
IAIN GRANT

1

W hen Sam woke in the middle of the night, there was a Viking on her lawn.

She'd slept through the first notification beep on her phone, waking long enough to register, contemplate and ignore the second. When the phone actually rang a few minutes later, she blinked in the dark of her bedroom and looked at the screen. It was a local Skegness number.

"Hello," she croaked, cleared her throat and tried again. "Hello."

She only caught half of the opening sentence. "What? Am I an adult?"

The man repeated himself.

"Am I appropriate?" She wanted to believe it was a nuisance call so she could hang up. "Do you know what time it is?" she said, rolling out of bed.

He did. He told her. It was ten minutes to midnight.

The man repeated the gist of what he had now said three times.

"Okay," Sam said, glancing through the gap in her bedroom curtains. "There's a Viking in my garden," she said.

The man asked her to repeat herself.

"Nothing," she said. "I'm on my way."

Sam dressed quickly and quietly. Dressing quietly was just a matter of habit. *Duncastin'* was a large house, with only two of them living in it. She checked the two notifications from her DefCon4 app. One was linked to the phone call she'd just received and the other was for a DefCon4 burglar alarm which had gone off at a property on the A158. She tied her hair back, swilled mouthwash, and made her way along the mammoth bungalow's serpentine central corridor towards the front door.

She paused by her dad's bedroom door. "Dad," she whispered. "Dad, I've got to go out. It's work. I won't be long."

There was no reply. She considered her options, then pushed the door open.

Her dad, Marvin Applewhite, was on his side, eyes shut, mouth hanging open. The light of his reading lamp caught the lines on his face in yellow light and illuminated the creased celebrity autobiography he had dropped as he fell asleep.

Sam was about to close the door again but was caught by his stillness. She looked at his quilt cover. She watched his buttoned pyjamas. There was no movement.

"Dad?" she whispered.

He mushed his lips noisily. "I'm not dead, you know," he murmured, eyes closed.

"I didn't..."

"You were thinking it." He inhaled deeply, eyes still closed. "Where are you going?"

"The police station. Oh, and there's a Viking in our garden."

"Anyone we know?"

"Possibly Ragnar Odinson."

He nodded against his pillow, trying to approximate sleep. "Why are you going to the police station."

"I'm an appropriate adult."

"Debatable," he said.

Sam closed the door. She went out onto the driveway.

"I didn't mean to startle thee," said Ragnar as he stepped from the gloom of the garden.

It was a point worth making. Ragnar Odinson had a potentially disturbing appearance. He was a broad-shouldered man, with powerful-looking arms that might have been even more powerful-looking in his youth. Time hadn't aged Ragnar so much as weathered him. His face was a tanned bronze, broken up by a city map of deep wrinkles. His brown-grey beard was long, heavy and braided randomly here and there. As the self-appointed leader of a Viking clan, he deliberately favoured leather and rough-woven garments, giving the overall impression of a Hell's Angel who enjoyed medieval re-enactments at the weekend.

The Odinson clan lived in a corner of a shabby caravan park with poor soil drainage and no obvious appeal. Their circle of static caravans had grown over the years and, with the addition of several makeshift sheds and outbuildings, turned into a small private compound; a miniature village.

Maybe in some dusty US state such a set up would be home to an apocalyptic cult, with enough weaponry to hold off the FBI. In this corner of Lincolnshire it was home to a man whose mid-life crisis involved delusions of being a Viking, and those children and grandchildren who were happy to play along.

Sam wasn't startled by Ragnar. The man was essentially harmless. If he liked you. And if he wasn't drunk. And if you didn't happen to possess something he fancied stealing.

"How long have you been standing out here?" asked Sam.

"I was cogitating on whether to knock or not."

"I meant, why are you here at all?" she said. "I've got to go somewhere."

His bushy eyebrows descended in scrutiny. "To the cop shop?"

"Yes. How did you know?"

"Giz us a lift and I'll tell thee."

Skegness police station was on the other side of town, a short trundle in Sam's company vehicle. She couldn't call her Piaggio Ape 50 a company car. It was essentially a three-wheeled moped with just enough cabin to cover the driver. No doubt DefCon4 had purchased these dinky vehicles for budgetary reasons, but in truth, in an urban environment, the thing was ideal.

However, as she rattled and hummed north along Skegness seafront, she did wish the vehicle had some sort of internal heating system. Spring nights were chilly on the Lincolnshire coast; the landscape was flat and exposed, with nothing standing in the path of the Siberian winds coming in over the North Sea. The town motto was SKEGNESS IS BRACING, which was unambiguous code for SKEGNESS IS BLOODY FREEZING. Beyond the promenade road the sea was black against the orange-blue night. The only lights were on the distant wind turbines and the even more distant cargo ships going to or from the Humber estuary.

Ragnar Odinson brought warmth and bulk to the tiny cabin (and a not unpleasant aroma of engine oil, woodsmoke, and herbs). Pressed up beside her, his gut made it almost impossible for her to turn the steering wheel clockwise. Sam's brain was already considering routes that featured only left hand turns.

The upshot was that Hilde, Ragnar's granddaughter, had been arrested.

"And with tha being her probation officer an' that, I thought tha'd know what to do," said Ragnar.

"Community payback overseer," Sam said automatically.

"Aye, that. And tha knows how to speak to the Saxons."

"I am a 'Saxon'."

"That's my point. And tha knows that she's as innocent as a lamb."

"I don't even know what she's been arrested for, Mr Odinson," she pointed out.

"But the Saxon coppers are always tryin' to fit us up. It's like them telegraph poles. Hilde didn't know the phone company wanted them back. They was just lying there."

"I know," said Sam, who had heard the Odinson version of events many times.

"But if tha could talk to them, get them t'see how she didn't do it—"

"Whatever it was."

"—Whatever it was. And give her this..."

As Sam tried to turn into Park Avenue, Ragnar shifted to pull something from his jerkin. The steering wheel locked and the whole column groaned as he leaned his bulk against it.

"Sit down!" Sam hissed, panicked, jabbing her elbow in his side to shift him.

The Piaggio Ape barely avoided a lamp post on the far side of the road. Sam swung it back round and into the police station car park. The Ape stalled across two parking bays. Sam decided that would do.

Ragnar dropped a heavy bundle in her lap. The contents clinked. It was wrapped up in a sheet of soft leather and tied off.

"Some trinkets of our peoples," said Ragnar. "Religious, like. To bring her solace in her time of woe."

Sam picked it up. It was heavy. "What is it?"

"Trinkets. Solace. Aye." Ragnar opened the door and backed out.

Sam got out too. "I have an official job to do here, you know," she said.

"But tha'll speak to them?"

"Sure."

Ragnar nodded and, with a grace unusual for a grandfather, padded away into the dark.

2

_____

Skegness police station on Park Avenue was an unimaginative grey cube of a building. Sam stamped some warmth back into her legs and went inside. The sergeant on the front desk was one she didn't know. Possibly a replacement for Sergeant Hackett who, understandably, hadn't been back in work since that unfortunate incident when his wife's head exploded. Sam was fishing around for her ID, about to explain who she was, when the side door opened and DC Camara walked in.

Lucas Camara was tall, lanky, and seemed to possess more than the usual number of joints. He struck Sam as being like an anglepoise lamp in human form. He had elegant hands and a shock of black hair which, like his name, spoke of some Mediterranean heritage.

"Ah," he said. "DefCon4 provides an appropriate adult service too?"

"It's surprising what they think I can turn my hand to," said Sam. "Surprising and tiring."

"Good," he said, turning on his heel and beckoning Sam to follow.

"We've called you in simply as a precaution," he said as they walked. "Normally we would request an appropriate adult only if we were questioning a minor, or an adult with identified learning difficulties."

"Right."

"We're going the appropriate adult route in case a smart-alec barrister decides to make something of the family's, er, idiosyncratic lifestyle, and Hilde's sketchy upbringing." He put a hand on an interview room door. "As I said though, it's all just a precaution. We caught her in the act, the goods in her hand, fragments of glass in her clothing that I bet will match broken glass at the property. We're just dotting the 'i's and crossing the 't's."

"Okay," she said. "Um, listen. Ragnar spoke to me outside."

Camara frowned. "He give you hassle?"

"Not at all," she said honestly. "He's just worried. He, er, asked me to give Hilde these." Sam held out the bundle.

Camara took it tentatively, placed it on a nearby shelf and untied it. Inside was a hammer, a chisel, a metal rasp and a handsaw. He laughed. "In all my years in policing, I've not seen anyone try to smuggle an escape kit into custody before."

"He said they were to give Hilde solace in her time of woe."

"I think it's traditional to conceal them inside a cake."

Sam shrugged. "Short notice. He means well."

Camara gave her a disbelieving look. He wrapped up the tool kit and opened the interview room door. "Here she is."

In the cramped space, across the table from a female police officer, sat Hilde Odinson.

In the 'good old days' of British policing, a lot of crimes could be cleared from police desks with the aid of the local village idiot. Young fools, grown adults with learning difficulties, and individuals with undiagnosed mental health issues would sign confessions for all manner of unsolved crimes. Some of the individuals were just being helpful (having been taught that one should *always* help the police), some might have been coerced. Heads knocked on police car roofs, fingers inconveniently caught in cell doors, an unfortunate tumble down the steps to the cells.

It didn't matter that they might have been incapable of such audacious crimes. It didn't matter if they had no actual grasp of the nature of the crimes. It didn't matter when they couldn't read the confessions they were signing, let alone pronounce some of the longer words like 'malice aforethought'. Confessions were signed, records were archived, and more than a few men swung for crimes they couldn't comprehend. But everyone could sleep a little more safely in their beds, so that was fine.

The appropriate adult service was an attempt to prevent such miscarriages of justice. If someone could not speak for themselves, or could not understand the magnitude of the trouble they were in, an appropriate adult would be present to help them understand and, if necessary, speak on their behalf. More often than not, appropriate adults were brought in by the police themselves, to forestall any later accusations of wrongdoing.

Hilde Odinson was young, but she was not a child. Her education had been sparse and strange, but she had no learning difficulties. As for mental health issues, she was possibly the most normal and well-rounded of the entire Odinson family. But that was the problem with families: everything was relative.

Sam said hi to Hilde. The young woman gave her a brief nod of greeting.

"Hilde has been arrested on suspicion of burglary," said Camara. "She has declined to have a solicitor present. Sam Applewhite is here from DefCon4 to act as an appropriate adult."

Hilde gave Sam a look.

"I'm here to—" Sam tried to remember the wording she had hastily read on the way over. "—to support, advise and assist you in communicating with the police – should you wish to – and make sure you are treated fairly with regards to your rights and protect you from potential intimidation or bullying."

"Not that we do any of that here," said Camara. He smiled, but it was wasted on Hilde.

With the four of them sitting at the table, Camara began the tape recording and introduced everyone present by name.

"Let's be quick about this," he said. "At ten fifty this evening, police were alerted to a break in at Candlebroke

Hall. At eleven oh-one precisely, a police patrol car found you running across the grounds of Candlebroke Hall towards the exit. You were carrying this in your hand."

Camara placed a transparent evidence bag on the table. In the bag was an animal horn. It made a solid thud as it hit the table. It was pale brown, a single elegant curve, and nearly the length of Sam's arm. Narrow gold bands circled it at several points along its length.

"Is that a drinking horn?" said Sam.

"This is a jewelled and frankly unique aurochs' horn." Camara caught Sam's look. "A giant cow that used to roam this country thousands of years ago. I had to look it up. This horn is part of the collection of antiques and wotnot kept at Candlebroke Hall. Her Ladyship herself has identified it as such. All we need to ascertain is the sequence of events which led to it being in your hands at the time of your arrest."

Camara paused, keeping his gaze on Hilde. Sam tried to not appear as if she was joining in with the staring. Hilde looked at the table and said nothing.

"Perhaps you have an actual question to ask, detective?" Sam suggested.

Camara inclined his head. "Hilde, can you describe your actions around ten-fifty this evening?"

Hilde said nothing.

"Can you tell me how this horn came to be on your person?"

Nothing.

"What were you doing at Candlebroke Hall in the middle of the night? How did you get there?"

Nothing.

"How did you know this horn was in the cellar storeroom? Who told you it was there?"

Nothing.

Camara adjusted his pose. "Hilde, you have prior convictions for theft. This is an act of burglary and, given the value of this horn, you will be tried in a crown court and sentenced accordingly. You will go to prison if convicted. When you were arrested, the officer told you that you don't have to say anything, but it may harm your defence if you do not mention, when questioned, something you later rely on in court. I am going to ask Miss Applewhite to explain that last bit to you." Camara raised his eyes to Sam.

Hilde spoke before Sam could. "I didn't do it."

"Right," said Camara slowly. "The evidence suggests otherwise."

"And you says I'm a thief, but I weren't."

"Is that so?"

Hilde looked to Sam as though she would back her up on this. "I didn't know the telecoms fellers were using them poles or the wire," she said. "They was just lying there. You shouldn't leave things lying around if tha doesn't want people to take them."

Sam nodded. "To be honest, the telegraph poles *were* just lying around."

"Finders keepers, ain't it?" said Hilde.

Camara held up the bejewelled horn. "And where did you find this?"

"And they had a tiger for a guard dog. That ain't right."

3

For an hour, Sam was an appropriate adult to a mostly silent Hilde Odinson. When DC Camara brought the interview to an end and Hilde was returned to the cell, Sam and Camara met in the corridor. A clock on the wall showed it was nearing two a.m. Seeing it, Sam immediately yawned, as though her body wanted to let her know its views on being up at such an hour.

"I could offer you a coffee, but I'm not going to," said Camara.

"Because you hate me?"

"Because our coffee is awful and if you drank it you'd hate me. I don't want you subconsciously judging me on the quality of the station's coffee."

Sam glanced in the direction of the custody cells. "Do you need me on your side?"

"Hilde can stay silent all she wants. The evidence is clear cut."

"Could she be telling the truth?"

Camara still held the evidence bag. "A convicted thief is found with a jewelled drinking horn, less than half a mile from the house where it was stolen, with glass from the broken window on her knees."

"Have you considered she wasn't necessarily alone?" she said.

Camara smiled patiently. Of course he'd thought of it.

"I'm meeting forensics at the scene now. What's the betting that daddy Sigurd's or Uncle Yvgne's, or even grandpa Ragnar's fingerprints can be found near the break-in? We wouldn't normally go to such expense with a simple burglary, but this is a high value item."

Sam looked at the horn. "How much is it worth?"

Camara shrugged. "It's the horn of a giant extinct cow, wrapped in gold and gems. Not the kind of thing you could pick up at a car boot sale."

Sam involuntarily wrinkled her nose.

"Don't believe me?" he said.

"Trying to stop yawning," she said.

"Well, we're done with you for now. We'll call you again in the morning if we need you. Get some rest."

Sam took out her phone and checked her app. "An alarm's gone off at one of our properties. I'm meant to 'respond and secure the site'." She looked at the address of the property on the A158. "Candlebroke Hall, you say?"

"Yep."

She sighed. "Can I offer you a lift?"

"I've seen your company car," he said. "Maybe I can offer you a lift."

. . .

CAMARA TURNED up his car heating as they drove the eight miles inland towards Candlebroke Hall. Sam appreciated the warmth but it made her drowsy. She talked to keep awake.

"How long have you been in Skegness?"

"Two years." His hands moved smoothly over the wheel as they turned onto the dual carriageway. "I served in uniform in Boston originally and came here after moving to CID. You?"

"Not much more than a year," she said.

"Oh, I thought you were from the area."

She gave a short laugh. "I'm the classic kid from nowhere. I grew up anywhere my dad was performing. I've seen more seaside towns and provincial theatres than is healthy. Spent various chunks of my childhood in Skeg, then my dad chose to settle here when he retired from stage magic."

Camara made an interested noise. "Chose Skeg?"

"More the spin of the roulette wheel, I guess. Skegness was where he was when everything stopped moving. And I came back here to help him out."

"And how is the retired Mr Marvellous?"

"In rude good health. Frankly indecent good health. Whatever time I get home he'll be in the kitchen, whipping me up some eggs, singing showtunes and ready with a showbiz story about the Barron Knights or Lenny Bennett that I've heard twenty times before."

"Who?"

"Well, precisely."

The main road out of town was deserted. Camara's car slipped up to the speed limit.

"What's your take on the Odinsons then?" he asked. "Were you aware of them when you lived in Skegness before?"

"They were more of an urban myth," she said, smiling. "Don't forget to lock your bike up or the Odinsons will nick it. Don't walk home in the dark or the Odinsons will have you."

"Really?"

"Oh, I think it was just general class prejudice." She looked out of the window at dark hedgerows and the shadows of villages. Through the dark she caught momentary sight of the high sails of the old windmill at Burgh le Marsh. "Mostly the Odinsons get by on the crap the rest of society has discarded."

Camara slowed for a roundabout and turned off onto a narrow unlit lane. Ahead, visible as a looming shadow against the night sky, was Candlebroke Hall.

LADY KIKI LETTUCES sat in the Steward's Room on the Hall's ground floor. The Steward's Room was not part of her private apartments – red sashes marked the areas that paying visitors were not allowed to enter – but the room had the advantage of looking down the driveway. From here she saw the lights of the approaching car. The policeman posted on the front door stepped down to meet it.

Kiki sipped her purple zinger tea and took a deep cleansing breath. "The detectives are here," she said.

Antoine sat up on the chaise longue. He had come to the house in a silk wraparound jacket with loose billowing sleeves. Kiki couldn't be sure if it was a short dressing gown or a piece of flamboyant daywear. "You only have to give them as much time as you wish," he said. "They can't keep you up all night. You have an interview and a photo shoot tomorrow. You need your beauty sleep."

She scowled at him. Beauty, she could have told him, relied on far more than a good night's sleep. After four decades of modelling, acting and being the ever photogenic starlet about town, Kiki knew true beauty required willpower, restraint, hard work and money. But he was right. If she didn't get to bed soon, she would have bags under her eyes for the centre page photographs in ... in...

"What magazine is it tomorrow?"

"I'm your confidante and personal psychic," said Antoine, "not your secretary. Go talk to the detectives. Give them the basics then excuse yourself."

Kiki went to the door and paused. She closed her eyes.

"The door handle's right there," said Antoine.

"I'm composing myself," she said.

When meeting new people, be it journalists or policemen, she felt one should project the best possible image of oneself. First impressions counted. It did not matter that she was tired, that it was the middle of the night. She had filmed night scenes for the original 1980 *Humanoids from the Deep* (tasteful scenes, before the producer had spiced up the film with random nudity in post-production). Kiki had made sure she was upbeat and professional throughout those night scenes, which wasn't easy on a windswept

Californian beach when you were dressed in a bikini and had to act against a man in a rubbish fish suit.

"You stay here," she said.

"Not going anywhere, my angel," said Antoine.

Kiki opened the door and, once more, stepped into the metaphorical limelight.

4

Sam and Camara entered a large reception hall. Black and white marble made an eye-bending chess board of the floor. Lamps on sideboards provided insufficient illumination: their yellow light barely reached the panelled ceiling.

"Wow," said Sam.

"Think of the heating bills," said Camara.

"My late husband's ancestors would have entertained visiting dignitaries here," said a woman as she entered the room, "but it's been some time since we've had any parties."

She was tall, with ash blonde hair. Sam would have been tempted to place her in her mid-sixties, but not many sixty-somethings could pour themselves into a slim, figure-hugging leopard print jumpsuit. Not many women would choose to rock a leopard print jumpsuit and high-heels in the middle of the night.

Camara walked swiftly over to her, hand outstretched.

"My Lady, I'm DC Camara from Skegness CID. Sorry to further disturb your evening."

She held out her hand, palm down for him to take. He took it, nodded like he almost thought about kissing it and gave it a limp wiggle.

Sam had her work ID in her hand. "We're not together. I'm Sam Applewhite. DefCon4. I've come to check and reset the alarms."

"About time!" she said. "It's been hours. The alarms have been driving us mad."

Sam made a show of cocking an ear. The house was silent.

"*Were* driving us mad."

"Apologies for the delay, Lady Lettuces. The local office is a bit understaffed."

"*Lay-tooses.*"

"Pardon?"

"It's pronounced, Lay-*tooses*. Not Lettuces. My late husband delighted in telling people about its French origins. I find it much simpler if everyone calls me Kiki. My stage name was Kiki Harris."

She looked from Sam to Camara, scanning for a reaction. Sam wasn't sure what she was hoping for. However, she had noticed the woman mentioning her 'late' husband twice in thirty seconds. Maybe if she was a beautiful, sixty-something widow, she would want people to know she was single.

"Lady ... Kiki, if you could show me where the alarm control panel is," said Sam.

"And then we'll take a look at where the burglar broke in," added Camara.

"Yes. Let's." Kiki led them out through a side door.

She had to pause a moment to move aside a red sash barrier – "Can't have the public wandering willy-nilly," she said – before crossing a hallway with a grand staircase leading up, and narrower servants' stairs leading down. Sam followed her down the curving steps into a cellar corridor.

There was a DefCon4 cabinet in a recess. Its door hung ajar.

"The racket was unbearable," said Kiki. "Antoine nearly took a hammer to it."

"Antoine?" said Sam.

"And now the scene of the break-in," said Kiki. "I hope none of this will take too long."

As the sound of Kiki's and Camara's footsteps on the stone floor receded, Sam inspected the alarm panel. Sam was only as technical as she needed to be. She was not involved in the installation of alarm systems, but could read a downloaded PDF file as well as the next person. She swiftly followed the resetting instructions.

Candlebroke Hall was a huge residence. Its alarm system was broken down into eight separate zones, with up to ten sensors per zone. Each sensor had been labelled, which wasn't always the case with these things. In a grid of happy green lights, there was one red light and one flashing orange light: Summer room exterior door and Cellar storage room. A tap of code into the control panel and a press of the reset button should have turned both lights green. They flashed orange.

"Okay," said Sam. She flicked to the relevant screen on her phone. Flashing orange meant *Sensors not aligned.*

She closed the cabinet and went in search of the nearest sensor. There would be old kitchens and former servants quarters down here. Candlebroke Hall was open to National Heritage visitors. Chances were some of the rooms would have been made up to look how they had appeared in decades past. Probably a mannequin of a portly cook in a frilly apron and bonnet whipping up a fake plastic cake in another room right now.

The cellar storage room was obvious when Sam spotted it. It was behind the dark green door with splinters of broken door and frame scattered on the floor. Someone had taken a heavy implement, a crowbar or a pick, to the gap between the lock and the latch and forced it open.

Sam grunted. There was no point kidding herself. It wasn't someone; it was Hilde.

She pushed the door open with the back of her hand. In the corner of the frame was the metal plate of the alarm sensor. The room beyond was broad and deep. Shelves were filled with lidded cardboard boxes. Sam stepped in and carefully lifted the lid of the nearest and saw china ornaments wrapped in masses of tissue paper. By one wall, there was a dusty glass cabinet containing mounted fencing blades. Further along there was a series of canvas picture frames stacked together like books on a shelf.

Sam vaguely recalled stories of how, during the World Wars, national treasures had been squirreled away to hidden vaults to protect them. This felt like a similar thing, on a smaller scale.

She reached for the next box to look inside.

"I would ask if you're meant to be here," said a deep and mellifluous voice behind her.

Sam whirled around. A man with a heavy moustache, and an embroidered silk wrap about his torso stood in the doorway.

"Jesus! You scared me!"

"But all of us are exactly where we are meant to be," he said. "And, no, any similarities between me and the Son of God are entirely coincidental."

He grinned. He had perfectly even teeth, like an American. There was no reason why such a smile shouldn't be disarmingly charming, but it just looked creepy.

"Er, I'm checking the alarm system," said Sam and pointed at the door. A part of her wanted to add, "If I scream, the police will come running," but she wasn't a coward, or an idiot.

"Ah. The alarm," he said, nodding as though she had said something truly wise and meaningful.

Sam gestured to indicate she needed to leave. She didn't like his brief hesitation before stepping aside.

In the corridor, she turned. "Is that—?" She waved at his open silk garment. "Is that a shirt or a dressing gown?"

"What do you want it to be?" he said.

Sam wasn't going to engage in that kind of twaddle at three in the morning. She found the stairs and went in search of the 'summer room'. She found Camara and Lady Kiki Lettuces ('Lay-*tooses*' she smirked inwardly), in a room that was part elegant parlour room and part library. Kiki stood with her arms crossed while Camara inspected the open French windows.

He glanced up at Sam. "Look." He pointed with the tip of a pen: a pane of glass dangled loose from the door. Sam stepped closer. The pane was smashed but held together by a web of sticky tape. "She taped over the window before punching it in and reaching through for the door handle. Deadened the sound."

"Clever," said Sam.

"Clever?" said Kiki, browed furrowed in irritation.

"Criminal and wrong and bad," said Sam. "But clever." It was the kind of thing Hilde would think of.

Camara made a humming noise. "She tore the strips with her teeth. Here. There'll be DNA samples."

Sam jerked her thumb back towards the stairs. "The cellar door was broken in. You've got a lot of valuables down there." She looked at the room around her – the antique yellow armchairs, the oil paintings above the doors, the brown hardback volumes behind the glass fronts of the oak display shelves. "Got a lot of valuables in here, too." She turned around. "Makes you wonder why she went to all the effort of breaking into the cellar."

"Thieves stealing to order," Kiki said simply. "Who knows what they might have taken. They'll steal anything not nailed down. We had an oak tree stolen from the grounds last year. An oak tree!"

Camara stepped back from the door. "We stay out of this room until forensics have been. Lady Lettuces, would you be able to check if anything else has been taken?"

Kiki gave him a wide-eyed look, hands outstretched as she turned about. "What? The whole house?"

"Maybe you have an inventory?"

"That's the kind of thing Phoebe deals with."

"Who?"

"The National Heritage girl. She'll be here in the morning. She might have an inventory."

"Right. National Heritage run the house, yes?"

Kiki made an unladylike lip-blowing noise. "If you can call it that. But, yes, she 'runs' things—" she made air quotes with lustrous red finger nails "—and I have my own private apartments upstairs. Speaking of which..."

"Of course," said Camara. "Sorry to have kept you up."

Sam interjected. "The alarms are reset, but I will need to come back after the police have finished. To reset the sensors in here and downstairs."

Kiki nodded. The sparkle in her eyes slipped away, For a moment she looked like a tired old woman. "Yes. I understand. Phoebe starts at nine." She gave each of them a formal nod and left.

"But it's a good point," said Sam.

"What is?" said Camara.

"Why bother to go downstairs to steal things when there must be thousands of pounds of stuff they could take from this room alone?"

When Camara smiled there was genuine amusement in his eyes. Sam hadn't made a detailed study of his smiles, but it seemed most of them didn't manage to stretch up to his eyes. "Gee. I can't think why a family who are obsessed with the Viking way of life would specifically want to steal a shiny drinking horn."

"I think they buy most of their Viking tat from that crystals and incense shop in Lincoln."

"And do they have giant bejewelled horns in that shop?"

"Fine," she said, knowing he spoke the truth. But a spark of loyalty to Hilde remained. "You do know she's one of the good ones, right?"

"Is she?"

"She has an honest job, a paying job, helping out in that junk shop by the seafront. She actually has a moral compass. It might be wonky, but she has one."

"I don't deny it," said Camara. "You think everyone we arrest is a villainous scumbag? Do you think all those other housebreakers we haul in are evil to the core?" He shook his head. "They all love their mums. They all want to do right by their girlfriends. And if you talk to them, you'll hear they wouldn't have got into trouble with the law if only—" His large, expressive hand twisted up and away, suggesting the infinite possibilities. "Go to Lincoln jail, Sam. Go to North Sea Camp prison. Place is full of such people."

Sam looked at him. "You have a poetic soul. For a policeman."

"I'm tired," he said. "Neurons misfiring in my brain. I'll be back to my robotic authoritarian self after some sleep."

After a night with almost zero sleep, there comes a sweet spot in the new day when both the brain and body agree there's no point complaining. The yawning stops, the head clears and one can just get on with the day. This is of course a convenient lie and, at some point, the brain or the body would call the other's bluff. For now, with the sun rising over the glistening sea as she drove home, Sam was awake and functioning.

The town was quiet, barely stirring. There were virtually no holidaymakers in early spring. Half the businesses near the seafront would remain shut until the Easter bank holiday and the rest were in no hurry to greet the day. The pier was open, its neon signs flickering, but the fairground was silent, rides frozen in the positions they'd held all winter. Around the clock tower and promenade, pubs and cafés were opening to serve warming and artery-clogging breakfasts to the locals. Sam caught a whiff of cooking oil and her stomach rumbled in response. If she was lucky, she might catch her dad in the act of preparing a fry-up.

She parked outside her dad's house and went up the stepped path to the front door. There were no enticing cooking smells as she entered, just the tang of hot coffee.

"The midnight rambler returns," said Marvin Applewhite. He sat at the kitchen breakfast bar, a cup of coffee in his hands and a plate of toast crumbs in front of him. He was already dressed for the day, although Sam wasn't sure what the day held for a retired stage magician.

There was a red handkerchief with an array of cogs and other broken watch parts spread on it.

"Get angry with your alarm clock again?" said Sam.

"Why have an alarm clock when you have a daughter sneaking into your room and disturbing your sleep?" he said.

Sam felt the coffee pot. It was barely warm but she poured herself a cup anyway.

"I'm revisiting the destroyed then restored wristwatch trick," said Marvin. "You think your friend Delia would have some old watches in her shop?"

"You've remembered how to do the destroying bit but can't get the watch to magically put itself back together?"

"Ha ha," he sang. "Even when performed correctly, you need a broken watch or two for effect. You can't just tell the audience that the watch has been pulverised. You need to make it look convincing."

The coffee was even colder than expected. Sam grimaced at the first swallow. "Delia should be able to sort you out. I ought to give her a call: her backroom engineer has been arrested."

Marvin frowned. "The Odinson girl?"

Sam nodded. "Burglary, up at Candlebroke Hall. I was there for the alarms. Met Lady Lettuces herself."

"Lay-tooses?"

"It's French, apparently. Kiki."

Marvin put his cup down heavily and tilted his head. "Kiki Harris."

"That's her. You know her?"

"Of her. We rarely moved in the same circles. She was a model or an actress back in the day. I think she was even a Bond girl."

"Which film?"

Marvin rolled his eyes. "They're all the same, aren't they?"

"And now she's the lady of Candlebroke Hall."

"Married the baronet when her looks started to fade."

"She's younger than you!" Sam laughed.

"And the acting world is uncharitable to women beyond a certain age. I'm sure she made the move from acting to marrying an elderly aristocrat with a heart condition at exactly the right moment."

Sam sniffed. "Well, I'd say she still looks pretty spectacular for a woman of ... senior years."

"How spectacular?" said Marvin.

Sam looked at him straight. "Is my elderly dad going to try charming the grey-haired hottie in the crumbling mansion?"

He shrugged. "I've still got needs, you know."

She grimaced. "I don't want to hear about your needs. You need a watch from Delia's shop. I need a shower before work. If you're ready when I am, I'll run you down to the pier."

6

"*So Lady Lettuces, tell me about your daily beauty regime.*"

"*Kiki, please,*" said Kiki in her mind, giving the imaginary interviewer a kittenish smile as she descended the grand staircase. "*I've never been one for too much formality.*"

"*You certainly don't seem like I imagined the wife of a baronet to be.*"

"*Oh, and what did you imagine?*"

"*A frumpy horse-faced woman with an entitled 'jolly hockey sticks' public school education and an unfortunate predilection for tweed jackets and cardigans. And yet you, Kiki, you are a wonderful contradiction: delightfully down-to-earth and yet with the glamour and personal style of a Hollywood icon. And, may I say, more than a little sexy.*"

Kiki paused to admire her reflection in an ancient, discoloured mirror at the foot of the stairs. She couldn't spot any damage done by a disturbed night's sleep.

"Sexy? What a cheeky young man you are," she giggled.

She went out through the summer room door. The police people had been and dusted for fingerprints and wotnot, leaving behind a pair of French windows with one pane missing. Something for Phoebe to deal with. The girl should do something to earn her bloody wages.

The sun was just rising over the trees. Curly mists hung over the rear lawns. It was a short, cold walk from the side of Candlebroke Hall to the beginning of the *Barfusswalk*. Not long ago it had simply been the perfectly adequate 'cherry walk' as laid out by her father-in-law. Now it was an ugly, fenced off piece of hipster nonsense. An eyesore, to be frank.

"*You were telling me about your beauty regime,*" persisted the imaginary interviewer.

"*You would not believe me if I told you,*" Kiki mentally replied.

She took off her shoes, stowed them in the bag containing her towel and wash kit and pushed through the gate into the *Barfusswalk*. The first section was bark chippings: soft underfoot with only the mildest discomfort. It was a mild introduction to half a kilometre of highs and lows, but Kiki despised it on principle. A German health fad, installed for the entertainment of visitors. She reached the end of the bark chippings and stepped onto the gravel. She kept telling herself, as she did every day, that what she was feeling was merely discomfort, not pain. In spite of the fact it made her want to shout out loud. There might be visitors in the grounds so she could not indulge in some heartfelt yelling and cursing, but inside she was screaming with frustration. It wouldn't be so bad if the promised health benefits would manifest themselves, but Kiki had failed to notice improved circulation or a serene glow of inner peace.

She moved off the gravel onto an all-too-brief stretch of soft moss. She knew she should practise mindfulness and luxuriate in the blissful relief, but she also knew what was coming next and just wanted to get it over with. Dawdling on the moss was not an option. She heard movement behind her and realised someone else was walking the trail.

She moved aside and turned to see who it was. It was Phoebe. The National Heritage liaison had her trousers rolled up over her rather manly knees.

"Good morning, Kiki, so nice that you're getting a chance to enjoy the facilities."

"I am not enjoying the facilities. I am enduring them," said Kiki through gritted teeth.

"Isn't the *barfußweg* a refreshing way to engage with nature, *ja*? So authentic!"

There was something perfectly insufferable about the enthusiasm of the young. Kiki felt you shouldn't be able to offer a deep or heartfelt opinion on a matter without the experience which came with years. You couldn't declare a bottle of wine to be divine unless you had sampled a cellar full. You couldn't describe a sunset as wonderful until you had seen a thousand. And you had no right to speak of the authenticity of an experience (whatever that meant!) if your life experiences amounted to three years at a provincial university and a few rail trips around Europe.

Phoebe Chiddingfold had come in as Candlebroke Hall's National Heritage manager with a head full of ideas and zero business experience. When she donned her fleecy top with the cutesy National Heritage logo, she became a fanatical warrior for the cause. To wit: turning Candlebroke Hall and every stately home and historic building in the land into a monstrous middle-class tourist attraction with gift shops and tea rooms, and ample parking for coach parties. No consideration for the financial well-being or quality of life of the poor people who were forced to live as tenants in some tiny portion of what was once their own private home.

"This must be so cleansing after the trauma of last night," said Phoebe. She pulled a simpering face and put her hands on Kiki's arm. "It must have been frightening for you."

"It was tiring, Phoebe," Kiki snapped. "An unwelcome and unacceptable interruption to my night. Why is it that when *your* alarms go off, *I* am the one who has to get up to deal with the racket?"

"Quite right," said Phoebe. Up close, Kiki could see the pale girl had beautiful skin. If only she'd do something about the rest of her appearance. "The police will be here soon and I will be utterly at their disposal for the rest of the day."

"I have that interview later, have I not?" said Kiki.

"Interview?"

"The photographer?"

"Oh, yes," said Phoebe. "Are you happy meeting with him?"

"It's why he's here, isn't it? What magazine was it again?"

"*British Sights and Scenes.*"

"Don't think I've heard of that one."

"It has a large circulation in the US, apparently."

Kiki nodded. "Those yanks do love the Brits, don't they?"

Phoebe looked ahead. "We're coming up to my favourite part now. The soft mud."

Kiki made a noise of revulsion.

"You know it gets mentioned in fifteen per cent of our reviews?" said Phoebe. "Such a worthwhile investment."

"Worthwhile investment?" Kiki could stand it no longer. "Phoebe, do you know why I make this wretched walk every day?"

"Because it's a balm to mind, body and soul?" quoted Phoebe from the website.

"No, you ridiculous child. I do it because there's a working shower at the end of it. Actual, functional washing facilities!" She lifted up the bag she carried. "Towel, soap, shampoo. Now ask yourself, why is Lady Kiki Lettuces, former screen star and catwalk model, driven to such extreme measures when she lives on the premises? What can the answer be, Phoebe?"

Phoebe sighed. "Is this going to be about the plumbing again?" she asked.

"Of course it's about the plumbing. Or the utter lack of it."

"Kiki, you know we've had the standards people out twice in the last year, and they have declared it adequate both times."

"Adequate for the age and type of the property."

"Yes, of course."

"So, if this was a nineteenth century miner's cottage, an outdoor privy would be adequate?"

"Exactly," said Phoebe brightly.

"It's not adequate for me," said Kiki. "I bet it wouldn't be adequate for you either, if you had to live with it."

Phoebe squidged through the oozing mud of the *Barfusswalk*. "I do hear you, Kiki, but as our German friends might say, *Leben ist kein Ponyhof*."

Kiki gave her a furious look.

"Life is not a pony farm," Phoebe translated. "I'm learning German on my LingoLingo app. Money has to be carefully allocated and having an award-winning tea room at Candlebroke Hall doesn't come cheap."

Kiki picked through the filthy mud on tiptoes as daintily as she could. The temptation to pick up a lump and hurl it at the stupid girl's face was strong. "Can you at least get the roof looked at before winter?"

"Oh, is it leaking? Send me some pictures and I'll file a report."

"You want me to wait until it rains so I can send you a picture of the leak?"

"Ideally."

The girl was so hopelessly optimistic and utterly naive. Wherever her reports ended up, they clearly dropped into the lap of someone who was not prepared to spend any money on Kiki's living quarters.

"What I don't understand," said Phoebe, "is why you do the *barfußweg* every time if you just want to use the showers."

"Because you installed a turnstile to prevent me coming in here the wrong way," said Kiki. "If I was as athletic as I was back in my Bond girl days, I'd jump over it, I can tell you."

"Oh Kiki, you are funny."

Nine o'clock found Sam in her office and functioning on one hour's sleep, an invigorating shower, and her first coffee of the day. The office cafetière and its knitted cosy were gifts from Delia at the junk shop. As she savoured her coffee, Sam made a mental note to contact Delia to let her know her assistant had been arrested for burglary.

The DefCon4 office was glacially cold in the winter months, and not much better in early spring. Some decent heaters or hot-blooded colleagues might have warmed the place up, but these were in short supply. Although there were four desks, Sam had been the only human to occupy any of them during her tenure as a DefCon4 employee. But she wasn't alone. A spikey powder puff cactus named Doug Junior sat on one of the desks. He'd stepped in when his predecessor, Doug Fredericks, gave up his prickly life in the line of duty. Doug Junior was a rookie, but Sam could tell he would shape up and be a valued member of the team.

As well as being cold, the office was redundant. Her many and varied orders from her employer were delivered to her via phone app. The byzantine corporation could get its talons into her twenty-four hours a day. It also tracked her location (again via the app) and demanded she attend the office during regular working hours. The only use Sam had for the place was that, at five p.m. she could stomp down the stairs to ground level, leave, and pretend she had finished for the day.

The office did have some other functions, of course. There was the filing cabinet containing Sam's fat folder of expenses receipts, a mysterious sealed file entitled OPERATION BUDGIE that she was forbidden to open, and a big wad of employee policies and manuals she was supposed to know off by heart. It was also used as a dumping ground for all the materials and equipment delivered by courier. Not useful items like pens or pencils, torch batteries, or first aid kits, but a random assortment of specialist equipment and experimental devices. This week alone, Sam had received a pair of high-power binoculars with night vision, a suit of tactical body armour, and a set of follow-me drones that were, according to the accompanying packaging, the successor to police and security bodycams.

On the wall behind Doug Junior's desk was a cork noticeboard, on which she had pinned an Ordnance Survey map of Skegness and the surrounding area. Next to it was a half-completed family tree of the Odinson family, constructed from photographs and several yards of string.

Photographs of Ragnar Odinson and his frankly

delightful wife Astrid were pinned at the top. There was an almost complete row of sons and daughter underneath. Many of those images came from a single photo from the local press: the whole Odinson clan on Skegness beach in front of their Viking longship. They were in celebratory pose, drinks in hands, after the first sea-trial of their boat (during which they had, coincidentally, rescued Sam from a grim wet death in the North Sea). Each of the Odinsons was clearly labelled, as it was not always easy to distinguish one from another by looks alone. The mostly middle-aged sons – Sigurd, Hermod, Gunnolf, Yngve and so on – had grown into hairy biker types whose individual styles were subtly different, ranging from hobo Santa, to trash-heap wizard to embittered roadie. The women were even more uniform in appearance, all being generally wan, skinny and miserable. The row of grandchildren underneath was less clear. Sam had some grasp on those she had met in an official capacity (Torsten's propensity to get into pub fights had kind of imprinted him in her mind), but many were a mystery.

There was a photograph of Hilde. It had been taken by Sam herself, on the beach, further up the coast at Wolla Bank. Hilde held a piece of string, on the end of which, out of shot, was a kite. It was a windy day. Her hair, that which wasn't tucked under her beanie hat, was pulled across her face in strands. Hilde was looking at the camera and smiling, an unguarded, open-mouthed grin of delight at doing something as simple as flying a kite.

Sam checked her work schedule.

The burglar alarm call for Candlebroke Hall was down as *Incomplete*. The appropriate adult job for Lincolnshire police was marked as *Open*. There were some routine hygiene and cleanliness checks to be made on a hotel currently used to house asylum seeker families, and smoke alarm checks to be made at the theatre complex on the seafront. Not the busiest day in all.

Sam could have taken the opportunity to use the gaps to get her head down and sleep, but she didn't want to do that. She looked to Doug Junior.

"What say I go over to the Odinson's place later and tell Ragnar in no uncertain terms that if any of his idiot sons were behind the break-in at Candlebroke Hall they need to get their arses down to the police station tout-bloody-suite and make a full confession, instead of letting Hilde take the rap?" She took a swallow of coffee. "Yeah. That's what I thought too."

KIKI WAS SHOWERED, dressed and ready for the day, but she was still left with that grubby feeling she was camping in her own home. Applying make-up and fixing her hair in front of her dressing table mirror alleviated some of that feeling. The make up might not have been Chanel or Mary Arden, but a skilled artist could do wonders with the most basic of materials. Young Kiki had been in more movie set trailers than she could recall, and always had a cordial and professional relationship with the make-up artists. There was that one time, on the set of *Malibu Bikini Shop 2,* where the entire team had gone down with food poisoning from a warm egg salad left out in the California sun. Kiki had led the bikini girls in applying their own slap.

Made up and ready for the day, Kiki left her horrid apartments and went downstairs. She had teamed a vintage safari suit with a leopard print chiffon scarf. It was, she thought, a whimsical yet stylish throwback to her heyday. It would prompt some amusing questions from the magazine interviewer.

She could hear voices from the basement. Antoine had told her to leave the business with the police to Phoebe. Even though Antoine was not the boss of her, she had agreed. Nonetheless, she could not resist.

In the cellar store room she found Phoebe talking with the lanky detective, Camara. The detective had to stoop slightly to avoid clonking his head on the ceiling beam in the room of carefully wrapped antiques. Phoebe was by the tiny desk area near the door, searching for something that did not appear to be there.

"This makes matters a little complicated," said Camara. Kiki could hear the understatement in his voice and a chuckle escaped her lips. Camara turned. "Ah, Lady Lettuces."

"Kiki."

"Kiki. Miss Chiddingfold and I were just making a list of items stolen in last night's burglary."

Phoebe gave up searching the desk with an irritated sigh. "Kiki, you wouldn't happen to know where the files detailing what's actually stored here might be? No, why would you?"

Kiki gave her a helpless smile and drifted over to a shelf where a porcelain figurine was visible through its tissue shroud. She gave the detective her best wistful look. "This used to be in Julian's study. Julian, the baronet, my late husband. Meissen, I believe."

"Valuable?" said Camara.

"Beyond words."

Phoebe seemed furious with herself. "I've seen the file. A yellow document wallet. It's a full inventory. It was here."

"Did the burglars steal that as well?" suggested Kiki. She just slipped it into the conversation, perfectly naturally. She was pleased with herself.

"Could you show me where the horn would have been kept."

Phoebe worked her way down an aisle. "Early modern and medieval items are kept together here. We had the horn on display once, as part of our *History of Drink* exhibition. Sold a lot of tea and local beer that month, I can tell you. The drinking horn I recall being among the – ah!"

Kiki watched from afar as Phoebe opened a lidded cardboard box. "Drinking horn, colloquially known as the 'Thunderhorn'. A gift to the Lettuces from the baronet of Middle Hill in the eighteen-fifties."

"So, the horn in question is definitely stolen," said Camara.

"The box is empty," said Phoebe, plainly.

Camara opened the box next to it, and then the next one along. "So's this," he said, opening a third.

Phoebe looked inside and found a slip of paper. "Medieval wood carving of Christ enthroned. Oh, God."

Kiki could see the girl's hands trembling. Phoebe began plucking off lids with a feverish energy. It was both disturbing and fascinating to watch as lids and fragments of packing tissue went flying. By the time she was done, Phoebe had found two more boxes with their contents missing. Phoebe staggered in shock, literally staggered. Camara had to put out his hands to hold her up.

He turned to Kiki. "It seems you may have suffered a more significant theft than previously realised."

"And don't forget the tree," said Kiki.

"What tree?" snapped Phoebe, fizzing with miserable energy.

"The oak tree," said Kiki with exaggerated calm. "It was stolen last year. Christmas time. Perhaps I could show you, detective?"

He hesitated before politely relenting. "Yes. Please."

"And Phoebe can take herself off and calm down," said Kiki. "I hear we have an award-winning tea room somewhere. Detective?"

Phoebe threw her a wild look.

Kiki led Camara upstairs, away from the store room and out through the armoury and onto the rear lawns. She watched the pensive look on his face.

"I'm sure it will all be sorted out soon enough," she said, lightly.

He laughed, briefly. "It's not often the victim doesn't know what's been stolen. There must be a complete household inventory somewhere. For insurance purposes, if nothing else."

"I do recall something being done shortly before my late husband signed Candlebroke Hall over to National Heritage."

"Do you remember when that was?"

Kiki tried to recall. "It certainly wasn't this century."

"Ah."

Weak spring sunshine was burning the last of the mist off the lawns. Candlebroke Hall was three high storeys of eighteenth century grandeur in brick and stone. The immediate grounds encompassed several formal gardens, an orchard, a churchyard, various outhouses, stables and cottages, an ice house, two ponds and a great number of trees. The original estate, comprising a deer park, a sheep farm, and several hundred acres of arable land, had mostly been sold off to private buyers. At one time, the Lettuces had owned all the land between here and the sea, eight miles away. There was even an edict from some mad Georgian king (she couldn't recall which one) that the estate stretched out halfway across the North Sea. It was of little note, although she recalled the company that installed the wind turbines offshore from Skegness had been obliged to pay some form of peppercorn rent for their use of the seabed.

"We will need to act fast if we are going to stop stolen goods being lost to the black market," said Camara.

"Do you know where to look?" she asked innocently.

"I've got some ideas."

She gestured ahead. "The tree."

Camara looked suitably surprised. Perhaps he had thought she had meant a small one, uprooted and carted away. Fir tree growers often had a problem with Christmas tree thieves during the festive season. Perhaps he had pictured an off-season version of that.

He stared at the stump. It was fully six feet across: a ragged mess of hacked wood. Camara looked up as though viewing the ghost of the fallen tree. "This would have been ... enormous."

Kiki agreed. "Several tons of mature oak."

"And someone did this in the night."

"Daylight robbery, apparently," said Kiki. "Members of the public even saw it happen. A bunch of rough types with chainsaws and trucks cut it down and carted it away in pieces. Can you imagine who would do such a dastardly thing?"

"I've got some ideas," said Camara.

8

R agnar Odinson was illuminating the chapter heading for his book SON OF ODIN: LIVE YOUR LIFE THE VIKING WAY, when his granddaughter Freyella burst into his caravan. Ragnar's book was an on-going handwritten reflection on Viking life, and a source of great solace at times of difficulty. He drew the intricate chapter illustrations in biro on colourful post-it notes. He did this partly because he felt the luminous post-its made his drawings stand out, and partly so that if his work was ruined by – say – the loud interruption of a grandchild, he could rip the note off and start again.

He glared at the ruined representation of the horse, Sleipnir, then at the girl standing in the doorway of his caravan.

"Ragnar, there's a tiny ice-cream van coming," she said.

"Tha's supposed to knock!" Ragnar growled.

Freyella rapped loudly on the doorframe. "There's a tiny

ice-cream van coming. And it's not playing the tune to say they've sold out."

Freyella was ten years old and entirely unafraid of Ragnar's temper. There were few Odinsons who did not fear their chief, all of them women, and Ragnar could not help but love them for it.

He pushed himself away from the hinged flap of Formica that served as his writing desk and stepped outside. Mud squelched beneath his boots.

The Odinson compound was, like the best of fortifications, composed of several rings of defences. Sturdy fencing, on temporary permanent loan from a building site somewhere, cordoned off the corner of the Elysian Fields Caravan Park which the Odinsons occupied. Within that was an almost complete ring of parked caravans, mostly empty, forming a screen against the prying eyes of strangers. Within that were the sheds, workshops and drinking halls of the tiny settlement.

The compound's open centre was a muddy mess, churned up by truck tyres and picked over by the family's free-roaming chickens and goats. There was usually a two to three week period in late summer when the mud dried into a dusty and reeking crust of earth, but the rest of the time it was a boggy morass.

Ragnar walked in economic strides from his caravan to the compound entrance. Young Torsten stood on guard behind the length of chain which served as a barrier. His muscly tattooed arms were firmly crossed in front of his broad chest. Beyond the chain, its engine puttering, was the little van belonging to the DefCon4 woman, Sam Applewhite.

"That's not an ice-cream van, tha daft apeth," Ragnar said to Freyella.

"Are you sure? That's what a man who doesn't want to pay for ice-cream would say."

"Too clever by half," he muttered.

Sam stepped out and walked down to meet him. There was a serious look about her. Ragnar had a soft spot for Miss Applewhite, and not only because she also appeared to be unafraid of him. Sam dealt with the Odinsons as she did with everyone else, without fear or favour. Cops and crooks, lords and outlaws, it was all work to her, part of some great social dance.

"How's my granddaughter, Saxon?" he called out.

Sam looked at Torsten, then Freyella, then Ragnar. "Not telling the police anything."

"Good."

"And about to be charged with burglary."

Ragnar tssked and stroked his beard. "This is a bad business."

"You think?" she said. "She wasn't acting alone, was she?"

"I have put the question to my kin," said Ragnar, "and I've put my kin to the question."

"She didn't drive out to Candlebroke Hall."

"She doesn't have a vehicle."

"You think how far it is from here to there. And she was caught with that horn on her?"

"What horn?"

"Big jewelled drinking horn from a ... whatchamacallit? Extinct cow."

"Aurochs..." said Ragnar hollowly. He felt a chill that had nothing to do with the weather. It had only been the other week when he'd been drinking from his own favourite horn and declared a fervent wish to have another one to match his favourite drinking vessel.

"That's the only thing they found on her," Sam said. "Whoever she was with might have slipped away unseen, but if there's anything else missing from that house, the police will know exactly where to come."

Freyella was tugging on Ragnar's jacket and pointing. A snaking line of police vehicles was making its way through the caravan park.

"Odin's balls!" he swore.

"Farfar!" said Freyella, in pretend dismay.

Ragnar turned to Torsten. "Get Gunnolf and Hermod!" Torsten hesitated a second. Ragnar gave him a mighty shove. "Run!"

"So you do have something to hide," said Sam. There was a hard and victorious note in her voice, but Ragnar was wise enough to know she meant no malice. She was concerned for Hilde's situation, and rightly so.

Ragnar strode back into the compound proper and cupped his hands to his mouth. "Saxons! *Saxons!*"

Men and womenfolk spilled out of caravans, climbing into clothes as they came.

Ragnar marched up to Yngve's truck. Yngve stood above him on the running board by the door.

"Tha got owt illegal in tha truck?" said Ragnar.

"Dad. Ah don't know what the others have—"

Ragnar silenced him with a slap on the thigh. "Has tha got anything illegal in tha truck, boy?"

Yngve began to shake his head, paused, took a fat roll-up from under the lip of his bandana and passed it to Ragnar. Ragnar tossed it away.

"Now, get thaself out there. And drive like tha's got something dodgy on board."

"How do I do that?"

Ragnar shrugged. "Drive like tha usually does."

Yngve started up and made for the compound exit. As soon as he was through, he swung wildly around the tiny DefCon4 vehicle and drove at the police vehicles. There was a bloop of sirens and Yngve came to a halt in front of the lead car. Officers were already getting out.

"If you're hiding something, Ragnar..." Sam shouted from the gate.

"I'm *always* hiding something, Saxon," he yelled back and waved his nearest and burliest relatives over. "Right, lads, we've got work to do and minutes to do it. And it'll require some heavy lifting."

SAM GAVE a wave as Camara's swanky saloon pulled up by the compound entrance. A police car was directly behind. Two vans blocked Yngve's truck further down the track. Yngve was doing a good job of putting up a front while the police poked around his cab.

Camara stepped out and gave Sam a coolly scrutinising look. "And what are you doing here?"

"Part of my role as appropriate adult. Come to feedback to the family."

"I don't like finding people where I don't expect them to be."

"Never had you down as a neat freak," she said, turning to her van. "I shan't get in your way. I'm off now. Looks like Ragnar's ready for you."

RAGNAR ODINSON CROSSED the compound to meet the Saxon police detective, Camara. "Hold up! I'm coming!"

The DC had an official-looking piece of paper in his hand. "Ragnar Odinson, I have a warrant to perform a search of these premises. We believe there may be stolen goods here, including a wooden carving of Christ enthroned, a number of brass candlesticks, sketches by William Logsdail and other items yet to be identified."

"Oh aye?" Ragnar replied as though this was perfectly normal. "Come on in and tek a look round. Kettle on, Astrid!" He beckoned to Camara to follow him into a caravan. "Astrid's just mekking a brew."

"No thank you," said Camara. "I'm sure we'd all prefer to get on with the search."

Ragnar made an expansive, welcoming gesture, and gave the policeman a wide smile. "Never let it be said that Ragnar Odinson failed to support an investigation."

"I think you and I can start walking the perimeter."

"Gladly."

Ragnar led him along the inside of the high mesh fencing marking the border. He pointed out landmarks on the way, enjoying his role as tour guide. "One of my sons Sigurd lives in this one here. The one next door belongs to Ogendus, who you'll be familiar with as he was locked up by your lot. Hilde's workshop lies empty over there to the left of the Mead Hall."

"Mead Hall?" asked a copper.

"Aye, we partake of mead in there."

"What's mead?"

Ragnar turned to face Camara. "Has tha brought a bunch of ignoramuses out 'ere? If these daft sods don't even know what mead is, how do you expect them to treat us and our beliefs with any due respect?"

Camara sighed. "These men aren't familiar with your, ah, beliefs."

"Mead is the sacred drink of our Viking forebears. It is brewed and consumed with great ceremony, and I will not tolerate your casual scorn! Come!"

He led them on round the perimeter to where the dingy mudscape of the compound butted up against a brook. Here the grass grew high and wildflowers bloomed. Six square box hives stood in a grid in the area. A few bees drifted about the place.

"Our honey production centre," said Ragnar.

Among the hives, on a stripey seaside deckchair, a white-bearded Odinson snoozed. Bees buzzed about him, even crawled across his grubby white shirt. He seemed gently oblivious.

"Bjorn here is our keeper of the bees," said Ragnar.

Camara walked the fence to where it crossed the wildflower meadow. "Where's that map?" he called. Someone passed him a furled-up sheet and he opened it out. He pointed to a pencilled outline. "This is what we believe to be the perimeter of the property you and your people habitually occupy."

"Habitually occupy," Ragnar repeated, rolling the words across his tongue. "Tha talks like a blummin' dictionary."

"I choose my words carefully," said Camara. "You certainly don't own the land."

"Oh aye? As free men living in Saxon lands I reckon that depends on—"

"It depends on nothing. The question of ownership is not up for debate. Now the line on the map would appear to enclose a much greater area than the one we just walked around."

"So tha map's wrong?"

"I don't believe so, no. I wonder if perhaps you haven't taken us around the actual outer edges of the land you occupy?"

Ragnar pointed at the fence. "We walked it, didn't we?"

Camara half smiled. "Yes we did. I notice this fence is composed of linked metal panels which drop into these cement blocks."

Ragnar didn't bother replying. The Saxon policeman was stating the obvious, probably for the benefit of his colleagues.

"If I think laterally," continued Camara, "it might occur to me that a fence like this could be moved in a hurry, with a few burly men like your sons lifting all of the pieces into place. In fact, if I examine some of the weeds entwined in the mesh, it looks to me as if they've been recently uprooted, which makes me think I might be on the right lines."

"Tha's a proper detective, looking at weeds an' all. Tha's lost me." Ragnar shook his head.

Camara turned to the nearest officer. "Tape off the *correct* boundary and search on the other side of that fence."

"Ah, I see tha's interested in the extended compound," noted Ragnar. "You should've said."

9

K iki descended the front entrance steps of Candlebroke Hall as the photographer took pictures of the house from the front lawn. He had a long fat lens on his camera. It almost made Kiki shiver with excitement. One rarely saw real cameras these days. It was all mobile phone technology, wasn't it? A real camera – bulky, black – made her think of paparazzi: snapping photos of celebrities as they came out of nightclubs. Caught in the moment, Kiki turned, extended a shapely leg, and gave a half-delighted, half-shocked smile at being caught in a 'private moment'. The photographer snapped a few more, then reviewed his pictures in the viewfinder screen thing.

"Very impressive," he said, nodding to himself while wiping his nose with a hankie.

Kiki approached him. High heels on soft lawns were not ideal, but she was a professional. Heels were wonderful. Four extra inches, and she was slightly taller than this red-nosed man in a tartan scarf. Other women her age were becoming hunch-shouldered old ladies, but Kiki was still a tall leggy blonde.

The photographer looked up. "How do," he said, sniffing. "Leland Watts, *British Sights and Scenes.*"

"Kiki Lettuces," said Kiki, holding out an elegantly limp hand for him to take. "*Née* Harris. You can call me Kiki."

He looked at her. "Oh, you're the lady of the house!" he said after a moment, belatedly taking the hand. "Pleasure to meet you."

She looked about for his potential colleagues. "I was expecting an interviewer."

"Just me I'm afraid." He sniffed again. "Me and my cold. Apologies. I do have some questions, though."

"I should hope so." She giggled playfully. "Shall we do this indoors, or take a stroll around the grounds? Leland, was it?"

"I'd prefer to take some exterior shots," he said.

She nodded at the wisdom of this. "Natural light. They do say there's something special about the light along this coast. This way." She led him back to the gravel path and around the east side of the house, away from the tourist entrance, the tea rooms and the National Heritage shop.

"So, how long have you lived here?" asked Leland.

"A good question," she said. It always did well to put the press at their ease. "I married my late husband, the Baronet Lettuces, in ninety-one. Seems so long ago now that I say it. It was a major change for me. After a successful career I was aware that married life meant I was settling down, after a fashion. But that's love, isn't it? Love is sacrifice. The film and television roles I had to turn down in those early days." She gasped at the scandalousness of it all.

"Television?" said Leland.

"Oh, yes. I was *very* busy before all this came along. Mostly guest slots. *That's Life. Blankety Blank.* Les Dawson had us all in stitches. But I had acting roles too. I was in *Lonesome Dove*, you know."

Leland was frowning. The poor lad was probably too young to remember.

"An American western mini-series. Robert Duvall was the lead. I had no opportunity to speak with him – we were all so busy. My part was reduced to a non-speaking role. Technical reasons, you understand."

"I see."

She wasn't going to mention the 'technical' reason was her attempt at a Texan accent was 'technically' awful. She wasn't ashamed or anything – it was a charming story in its own way – but she didn't need to tell him everything up front. Let him dig a little.

Leland took a few idle snaps of the house as they walked on into the spring flower gardens. The hyacinths were starting to bloom in whites and pinks and purples.

"Have there been any alterations to the original house?" he asked.

She nodded, pleased with his subtle questioning. The last few interviews she'd done with cult movie YouTubers would just leap to "Did you do that topless scene in *Humanoids*?" or "How did they make your hair look weightless in James Bond?"

"A woman likes to put her own personal stamp on any

home she owns," she said. "In my LA days, I wouldn't live in any place that didn't have its own hot tub. We looked at putting in a hot tub here, but Julian wasn't keen, and those listed buildings people can be sticklers for the rules. Nonetheless, I like to think I have brought my own sensibilities to the place. A bit of fun."

"Uh-huh," he nodded absently but didn't press her further, which was possibly just as well. She had no desire to tell him she now lived in a handful of dingy rooms in the furthest corner of the top floor.

"And the outside?" he said. "All original?"

"Built in seventeen hundred. On the grounds of the old Candlebroke Castle. It played a part in the Civil War. If we walk down to the church, we can see where the royalists were all slaughtered as they attempted to retreat to the castle walls. Apparently, they were trapped against the parish gate, which only opened one way. In their panic they jammed it shut. They say Julian's ancestor, Ingram Lettuces, was bludgeoned to death with his own wooden leg."

"Really?" said Leland and blew his nose again.

"Such a rich family history. Not 'rich' rich, you understand. It's so easy to accidentally equate a stately home with vast reserves of hidden wealth."

The photographer gestured across the pond to the formal gardens on the other side and the people wandering about. "You get a lot of visitors?"

"We're very popular."

He sniffed snottily. "Do they get in the way? Are they, um, allowed to roam freely?"

Kiki laughed. "Oh, Leland. There is a contract between a

famous person and their public. They pay our wages and we belong to them. I love having members of the public here. I love bringing joy and glamour into their lives."

She had told the lie so often to herself and others that it didn't feel like a lie anymore. God, how she'd love to kick them all out, seal the gates, reclaim her home, and live the life of sedate luxury a woman of her standing deserved! But, no, here they were, traipsing around, poking at the fixtures, stealing plant cuttings when they thought no one was looking, and consuming industrial quantities of cream teas in the café. Treating her home like some theme park for the middle aged.

"It's an absolute delight," she said.

10

As Camara and Ragnar entered Hilde's workshop, Sigurd came running forward and tried to insert himself in front of them. "Tha shouldn't be in here, not without Hilde's permission," he said.

Camara gave the man a quizzical look like he was trying to place him. "You're Hilde's dad, right?"

The man twisted his fingers through his plaited beard nervously. "No comment," he said.

Camara restrained his smile. "You're not being questioned, Mr Odinson."

"No comment."

"Your daughter," said the Saxon copper gently, "is being well-cared for while she's in custody."

"She ain't done nothing," Sigurd blurted.

"And on that unlikely opinion, you and your daughter agree." Camara made sure his gaze took in both Sigurd and Ragnar. "She was apprehended with stolen goods. Unless somebody else wants to come forward and admit their part in what happened..."

Ragnar watched his son. Sigurd, like all the others, had sworn he had played no part in Hilde's misadventure. Ragnar had made them all swear on the holy image of Thor's hammer. None would dare lie.

Camara pushed past into the workshop. "What's this?" he asked, pointing at the workbenches forming a horseshoe shape around one end of the room.

Hilde generally kept the place tidy when she wasn't at work. At the moment, the benches were covered in animal horns. Small ones, large ones, even curly ones. Some were in pairs, a couple attached to skulls, a few odd ones. There was an unwholesome stink in the room, somewhere between burnt hair and marmite. Ragnar knew it must be coming from the horns, but it was sinister and overpowering. He could see some of the police officers already looking queasy.

"Can't say as I rightly know," said Ragnar truthfully.

"This?" said Sigurd. "It's one of the art workshops that the young 'uns have been doing. Hilde likes them to work with so-called 'found objects'. The kids wanted to make drinking horns for their squash."

Camara stared hard at the selection of horns. "You wouldn't be attempting obfuscation, now would you?"

"Tha's a proper walking dictionary!" cackled Ragnar.

"By which I mean you knew we'd be investigating one stolen horn, so you've dug out all these substitutes to confuse the issue."

Ragnar nodded. "And are you?"

"Am I what?"

"Confused."

Camara glared. "You're on thin ice, Ragnar. Don't push it."

Ragnar literally lifted his feet to look at the ground beneath them and grinned. Camara stalked off but came up short against a large form draped with camouflage netting. He lifted an edge.

"Ah! The wonderful *Sandraker* longship. This netting – would it be military netting?"

"Army surplus," agreed Ragnar.

"Did you check it was surplus before you took it?"

Ragnar helped Camara roll the netting back out of the way so he could access the step ladder to climb on board the *Sandraker*.

They both stood on the deck and Camara walked between the rows of benches. He had actually been on board this ship once before, when it had been pressed into service to perform an impromptu sea rescue. The *Sandraker* had acquitted herself with pride, testament to the quality of its design.

"I have to hand it to you, Ragnar, this is a fine ship," said Camara.

"Aye, it is that."

"It's top quality throughout. All solid oak, unless I'm mistaken. No plywood anywhere."

"Oak is Odin's sacred tree. Important to our Viking heritage."

Camara gripped the rail, testing its strength. "Makes a statement, you might say."

"Aye," said Ragnar.

"If it could—" Camara gave the railing a thump "—what tales would these oak beams tell?"

Ragnar did not like the tone to his voice.

"We also happen to be investigating the theft of an oak tree," said Camara.

Ragnar scoffed. "Can you really steal a tree, officer?"

"Did you know the genetic fingerprint of a tree is unique, Ragnar? I expect the lab will find an exact match between these planks and the stump of an oak tree that was illegally felled and stolen from Candlebroke Hall."

"Ah, you've lost me with yer fancy science."

"I'll be back to explain it to you more slowly when – sorry, if – we find a match. You do know what that will mean? Apart from the crime committed by illegally felling a tree planted to commemorate the battle of Inkerman – did you know the tree had a name? There were two, Balaclava and Inkerman, planted after the Crimean war – apart from that, it follows this ship is stolen goods and therefore does not belong to you."

Ragnar was shaken, but he maintained his composure. "Tha's backing the wrong horse here, I can tell thee. And I'll not consent to you damaging her, neither."

Camara held up a long splinter. "This is all I'll need for now."

Ragnar growled. "Tek yer samples, then! Is this what happens when you can't find the made up things on your warrant, eh?"

"Not at all," said Camara, slipping the splinter into an evidence bag. "Just a happy coincidence. Your sins will find you out in the end, Ragnar."

11

Kiki stomped through the house, looking for Antoine. She stomped through the main doors, two floors up the sweeping staircase, through the book lined corridors and into the 'lady's chamber' that Antoine often used as his private meditation room. The damned man wasn't there.

Kiki was tempted to give up her search. It had been a horribly disturbed and fraught night, with a fruitless day following. It would be easy for her to retire to her apartment, mope and mutter over a glass of Co-Op white in front of the telly, but she resisted. If Kiki Lettuces *née* Harris was tough enough to be one of Hugo Drax's space babes in *Moonraker*, then she wasn't going to give up so easily. She stomped back along the corridor, down two flights of stairs, out the front door and round to the menagerie.

The menagerie was in the space between the kitchen gardens and the Orchard gallery, mostly screened by a row of conifers. Members of the public were not granted access to the area. Kiki treasured every square inch of privacy to be found at Candlebroke Hall, but the menagerie was not truly hers. This was Antoine's little kingdom. There were the snakes in the converted stables, and a lemur enclosure with its family of twelve, but the real star of the menagerie – the reason for its existence – was the tiger, Hugh.

Antoine was sitting on a canvas fishing stool outside Hugh's enclosure, hands on knees, simply staring at the beast. It was not the first time Kiki had found him doing it. She didn't know what he got from the experience. It was just a damned cat, and a saggy, thin-chested, moth-eaten one at that. Hugh lay on his raised wooden platform, staring out at nothing at all.

Antoine had not noticed Kiki's arrival, giving her an opportunity to collect herself and sashay forth like she was stepping onto a catwalk.

"Can you believe that man?" she spat with actorly anger.

"I can believe all manner of things, *ma cherie*," said Antoine, finally looking up. "What happened?"

"It took me a full half hour to realise he wasn't even recording the conversation."

"The police?" said Antoine.

"The magazine interviewer. Chatting away we were. I was giving some wonderful soundbites and..."

"He wasn't recording? Perhaps he was doing it on his phone."

"He was not," she sniffed, affronted by both the interviewer's unprofessionalism and Antoine's assumption she was wrong. "I don't appreciate having my time wasted."

Antoine was on his feet, her hands in his. "You are agitated, my love."

Antoine was twenty years younger than her and possessed looks that, if not exactly handsome, were certainly distinctive and masculine. She wasn't in love with him – she had questioned herself deeply on this point, concluding that even if he ditched his silly moustache (which might have been an attempt at a Burt Reynolds or Tom Selleck, but had long ago slid sideways into porn star territory) she still wouldn't love him. Nonetheless, she had to suppress a shudder of pleasure as his gentle fingers explored and caressed her skin. The attentions of a handsome man were sometimes hard to resist.

"You're upset," he said and dipped into his pocket for an ointment jar. "A powerful herbal remedy, blessed by angels. Perfect for soothing the nerves."

"Isn't that the one you gave me for the bags under my eyes?"

"A *powerful* herbal remedy," he insisted, swiftly rubbing the cooling paste onto her hands. "Stress and anxiety will be the death of you otherwise."

"Can you see that?" she said. "Is that the future?"

He smiled as he shook his head. "You know you will die surrounded by riches. The stars themselves will weep at your passing."

"I bet you say that to all your rich widowed girlfriends."

"I have no other rich widowed girlfriends."

She snorted. "I'm sure you have a string of them, you widow-wooer."

"Widow-wooer, is it?" he grinned.

"Serial widow-wooer."

Antoine slipped the ointment away into a pocket. He let her go and turned back to the tiger. "I was just contemplating his aura. Such vitality."

Kiki tried to frame a sympathetic comment, but found nothing. "He does nothing but lie about. Like a rug."

"Hugh's an old man now. Twenty years of age. No wild tiger ever lives that long."

"Ah, maybe he will be a rug soon then." She immediately regretted the comment when Antoine shot her a wounded look.

"Tigers have a purity of spirit few animals can match. The things this great beast has seen."

Like the look of terror on Antoine's former assistant's face the moment before it was bitten off, thought Kiki.

"The Chinese revere them," he said. "One of the super-intelligent animals of Chinese mythology."

"I know."

"*Hoo* is the Chinese word for tiger. Stupid promoters at our first show billed him as 'Hugh' instead."

"You may have mentioned it."

Antoine didn't notice the boredom in her voice. "Tigers offer spiritual protection from the Three Disasters: ghosts, fire and thieves."

Kiki stroked her forearm where Antoine had touched her, feeling the give in her flesh. "I don't fear my ghosts."

"You have your late husband watching over you," said Antoine smoothly. "And me as your spiritual guide. Are you looking forward to our livestreamed internet ghost experience next week?"

"Let's get this week over with first." She looked back in the direction of the house. "Both Phoebe and the police know there are antiques missing."

"Do they know what?"

"Apart from the jewelled horn thing the girl stole, no. Phoebe made some guesses, but without the insurer's inventory— You still have it?"

Antoine retrieved the yellow document wallet from under his stool. "I'll burn it eventually. For now, I'll keep it safe." He nodded at the tiger enclosure. Hugh's concrete and wire-mesh home was made up of several distinct zones, separated by gates and sliding doors. Antoine treated his pet and one-time co-star with wary respect, needing to be able to isolate Hugh while it was cleaned out. In that maze there were a few brick structures, including Hugh's cave-like den. The largest was a sturdy shed with a locked door, a perfect storeroom for anything Antoine wished to keep hidden. No one would be foolish enough to go snooping around inside tiger cages.

"Indeed," he said. "And as long as I do, we are perfectly safe."

He sounded assured and unworried. Kiki wished she could share his confidence.

12

The police called Sam again as she sat in her office at the end of the day. She would have strenuously denied she was asleep at the time of the call, if challenged. Being awake for twenty-three of the last twenty-four hours was a reasonable excuse for anyone caught napping. If her employer's app wasn't tracking her location, she might have been tempted to spend her afternoon at home, 'working' from her own bed. But even as she sat up groggily, two pink indentations in her cheek from where her head had been resting on a lever arch file, Sam was preparing her denials.

"Nnnnh," she grunted. "Sorry?" She listened for a moment. "Appropriate adult. Got it."

Five minutes later, she was in her Piaggio Ape. Ten minutes after that, she was in the police station car park. She caught her reflection in the Ape window and tried rubbing the indentations from her cheek. Another five minutes and she was sitting in an interview room next to Hilde Odinson.

"How you holding up?" she said.

Hilde shrugged. "They gave me sandwiches for lunch."

"Any good?"

"Cheese *and* ham," said Hilde as though this was a minor revelation. "*And* the cheese was grated."

"That's nice?" said Sam, not entirely sure what Hilde's take on grated cheese and ham was.

"It's a bit like being on holiday," said Hilde.

Sam looked round the interview room. It was compact, almost oppressive in its austere dimensions. The grey-blue walls were peeling near the ceiling. It didn't immediately strike Sam as being a single bit like being on holiday; although thinking back to some holiday camps she had frequented in her childhood, there were similarities.

DC Camara entered and, with a female officer, sat on the opposite side of the table. Camara had a file of notes which he scanned as he started the introductions for the benefit of the tape recorder.

"Evening, Hilde." He sounded as tired as Sam felt, but she reckoned Camara hadn't fallen asleep on office stationery at any point in the day. "It's been a busy day. So far, you've not provided us with any assistance regarding what happened at Candlebroke Hall last night, so we've had to piece things together ourselves."

Hilde stared blankly ahead. Camara opened his file.

"You were found with one jewelled drinking horn, known as the 'Thunderhorn', in your possession when you were picked up. This is one of a number of items – exact number yet to be determined – that have gone missing from a locked room at Candlebroke Hall. Although, we have not found any relevant fingerprints at the crime scene, we are testing saliva found on Sellotape used on the window, and expect to make a DNA match. What we also found, by a beech tree not far from where you were arrested, was a bag containing numerous tools—" he slid a photograph across the table "— including what I take to be homemade lockpicks, gloves and – *quelle surprise*! – a roll of Sellotape. Your fingerprints were found on several items in that bag. What can you tell us about that bag, Hilde?"

Camara patiently waited for any form of response. Hilde kept her mouth closed.

"We paid a visit to your family home with a search warrant," he continued. "We spent some time in your workshop."

He paused, watching for an angry response. Hilde held herself still.

"It was educational," he continued. "Although we found items potentially linked to a number of crimes and took samples for analysis, we did not find anything that might be from the Candlebroke Hall collection. Would you be able to tell us where those items are?"

Hilde maintained her silence. Camara nodded.

"To summarise, you were arrested with stolen goods in your hand a short distance from the scene of the crime. Your fingerprints are on the tools used to gain entry, and we will soon have DNA evidence placing you at the scene. The courts will not require anything more to convict you of the theft of *all* the items. What you can do, to make the situation better for yourself and demonstrate your willingness to co-operate, is tell us who was there with you and where the stolen items are now."

"There was no one else," she said.

"You were alone?"

Hilde was silent once more. Part of Sam wanted to tell her she needed to tell the police something, that this silence was only compounding her guilt. But Sam's role was only to ensure Hilde's rights were being upheld, and the police had been scrupulously professional in that.

Camara tried a number of other questions, but Hilde didn't budge. The DC yawned and, as he apologised, Sam felt a yawn come over her too. She blinked hard, clenching her jaw to hold it back.

Camara leaned back. "Hilde Odinson, I am charging you with burglary and going equipped for burglary. You will be kept here until you can be brought before a magistrate who will decide if you are to be remanded in custody, or released on bail pending trial. Interview terminated at six twelve p.m." He turned off the tape machine and closed the file.

"We'll find those other items, Hilde. Whoever is hiding them for you will be charged with handling stolen goods. I'm sure Miss Applewhite will pass messages to anyone who needs to come forward to the police." He stood and left.

"I'll give you a moment, if you wish," said the policewoman and left too.

Sam looked at Hilde. Hilde met her gaze.

"Have you got something to say?"

Sam puffed out her cheeks. "I think you're possibly an idiot. They could lock you away for this. A long time."

Hilde's stare was hard and unyielding. Sam was reminded however much she had got to know Hilde, they weren't friends. Sam was just another Saxon, with laws and rules that the Odinsons had no care for.

"I did not steal the horn, Sam."

"Oh, come on! I saw—"

"I did not steal it. I swear."

"Then you tell the police which of your idiot cousins or uncles was there and—"

"I was alone."

"That just doesn't make sense!" Sam snapped. "If they've misread the whole situation, you need to tell them."

"No. They won't listen. You tell my Farfar Ragnar that I didn't do it. I swear it on Mjolnir."

Sam let out a tired laugh. "Do you even believe that Viking stuff?"

"Then I will swear it on your Saxon god. Believe me."

Sam wasn't sure she had any gods, Saxon or otherwise. She nodded anyway. "Okay, I believe you." Weirdly, it felt like the truth.

13

O utside, leaning on the side of her van where the sharp evening breeze would keep her awake, Sam phoned Delia.

Delia picked up and Sam was immediately assaulted with the sound of tea-time at Delia's house. In the background, one young voice was declaring its hatred of peas, while another was singing a song with no discernible tune or words.

"Did I call at a bad time?" said Sam.

"There are no good times. What age do children leave home again?"

"I still live with my dad."

"Yeah, but he's a wizard and has a mansion."

"It's a bungalow."

"Still a mansion, just without stairs."

Sam turned up her collar against the wind. Enlivening breeze was one thing, wind chill was another.

"I was at a proper stately home today. Candlebroke Hall."

"Heard it's nice."

"Because your number one backroom employee was arrested for trying to burgle the place."

There was silence on the line, except for the sounds of vegetable-themed outrage and youthful warbling. *"Why would she do that?"* said Delia eventually

Sam wanted to say, "I don't think she did", but it was only a gut feeling so she quashed it. "She's not co-operating, but they've got evidence."

"Shit."

"Yep. What's more, they haven't recovered all the stolen goods."

Another pause. *"Is this the bit where you tell me the police are going to raid my shop in the belief I was in on it?"*

"It's a possibility."

"I'd enjoy being a cat burglar. I'd wear a sexy spandex outfit."

"I've seen you in spandex."

"Don't mess with my dreams. Shit! Why'd she do it, Sam?" There was genuine distress in her voice. Hilde was an easy person to like.

"I'm going to look into it," Sam said.

"Like, officially?"

Sam had no idea. "DefCon4 handles the alarm system at the house. I'm going out there again tomorrow. If there's any doubt, any chink in the police evidence..."

"Thanks," said Delia, then yelled, *"Don't think I can't see you trying to hide them under your beaker! I am not going to be cleaning mushed up peas off this table again!"*

"I'll go. You're busy."

"It never ends," said Delia.

KIKI UNLOCKED HER APARTMENTS' front door. She had to put her foot under the door's drip flange and heft it up and to the right for the lock to line up. It was a workable system for as long as a) she kept a pair of shoes she was prepared to scuff handy, b) the drip flange had not rotted entirely away, and c) her foot muscles could withstand the weight of the door. Common sense suggested some maintenance was in order, but apparently it hadn't yet made the priority list.

She went inside and inhaled. The smell of home was a mushroomy dampness.

Her private apartments were on the top floor of Candlebroke Hall, three rooms which were officially designated the *Withdrawing Chamber*, the *King's Bedchamber* and the *Inner Chamber,* but had nothing regal about them. The only chambers they resembled were dank caves. In this upper corner, beneath the leaky flat roof, damp was an ever-present feature. The stone of the walls was never properly dry, even in summer. If an item of clothing or soft furnishing didn't get washed and aired on a regular three month rotation, it would succumb to mould.

She looked at her watch and calculated she had time to put the machine on, as she did most days. The water supply was so poor that a washing cycle would bang the ancient, leaky pipes for a solid three hours. She had used rolls and rolls of duct tape to make temporary repairs, but still the pipes leaked and still they banged.

Before she could use the washing machine she needed to check the water tank on the roof. She climbed the access ladder and emerged onto the flat roof of the south wing. A stiff breeze whipped around the flagpoles. The centre of the roof was taken up with a vast, low-domed skylight, a grid of Victorian glass that allowed better illumination into the upper halls. Now, the dim electric lights within cast a glow across the rooftop space.

All of Kiki's running water was fed from the tank, which collected rainwater from taller central parts of the building. She couldn't drink it, obviously, but it fed the bathroom. The cover for the tank was made from lead, and the ancient clips holding it in place were long gone. It became dislodged on a regular basis, and washing clothes in dead pigeon soup was an experience Kiki never wanted to repeat. She satisfied herself there were no dead things in the water and went back down the ladder.

She put on the wash and went into the kitchen to make herself a meal. There was a microwave oven and a single electric ring wired directly into the wall, but she strongly believed microwave ready meals were slops she would never stoop to. She had tried various plug-in appliances over the years, but anything that drew enough current to cook food would inevitably trip out her electricity. Tonight, she was preparing a piece of salmon with vegetables. She would cook the vegetables, then try to keep them warm while she pan fried the salmon.

National Heritage had provided a dispenser for drinking water, and she used this to cover the potatoes in the saucepan. She used it to wash her face and brush her teeth too, and would tell anyone who listened that she used Evian to maintain her complexion (even though the stuff in the water dispenser was cheap, non-branded stuff).

As the washing machine set the pipes rattling. Kiki opened a bottle of Sauvignon Blanc to go with the salmon, trying not to think what this meal would have been like when Julian was alive. She sipped her wine and sighed. In the years before National Heritage ran the place she'd lived in relative comfort in the main house. In those days she'd have wandered through her dressing room, picked a designer outfit and some statement jewellery to wear, and there would have been a nice Gavi to go with the salmon, instead of this supermarket plonk. She told people she had embraced minimalism, but in truth she'd had to sell many of her lovely things because she didn't have the space to keep them. Phoebe had suggested creating a display in the main house, featuring some of her lovely outfits, which might help with the storage problem, but the thought of tourists pawing her clothes with curiosity or envy was more than Kiki could bear.

It turned out her particular style of minimalism favoured the clothes she'd kept from the seventies. Man-made fibres were less susceptible to the moths and the mould. Safari suits and kaftans were sufficiently vintage to be interesting and exotic, rather than just old-fashioned, and she liked to think her wardrobe reflected her circumstances: seriously constrained, but as stylish as it was possible to be.

Yet it didn't matter how well she tried to maintain some semblance of her stylish lifestyle, that facts were unassailably clear: she was a woman of advancing years, living alone in a tiny damp flat, without running water or reliable electricity. While the wealth of generations of aristocrats sat gathering dust in the great house below her.

Legal or not, those treasures were morally hers. She'd married the bloody baronet, hadn't she?

She sat on the settee with her salmon and lukewarm vegetables and flicked through the television listings. On the Horror Channel they were showing *Slaughter High*. With a grunt of humourless laughter, Kiki put it on.

She downed half her glass of wine before the opening credits had even finished. It wasn't one of her films, but she'd auditioned for the role of scream queen Carol. The part had gone to Hammer Horror starlet Caroline Munroe, in what Kiki just knew was some backroom deal between producers. Caroline's character would get killed by javelin in the final act, which brought some consolation, but not enough.

"What's she got that I haven't, huh?" she said to the empty flat. She already knew the answer: running water, electricity, and a zero percent chance of having her clothes washed in dead pigeon soup.

14

Back to Life had a prime position on Scarborough Avenue, on the corner across from the entrance to Skegness Pier. It was Delia's heartfelt view that the junk-slash-upcycling shop occupied an important niche between charity shop and antique shop, between jumble sale and craft fayre. Down to earth enough to be able to offer things of beauty at budget prices, artistic enough to inspire and amaze the casual shopper.

On a summer weekend, holidaymakers provided constant traffic for Delia's eclectic wares, bringing in the smells of donuts and fish and chips and candyfloss. On a springtime weekday morning, the rare opening of the shop door merely brought in the chill and the smell of the sea.

And policemen.

Delia greeted DC Camara with a smile. "Welcome!" She waved away his attempts to show her his ID card. "We met during that escaped animal fiasco at Otterside Retirement Village."

"Who could forget?" he said. "You're Delia."

"You're here to find clues, yes?"

"I am here to investigate."

"And prove Hilde's innocent?"

Camara made a rather wooden effort at looking round the shop. "So Miss Odinson works here part time?"

"Yes."

"How many hours a week would that be?"

"Ooh, an actual notebook!" said Delia, as he took a pad from his pocket. "You're an attention-to-details kind of a person then? I mean, you probably have to be, in your line of work. That's why I could never be a detective."

Camara nodded. "Hours?"

"Oh. yes. Well it depends what we've got on. Hilde runs some of the workshops, so some weeks she'll be here for fifteen hours or so, other weeks she'll just help me organise and process some of the things, so it would be a bit less."

"What exactly do you mean by 'process'?"

"There's a few things. She PAT tests any electricals for me."

"PAT?"

"PAT tests. It's the testing to make sure electrical things are safe to use. Then she does upcycling. She has a flair for it. We take some unpromising ingredients and make new things out of them."

"How much did she earn?" said Camara.

"I beg your pardon?"

The tall copper looked down at her. "Did you pay Hilde an hourly rate? Or a piece rate for work she did?"

"Everything was above board tax-wise."

Camara made a note.

"Or are you asking if she had money troubles?" said Delia.

Camara shrugged. It struck Delia as a particularly Gallic shrug, although she suspected that impression was influenced by his old fashioned raincoat. He was a bit too tall to be an Inspector Clouseau type. Definitely too tall and well-presented to be a Columbo style detective.

"So, would Hilde have access to everything here?" asked Camara, gesturing about with the tip of his pen.

"She would."

"And have you noticed anything going missing?"

"I most certainly have not!" said Delia, indignant. "Sometimes Hilde's taken something from here to use in a piece of work back home or wherever, but she would always ask first."

Camara spent some time at the counter asking questions about the till and the handling of money. He pointed at the glass cabinet that sat at the end of the counter. "Is this here because it contains high value items?"

Delia see-sawed a hand. "Not so much high value as good candidates for last minute impulse buys. I put them in people's eyeline while they're paying."

Camara shook his head and headed for the main aisles. He walked past crockery and kitchenware, pausing a few times to examine a price label. He picked up a sandwich toaster and looked at the label on the plug.

"Are you aware of Hilde being in any trouble? Debts? Romantic problems?"

Delia laughed. "I believe that girl has a socket set where other people have a libido. No. No romantic problems. She's not motivated by money or material goods. Or romance. Hilde does things for her own reasons."

"Right."

"Speaking of romance, you do know that Sam Applewhite is single?"

He frowned. "Her and Hilde...?"

"No! I'm saying if you ever wanted to ask Sam out for dinner, I'm sure she'd give it some thought."

His pen paused. "Are you, by any chance, trying to embarrass me or otherwise weird me out? This is not the school playground. We are not eleven years old."

"None of us are as young as we'd like to think."

He looked about. "It strikes me you have a knack for selling things that would otherwise be hard to shift?"

"Thank you."

"On-line, eBay, auctions. That kind of thing."

"I suppose so."

"So, if I had something I needed selling, something that would be hard to move using conventional means..."

She was about to wax smugly about her entrepreneurial abilities when she grasped what he was hinting at. "Do I look like a fence to you? Upstanding member of the community. Skegness and District Business Guild Businessperson of the Year, me. Everything is above board."

He walked around the workshop, opening drawers and looking inside boxes. "The tools are all yours?"

Delia shrugged. "Mostly, I think. Hilde brings some things from home occasionally, if she needs something I don't have."

Camara pulled a photo from his pocket to show her: a leather tool bag containing work gloves, a handsaw, a roll of some tape and sundry other items. "Any of these items yours?"

She gave the picture a good long look. In truth, she had no idea if any of the items were hers or originated in the shop. Delia, like Hilde, accumulated tools like other people accumulated socks. They were bought or made or borrowed, hanging around long after they were past usefulness.

"No. Definitely not," she said. "She didn't do it, you know."

"Do what?" said Camara.

"Whatever it is you've arrested her for."

He smiled. It wasn't a cruel smile, just an acknowledgement of the game they were playing. "Did Sam Applewhite tell you I might drop by?"

"Would it be against the law if she did?" said Delia.

"None I can think of." He made a cheek clicking noise and turned away from the shelves. "I guess that will do."

"Have you seen everything you wanted to?"

"Yes, I think so." He turned to go, then paused. "There is just one more thing."

"What is this? Columbo? Is this where you blind me with a difficult question or some detecting brilliance?" asked Delia.

"What? No. I wanted to check. Was that sandwich toaster really only a fiver?"

"An absolute bargain," she said.

"I think I'll take it."

A GREY-HAIRED WOMAN in a bobbly National Heritage fleece pointed with both hands to an archway by the side of Candlebroke Hall. "Visitors entrance is this way."

"I'm going to the house to look at the burglar alarms," said Sam. She would have held up a tool bag as a demonstration of her vocational role, but since she didn't have or need one she held up her phone instead. It didn't have the same effect.

"You don't look like you're from a burglar alarm company."

"I get that a lot."

"You should have a uniform." The woman pursed her lips in thought. "A peaked cap. An orange boiler suit."

"Orange?"

The woman looked up, accessing the imaginary images of burglar alarm fitters of her mind. "Or red."

"I'll remember next time." Sam went up to the main entrance.

Down in the cellar corridor she reacquainted herself with the DefCon4 security control cabinet. Sam's experience with alarm systems and electronics could be generously described as on the job training. She had no background in technical matters. Her skillset came from following instruction manuals, and when that failed, looking for guidance (preferably with an accompanying video) on the internet. She could not count the number of times the day had been saved by an instructional YouTube video presented by a chirpy but reassuring bloke with a name like Tom or Gary.

This one, however, seemed relatively straightforward. She made a Bluetooth connection between her phone and the control panel. Now she had a web browser overview of the alarm system. As she had previously gleaned from the lights on the panel, only two of the alarms were not set. SUMMER ROOM EXTERIOR DOOR had been triggered at ten forty-six on the tenth of March. The alarm for CELLAR STORAGE ROOM had not been triggered at all. It was simply marked as *not set*.

This was unexpected but not unexplainable. Not been set properly in the first place, then triggered when the door was forced. perhaps.

According to screen and panel, there were no other issues. Sam simply needed to check the doors were properly closed and hit reset. The system would then resume its programming, with the alarms live between six pm and eight am daily.

Phone in hand, Sam went to the cellar storage room. The smashed lock had not yet been replaced but the door was closed. She opened and closed it, visually checking the magnetic contacts in the frame were aligned.

"All good down here," she said and went upstairs to the scene of the original break-in.

"Can I help you?" called a tour guide as Sam approach the French windows.

"DefCon4. Resetting the alarms," said Sam.

"Of course. I'm Phoebe, the National Heritage manager here. If you have any questions, do ask."

"If I get lost, I'll shout," said Sam. "It's a big house."

"A beautiful house," nodded Phoebe enthusiastically. "We've got a seed packet wreath workshop in the stables if you'd care to join us later."

"Sounds lovely," said Sam, but the woman was already chasing after a tour group who seemed to be on the verge of making a run for it.

Another thought popped into Sam's mind. As she made sure the French doors were properly closed she let the thought percolate. The smashed pane had been temporarily replaced with a rectangle of plywood. The door which Hilde had allegedly been coming through when she set off the alarm.

"Ten forty-six," Sam said to herself.

She looked at the clock on her phone as she walked back to the alarm panel. The walk took at least a minute.

She was still looking at her phone when a message came through from Delia.

YOUR DETECTIVE FRIEND CAME TO THE SHOP AND HAD A LOOK ROUND.
TOLD HIM YOU FANCY HIM AND HE SHOULD ASK YOU OUT FOR A DATE.

SAM PHONED DELIA STRAIGHT BACK. "I don't fancy him!" she said.

"*Give him a chance,*" said Delia.

"He's too old for me."

"You're the same age. You're being fooled by the height thing. He can't be more than thirty-five."

"You think I look thirty-five?"

"I was just putting in a good word for my single friend."

"Who says I'm even into men?"

"I've met your ex-boyfriend."

"Who I dumped."

"More fool you. Also, we've been drunk on the sofa together many times and you've never made the move on me."

"Maybe you're too old for me."

"You saying I look thirty-five?"

"How fast can you run?"

"Is age determined by speed now?"

"I've encountered a problem with the Case of the Stolen Drinking Horn."

"Proof that Hilde's innocent?" Delia's voice was suddenly serious.

"A problem," said Sam. "Needs testing out. If you've got time, could you meet me at Candlebroke Hall?"

"Anything."

"Okay. I'll meet you outside. I'll be looking for a beech tree."

15

Sam had found the beech tree by the time Delia trundled up the driveway in her dilapidated family car. Delia's hair was pulled back in a messy bun, tied off with a strip of patterned fabric. There was a pencil jammed into that mass of unruly hair.

"This is a beech, right?" said Sam. "At moments like these I realise I only know three or four trees for definite."

"Grey bark, horizontal marks. That's the one. I think the question on my lips is 'why?'"

Sam patted the rough bark of the tree. "Lucas Camara said Hilde's bag of tools was found by the beech tree and that she was arrested nearby at – I think I recall correctly – eleven oh-one."

"Uh-huh?"

Sam corralled the thoughts that had been circling her head. "The alarm for the outer door went off at ten forty-six.

The police were notified at about ten fifty and had Hilde in hand cuffs by one minute past eleven."

"Yes?" said Delia politely.

"That's precisely fifteen minutes from alarm to arrest."

"Indeed."

Sam pointed at the house, rising above the trees, half a mile away. "Fifteen minutes to break in, sneak downstairs, break into the cellar, find the horn, come back up and run to this point."

"You think it can't be done?"

Sam jiggled her head. "It would be tight." She took off her jacket and passed it to Delia along with her card wallet and keys. "I'm going to run to the house and time it."

"And I'm going to drive, right?" said Delia.

"No – I'll get you to run back here so we've got two times to compare."

Delia chucked Sam's things on the back seat among the booster seats, drinking bottles and general rubbish. "Oh, no need to overdo it," she said.

Sam stood by the doors to the summer drawing room, getting her breath back while trying to look like she didn't need to get her breath back. Delia came round the corner, accompanied by a surly-faced National Heritage volunteer.

"Is this woman with you?" asked the volunteer.

"My assistant," said Sam, keeping her answers short so her breathlessness was less obvious.

"You run funny," said Delia.

"Everyone runs funny," said Sam and took a deep breath.

"That's why people don't like doing it in public." She held up her phone to show Delia the timer. "Seven minutes twenty-one. It's not easy over rough terrain."

"I think Hilde would have been faster."

"In the dark?"

The volunteer woman frowned. "Is this what you two do then?"

"This and drink colourful cocktails," said Delia.

The woman gave them a displeased look and left.

"Fifteen minutes minus seven is eight." Sam looked at the door. "Eight minutes to carry out the actual burglary."

"Doesn't sound unreasonable."

"Let's try it. Ready?"

Delia gave her a look. "Ready for what?"

"Ready to act like burglars." She reset the timer on her phone. "I've smashed the window pane ... I've reached for the door handle ... the alarm goes off—" she pressed the timer "—and ding-a-ling-a-ling." She opened the doors and stepped inside.

Delia followed, immediately adopting a stealthy half-crouch with arms held wide. "Did Hilde— Did *the burglar* know what they were looking for?"

"They didn't grab any of the obviously valuable stuff in here." Sam pointed at the pictures on the wall.

"This furniture would be worth a quid or two," said Delia.

"Maybe the burglar was only interested in transportable items."

They moved swiftly but quietly through the house

towards the stairs. Sam looked at Delia and her crab-like movements. "What are you doing?"

"I'm in character. I'm a burglar."

"You look like you've crapped yourself."

"I'm 'Snatch' McAndrews, international jewel thief. You're my sidekick, Pussy Pockets. We're being sneaky."

"The burglar alarm is already ringing. There's no point being sneaky."

Sam descended the stairs to the cellar. "Right. Here's the door. The burglar used a crowbar or something to prise it open."

"Huh," said Delia.

"What?"

"Legge cylinder pin lock." Delia tapped the door. "Nineteen fifties or sixties. Hilde could pick that easily."

"But our burglar's in a hurry." Sam put an imaginary crowbar in the frame, gave two imaginary yanks and opened the door. She flicked on the light switch, walked to the boxes in the corner, and took out an imaginary horn. "Back to the exit."

Once they were at the doors to the summer drawing room again, Sam stopped the timer. "Twelve minutes. But we faffed about."

"Never underestimate the faffing," said Delia. "As you said, Hilde was doing this in the dark. And she was scared. And unless she'd been here before, or had a map, she wouldn't find the cellar so easily."

"Twelve minutes plus seven is nineteen," said Sam.

"And she was arrested fifteen minutes after the alarm went off."

The two of them quietly considered the possibilities.

"It was impossible for Hilde to commit the crime in the time she had," said Delia.

Sam nodded. "Yet she was clearly here. And she got the horn, somehow."

"But it was impossible all the same."

Sam knew their experimentation method was suspect and would do little to dissuade the police, but the facts confirmed her suspicion that something was not right at Candlebroke Hall. She would tell Camara anyway.

Delia took a buzzing phone from her pocket. She answered without hesitation. There were lots of "Uh-huhs" and subdued "Okays" and a final "Of course, you can come back, as soon as you're ready." She looked at Sam. "Hilde's out on police bail."

"Good," said Sam earnestly.

"And they've arrested Ragnar for stealing an oak tree."

Sam thought about it. "I did wonder where they got the wood for that ship of theirs."

Her phone pinged. A new job had appeared on her DefCon4 app. "You have got to be kidding me," she whispered.

"Problem?"

"A job." Sam read from the screen. "Police evidence collection. One Viking boat."

16

Kiki heard the rustle of bushes and turned, prepared to give a stern rebuke to a wandering member of the public who had strayed into a private area. But it was the young detective, Camara.

"Forgive the intrusion," he said, stepping onto the path by the tiger enclosure.

Antoine stood swiftly. He looked like a schoolboy caught doing something unspeakable behind the bike sheds. He might have been a stage performer, but he didn't have an actor's self-control.

"Not interrupting anything, am I?" said Camara.

"We don't often get people back here," said Kiki, offering him a hand.

"Miss Chiddingfold – Phoebe – told me you'd be here."

"I don't think you two have met," said Kiki. "Detective Camara this is my friend, Antoine de Winter. Antoine, this is Lucas Camara."

"And this is Hugh," said Antoine, gesturing to the creature sleeping on his platform in the cage.

"Who?" said Camara, who clearly hadn't spotted the beast.

"His Chinese name, yes."

Camara finally clocked the mangy tiger. Kiki thought it was poor show for a detective to be so unobservant, although the greying geriatric thing was hardly attention-grabbing.

"Ah – the tiger guard dog," said Camara. He frowned. "Do you require a special licence for this?"

"A Dangerous Wild Animal licence as granted by the council," said Antoine smoothly.

"My late husband kept a number of animals here," said Kiki. "I was able to help Antoine out when he was looking for a home for Hugh."

"We used to work on stage together," said Antoine.

"You and Lady Lettuces?" said Camara.

"Hugh and I," said Antoine. "But that was a long time ago and the past is a different country. Psychic phenomena and mentalism are my metier these days."

Camara nodded. "I think I may have seen posters for some of your shows at Carnage Hall."

"I'm waiting for the day the police call, asking for my assistance in an unsolvable case."

"Yeah. Not sure that ever happens." Camara clasped his hands together, eager to move on. "In fact, I have come to speak to Kiki about some stolen property."

"The burglar has told you where she hid the loot?" said Kiki.

"Not that, no. We still have questions with regard to the

burglary. But our investigation has tangentially led to us running tests of some wood."

"Wood?"

"I'm pleased to say we have found your stolen oak tree. Well, timbers, as it now is. Normally, we'd return stolen property immediately but, well, it's been turned into a longship."

Kiki found this a little difficult to process. "Longship? As in...?"

"A Viking boat," nodded Camara. "Obviously, there's no way to restore your beautiful tree, but I did discuss the matter with Miss Chiddingfold. She thought that she – you, National Heritage – might want the boat. Have it *back*, as it were."

"Why would we...?"

"It is a beautiful boat."

Kiki wanted to say she had never heard anything quite so ridiculous. But then she could picture Phoebe's response to having a huge, decorative ... *installation* in the grounds of Candlebroke Hall. An item whose value might extend beyond the cost of its component parts.

"I could have predicted this," said Antoine.

In the cage, Hugh yawned, revealing three-inch canines and a fat pink tongue, then he went back to sleep.

If Sam had to think of a single word to describe her job, on a good day she might pick 'varied'. On a bad day, the word would be much more earthy. She had no idea what might appear on her scheduler app. Today's task had been outsourced from the Lincolnshire police, requiring the transportation of a Viking longship. Sam only knew of one longship in the area, and the details confirmed she was to pick it up from the Odinsons' compound and transport it to Candlebroke Hall.

She called Camara.

"Yes," he said. "*It's the sort of specialist job we always outsource. We're just not equipped to do that sort of thing. I guess you can rustle up some expertise from elsewhere in your organisation, can't you?*"

"You'd think so, wouldn't you?" said Sam. "I'll make some arrangements."

"*Oh, and what's this message about how hard it is to run in the dark?*" His tone did not sound promising.

Sam explained. "Simply put, detective, to be able to get downstairs, steal the horn, get out and run out to where the police found Hilde is nigh on impossible given the times recorded by the alarm system and the arresting officer."

There was a silence on the line. Sam could picture Camara massaging his brow or slowly rolling his eyes. "*Nigh on impossible. And yet, we are going to have concrete evidence placing Hilde at the scene and – this is key – Hilde had the stolen property on her.*"

"Something else was happening."

"*What? If you put another person at the scene it doesn't affect the general narrative or prove her innocence. Are we looking for some rocket-powered roller-skates we've not yet uncovered?*"

"You're mocking me."

He sighed. "*Sorry. Your diligence is appreciated. But nothing's changed. You've given me one piece of evidence that argues against our version of events, while I've got a slew of physical evidence that backs it up. So, thank you, Sam but I've got other things to..."*

"Yeah, yeah, sure," she said. "Sorry to bother you."

Deflated, she killed the call. She spent a few minutes browsing the internet and started to get a feel for the cost of transporting something like a boat. Then she cross-checked with the budget DefCon4 had allocated. There was a significant difference. She made herself a cup of tea and braced herself to phone head office.

DefCon4's labyrinthine phone system seemed designed to keep actual human contact as far out of reach as possible. Sam spent what felt like hours negotiating the perplexing option menu, usually coming back to her starting point. She constructed a flow chart as she went in an attempt to hit on the winning combination. Winning the lottery might have been easier. She was poised to thumb re-dial yet again, when there came a clunk and the voice of a woman.

"Hello, can I help you?"

Sam had to gather her thoughts. She had been so focused on solving the phone problem, the original reason for the call had slipped to the back of her mind. "Hi, it's Sam Applewhite calling from the Skegness office. I have a query on a task that I've been assigned."

"Have you checked with your branch manager?"

Generally, Sam found it was hopeless to try and convey to the employees at head office exactly how desolate and unpopulated the Skegness office actually was. She glanced across at Doug Junior, her stand-in colleague when she needed a chat. He was very supportive, for a cactus.

"Yeah, I've discussed it with everyone here," said Sam truthfully, "and it's unanimous, We need some guidance."

"Give me the task reference and tell me what the problem is."

Sam gave her the code. "It's a massive, specialist job. The budget I've been allocated is less than a tenth of what I'm going to need."

"Hm, you're to collect evidence secured by the police."

"It's a ship."

"According to my information, it is a sailing vessel with less than three masts, so it's a boat."

Sam tapped the desk in frustration. "It's a very large boat then. It still needs specialist equipment."

"Am I right in thinking," came the voice, in a tone suggesting she knew she was right, *"that you are located near to the sea? You will simply need to borrow or hire a boat trailer and use your company vehicle to tow it to its destination, which appears to be less than ten miles."*

"It's not a question of the distance—"

"—If I can be of any more assistance, don't hesitate to get back in touch." The woman hung up.

17

T horoughly depressed by the logistics of the 'evidence collection' job, Sam decided to spend an hour in Cat's Café with a warming hot chocolate while she mulled over her options. Outside the heavens had opened and Skeg was being treated to a hearty downpour. The entrance to the Skegness DefCon4 office was squashed between the *Who Do You Ink You Are* tattoo parlour and Cat's Café. Sam stepped out, locked the door, took a step to the left, and entered the café.

Behind the counter, Cat whirled and gasped in horror.

"It's only me," said Sam.

"Oh, I know," said Cat cheerily. "I'm just practising my shock reactions."

It would be perfectly normal to enquire "Why?" or "What the hell?", but Sam had learned better. Asking Cat such a thing would undoubtedly lead to a lengthy monologue about her latest project with Skegness Operatic and Dramatic

Society. Cat, when not half-heartedly running a cheap café, was an aspiring actress and playwright and would tell anyone who cared to listen. And those who didn't.

"Hot chocolate," said Sam. She looked at the rain. "With all the trimmings."

She took a seat at a window table and thought how she could approach the mammoth task of moving the Odinsons' longship.

The DefCon4 woman's suggestion of towing the ship with her company vehicle was laughable. Sam didn't know where to start. Her Piaggio Ape 50 could not even support the weight of a towbar. Hitching something onto the back would almost certainly result in it rolling backwards down the least incline. Or pulling the back off the van.

Sam tried to picture what sort of a trailer would be needed to hold a longship. Maybe she should call someone at the boating club, just to see if they had any ideas.

The hot drinks machine gurgled and hissed.

"What was that?" said Cat with a strangled yelp.

"My drink," said Sam.

Cat eyed the machine suspiciously. "Or is it the scraping fingernails of dead children trapped in the wall?"

"Definitely the machine," said Sam.

Cat shrugged. "I'm just trying to get into character. I've got—"

"Oh, phone's ringing!" Sam lied and put her phone to her ear. She kept up a pretend conversation until Cat retreated. Then she phoned the Skegness Boating Club to see if they could help with the longship problem.

Sam was passed around to a few different members who

asked her an array of questions she need to look at the ship to answer – like the depth of the keel and how the masts were held in place. She had a suspicion the questions were mainly being used to bat her away. And no matter what the answers were, nobody would be equipped to help her. They'd be even less inclined to help once they realised the job would entail going into the den of the Odinsons.

As she sipped hot chocolate, she logged onto a website that was a platform for offering casual work. It was designed to match the task with local people who matched the profile. She thought for a few minutes and made two listings.

- *WANTED: SOMEONE WITH AN AGRICULTURAL HEAVYWEIGHT LOW-LOADER, AVAILABLE TO DRIVE A SHORT-HAUL LOAD FROM SKEGNESS.*
- *WANTED: FIFTEEN STRONG MANUAL LABOURERS, NEEDED FOR A LOADING AND UNLOADING JOB NEAR SKEGNESS.*

IT WAS A POPULAR SITE, so she was confident she would find some help. Indeed, before she'd finished her hot chocolate, her inbox dinged with replies. She selected the ones which seemed like the best fit and added them all to a group chat, so she could summon them when she needed them.

There was the smash of a plate from the kitchen and a scream.

Sam leapt her feet. "Cat! Cat, you okay?"

"The horror!" Cat replied in a weird, screechy dreamy voice. "The horror!"

Sam held her tongue for a second in case the first thing to come out was a string of obscenities. "Cat! Are you hurt? Or are you just messing about?"

"Why won't the spirits leave me alone?" Cat trembled.

Sam put a couple of pound coins on the counter. "Thanks for the drink, Cat. I'll see you around."

"Thank you," said Cat cheerily. "Don't forget to post a review."

18

The rain had gone by the following afternoon, leaving clear, cold skies over the coast. Sam drove down to the Elysian Fields Caravan Park to visit the Odinsons. She parked her tiny van next to a dusty mobility scooter and walked into the compound.

It felt more as if she was stepping into a medieval village or a strangely bohemian shanty town than a caravan park. Joined-up scraps of guttering carried rainwater towards a polytunnel. She'd never been inside, but guessed someone was growing vegetables, or something more recreational. There were covered walkways between some of the caravans, all made from salvaged materials as far as Sam could tell. The medieval feel was further enhanced by scraps of fluttering bunting, embroidered with runes. Was that the work of Astrid, Ragnar's wife?

A rangy Odinson strolled over to her. She recognised the red bandana. It was one of Ragnar's sons.

"Afternoon, Yngve."

He gave a brief nod, and the roll-up in the side of his mouth twitched. "Aye."

"I need to speak to someone about the longship. You know that the police are impounding it?"

Yngve gave a brief sneer and walked away into the compound. He returned a few minutes later with Ragnar, who was accompanied by Hilde. The Odinsons stood in a defensive line.

"You want to know summat about the longship?" Ragnar asked.

"Nice to see you out of custody, Hilde," said Sam.

Hilde smiled at Sam but made no move to step any closer.

Sam produced a letter given to her by Camara. "I have instructions to collect items as dictated in this letter. Specifically, your longship."

There were hisses and mutters and from somewhere a shout of, "You think we're gonna let ya?"

Sam smiled grimly. "You don't have to let me," she replied loudly. "But then I'll have to ask the police to come and help me. You don't want that."

There were more hisses and mutters, more anti-police than anti-Sam. She looked at Ragnar.

"I've seen your ship in action, Ragnar. Close up. It's a thing of beauty. You know I will do my best to ensure it's unharmed."

Ragnar pawed his beard with sad thoughtfulness.

Yngve smirked. "Might need a bigger van."

Sam ignored him. "I've come to assess the job. I'll need to

get some details from you. Depth of the keel, what can be done with the mast and so on. Perhaps you'd lead the way, Ragnar?"

Ragnar and Hilde walked silently away. Sam followed. She could hear Yngve behind her, rapping on doors of the caravans they passed. She sighed, knowing this was about to become a major spectacle. She would just have to work hard to keep a professional demeanour.

They arrived at the longship and Ragnar turned to Sam. "Right. Reckon tha can pop that in yer handbag then, lass?"

Sam caught Hilde rolling her eyes at Ragnar's casual sexism.

"You've got other things to worry about, Ragnar," said Sam. "You and Hilde got court dates, yet?"

"I'm not afeared of prison," he said, but Sam could hear the hollowness in his bravado.

She gestured to the ship. "Have you removed all of your belongings from the ship? Astrid's cushions and so on?"

Ragnar huffed and pointed at a couple of the younger people who were crowding around. "Hop on board and gather up anything that's removable."

Sam walked around the ship, checking it out. It was resting in a wooden cradle. Sam knew the ship would stand upright on the beach, because she'd seen it, but thought the cradle would be useful to help transport it.

"The cradle," said Ragnar, watching her face, "is not made from oak. It stays here."

Sam had been sizing up the task in her mind's eye. She could actually see it fitting on the back of a low loader if the cradle was in place. She continued to walk around the ship, trying to think of an alternative. Could she wedge it in place with bags of sand or something? She pulled out her phone and tried to calculate what it would cost for a builders' merchant to deliver a pallet of large bags. How would they get them into place around the ship? Could a crane lift them on with enough precision? She would need the crane to unload it, as well. It was starting to sound complicated. And expensive.

"What about the mast?" she asked. Can it be taken down?"

Hilde nodded. "We can release it with about thirty minutes' work."

"Please do," said Sam.

Hilde moved towards the ship, but Ragnar clapped a hand on her shoulder. "Hold up. We're not obliged to do that. If there's work to be done, reckon it's on you, lass."

Hilde looked pained. "Farfar," she whispered. "She's on our side."

"And taking our ship?" Was that a sudden choke in Ragnar's voice? Was he looking away to hide a sudden tear?

"Fine," said Sam.

She'd had some speedy responses to her posts on the jobs site. It was time to call them in. She went to the web group chat. Theoretically, most of her labourers were on standby, flat rates of pay already agreed, so she might as well see if she could organise them sooner rather than later. She sent a message to them all.

She was surprised to hear a chorus of nearby dings. Numerous Odinsons pulled out their phones.

Sam checked some of the user profiles on her virtual

team. "You!" she said, pointing at Yngve. "Are you *GunNRoses49*, by any chance?"

Yngve nodded and glanced across at Ragnar, who clearly hadn't caught up with what was going on.

She pointed at the twins, Gunnolf and Hermod. "And you two! You're clearly *TwinTurbo*."

They nodded as well. Sam huffed with frustration. Her band of trusty labourers were all Odinsons. Why hadn't she seen that coming?

Something else occurred to her. "Wait, is the low loader yours as well, Yngve?"

"Aye, sort of," said Yngve. He got a kick in the ankle from a young girl standing behind him. "I mean, definitely ours, aye."

"So the people that I've hired to remove your ship are all of you?" she said, realising the enormity of it. "Well, that's a bit of a pickle, isn't it?"

Ragnar beamed around at his family as he finally caught up. "Nice work!" He turned back to Sam. "Seems you should go and tell the police the boat will need to stay here, as there's nobody capable of moving it. And I don't know what they were thinking, getting a girl to try and move a bloody great ship, anyway."

There was silence, broken only by a girl's voice muttering, "Sexist, isn't it? No call for that."

Yngve kicked at the wet earth. "If we did move the ship for you..." he said, slowly, cautiously, like a man in a minefield, "we would still get paid, wouldn't we?"

"What?" growled Ragnar.

"A full day's pay is a full day's pay," said Hermod with equal caution.

"It's our ship!" said Ragnar.

"And it's a lot of money," said Hermod.

"Mutiny! Sedition!" Ragnar stalked forward and gave Hermod a shove. The huge man mountain barely moved. Ragnar gave him a furious, mad-eyed squint and shoved him again. Hermod took the hint and dutifully fell over. "I won't allow it! No man here is to raise a finger to move that ship! It's our bloody ship!"

Sam, whilst not devoid of sympathy, had had enough. "Ragnar, I'm sorry to tell you the police have made it clear to me that my task is to recover the wood that was stolen. They do not care whether the ship is intact or not."

"Eh?"

"I have a Plan B – would you like to know what it is?" She turned in a semi-circle, challenging all of the Odinsons, like she hadn't just invented Plan B on the spot. "It's to drive into town, hire a chainsaw and a skip, and come back here and reduce your ship to matchsticks so it will fit in that skip. One way or another, I will be moving this ship."

Ragnar pulled a face. It took him a good while for his anger to circle the airfield and make a landing at Calm and Reasonable Central. He made patting movements with his hands.

"Talk of destroying my ship is more than insulting. It's a blow to our freedom to express our religion – nay to our way of life. I won't have it, I tell thee."

"Farfar, there might be another way of looking at this," said

Hilde. She walked forward and pointed at the ship. "*Sandraker* needs to be moved. We can resist and complain, but other Saxons will come. What we need to do is make sure it's moved by people who'll care about it and do it properly." She looked over at Sam. "Obviously we'll get the money for the job as well."

Ragnar looked at Hilde and his expression softened. "Well, money's money I suppose. Let's make sure it gets there safe. Then we know we can bring it back when t'day comes that our property is rightfully restored to us!"

19

The collective muscle power of two dozen Odinsons was an impressive thing to behold. What seemed immovable by human hands was easily transported by many. Working as one (and it was pleasantly surprising to see that the workshy and generally uncooperative Odinsons could work as one) the family hoisted their longship up to shoulder height and carried it forward onto the back of Yngve's flatbed low-loader.

As various men lashed it into place in the darkening evening, Sam took Hilde's elbow and steered her aside.

"What happened at Candlebroke Hall?"

Hilde flashed her a dark look. "Is tha wearing a wire?"

"What? No. I know things don't add up there. You didn't break in, go down to the cellar, steal that horn then run out to where the police arrested you. You didn't have time."

"I know. That's what I told the police."

Hilde said it so matter-of-factly that Sam was stumped.

"You are going to be tried and convicted of burglary," she pointed out. "They haven't even listed all the items you've supposedly stolen yet."

Hilde nodded.

"You are going to prison."

Hilde nodded again.

"Prison is not a nice place. I know from experience."

Hilde's eyes widened.

"*Work* experience," said Sam. "DefCon4 manages a number of prisons. God help anyone who ends up in one of them."

Hilde's nod this time was solemn and resigned. It was infuriating.

"What are you not telling me, Hilde?"

Hilde had had enough. She looked away to the men working on the longship. "Torsten! Not round there! That strap'll snap the masthead off on the first corner tha comes to!"

Hilde marched off to organise the men's efforts. When it came to work tasks, the Odinsons seemed to have two settings: 'Leave it, it'll be fine' and 'When in doubt, do it again'. There was no middle ground. The longship was starting to look like Gulliver pinned down on the sand by a thousand Lilliputian ropes.

"I will stand in the prow as we go," declared Ragnar. "A Viking chief should captain his vessel, whether over sea or land."

"No, you will not, Ragnar," said Sam.

"Tha'll not be telling me what to do," he retorted. "The

police'll see me arrive at their compound proud and unbroken."

"One, you'll be breaking the law, standing up there. Two, we're not going to any compound. This boat is going to be taken to Candlebroke Hall."

There were general murmurs of confusion and disdain.

"It's where the wood came from," she said. "And they've got the space. I'm not going to rock up at Candlebroke Hall with their stolen wood—"

"Harvested!" shouted a voice.

"—Stolen wood with the man who allegedly stole it standing proudly on top. Now, get down, Ragnar. Kiss your boat goodbye and stop making a fool of yourself."

Grumbling but chastised, the man clambered down.

Sam climbed into the cab with Yngve. Odinson men piled into various vehicles so they could help with the heavy lifting at the other end.

"Okay, let's go," said Sam. "See if we can get this job completed before midnight."

Yngve noisily put his vehicle into gear. "Just so tha knows," he said. "Most of us were there helping Ragnar steal the wood in t'first place."

"Really?"

He sniffed. "Fact, we used Hermod and Gunnolf's Super Duty to carry it."

Sam looked back at the cherry red truck with flame decals on the side. It was an unmistakeably distinctive vehicle.

"It's a good job we're doing this in the dark then," she said without any confidence at all.

20

Phoebe, who did not seem to approve of Antoine hanging around Candlebroke Hall, was somewhat taken with his YouTube seances and ghost hunts. He had a modest following on the internet, and Phoebe felt it encouraged a buzz of interest in the stately home.

Politely, Phoebe insisted Kiki should be present at Antoine's seance broadcasts. Kiki understood there were people who remembered her glory days, and a glimpse of a former movie star in a stately home would draw in a certain crowd.

From her wardrobe, she selected a diaphanous gown in a striking sapphire colour. It would flutter spookily in any draft, which could help with the show. She also raised a small prayer of thanks to the designers of the seventies for their love of polyester: this dress would never succumb to the moths or mould. She slathered herself in Oil of Ulay, as she had for decades. She ran her fingers up and down her face, enjoying the ritual, and smiling the self-satisfied and slightly mysterious smile she would have worn if they'd ever used her for the Ulay advert – as they should have done. She used curling tongs to tease body into her hair.

She turned on the antique washing machine, left her rooms, and went down to meet the others in the first floor winter dining room. Antoine had already dimmed much of the lighting, down to replacing some of the lightbulbs with low wattage ones. Kiki coughed lightly as she stepped into the room, so that they turned to look.

"Kiki, darling, you always look so at home in your vintage treasures!" Antoine said, moving forward to kiss her hand. He was dressed in a suit of navy blue and gold brocade. Even under partial lighting it looked brash, but Kiki knew when the lighting was fully dimmed, it would look rich and exotic.

The door opened and the young am dram woman from the town entered. She was dressed in the sort of clothing Kiki liked to call 'Fairtrade hippy', with a long swishy skirt that had tiny mirrors embroidered into it. The top was made up of multi-layered pennants in shades of a muddy purple. If Kiki had been liberal with her use of eyeliner, Cat had taken it to a new level.

"I love the atmosphere of this place," she said. "It gets spookier every time I visit, Mr de Winter." She gave a girlish giggle and pretend shudder. "Kiki. Wonderful to be working with you again. I've had six energy drinks today to keep me alert and ready."

Antoine walked over to the table and picked up what Kiki knew better than to call a selfie stick – last time he had wittered on at length about gimbal stabilisers and whatnot. It was a fancy selfie stick, and Antoine loved using it. There was a neat lighting rig attached to it, with a ring of LEDs. When they lit up, Antoine killed most of the dining room lights, casting them all in a dramatic glow. As Antoine turned on the camera he stepped straight into character, dropping his voice half an octave and pouring on his velvety charm.

"Good evening, everybody. I'm Antoine de Winter. I'd like to welcome you once again to one of Britain's most haunted stately homes, Candlebroke Hall. I'm joined this evening by Kiki Harris, well-loved model and actress."

Kiki inclined her head gracefully, making sure she did not allow her smile to slip. She had complained in the past that the phrase "well-loved model" made her sound like a second-hand car, so Antoine never missed an opportunity to say it.

Antoine turned to point out Cat. "We have Cat, who lives locally. Cat is sensitive to the spirit world and will provide a useful counterpoint to my own expertise. We also have Phoebe Chiddingfold, an historian and expert on Candlebroke Hall's past."

Kiki wondered if Phoebe had ever watched herself. Because the woman wore appalling clothes and no makeup, she now looked more like someone who belonged on a video warning about the effects of solvent abuse.

"So come with us as we explore this, the oldest part of the house tonight," said Antoine, walking to the door and beckoning his audience to follow. "We have the usual equipment. On screen live tracking of the time and local temperature. I have my hand-held EMF recorder, which detects any interference in the electromagnetic field. I have static cameras in place, as well as the one I'm using here, so I can show you the facts, and the truth." He said this last with profound sincerity. "Come with me as we try to contact some of the unquiet spirits of Candlebroke Hall."

Kiki, Phoebe and Cat all followed him along the corridor. There was no point in speaking at this point as Antoine would be overlaying the theme music as they walked towards adventure.

He pushed open a door. "Here we are in the playroom. Look around at the old toys. Imagine the generations of children who have spent time here."

Hardly any of the toys would have been played with by Lettuces children. Antoine trawled car boot sales and antiques shops for old toys and ornaments, just so he could set up scenes like this. Kiki knew he would cut in loads of spooky footage of the freaky-looking old toys because they set the mood.

"You'd like to think the childhoods of the rich and privileged would be idyllic, but it wasn't always so," he said ominously. "Sometimes things took a tragic turn."

Cat sobbed suddenly and Antoine swung the camera onto her. "What is it Cat, do you feel it too?"

"Poor little mite!" she sobbed. "He was so young!"

Kiki could have vomited at the girl's amateurish mugging. It was fine if you had the charm or looks to carry it off, but this shapeless wench had neither.

Antoine swivelled the camera back round onto himself. "Cat feels, *as do I*, the closeness of the spirit. I can report the room has suddenly become very cold. Do you feel that, Phoebe and Kiki?"

They both nodded. Antoine would make sure the thermal monitoring matched the story during the edit. As he had discussed with her before, this wasn't lying to the audience, merely "enhanced narrative visualisation."

"I can see him in my mind," said Antoine. "So clear. He is dressed in the most adorable blue velvet suit. He has blond hair and rosy cheeks. Do you see him Cat?"

"I see his little face!" wailed Cat. She was overcome with it all and plonked herself heavily onto a chair, racked with sobs.

"You can't sit on that, it's part of the exhibition," said Phoebe. "It's clearly stated on the sign."

Cat wasn't listening. She sniffled noisily and her wailing grew louder. Phoebe tapped her on the shoulder, and shook it when Cat did not respond.

"Cat. Cat, my dear," said Antoine. "I'm worried you're channelling too much of the negative emotion. Let me commune with the boy. I believe he returns to this room because he feels safe here, but he died elsewhere. In fact, that is what's kept him tethered to the earth if I'm not mistaken, the idea that this room is where he was supposed to be. He crept out one day, against the rules, because he wanted to ride his tricycle outside."

"A tricycle?" said Phoebe.

"He cycled out towards the stables where he fell into a well." Antoine let out a long, heartfelt sigh. "The poor lad drowned, but his final thoughts were how angry his mother would be when she discovered he had left the room. He's been trying to return ever since."

"So when was this?" asked Phoebe. "It would be

interesting to cross-reference with our historical records, to see who he might have been."

"I'm sensing a name," said Antoine, his eyes closed, waving a hand airily above his head. "That might help, yes? It could be William, perhaps?"

Phoebe shrugged.

"Or perhaps Henry? William was a close friend. Henry? Henry, William and ... Charles. They were all great friends. They would play together in the rose garden."

"There was a son called Charles in the early eighteen hundreds," said Phoebe. "Although, if he had a tricycle, I'm not sure, historically speaking, it would be possible for—"

"There we are then!" declared Antoine. "Now, let us see if young Charles will communicate with us, and let us help release him from his earthly bonds."

"Yes! Charles, we're coming sweetie!" screeched Cat. "We will do our best to help you, poor soul!"

"Shush, we must see what else the spirit chooses to bring to us." Antoine continued his silent appraisal of the room. Kiki thought he looked like a bad mime act, but he claimed it came across well on the video. He went over to the far wall, and made a gasp of discovery. He brought his hand up to show how his fingers glistened in the light cast by his rig. "Look at this! Ectoplasm. The spirit is manifesting much more strongly!"

"Er, what?" said Phoebe. "Really?"

Meanwhile, Cat was sliding to and fro on the wall, as if re-creating a Kate Bush video.

"Mind the wallpaper!" snapped Phoebe. "That's hand-painted Regency!"

"There's more!" cried Antoine, his voice shockingly loud, as he sought to ramp up the tension by increasing the volume. "I'm getting something else now. Something different!"

Everyone froze in place, watching him.

"I ought to clean up that goo," Phoebe said quietly. "It might stain."

"I want the loo," whispered Cat. "Too many energy drinks."

"Charles, can you reach out to us?" Antoine called.

"On your tricycle," added Kiki helpfully.

"Come to see us here in the room," said Antoine.

Cat's quivering became more pronounced. She jigged up and down on the spot.

"He's coming!" said Antoine grandly.

There a loud horn blast from outside. In the tense gloom of the house, all of them jumped. Cat shrieked.

"Jesus!" hissed Kiki.

"Is that his tricycle?" said Phoebe, her voice strangled.

"With an airhorn?" said Antoine.

"Oh no," Cat wept. "Oh no, oh no."

Kiki walked to the window and pushed aside the heavy drapes. Bright headlights were swinging up the driveway and onto the gravel semi-circle in front of the house. The shape of the vehicle was confusing in the dark. It seemed to be carrying an inverted arch.

"Oh, it's people bringing the boat," said Phoebe, looking at her phone.

"I have to stop," Cat moaned softly.

"It's over," said Antoine, slowly. "We can put the lights

back on. The spirits have left the room. We will need to try again another day."

Cat shuffled. "Um, you know with possession, does it sometimes happen that a spirit enters a body and makes it have an embarrassing accident?" There was a puddle beneath her.

"It often does, my dear," sighed Antoine. "You're just lucky he went before he could do more damage."

"Lucky, yes," said Cat, staring at the floor.

"I'll get a mop," said Phoebe. "And someone please Google how to get ectoplasm stains out of hand-painted wallpaper. I'd best get down there and direct them where to put our delivery."

Antoine turned off his camera. "And cut," he said, wearily, since no one was listening to him anymore.

Kiki stepped forward to examine the ectoplasm on the wall. She got an unmistakeable whiff of Oil of Ulay and nearly groaned out loud. Had she left the bottle too close to the rattling washing machine? Had it slid and fallen? She could picture the bottle on the floor above, dripping through the floorboards. She didn't have money to waste on replacing essentials like face cream.

Kiki was torn between nipping back to her apartments to see what damage had been done, and going to offer personal supervision of the delivery of a longship that, without careful placement, would undoubtedly be an eyesore on her estate.

She went to the door.

"Oh, we're taking ten, are we?" said Antoine scathingly and hurried to catch up with Kiki. "I would like to get this whole televisual masterpiece shot in one night. Some of us have a living to make and significant debts to pay."

"Are we not making enough money together?" said Kiki, keeping her voice low. "Aren't there items for which your dealer has yet to pay us?"

"In light of the recent 'burglary', I've decided to keep a bit of a low profile. I will be visiting Vance tomorrow and chase payment for goods received. But there has been a bit of a snag."

"Snag?" said Kiki as they reached the ground floor.

"A friend on the force tells me the burglar alarm woman has poked some holes in the official story of what happened that night."

"A friend on the force?"

"I have my sources. And I have plugged the holes. Quite cleverly if I say so myself."

"Cleverly," said Kiki. Antoine was indeed a clever individual, although Kiki feared he was not always as clever as he thought.

21

Telling Yngve to stop a good distance short of the house, Sam jumped out and walked. The National Heritage woman, Phoebe Chiddingfold approached.

"You're the hauliers, yes?" said Phoebe, hand outstretched. She hesitated when she saw Sam's face. "Weren't you the burglar alarm woman?"

"I get around," said Sam. "I hope you were expecting the delivery of a Viking longship."

"Indeed." Phoebe moved sideways to get out of the headlight glare and see the ship more clearly. "It looks a beauty. I thought we'd set it down in the main lawns, nestling under the cedar trees. Do you think you can get it round the back through that gap there?"

"I think so," said Sam. If the Odinsons had managed to navigate the estate's tracks and gates when stealing the wood, they should have no problem doing the same to put it back.

"Excellent," said Phoebe. "I will see you round the back."

Sam returned to the cab. "Through that gate round the side," she said.

"Aye," said Yngve. "Reckon I know the way."

He put his vehicle into gear and, with a throaty rumble, drove round the gravel driveway circling the house.

The wide gardens and open spaces to the rear of the house looked ghostly in the dark. Huge shadows of trees swung about in the truck headlights. Hedges and outhouses made a dark silhouette against the blue-grey night sky. Yngve continued past the formal gardens to the trees further beyond. Sam belatedly realised he was automatically heading to the exact spot where his brothers and nephews had cut down Candlebroke's fine oak tree.

"Woah, woah. We'll just wait here, shall we?" she said.

"If tha says so."

"And when you're all out there, moving the ship, could you all be..."

"What?"

"A little less Viking-y. More normal. Not so suspicious."

Yngve touched his long beard and his bandana headscarf. "Stop being who we are?"

"For half an hour. Tell the others."

Three figures were making their way across the lawns. Sam went to meet them.

"Yes, yes," Phoebe was saying. "I thought it would look quite dramatic if we had it up there with the prow, the figurehead, facing towards the house."

"Having a dragon's head staring at me when I open my bedroom curtains in the morning," said Kiki Lettuces sourly.

"Now, Kiki, you know your apartments are at the front of the house."

"It's certainly a dramatic-looking beast," said the moustachioed man in a gaudy suit keeping pace with them. "Sign me up for the Viking funeral with the burning ship."

"We're not burning it," said Phoebe. "I thought it might work as a garden installation, perhaps with a rockery and plants around it. Or maybe a children's play fort, suitably adapted to meet health and safety needs."

"Oh, yes," muttered Kiki. "More children around the place. That's exactly what we need."

The man spotted Sam. "Ah, and here is our security expert cum haulage expert. This is her, isn't it?" He seized Sam's hand and held her fingertips as though he was about to pull her into a ballroom dance. "We met," he said, holding her gaze. "I caught you at your work in the cellar. Startled like a schoolgirl, weren't you? You're Sam Applewhite. I'm Antoine de Winter."

"Er, yes?" said Sam, not meaning to turn it into a question.

"I'm so glad you're here," he said. "We have something we must show you. In the house."

"Well we have this to unload first and—" She fell silent as Yngve came round the truck. His bandana had been replaced by a checked flat cap and he walked with an exaggerated swagger.

"Awight!" he said. "Ah's it goin', mate? I'm Gaz. Me an' the lads are 'ere to unload your boat. Bish, bash, bosh. Soon 'ave it done. Sweet as a nut." He jutted his chin at Phoebe. "Awight, darlin'?"

His – Sam hesitated to call it an accent – *vocal impression* seemed to be based fifty percent on Dick Van Dyke's turn in *Mary Poppins* and fifty percent on the worst *EastEnders* actor. If this was him trying not to be a Viking, Sam wished she hadn't asked.

Other Odinsons sauntered up. "This is Baz and Laz and the boys," said Yngve. "Show us where you want this thing puttin' and we'll get it done. Crash, bang, wallop. Bob's yer uncle, innit?"

Sam realised she was staring in open-mouthed horror.

"So, if I could show you at the house, mademoiselle..." said Antoine.

"What?" said Sam.

"The important thing I must show you."

He tried to pull her away but she resisted and waved at the vehicles. "I have to oversee..."

"Nah, we'll be fine, darlin'," said Yngve.

"Right as ninepence," added another Odinson in an equally awful accent.

"Fit as a butcher's dog," concurred a third.

"Apples and pears," agreed another.

Sam allowed herself to be led away as Phoebe and Kiki began to bicker over the placement of the ship. She put it from her mind and turned her attention to whatever it was this man wanted. "Something important in the house?"

"Yes. This way, my dear."

Walking across a dark garden with a strange man – a strange man with a porn star moustache to boot – raised a number of red flags in Sam's mind. But here she was, following him.

"Something about the burglary concerned us deeply," said Antoine.

"Oh. Right. What's that then?"

"We couldn't fathom out how the burglar managed to get in and out so quickly. The times didn't seem to add up."

"You noticed that too?"

He walked across the rear terrace, which was part-lit by lights from the house, and moved to a shady corner near some box hedging. "And then we saw this."

He pointed at a half-window down at ground level. It was less than a foot high, put in generations ago to give some light to those servants living and working below stairs.

"Here," said Antoine. He knelt and pulled. The window opened upward. Splinters of paint and wood littered the floor. "This was where she broke in."

This seemed nonsensical to Sam, although she didn't dismiss it immediately. The French doors to the Summer Room were an obvious break-in point. Having two didn't make sense.

"You can see it's been forced," said Antoine. "There's a bit of a drop to the floor inside."

Sam knelt beside him and shone her phone torch on the window. Close to Antoine, she could smell the man's cologne, musky but also heavily floral.

She touched the splinters on the ground. "Forced open with a crowbar."

"One assumes," he said. "There's no alarm sensor here so no one would have noticed."

The window was painted white, but among the splinters a different colour caught her eye. Flecks of dark green were embedded in some of the white wood. She picked them up and, lacking anywhere else to put them, prised off the rubber protective case on her phone and sealed them inside.

"Evidence samples?" said Antoine.

"Just thinking things through." She pushed the window up fully, hesitated but a moment, then climbed in feet first. She had to twist almost immediately onto her front and wriggle herself backwards into the small aperture.

"Mademoiselle...?" said Antoine.

"Lower me down." As the lip of the window rode up her torso, she held out her hands. His grip was warm and strong. She wriggled backwards. Suddenly all her weight was in his hands.

"It's a bit of a—" he grunted, then let go. She landed on her feet in the dark. "—drop," he finished.

Sam looked around. She was in one of the cellar corridors. "It's okay. I'm fine." She tried to get her bearings.

So, they'd found another break-in point. Did that mean the burglars had broken in twice? Or broken in one way and out the other?

She recognised the corridor ahead. She was close to the alarm panel, and here was the door to storage room. There was a light switch further along. She turned it on and the creepy basement level was abruptly a lot less creepy. They had finally got round to replacing the lock and latch, but not repainting the damaged door. The door was dark green.

There was a clatter on the stairs and Antoine de Winter appeared, evidently out of breath. "So," he said with finality.

"So?" said Sam.

"So. That explains everything."

Sam frowned. "Sorry, I don't understand why you're showing me this. Did I need to know?"

Antoine blinked, blustered and pointed down the corridor. "Maybe, as the, um, alarm expert, you'd consider putting an alarm on that window."

"Right. I see. I can certainly sort that out. You've mentioned this to the police? The business with the window?"

"As soon as we saw it."

"Very good." Sam moved past him and went towards the stairs.

He followed closely. "It seems clear," he said, "that the intruder broke in through the cellar window, purloined the valuables and exited through the Summer Room, thereby setting off the alarm on their way out rather than their way in."

"Why would they choose to do that?" said Sam.

"Small window. High too. Difficult to get out compared to getting in."

Sam thought on this as they climbed. "No," she said. "That doesn't work."

"It does."

"The Summer Room doors were broken from the outside. The tape on the windows was on the outside and the glass on the inside."

Antoine laughed. He kept laughing. One might almost think he was laughing to stall for time. "No. No. No, no, no," he chortled. "You've clearly missed an important point."

"Have I?"

"Yes. Obviously. So very obvious. We were meant to think

that." He raised his hand and twisted it so she could see both sides. "This burglar is evidently a master of misdirection." He flicked his fingers, and there was suddenly a shiny coin between fore and index finger.

"You're a magician," she said. "I didn't know."

"My dear," he said darkly. "I am so much more than that. I am an explorer of the spirit realms, a master of occult arts. I am a very dangerous man."

His eyes widened expressively. Sam was abruptly conscious that the house was quiet, and he was just a little too close. The smell of his aftershave was almost overpowering.

The quiet was broken by a banging door and the sound of heels on tiles. Cat almost staggered in, fighting to rearrange her long skirts. She looked up in surprise.

"Oh! I didn't see you there, Sam! Thought you were a ghost. What are you doing here? Forgive the smell, I don't feel all that well." The café-owner did look pale.

"You look awful," Sam agreed.

"Something I drank," said Cat.

"A powerful encounter with things from beyond the veil," said Antoine. "Perhaps I should drive you home, Cat. Miss Applewhite here has burly men to oversee."

Antoine put an arm around Cat's shoulder and swept her towards the front door. Sam watched them before heading out the rear of the house.

She had things to think about. Broken windows, and hammy performers too keen to share personal theories. His explanation just about covered the facts, but there was one matter they totally failed to explain. If there were green flecks of paint among the white by the window, then the same tool had probably been used to force open both window and cellar door. If fragments of green door paint had travelled to the window, and not vice versa, then the cellar door had been broken open before the window. And that made no sense at all.

She headed out across the lawns to the Odinsons unloading their ship.

22

Antoine performed a continuous coin roll over his knuckles as he walked down Roman Bank to the *Who Do You Ink You Are?* tattoo parlour. He used a stage magician's coin, almost too large for the purpose. The coin roll, or steeplechase flourish, had stayed with him all his life. He had learned it as a teenager, practising for hours at school and in his bedroom. Walking the coin down his knuckles and back had failed to impress the girls at school, but he'd found the older he got, and the older the girls got, the more they were susceptible to its charms. Older ladies were appreciative of a man who was good with his hands. Drunk Sharons and Traceys in the seafront pubs and bars could easily be won over with a flash of gold and an easy smile.

He'd kept up the skill throughout his career. For one, a good magician needed to keep practising the basic skills of their craft. For another, Antoine was attracted to the superficial symbolism of the coin: wealth, value and the duality of the two faces.

Everyone and everything had two sides. The public and the private. The mask worn in front and the secret face underneath. Part of his talent as a psychic (and there was a true talent to it, even for a fake psychic) was understanding faces. When he met people, either one-to-one or in a vast auditorium, Antoine was studying both of their faces. People thought they were presenting their public face, but the professional psychic could see through to the private one – the worries, the sorrows, the guilt, the pathetic desire to believe there was something more than this tawdry material world.

Skegness itself had a multitude of faces. It wore them in geographical layers, from the unspoilt if bleak coastline to the gaudy family-friendly arcades and amusements along the seafront; to the pubs and clubs and gambling spots mingling with them; to the vein-like alleys where the seedier elements lived.

Antoine liked the town. It had a transient air, communities drifting in and out, people coming and looking for escape and entertainment, and a glimpse of magic. Things Antoine was always ready to provide.

Vance, who owned the *Who Do You Ink You Are?* tattoo parlour was also a man of multiple faces. On the surface, he was a bargain basement tattoo artist with an uninspiring shop in Skegness town centre. Underneath, he was the finest dealer in black market antiques and artwork on the east coast. The two facets were so incongruous that it was quite possible no one suspected him.

Antoine paused before entering. Squashed between Vance's shop and the greasy spoon café was a doorway he had never noticed before. The glass pane was dusty and dull. Beyond, he could see a set of stairs leading directly upwards.

"DefCon4," he murmured, wondering where he had heard or seen that name before. It would come to him.

Antoine entered the tattoo parlour, the door giving an electronic two-tone beep. There were no clients waiting, no browsing customers. He could hear the low buzzing sound of the machine in the treatment room. He flicked through some designs in the portfolios while he waited, idly speculating on what tattoo he might have, if he didn't find the idea repulsive.

Would he have something mysterious, like the lettering from a Ouija board? As soon as he pictured the design against the backdrop of his skin, he found it simultaneously ridiculous and nauseating. He looked up at the designs on the wall and saw a tiger. Of course, that is what he would have. Except that he never would.

A jangle of curtain beads and a young slip of a thing came through, Vance behind them. "Leave it for at least five hours and then wash it with a gentle soap," he was saying.

The young thing cradled a forearm which was wrapped in a tattoo cover.

"Then moisturise, clean, moisturise, clean." Vance opened the door for her, watching her stroll away down the street. "She won't," he said, possibly to himself. "She'll have that wrapping off in the next twenty minutes to show her friends. Hideous fairy tattoo."

"Proud of your work there," smiled Antoine.

"Everyone gets the tattoo they deserve," said Vance.

"Karma in action." He nodded at the tiger tattoo on the wall. "Gorgeous, that one, isn't it? Tempted?"

Vance was a walking advert for his own craft, with tattoos and piercings over much of his body. A row of studs above his eyebrows had the effect of exaggerating his expressions. If Vance pulled a questioning face, as he was now, his studs arched cartoonishly up his forehead.

"Not today," said Antoine.

"What will be will be," said the tattooist unperturbed. "I hear you had a little trouble up at your place."

"Hmmm?"

"The police at Candlebroke Hall."

"Not my place per se, Vance. One of my many roosts. There was indeed a break-in. A valuable drinking vessel stolen by a girl, one of those idiot Viking poseurs."

"The Odinsons?" said Vance. There was an unmistakeable note of alarm in his voice.

"You know them?" said Antoine.

Vance nodded and went to his counter to put cash in the till. "So, this business with the police—" he was desperately trying to sound casual, "—it has no impact on our own business enterprise?"

"Shouldn't do. There may be some scrutiny of the comings and goings at the house but, no, they've got the little minx banged to rights. She'll be locked up before you know it. I've given a drinking horn to you to sell before, haven't I?"

"Have you?" said Vance.

"I keep meticulous records, Vance. I'm sure you do too. I know what I've got in storage, pending sale, I know what I've given to you. I was wondering how much you sold that horn for, and if you could sell another?"

"Items of extremely high value and rarity are harder to shift and our profit margins are lower. It's not a case of just bunging them on eBay or taking 'em to Skegness Fields car boot. You're a magician and—"

"A psychic and medium, Vance."

He bowed his head, eyebrow studs glinting. "Apologies, Svengali. I was going to say that what I do, whisking wondrous *objets d'art* to all corners of the world and making you a tidy profit, is a magic all of my own." He smiled. "I'm sure I owe you something." He opened the till, sniffing and rubbing his nose as he shuffled notes and receipts.

"People come to me and they put their skin, their bodies in my hands. They trust me. You want Chinese ideogram across your shoulders? I'm your man. A rosary bead and crucifix around your ankle? I've done a thousand. A picture of your dead dog, your children's names? You want a tiger across your entire back? And I'm a spiritual guy. The art moves through me. These aren't just pictures – these are tattoos direct from the universal consciousness. Everyone gets the tattoo they deserve and I am just a humble servant of the medium." He looked at Antoine. "*You* put your faith in me. Tens of thousands of pounds worth of the finest art and antiques. And I am just a humble servant." He put several scraps of paper on the counter.

"Scrimshawed poker dice box. Art deco hat stand. Genuine Louis XV mirror, nice bit of work that. Rosenthal ornament of three foxes. That's fourteen hundred and fifty I owe you." He counted out notes onto the counter. "I know this is probably small beer for you, sir, but it's a slow business."

Antoine didn't comment. Subtly ransacking and selling off the wealth of an English stately home should be more profitable than this, but it was hardly small beer. Antoine could tell him that internet videos of seances paid almost nothing, that psychic fairs paid barely more. Psychic shows at theatres, pubs and holiday camps barely broke even. Clawing his way back up from rock bottom after the disgraceful end to his stage magic career was proving long, difficult and degrading.

Antoine watched the money being counted out and acted like he didn't care. Even he had two faces: the successful and unruffled mystic, and the fallen stage magician who couldn't take his eyes off the cash in front of him.

23

During her mid-morning coffee break, Sam phoned DC Camara. He picked up as the kettle began to boil. Sam put it on speaker.

"Morning, Sam."

"Good morning, Lucas. Can I ask you something?"

"Is it another well-intentioned theory regarding the Candlebroke Hall break-in?"

"Maybe," she said, slowly. "I know I'm being annoying and I know you think I'm being naïve."

"I didn't say you were annoying or naïve."

"But you thought it."

There was enough of a pause to confirm her suspicions.

"You've got a question," he said. *"Ask away. Frankly, the paperwork's filed and it's the court's business now. The ceaseless work of policing this mean town has moved onto the next big case, but I will absolutely pretend to take your theories seriously."*

"Thanks," she said, happy to take that as a win. "Did you

hear they found another window where Hilde – damn it! – where *the burglar* might have broken in?"

"*Er, yeah. Think I saw something. It was added to the case data.*"

"They used a crowbar to break open the window. Or something like it." Sam poured hot water into her cafetière. "In the bag of tools found by the tree, was there a crowbar in it? Or anything like one?"

Camara sighed and there was a tippy-tap on a keyboard. "*No. No crowbar.*"

"Ah-ha."

"*Absence of evidence is not evidence of absence. That item could be anywhere. There's a lot of long grass on that estate. Dykes and hedgerows and—*"

"I don't think Hilde crowbarred that window at all."

"*Really?*"

"I think someone did that afterwards, to cover up that the timings of the burglar alarm and the arrest just don't work."

"*Like someone at the house?*"

"Perhaps."

Camara grunted. "*Do you know how many times I've attended a domestic burglary, a real and genuine domestic burglary, and people – I'm talking Joe and Joanna Average – have lied or messed with the scene of the crime in order to change the narrative? People who've left their front door open by accident and then forced it themselves to explain how someone managed to steal their VW Golf off the driveway without any signs of a break-in.*"

"But you admit it's a possibility."

Camara sighed again. This one was deeper. "*Sam Applewhite. I hear you're an intelligent individual.*"

"Thank you."

"*Then let's get this straight. A valuable horn was stolen. The valuable horn was in Hilde Odinson's hands. Hilde Odinson's DNA and fingerprints were found at the property. Everything else — everything! — is window dressing. Even if she didn't steal it herself — and she did — then she is guilty of handling stolen goods and possibly trying to obstruct justice in keeping the truth to herself.*"

Sam, feeling frustration rise within her, pushed the cafetière's plunger too hard. Coffee spurted out of the top. "I just think something dodgy is going on at Candlebroke Hall."

"*Undoubtedly,*" Camara laughed. "*People are dodgy. Aristocrats doubly so. But that's between them and the insurers.*"

"You're meant to uphold the law!"

"*I can give you the number of the fraud squad over at Nettleham if you want them to laugh at you too.*"

"Now you're just being mean."

There was silence on the line for a moment. "*I'm just concerned you seem to be on a crusade for justice for Hilde and the Odinsons.*"

"If she didn't do it—"

"*Then one of them did. Simple as that. They may act all quirky and folksy, but they are not nice people. Half of the men and some of the women have spent time inside.*"

"They're unconventional, true."

"*Criminals. Criminals is the word you're looking for.*" There was anger in his voice now. "*Stolen goods. Trees for goodness sake! Dangerous cut and shut vehicles. Probably drug dealers. Oh, and let's not forget affiliation with neo-Nazi groups.*"

"What?"

"You knew that, right? You've had Torsten on your community service sheet. Racially aggravated assault."

Sam was flabbergasted. "No. That's not... Are you sure?"

Camara chuckled but there was no humour in it. *"Take a long hard look at that family before you decide to fight for them. I'm sorry, Sam. I really am."*

Sam mumbled a farewell, hung up and stared at spilled coffee for a long hard time. She came to a conclusion.

"There's still something deeply dodgy going on at Candlebroke Hall." She looked to Doug Junior for confirmation. He always backed her up.

Sam poured her coffee, searched on her phone and made a call.

"Hi," she said, "Is that Miss Chiddingfold? This is Sam Applewhite from DefCon4. We manage the alarm systems and – yes, we delivered the Viking longship. I'm glad you like it." She nodded along while the National Heritage woman spoke. "I'm aware there's some confusion regarding what exactly has gone missing from the house and I was wondering if, for insurance purposes, you needed someone to do an inventory of the house?"

Sam continued to nod turning to her computer to find out how Phoebe Chiddingfold could make a formal request to DefCon4.

24

Once back at Candlebroke Hall, Antoine looked for Kiki in her apartments. Failing to find her there, he looked in the most obvious public rooms, even tried the café, blagging an Americano from the cashier as he moved through. Getting free coffee was a part of his routine. He hardly had to work at it any more – sowing seeds of doubt that the first cup of the morning might suffer from 'debris in the pipes'. He had generously offered his services to assess the quality of the day's first cup, and now the staff were conditioned to just hand him a coffee when he walked in.

He always took it elsewhere to drink, enjoying the conceit that he was master of this vast estate. Sometimes Kiki would join him and they would sip their drinks together before the crowds arrived. Kiki was fond of positioning herself directly underneath one of the signs declaring no food or drink should be consumed in the house, but then she had every reason to resent the rules imposed upon her in her own home.

He eventually found Kiki sitting on one of the stone benches on the rear terrace. She was wrapped in a faux fur leopard skin coat. She had a silk headscarf knotted over her head and wore a pair of sunglasses whose massive lenses covered half her face. She looked like Jackie Onassis, if Jackie Onassis was trying to hide from the paparazzi on the cold east coast of England.

"What on earth are you doing out here?" said Antoine.

"Thinking," she said, softly. She looked up and automatically took the coffee from him with a gloved hand. He'd barely had a sip but hid his irritation with ease. "Thinking and looking."

She nodded up the sloping lawns towards the trees, where the newly installed Viking longship was just visible beneath a canopy of cedars. A set of temporary metal barriers had been placed around it. "I don't like it."

"It has a certain gauche charm." He sat beside her. The cold stone instantly chilled his buttocks.

"Every day I feel that, more and more, I'm living in the ruins of a theme park. Viking longship, gift shop... What's next?" She removed the sipper lid of the coffee cup to drink it, unleashing a plume of steamy air.

Antoine dipped into his pocket and produced a plain brown envelope. "Your share," he said.

Kiki eyed but didn't take it. "How much?"

"Five hundred pounds."

Kiki blew out her lips, unimpressed, and sulkily sipped

the coffee. *His* coffee. "Five hundred. What's that going to get me?"

"It could get you a new washing machine, or replace the worst of the wallpapering in your rooms."

She twitched irritably. "For hell's sake, Antoine. I don't want a new washing machine!"

"What I meant was—"

"I'm not so petty. My dreams are bigger. I want to go away. I want to move. I want ... Lytham St Annes."

It took Antoine a few moments to process this. "Lytham St Annes? The seaside town?" He pocketed the cash again.

"Yes."

"By Blackpool?"

"Yes."

"You want to swap one faded seaside resort for another."

Kiki grunted. "Shows what you know. I'm talking about a well-to-do place. It has four golf clubs you know."

"You don't play golf."

"It's a vibrant little town. Affluent, with a buzzing cultural scene. Art galleries, tea shops. A lot of famous people retire there. I want a cottage with a sea view. Maybe Elaine Paige lives next door but one. Maybe Jan Leeming has the house opposite."

"That's your dream, is it?"

She took her sunglasses off. Her face, white in the cool air, looked more lined than usual, like frozen ripples of ice cream. "It is. My own quiet place, where I can live a quiet private life with just the right amount of hushed awe and respect from people in the streets. Five hundred pounds is not going to get me a deposit on that dream."

"There's the thousands we've already made."

"I have living costs, you know," she said fiercely.

Antoine gently took the coffee from her, placed it down and held her hands in his. Her red leather gloves creaked beneath his fingers. He assumed it was the leather and not the old bird's bones.

"We are in this together," he said. "We both need the money. We've both had a taste of the high life. I was let down by some unwise investments in the past. Fate has been cruel to you."

"It has," she agreed.

"We need to stay strong, stay together and try to make each other happy." He looked around to see if anyone was within earshot. "We're playing a slightly risky game here. Technically we're breaking the law, even though all we're doing is seeking to profit from the valuables your husband left you."

"He did. He did."

"We'll get through this and we'll make those dreams come true." He placed a chaste kiss on her cheek. It was icy cold against his lips.

25

Sam turned up at Delia's shop carrying donuts.

"Now this is a welcome surprise!" said Delia, removing her paint-spattered apron. "It's not someone's birthday, is it?"

Sam joined her at a table that had been spray painted over paper doily stencils to make a lacy pattern on the surface. Sam ran her fingers over the lavender-glitter paint and tried to picture who might want such a thing.

There was the sound of clanking and hammering from the back room. Delia saw her looking.

"Hilde's turning an old wrought-iron gate into a decorative umbrella stand."

Sam called out. "Hilde! I've brought donuts!"

The hammering paused. "Hot donuts?"

"Yes."

"I'll have one later. Prefer them cold." The hammering resumed.

"She all right?" said Sam.

"She's going to be convicted and imprisoned for burglary," said Delia. "She seems pretty balanced, all things considered."

"I've been given a new job at Candlebroke Hall," said Sam. "And I wanted to pick your brains on how I do it."

"Been given another impossible task?"

"I kind of inflicted this one upon myself. I'm checking the insurance company's inventory of the house and contents."

"Because of—?" Delia jerked a thumb over her shoulder towards the clanking, hammering Hilde.

"I want to investigate things for myself."

Delia bit into a donut and groaned with pleasure. "Delicious. So, an inventory sounds pretty straightforward. What's bothering you?"

Sam dropped a heavy ring binder on the lavender doily table. "Well, part of it is the sheer scale of the thing. I've got this old inventory from thirty years ago when National Heritage took it on. They'd lost the one at the house, but old Baron Candlebroke or whatever left a copy with his local solicitor's office. It's not numbered, but it looks to me like it's got tens of thousands of items on it."

"Oof!" Delia licked donut sugar from her fingers. "Well at least you have a starting point. You can look at each thing on the list and tick it off as you find— Yeah, maybe that will be difficult if there are that many things."

"And this inventory, you wouldn't believe how unreadable it is. It's like the person who wrote it was trying to channel a Ye Olde Englishe vibe or something, with mad words and abbreviations."

"Try one on me."

Sam opened the hefty wodge of badly-photocopied documentation. She had hoped for something that might point her towards a digital, searchable copy; but it seemed as if the inventory was prepared by a firm of estate agents-cum-auctioneers who had not only all died since the work was undertaken, but who had treated technology with deep suspicion when they were alive. She flicked past the verbose introduction to the house and its history, which contained nothing of practical use.

"It's like they started off listing stuff in alphabetical order, but after a while decided that was too hard. Lots of things at the start begin with 'a', then it all goes to pot around page six. Right, what do you make of this: 'aundyrone pr, C17, brass+iron w. engr. putto masks'?"

Delia looked thoughtful for a long moment, then shook her head. "No, I got nothing. Let me see how they're spelling that first word." She peered at the entry. "I suppose it might be a way of spelling andiron."

Sam looked at her. "If that's a joke, I'm not sure I understand."

"Andirons? Fire dogs?"

"Now you're just saying words."

"Fire dogs are those things you have at the sides of an old fashioned fireplace, so you can put the logs across, on top of each other."

"Huh. I will look out for them. So 'pr' is a pair, I get that. I will have to try and figure out the business with the masks when I find them."

"I hate to say this, but you're likely to find quite a few fire dogs in a house like that," said Delia, as she turned more sheets and shook her head at the incomprehensible language. "Who on earth says 'chardger' instead of 'big plate'?"

"Big plate you say? Maybe I should make some notes. Or you could scribble on the pages in pencil?"

"Can do. Is this a copy then?" Delia rootled on a shelf to find a pencil.

"I've got two copies, both equally smudged and blurry. Nobody knows what happened to the original."

Delia pored over the document and made a few notes. She shook her head and made tutting noises. Sam ate a donut to distract herself. They were from the kiosk down by the pier slipway. In early spring, there were few tourists to buy popcorn and candyfloss and red sweet dummies but, all year round they did a brisk trade in hot drinks and greasy donuts. The sugary hit gave her a surge of optimism.

"Maybe it won't be so bad," she mused.

"It's going to be horrendous," said Delia quietly.

"Some confidence boost this is turning out to be. No more goodies for you."

Delia gave her a wounded look and snared another donut, putting it on a high dresser next to her. "I just meant this document is possibly making it harder than if it didn't exist. Whoever wrote it must have been hell bent on writing it in code that only dusty old antique people or academics could understand. I'm getting about half of it, and I reckon I'm doing well. They're not even using the same abbreviations consistently. They use 'pt' to mean 'part' and 'point' and possibly 'pint' as well."

"It's about context though," said Sam. Going back to head office and saying that the task was impossible was not an option she was prepared to contemplate. Particularly since she'd suggested it. "There must be an organised way of doing this."

"Well," said Delia, thoughtfully. "If it was me, I would try to round up all the things that are of a particular type. Take the fire dogs. Get them all into the same room. Then at least you can see what you've got in terms of fire dogs, and how they match that document."

"Ah. Well, I'm strictly forbidden from moving things around," said Sam. "National Heritage are insisting I do not disrupt the displays."

Delia pulled a face. "Well that's going to make things a bit difficult. How are you supposed to work in the public rooms?"

"My current plan is to take lots of videos," said Sam. "I have about two hours before visitors can go in each morning, so I'll blitz as many of the public rooms as I can in that time. Take videos and watch them afterwards – see if I can figure out what I'm looking at with the aid of the pause button."

"Oh my golly gosh, that will be unmissable watching."

"Are you being sarcastic?"

"No. It will be fascinating. Please tell me I can come round and help you go through the footage?"

"Really?" said Sam with a grin. "That would be so great. I'll supply wine and, er, popcorn."

26

The National Heritage woman, Phoebe Chiddingfold, stood on the front steps of Candlebroke Hall to greet Sam as she arrived the following week. There was a delighted smile on Phoebe's pale face.

Sam didn't know how to categorise the woman. She was probably Sam's own age, or a couple of years younger, but there was something inescapably juvenile about her. Phoebe seemed mature, educated and well-mannered, and physically she was a shapely and healthy specimen of adult womanhood and yet— Sam felt the woman had gone straight from girlhood to womanhood, failing to pick up something essential en route. Phoebe Chiddingfold seemed oddly *unfinished.*

"I bet you can't wait to get cracking," said Phoebe. "Immersing yourself in this gorgeous treasure trove!"

"Er, yes," said Sam, lugging the unwieldy plastic case she'd brought with her.

"To tell you the truth, I'm a little envious."

"Have you never been tempted to create an inventory yourself?" asked Sam.

Phoebe laughed. "I simply don't have the time. I'm constantly on the go with visitor engagement and the admin. Besides, you have the backing of a massive company. You can tap into all sorts of extra help."

Sam wasn't about to correct her. She nodded politely and followed indoors.

"So, we have a local poet doing a reading event in the Library today, which as you know is on the first floor. My suggestion is you start work on the ground floor this morning. There will be no visitors in the hall until ten, but you can have until ten thirty in the ground floor public rooms, as they should be fairly quiet."

Sam smiled, unsure if she was supposed to express gratitude for being permitted to do her job.

"Obviously you must leave everything as you find it," said Phoebe. "Now there aren't so many of the high value items on the ground floor, so you shouldn't have any problems with the alarm—"

"How do you know?" asked Sam.

"Sorry?"

"That there aren't so many high value items on the ground floor? You don't have an inventory."

Phoebe laughed. "Well, yes. But we've got some very special things on the first floor, like the Wissing and the Vanderbanc. Those things are wired into the alarm system."

Sam wondered how the insurance valuations were carried out, but it wasn't her concern. She was not expected to make any judgement on value, simply create a list.

"What about access?" she asked. "I guess there are things that are inside cabinets?"

"I'll show you the key safe," said Phoebe. "It's all labelled by room, so you should find everything that you need."

Sam was left to start work when Phoebe disappeared to prepare for the poetry event. She decided she would begin at the far end of the East Wing and work her way room by room around to the West Wing. There was a pair of bedrooms with an attached sitting room at the end of the ground floor. Presumably it was a useful space to accommodate older members of the family, without the bother of stairs. Sam started in the furthest bedroom. There was a pleasant bay window overlooking the grounds, so even the bedridden could enjoy the carefully cultivated vistas of Capability Brown. The room was decorated in a style that Sam didn't think was Victorian. What came after Victorian? Arts and Crafts maybe? A quick scan revealed the room was not quite so mind-bogglingly rammed full of things, so Sam looked forward to trying out her technique on it. She'd been to the key cupboard and taken the keys for the first three rooms on her list, putting them in three separate pockets.

"Bottom left is South Garden bedroom," she murmured to herself, pulling out the correct set of keys and placing them on top of a small cupboard. Thankfully, each key had a label. She wouldn't need to open the acrylic lid on the sewing box, as she could see the contents clearly, but some of the cabinets held dainty ceramics, and she should check them for makers' marks.

Sam set down the large plastic case she'd brought and opened it. Inside were three follow-me drones. Individually they were little larger than her splayed hand, much smaller than the security drones DefCon4 had previously sent her to road-test. As best as she could understand from the accompanying paperwork, these were meant for DefCon4 staff to use when transporting cash and valuables. Previously she'd used bodycams (and was wearing one now) but the follow-me drones could follow and film the security operative, giving a more global view.

Sam wasn't sure the average security guard wanted three buzzing drones following them around like a cloud of horseflies. She also suspected the drones would make irresistible targets for certain anti-social types. If she tried to use them in public they'd soon be on the receiving end of well-aimed stones.

But in here, instructed to scope out whatever room she was in and record everything they saw, they might just produce some good reference footage.

She placed the first in her hand, turned it on and with an "Up you go," watched it take off and begin circling the room. She launched the other two and watched as her trio of aerial spies felt out and explored the shape of the room.

Sam switched on her body-cam and began to record.

"We're on the ground floor, and this is the South Garden bedroom." She scanned the room to capture a broad context then inspected each item in turn. "A wooden dressing table with a tilting mirror and a pair of candle holders. Let's open the drawers to see what's inside."

It turned out they were empty, so she moved to the items on the top. "A set of brushes and hand mirror with embroidery on the back. A glass tray with some other glass things." She had no idea what they were. "A vase maybe? And some pots with lids. And a pair of candlesticks? A perfume bottle." She moved on. She weirdly felt like she was playing one of those childhood memory games with an assortment of objects on a tray she needed to memorise.

'*And a cuddly toy!*' Marvin would have shouted, in reference to that game show Sam had no recollection of.

"A wall hanging showing a garden scene in greens and gold," she continued. "Would you call that gold? Bronze maybe. A tall cabinet housing a ... a garment." Sam thought perhaps she should take a closer look, in case it had a label. It was some sort of an evening dress, embellished with beads. It was faded but undeniably beautiful. She paused to look for the key. "Opening the cabinet to check on this thing." She opened the door, which made a barely audible *pfft* as it swung. She reached a hand inside to lift the collar, where a label would normally be found. As she touched the collar it came away from the body of the garment, without the slightest hint of resistance, as if it was made of tissue paper. Sam snatched her hand away in horror and stared at what she'd done. She put her hand over the body-cam lens and quickly locked the cabinet. She snapped a picture of the dress and sent it to Delia who immediately phoned her back.

"*Nice piece, looks like silk.*"

"I might have torn it," hissed Sam. "It's really delicate."

"Yeah, that looks like some sort of climate control cabinet."

"Can I fix it?" asked Sam. "There's some sewing stuff in here."

"No! Don't touch it! Seriously. Keep that cabinet shut and your hands off! A conservator could fix it, but you can't. Now, can you see the damage with the door shut?"

"No, not really."

"Then my advice is to move on and never mention it. The rest of the garment is probably not perfect anyway. Why did you even open the door?"

"I thought there might be a label I should look at."

"Don't touch any more textiles unless you can tell it dates from the last seventy years or so. You might find labels in more modern things, but not in an Edwardian evening gown."

"Great advice, thank you."

"How many rooms have you done so far?"

"I'm about one percent through the first one."

"You're doing great, press on!" said Delia with a brightness that oozed fakery.

"Will do!"

She realised after another thirty minutes that her vocabulary was seriously lacking when it came to the many and varied trinkets adorning Candlebroke Hall. She was starting to understand why the writer of the inventory had gone to town with the flamboyant wordery.

She worked through the contents of a bureau, moving a series of pens across the folded-down flap of the desk, trying to describe each one. "Another fountain pen, silvery coloured. Another fountain pen, would you call that black, or dark blue? A folded document – a list of horses at an auction in 1878. Another folded document – a plan for a garden layout. A sketch of a frowning woman, unsigned, uncaptioned."

A drone buzzed gently past her head and she wondered how long she'd spent on the task.

"A cardboard box containing ... what are these things called? A slide rule, that's it! A case containing a compass. No, wait, my dad would insist that it's a pair of compasses! Also it has some accessories." Sam did not want to speculate on what the accessories were. She put the box aside, then paused as she heard a noise.

She turned to see a boy of around ten racing through the room, chasing after her drones. "Oh cool!" he said and leapt inexpertly to try to catch one.

He ducked under the rope to join Sam at the bureau. He picked up the pair of compasses and walked them across the desk.

"Don't do that." Sam took them from him.

"You can't touch me. Strangers aren't allowed to touch me."

"You shouldn't come behind the rope. Surely you know that?"

"You did."

Sam grimaced, nipped under the rope and urged the boy to do the same.

"Can I have one of your helicopter drones?"

"No you can't. Where are your parents?"

"Listening to poetry. We are encouraged to explore the house and learn all about our cultural heritage while the event takes place." He spoke in the manner of someone who had been told those exact words, possibly by Phoebe.

Had Phoebe knowingly unleashed small, unsupervised people on the house? Was she mad? Sam wondered if this young man had made a massive nuisance of himself at the poetry event, and setting him loose was the lesser of two evils.

She had to get him away before he vandalised something precious. Sam felt her face redden as she thought of the dress.

"You know, you can buy these drones in the gift shop," she lied. "They're only a quid."

"Really?" His mouth wide with joy he ran from the room, yelling, "Mum! Mum!"

27

"She's here again," said Kiki, interrupting Antoine's meditative contemplation of Hugh.

The old tiger was awake for once and his great head was turned towards Antoine. He held Hugh's rheumy gaze in his and pondered on the power of this wonderful beast. At times like these he realised how intense Miranda's awe and terror must have felt when Hugh slipped his chain and charged at her across the stage. Such thoughts gave Antoine thrilling shivers.

Kiki's interruption was not a welcome one. "Who is here again?"

"The woman," said Kiki shrilly.

Antoine nodded. "Okay. We've reduced the possibilities to fifty percent of the population."

"The woman from the burglar alarm company."

"Here to fix an alarm to that window no doubt."

Kiki stepped closer, her furs bunched around her. Hugh

looked at her and sniffed the air. The poor boy had cataracts. She probably looked like a fluffy bear to him.

"She's doing an inventory," she said, as though she was delivering the most terrible news possible.

It was not good news. "Inventory? Why?"

"Hired by the insurers. Or the police. Or maybe Phoebe. But she's tallying everything up, we're going to be found out, and at least one of us is going to prison!"

Ignoring the 'one of us' comment, Antoine gently took her hands in his. He realised his right hand was smeared with beef juices from feeding Hugh, but hoped she didn't notice.

"Don't worry, *ma cherie*. We are in no danger." He didn't know if this was true, but he needed to say it regardless. "A bit of magical misdirection. A bit of bamboozlement. A bit of neuro-linguistic programming and she will be putty in my hands."

Kiki pulled her hands away sharply. "Oh, going to turn the charm on, are we? Off wooing younger women?"

He tutted and shook his head. "She's a child, Kiki. I have eyes for no one but you."

She softened, but not enough. "You are a slippery one, Antoine de Winter. And not as smart as you think." She stalked off unhappily.

"That's just what I want people to think," he called after her. He looked to Hugh. "Women, eh?"

Hugh produced a deep rumble of agreement. It might have been indigestion or flatulence, but Antoine knew it was agreement nonetheless.

He brushed down his hands and began his own slow

walk back to the house. So, Sam Applewhite was back. It didn't necessarily mean anything. The multinational company she worked for managed the estate's security systems. There was no reason why they wouldn't also be contracted to collect evidence following a burglary. Antoine knew how to manage people, no matter who they worked for.

Kiki, on the other hand, was a mild concern. Hysterical older women did not make ideal partners in crime. She needed managing, calming. He found himself gazing up towards Kiki's apartment, contemplating the roof space above it. Kiki only mentioned the roof when she was grumbling about the water tank, but it was actually quite a large open space. Private too.

He'd brought up this subject in the past, asking Phoebe why Kiki shouldn't have a bijou roof garden up there. Phoebe's immediate response had been that it would spoil the appearance of the building. Kiki had once hung a tea towel out of a window to air; Phoebe had made her go and remove it, as it was within visiting hours.

Antoine couldn't see the water tank from where he stood. Much of the rooftop was hidden from view, either because of the angle, or perhaps the low wall surrounding the roof. There was clearly a sizeable blind spot.

There were two National Heritage gardeners contracted to look after the grounds. He could see them currently up by the Viking longship. They'd been digging in foundations around the grounded boat and creating a rockery as part of the supports. They were currently planting clumps of high grasses.

One saw him approach. "Now then. What d'you reckon? Swaying grasses to replicate the ocean waves."

"Ah, yes," said Antoine, disinterested. "Very clever. I've got a job for you. You know those pots over by the stables? The planters with the lavender? Need you to move two of them to another location. It's going to need a bit of lifting, so it'll take the pair of you."

Antoine batted away their brief flurry of questions with his commanding presence. His old assistant, Miranda, had once unkindly described him as being 'insufferably overbearing', but she hadn't comprehended the enormity of his charismatic magnetism. People did what he said. That was all that mattered.

"Yes, put those down. Leave them there. Stables. Pots. I will see you at the house."

As they headed off, grumbling to each other, Antoine proceeded up the lawn to the house. The first visitors of the day would be arriving soon. He saw Sam Applewhite in the summer room, adjacent to the terrace, where she appeared to be working methodically through a china cabinet. Three hovering electronic drones circled the room above her. He saw the glinting camera lenses. Antoine was impressed by her idea of videoing the rooms. It was impressive, yet annoying. It was likely to confound some of the ideas he was considering to disrupt her inventory. He had been contemplating moving some of the items – the Meissen figurines for example – so that they got counted twice. Not an effective tactic if Sam could just go back and watch the video to spot the deception.

She looked up and saw him watching.

He walked in through the French windows. "Good morning, Miss Applewhite." He went with a slight nod. He'd learned that a full bow was often met with ridicule, but he liked to make a good impression.

"Er morning, um—"

"Antoine."

"Antoine..."

"Antoine de Winter."

"That's right." She returned her attention to the contents of the cabinet.

"I've just enjoyed the most exquisite cup of coffee," he said. "These new Sumatran beans they're using in the café are excellent. I'm on my way to go and tell them how much I enjoyed it. I always find it's good practice to reward service workers with positive feedback. Can I get you a cup?"

Sam blinked. He couldn't tell if she was overwhelmed by the offer of a free coffee or impressed with his shirt. That morning he'd selected Italian silk in a vibrant shade of purple, leaving it slightly unbuttoned so that a few chest hairs curled into view. He was a bold dresser and liked to make an impact.

"That's very kind," she said. "But I had a drink a short while ago, thank you."

Antoine smiled, certain it was the shirt that had knocked her off her feet. "It's a hell of a task you've got here."

"It is."

He glanced at the drones and smiled for whatever future audience might be watching. "Just let me know if I can get you anything else to keep you going."

She smiled at him. "Thanks, I reckon I'm fine for a bit."

"Of course, but if there's—"

"Oi, mate!" one of the gardeners called from the terrace. Antoine looked round. The pair had the planters balanced on one of those wheely trucks. "Where'd you want these then?"

"Excuse me," said Antoine and with another tiny, chivalrous bow, withdrew.

He definitely needed to get closer to what Sam Applewhite was doing. If he cultivated her company perhaps he could gain some insight into her thought processes, and exploit them. Or if an opportunity arose to delete some of those videos, that would be equally useful.

"With me," he said to the gardeners and gestured for them to bring the planters inside.

"We can't bring the truck in there," said one.

"You're absolutely right. Thank goodness for good old-fashioned manpower. Chop chop, gents."

Ignoring the mutters and groans he led them through to the upper levels while they carried the first of the planters in.

"We're spilling soil," said one.

"You can sweep it up after," Antoine replied. "Make a mental note."

He'd been worried Kiki's door might be locked, but she frequently left it open. She would often insist she had nothing worth stealing. Leaving the place unlocked was a way of wearing her poverty on her sleeve.

"Come on, this way," he said to the gardeners. "Make sure we don't spill any soil in here though. These are a lady's chambers."

They carried the first planter through the paraphernalia of Kiki's life.

"Now, it needs to go up here," he said, pointing at the ladder up to the roof. "I'll pop up and clear a path for you."

The two gardeners stared at the ladder and at the enormous planter. "How we gonna do that?"

"You're strapping lads. You'll be fine."

"Will it take the weight?"

Antoine wasn't sure if they meant the ladder or the roof. "Yes, of course it will. Get a move on now, will you?"

He left them shuffling and grunting as they manhandled the planter, hefting its weight between them. He walked across the roof and tried to picture just how large the blind spot might be. He paced out a space that looked about right.

"Brilliant work lads," he said as they appeared at the top of the ladder and somehow got the planter onto the roof. He pointed. "Pop it over there, will you?"

They manoeuvred the planter into place, groaning with relief and massaging their arms.

"No time to lose," said Antoine. "You need to go and get the other one."

He followed them outside, so he could check the planter was unseen from below, delighted to see it was completely invisible. He had another thought. While the gardeners were grappling with the next planter, he went to the café terrace and took a chair from one of the outside tables. The faux-wrought-iron wouldn't have been his first choice for a rooftop haven, but it was available. He carried it into Kiki's apartment and left it at the bottom of the ladder for the lads to carry up.

Ten minutes later, the two planters and the chair were in

place. Antoine clapped the two gardeners on the shoulders. "What a fantastic job you've done! Many thanks."

They grinned back at him.

"Tell me something. Did the two of you, by any chance, create that wonderful trelliswork arch I've seen in the South Garden?

"Yes, we make all that."

"I have a design in mind for this area here. I wonder whether it might be something you could knock up?"

28

F riday night at *Duncastin'*. Marvin Applewhite opened the front door. A gusty breeze blew in, bringing Delia with it.

"A horrible night to be out," she said.

"Then you'd best come in," said Marvin.

"I've brought snacks." She rustled a carrier bag. "*Twiglets* and *Pringles* and chocolate fingers." She pulled out a packet of knobbly crisp snacks. "*Nik Naks* while we're looking at Sam's knick-knacks."

He ushered her through and took her coat. "I'm not entirely sure what we're meant to be doing." He followed her through the twisting central hallway of the sprawling bungalow, to the lounge.

"I think it's going to be a sort of virtual Bargain Hunt. Hope you're good at spotting antiques."

"I knew watching all that daytime telly would come in handy one day," he said.

Sam had been busy. She had connected her laptop to the television, photocopied several sheets and, most importantly, made a tall pitcher of something frothy with ice cubes floating in the top.

"What's all this then?" asked Delia.

Sam moved in the manner of someone who was still shrugging off her week-long professional demeanour and hadn't yet switched to her chilled-out, casual, weekend equivalent of 'onesie and slippers' persona. She laid out the papers and put pencils neatly beside each set. She set out drinking glasses.

"This is an alcoholic concoction that I call Antiques Roadshow," she said.

"Got half a bottle of port in it," said Marvin as an aside. "I might stay well clear."

"And this," she said, gesturing at everything else, "is Antiques Bingo!"

"A game suitable for all ages?" asked Marvin.

"There are prizes."

"Ooh."

"For you, that's mostly love and respect," said Sam.

"Not a date with Kiki Harris then?"

"Who?" said Delia.

"Lady Lettuces of Candlebroke Hall," said Sam. "She was a minor actress in her time. Dad's been zipping backwards and forward through a Roger Moore James Bond DVD and fantasising."

"She makes it sound sordid," Marvin said to Delia.

Delia poured drinks and emptied snacks into bowls while Sam explained what they were going to do.

"This is the video I took at Candlebroke Hall. There's up to four feeds on the screen at once. You've got different portions of the inventory. You see something on your list, tick it off. But it needs to be verified by our panel of experts."

Marvin looked round expectantly.

"Is that me?" said Delia.

"And me," said Sam. "You're the antiques expert—"

"I didn't say expert."

"—and I'm the one who has got to sign off on this thing."

"Sounds like I'm already at a disadvantage," said Marvin. "Just a small one for me, Delia."

"Not a fan of Sam's cocktails?"

"Normally, I'd say any port in a storm, but I've seen what Sam has done to this port." He took his glass.

"Ever considered a career on stage?" said Sam.

"Funny you should say that."

"At least something is." Sam clicked on her laptop and video footage appeared on the screen. "I tried to use computer software to match images to the text inventory, but it seems the AI just aren't smart enough. You, dear ones, are the much need human element."

"Oh, very fancy," said Marvin. He sipped his Antiques Roadshow and winced.

"Nice granite-topped table there," said Delia. "Not on my list, but very nice."

Marvin peered at his list. "What's an arbalest?"

"A type of crossbow."

"Ah. I'll look out for it."

Sam sorted through her papers, continuously rotating them.

"We need those bingo dabber pens," said Delia.

"I think I've got some somewhere," said Marvin.

"Really?"

"Oh, yes. I've bingoed in my time. Is that the right verb?"

Delia suddenly bounced up and down in her seat. "Tortoise-shell snuff box!" She waggled her pencil and pointed at the item about to drift off screen. Segments of actual tortoise shell made up the top and side of the small box. "Is that a snuff spoon with a tortoise foot as a handle too?"

"Bit tasteless," said Sam.

"This is the rich we're talking about. There's nothing tasteful about it. Poor thing." Delia circled it on her sheet and took a swig of cocktail. "Mmm, bitter," she coughed.

"Crystal chandelier," said Marvin, pointing.

"Which one, dad?" said Sam.

"This one?" he said, hopefully pointing at his sheet.

"Bishop's chair (badly savaged by dog)," said Delia, pointing with one hand and circling with the other.

"Is that the dog?" said Marvin, pointing at a stuffed creature.

"I've got mounted ocelot on my sheet," said Sam. "Is that it?"

"Definitely not. That's far too small. More of an ocelittle."

Sam gave him a frank look. "If you're going to treat us to music hall quality patter all night you can go to bed."

"Do I take my drink with me?" he said.

"No."

"That's all right then."

"Oh!" said Sam. "I've got pine marten here too. Could it be a pine marten?"

"It's a pine marten," Delia agreed. "Look at its sad face. Poor thing." She raised her glass and took a mournful swig. "God rest its soul."

"I've got hardwood decorative sideboard, damaged by gunshot," said Marvin. "Is that what that is?"

"I thought that was woodworm," said Delia, peering at the screen.

The images and discussion were inconclusive. Further on, in other rooms, Marvin ticked off Georgian silver sugar tongs and a lithograph of the Dorset coast. There was some disagreement as to whether a metal dish was a giant punch bowl or a dissenting baptismal font.

"That's an eighteen-thirties Toby Jug caricature of Lord Henry Petty," said Delia. "Would you say that's a caricature of Lord Henry Petty?"

"I didn't know him personally," said Marvin. "I know I look old..."

"That is a bust of Wellington carved from whalebone though," said Sam and wrote short notes on her paper.

"Poor whale," said Delia. "God rest its soul." She raised her glass and the others followed suit. The cocktail was decidedly bitter and drying and not all that pleasant, but it was surprising how swiftly it went down, and it would have been rude not to toast the memory of a poor creature killed to make vulgar ornaments.

An elephant foot umbrella stand in an upper hallway was toasted. An ostrich feather lamp was toasted. A pair of ivory shoe horns was the subject of some debate.

"Do we toast it once or twice?" said Delia. "There's two of them."

"Probably from the same elephant," said Marvin.

"Can we be certain?"

"I'm now picturing star-crossed elephant lovers, cruelly separated in life, but brought together in death."

"No one pictures star-crossed elephant lovers," said Sam.

"Two sips, just to be certain," said Delia.

Sam paused the video. "I need to take a break," she said, a little woozily. "I need to make sure we've noted down what we've noted and where we've noted it. And that drone footage is making me queasy."

"Oh, it's the video doing that, is it?" said Marvin. He was still on his first glass of Antiques Roadshow. Sam and Delia were on their third, possibly fourth. "I'm going to put the kettle on."

"I don't think it'll fit you," said Sam.

"And you accuse me of sub-music hall patter!" As he stood, his attention was caught by a person in the corner of one shot, just passing through the room. "Who is that?" he said.

"That?" Sam blinked and looked. "That's, um, Antoine de Winter. He's a sort-of hanger on around the hall."

"Tony bloody Winters," muttered Marvin.

29

With a level of effort he had not had to exert in years, Ragnar got all of the adults of the Odinson clan into the mead hall. The very act of bullying and cajoling them all to be there had sickened him to the pit of his stomach. It was like holding a basket of eggs while the basket unravelled strand by strand; like trying to bail out a boat full of holes. The fact that he had to exert energy to bring his family together told him it was coming apart at the seams.

"Now," he declared to the full hall in the light of the central fire, "some bugger's goin' a tell me what's going on? Thing's ain't been right for a goodly while now."

Sons and daughters, nephews and nieces all looked sheepishly towards one another.

Then, out of nowhere, a young wife whose name Ragnar couldn't quite recall, said, "Me an' Kalf are thinking of getting a caravan at that nice new caravan park near Ingoldmells."

"We are not," squeaked young Kalf, alarmed at being called out. "I mean, we're thinking about it, but only thinking 'bout it. 'Sides, Torsten's thinking of joining the army."

The accusation ball having been tossed, it was Torsten's turn to look worried. "It's talk, only talk," he said hurriedly. "But, okay, I'm thinking about it. Maybe I need to get—" he swallowed hard "—a proper job."

"A proper job?" said Ragnar.

Ragnar's son, Yngve, stood up. "Ah've been thinking, dad. Maybe me and my boys might like to live in a proper house."

"What?"

"None of us are as young as we used to be, and maybe..."

Ragnar was shocked to see slow, encouraging nods from some of the others, but Yngve didn't have the guts to finish his sentence.

"Maybe it's time to stop being Vikings," said a voice from the darkness.

Ragnar didn't see who it was but the fact that no one leapt up in outraged disagreement was like a bullet through his heart.

"Stop being Vikings?" he said. "But that's everything we are. Look at us." Ragnar flung his arms wide. "This is our land, our mead hall. Our mead!" He held a drinking horn aloft.

"This is a caravan park and this is a shed," said Sigurd.

"You tek that back!" snapped Ragnar. "It's a mead hall."

"And tha horn is just summat tha bought from Runesplicer's shop in Lincoln," said Hermod.

"Aye," said Magnus. "It's all just bloody trinkets."

"And the one true Viking thing we made for oursens was taken by the Saxons!" spat Hermod.

"And you let them," added Ogendus.

And there was the crux of the matter. In the face of the Saxons, even though none of these cowards had stood against them, the fact that Ragnar had let the Saxon woman, Sam, take their ship from them was a bitter mortal blow to their community.

"It were a bloody good ship," said Yngve.

"We was gonna go raid Cleethorpes," said Gunnolf.

"We could build another," said the voice of Hilde. She was barely heard above the hubbub of discontent, so she repeated herself, louder. "We could build another."

"What? And let the Saxon's steal that one too?" sneered Ogendus.

"We want our ship back or we ain't no Vikings," said Hermod.

"We've been wronged and we deserve justice," said Sigurd.

"We should get the lawyers onto them," said Torsten.

"But not Saxon lawyers!" shouted Yngve.

There was a massive grumble of disgust against the very notion of Saxon lawyers.

"We need our ship!"

"We need Viking justice!"

"And we need it now!"

Ragnar looked at the shop-bought drinking horn in his hand and pondered.

30

By the end of the following week, Sam had finished working through the ground floor rooms at Candlebroke Hall. She pulled out the floor plan to decide where to go next. Should she tackle the outbuildings before moving upstairs? Maybe it was a good idea to do those while the weather was fine. The old floor plan showed a building marked as the Groundkeeper's Cottage. She would start there.

The Groundkeeper's Cottage turned out to be a building that backed onto an old tennis court surrounded by a chain link fence. It made sense, Sam decided. If you were rich enough to have tennis courts and a ground keeper, you'd definitely put them together. She wondered if they had one of those machines for painting the stripes on a tennis court, they always looked like a lot of fun.

The sky had darkened as she'd walked across, which was annoying. Perhaps she should quickly scope out the outside, and work her way indoors when the heavens opened. She had the keys ready in her hand. Some of them looked new. She headed for a gate in the chain link fence.

There was a sign on the gate:

ACCESS FORBIDDEN.

AUTHORISED PERSONNEL ONLY.

NOT OPEN TO THE PUBLIC.

SHE'D GROWN USED to ignoring all of the signs warning the public away. She was, after all, definitely authorised. If anything, her job made her over-authorised. There were days when she wished someone else could take over some of the security management, health and safety, and general authority holding her job required. She pulled the gate closed behind her. After a moment's reflection, she decided she should lock it. She'd discovered visitors to Candlebroke Hall would follow her into places that were clearly off-limits.

There was another gate inside, which Sam found irritating. What was the point of this little ante room? Maybe there would have been a rest area in here. She pictured a bench seat with a pile of fluffy towels and Robinson's Barley Water. She found the key to get through the second gate, but she left this one open, as nobody would be following her. The grass inside was definitely not Wimbledon quality. Scrubby earth gave way to a concrete slab after a few yards. There was a massive log on the other side, like a sideways tree, although it was silvery grey with age.

Sam's phone went. "Hi Delia."

"There's another video on the internet where they mention DefCon4 taking the ship away, I thought I'd let you know."

"Do I look an officious idiot in this one?"

"Maybe. But you can't see your face, so..."

Sam walked a few yards before pausing. Something about this space wasn't right. She had a strong feeling her subconscious was trying to tell her something. It was the smell that tipped her off. A deeply musty, cloying fug clung to the place, even though the cage was open to the elements. She paused to take in the ambience. Cage...

This space seemed more like a zoo cage than anything else. A rubbish, old-fashioned zoo cage, but yeah, that's what it felt like. The entrance to that building over there was a darkened archway. There was something shiny that might well have been a food or water container.

"Hold on..."

Sam backtracked towards the gate. A low growl stopped her. There was something on the log, something huge and covered in untidy spiky fur. A tiger had appeared on top of the log.

"Shit," she whispered.

"What's the matter, Sam?"

Had it always been there? Its body was flat, like someone had let all the air and life out of it. And its fur – surely its fur was meant to be a lustrous fiery shade you could see a mile off! –was a dull, dead leaf orange. It looked like a poor specimen, but those partially exposed teeth looked to be in fine working order. Its head was the size of a pumpkin. Sam's mind screamed. How could such a huge thing be allowed to exist?

"Tiger." Sam spoke through clenched teeth, as if she was operating a ventriloquist's dummy. She was worried if she moved a muscle the tiger would leap on her.

"*What?*" said Delia.

"Tiger tiger tiger."

"*It sounded like you said* tiger. *What's up?*"

"In a tiger cage," said Sam.

"*Who is?*"

"I am."

"*Why?*"

"No idea what to do."

"*An actual...? Christ! Who should I call? No time, no time. Fuck! Wait, let me google what you should do. Hold on.*"

"Google?"

Sam held on. She tried to suspend her breathing in the hope it would make her invisible.

The mangy old tiger raised its head slightly so it was in a slouched seating position, but seemed content to just look at Sam for now. She knew, just knew, it was toying with her and she wanted to scream. She also wanted to pee. She didn't dare pee herself, immediately convinced the scent of urine and fear would cause it to attack.

"*Right, right. Here we go. This is what you need to do,*" said Delia. "*Right. Do not run.*"

"Not running," muttered Sam.

"*Apparently they like a chase.*"

"Definitely not running."

"Also, do not approach it. That's common sense. So is don't antagonise it. Christ, I could have written these. Ah, here's one I wouldn't have come up with. Do not urinate in its territory. Got that?"

"Mm," said Sam, glad she hadn't weed herself. She hoped that there might be something more practical on Delia's list. "I think I can get back to the gate. I'll take it slow."

"Right. Good. Stand up tall. It needs to know you're a human and not a, I don't know, antelope."

"Are there many antelopes in Skegness?"

"Don't make eye contact, but do keep facing it, they like to attack from behind."

"Okay." Finally, some actual advice. Sam kept her eyes lowered but her head high. She inched backwards and sideways towards the gate. She made good progress. Then the tiger moved. It wasn't in a huge hurry, but it seemed interested, and strolled towards her. It practically flowed. Okay, maybe like stodgy porridge that had been left on the stove too long, but the muscly beast moved with a languid smoothness that told her it could pounce faster than she could run. At Sam's current rate of progress it would easily reach her before she made it to the gate. "Shit."

"Noise might work, but it has to be brash and surprising."

"It's going to hear some screams soon."

Sam could see no immediate way of making a noise, other than shouting. Would it misinterpret that and chase her?

Heavy drops of rain started to fall. Sam wondered if it might make the tiger decide to go back inside its shelter, but it showed no sign that it was bothered.

A new voice made Sam flick her eyes sideways. "You're doing great. Keep going, very slowly."

Over by the other building was Antoine, just visible through the dark arched doorway. He was moving slowly into the enclosure. Sam didn't dare speak to acknowledge his remark, or indeed emphasise she had no intention of breaking into a sprint.

"Is someone else there with you?" asked Delia on the phone.

"Uh huh," breathed Sam. She inched towards the gate.

Antoine had a bowl of feed. He replaced the metal bowl and backed into the arched doorway, fastening a gate across as he retreated inside. Then he clanged the empty bowl loudly on the floor. "Come on! Dinner's served! Come and get it, Hugh!"

Sam was relieved to see the tiger was clearly interested. It turned its head, gave her one last glance – a glance that transparently said, 'Yeah, I could have you if I wanted, little mouse, but I'm gonna go check out this bowl' – and trotted over to inspect its bowl in much the same way a domestic cat might. She covered the last few feet to the gate at a brisk pace and closed it behind her.

"I'm out!" she breathed into the phone.

"Thank God!" said Delia. *"Who was that?"*

"Antoine. He seems to know the tiger."

"Yeah? Well, ask him why the fuck he's got one in his garden," said Delia. *"Now, is he good looking?"*

"What?"

"There's nothing like a near miss to send your heart all a-flutter."

"I thought you were trying to fix me up with Camara."

"You've got to throw a lot of darts before you pop that balloon, dear."

"Well, actually, he's a bit— Oh, hi!" she said as Antoine came round to her.

"You met my lovely Hugh then," he said with a playful waggle of his eyebrows. Then his face took on a serious expression. "But please, tell me that you're all right? An experience like that can be very distressing."

"I'm fine, I was just—"

"Please? A cup of sweet hot tea?"

"No, thank you, I should—"

"It would be my pleasure."

"Go on, he's a proper smoothie, isn't he?" Sam had forgotten Delia was there, enjoying the drama.

"Er, yes. Sure. A cup of tea would be very welcome," said Sam. "Bear with me. I've got a friend on the line," she indicated the phone.

"Of course." Antoine backed away with a bow.

"I know you were about to say he's old, but maybe that's what you need in your life. Someone who's been around the block and knows all the moves."

"Moves? I'm going for a cup of tea!"

"I can't help it. Your day has been so much more interesting than mine. I haven't been in a tiger's— How did you manage to end up in a tiger's cage by the way?"

"I'm putting that down to poor signage. One thing I will be telling Antoine is the no entry sign on the enclosure really ought to mention that there's a tiger in there."

"Oh, I don't know about that. It's a pet, yeah?"

"What?" Sam was fairly sure pet tigers were not allowed in the twenty first century.

"*Well, did* you *know there was a tiger at Candlebroke Hall? Anyway, off you go for your tête-à-tête. I expect a full update afterwards.*"

Delia rang off and Sam went to catch up with Antoine, her curiosity piqued. What kind of person had a pet tiger?

As she approached, Antoine cocked an elbow to offer his arm. Normally, Sam wouldn't take the arm of any strange man, particularly one with a definite penchant for shiny shirt fabrics, but the near-death experience had brought out her generous side. She looped her arm through his and walked in step with him towards the Candlebroke Hall tea rooms.

Antoine swept her in, ignored the queue of customers, and gestured imperiously to the woman at the till. "Two teas, Caroline. Lots of sugar."

"I don't need sugar," said Sam.

"You're in shock, dear. Sugar is the answer."

Sam didn't argue. Once she'd regained her composure, she might have a word with him about letting people make their own decisions, but right now it was at the bottom of her to-do list. Somewhere below relieving her terrified bladder and screaming at the horror of what had just nearly happened to her.

He ushered her outside onto the terrace. The cold breeze and intermittent raindrops felt good on her face. Sam took the sipper lid off the tea. It was lip-tinglingly hot, but Antoine had been right about the sugar.

"Can I ask a foolish question?" he said.

Sam looked at him and his serious face. His eyes had a

sort of half-lidded stare, which either meant he was giving her a smouldering look or he had some sort of eye problem. She laughed. He was surprised.

"I'm sorry," she said. "Yes. Yes. I know. I shouldn't have walked in there. I saw the sign, thought it didn't apply to me, and..." She shook her head and laughed again, embarrassed. "I'm an idiot. I was just trying to do my job."

"Don't apologise," he said. "I get it, you're a task-focused person. I respect that."

"But to answer your question, I had no reason being in there, did I?"

"That wasn't what I was going to ask," he said and raised an eyebrow.

"Oh?"

"After such a shock, I wanted to offer you a chance to decompress."

"I feel like I might burst with shock, I have to say."

"Then let me buy you dinner tonight."

"Dinner? Tonight?"

"Or another night. Whatever. No strings, just a meal and a chance to chat. I, for one, get rather starved of company in my line of work. I wonder if you find the same?"

Sam paused and thought for a moment. "Well, I'm not sure—"

"If it might influence your thinking, I've been desperate to eat at that lovely Italian on Roman Bank for some time, but I don't like to dine out alone. You'd be doing me a big favour."

Sam did want to question him further. He'd have insights into all the secrets and goings-on at Candlebroke. And it would get Delia off her back. And she did like food. And, though this middle-aged man held no attraction for her, it would be just a dinner.

"All right. That does sound nice. I warn you that I'm likely to fade fast. It's been such a busy week that I really can't manage a late night."

"I completely understand. Allow me to make a reservation that will accommodate an early night." There was the smallest wink and twinkle in his eye as he spoke.

"Have you got something in your eye?" asked Sam.

He put a hand to his face, the movement involuntary.

"Miss Applewhite!" called a voice from along the terrace. It was Kiki Lettuces.

"I'd better go and check," said Antoine. "About the eye, I mean." He slinked away as Kiki approached.

The older woman glared suspiciously at Antoine's retreating back. "Has Mr de Winter been bothering you?" she said.

"No. Not at all," said Sam honestly. "He saved me from being a tiger's lunch."

"Hugh? What on earth were you doing in there?"

"Trying to do the inventory, if you'd believe that."

"Must be fascinating work. Are there any unusual items that you've discovered? Or perhaps seen on the inventory?"

"The old inventory isn't all that useful," said Sam. "I'm struggling on. So, have you been out somewhere? That's a nice outfit."

"This old thing?" laughed Kiki. "I wore this when I auditioned for *Dempsey and Makepeace*. Of course, Glynis Barber got the part. I believe she based some of the character's outfits on what I was wearing, though, so it was a successful casting call in that sense." She laughed again, to show she was a good sport.

"This is just like being at home," said Sam. "My dad's got a million stories like that."

"Is that so?" Her expression altered subtly. "Applewhite —? Your father's Marvin Applewhite?"

"He is."

"A stalwart of the variety scene. Goodness me, we would have mixed in similar circles at some point, I'm sure. I would genuinely enjoy the chance to hear some of his stories."

"Funny you should say that. He'd probably be keen to meet you too."

31

S am sat in the kitchen with a glass of wine while Marvin cooked his famed beef stroganoff and talked about how many notable personages he had prepared this particular dish for. It was the soundtrack of her childhood, and she loved knowing every word. After a close encounter with the business end of a tiger she needed some comfort food, comfort wine, and some nostalgic monologuing from her dad.

"Tell me about Antoine de Winter," she said.

Marvin stopped. Beef slices sizzled softly in the pan. "Why?" he said.

She shrugged. "I'm just saying. Tell me about him. You knew him as Tony..."

"Tony Winters. That used to be his stage name. I don't want to talk about him." He said it with uncharacteristic abruptness.

"Gosh. A celebrity you don't want to talk about? What has come over you?"

"If you can't say something nice about someone then you should say nothing at all."

Sam tilted her head to one side, then the other, and made theatrical 'Hmmm' noises. "No. Still doesn't sound like my dad."

"I said I don't want to talk about him!"

And that was that.

Dinner was subdued if delicious. A few genuine compliments across the kitchen table mellowed Marvin.

"You put fresh herbs in this?" said Sam.

"Never do," he said. "Apart from what grows in the garden, we never used to have fresh herbs. Back in the day, we didn't have half the ingredients you have now. You only saw rice in rice pudding. Spaghetti was considered exotic. Do you know when I first saw pitta bread?"

"Was it nineteen eighty-nine?" asked Sam innocently.

"It was. Berlin Wall came down. Pitta bread. It was like a revolution."

Sam tidied the pots away. There was shop bought crème brûlée for pudding. Sam ate half of hers, then begin reading through the Candlebroke inventory while she finished her glass of wine.

Marvin laid out a green velvet sleeve on the table. Sam could immediately sense a trick about to begin. "Hello, madam," he said in his stage voice. "We've not met each other before, have we?"

"Never seen you before in my life," she agreed.

"Would you happen to own a simple wristwatch, madam?"

"No, because I'm not from the past," she said honestly.

He humphed. "Oh, then this must be your watch here." He laid out a gent's wristwatch with a leather strap.

"News to me," she said. "But, pray, what are you going to do with it?"

"Why, I'm just going to look after it by putting it in here," he said, tucking it into the velvet bag. He gathered the bag up by the neck, and with three swift movement dashed it hard against the edge of the table. "I appear to have smashed it to smithereens."

"First I didn't have a watch, then I did, now it's destroyed. This is turning into an emotional rollercoaster."

"Knock it off, smart arse." He opened the bag and spilled watch bits on the table. "Oh, I am sorry. Whatever has happened?"

"One of the cogs went in my crème brûlée."

"Added iron in your diet? Here, let me sweep all the bits together and see what we can do with a little bit of magic."

A few flourishes, a bit of generic jiggery-pokery, and Marvin produced a whole watch before Sam's eyes. "Is this your watch, madam?"

"Would it be easier if I said yes?"

He gave her a stern look, but not much of one. "Did you see how I did it?"

Sam leaned back. "If you mean do I know how you did it, then yes, because I know you and your act. But was it seamless and capable of impressing crowds little and large? Yes, it was!"

"Thank you," he said and gave a bow. "I've been practising. Restoration – undoing damage done – can be one of the trickier forms of magic. What are the others?"

"It's a test now, is it? Um, making things disappear. Bringing them back. Transformation, transportation and the other one..."

"Transposition." He gathered and tidied away the effects of the trick. "And then there's penetration, prediction, escape and levitation."

Sam tried digging for the lost cog in her dessert.

"Tony Winters did an impressive tiger levitation as part of his act," said Marvin.

Sam deliberately did not look up. "Is that so?"

"Animals and magic are not an easy combination, if you're working with anything larger than a rabbit or a dove. But he managed it. A lot of mechanical effects and showmanship. He never displayed any true skills."

"You didn't like it?"

Marvin shrugged, uncomfortable. "Back then I would have simply said his material wasn't to my tastes. But what do I know? He was young. This must have been around the millennium. Magic performance in the twenty-first century ... who knew what people wanted? Animals on stage seemed very old fashioned, though. I worked on the variety circuit with Andy Robin and his bear, Hercules. They were a great pair. But it was a thing of its time."

"Clearly, Antoine's changed his act since then," said Sam. "And his name."

There was a darkness to her dad's expression. She

couldn't quite make sense of it. "His stage career came to a sudden and horrible end," he said.

"How horrible?"

He flashed her a look. "His assistant died on stage."

"I'm guessing you don't mean they had a deeply unreceptive audience."

Marvin shook his head. "I didn't see it, although I gather there's footage somewhere. I think it might have even been filmed as part of a straight-to-DVD spectacular. The trick was a William Tell themed escapology routine. The assistant was a young girl called Miranda. She was chained to a post on stage, an apple balanced on her head. Tony had a crossbow. I'm not sure how the trick was supposed to play out, but, as I've heard it told, the sound of the crossbow spooked a tiger who was on stage with them, and it lashed out. It hurt the girl, Miranda. At first. But she was tied up, nowhere to go. There was blood. The tiger was angry and excited."

"Oh, no."

"It came up at her, this tiger – had a stupid, boring name like Clive or Bernard—"

"Hugh," said Sam.

"That's it. Hugh. It came up and grabbed her in its jaws." His hand half-waved towards his face but seemed unable to complete the gesture.

"And what happened to Tony?"

"By all accounts, he just stood there and watched. Dumbfounded. While she was screaming and dying."

"Jesus..."

Marvin breathed in deeply. "Fifteen years ago now. At least.

But that put paid to the career of Tony Winters. The abuse he got in the press – all of it thoroughly deserved. He stood and watched." Marvin was growing angry. "When I saw Andy Robin wrestling with Hercules, it was Andy putting himself in danger. When that Australian nature guy got stabbed by the stingray, it was him putting himself in the situation. That poor assistant. I'd have never put Linda in any situation I wouldn't face myself."

"Did you know this Miranda woman then?"

"No. Didn't even know Tony to speak to until years after the event. He was halfway to becoming the psychic fraud he is now by that point."

"So, how did you come to know him?"

Marvin began to tidy away as though the conversation was done. He took her unfinished dessert and the wine glasses and pottered by the sink. "All I'm saying is that Tony Winters isn't a man you should trust. At all."

"I'm with you there," said Sam. "There is something supremely fishy going on at Candlebroke Hall."

"You think he was the burglary's inside man?"

"I don't know," she admitted. "I think it's bigger than you realise."

"Stately homes are deceptively large."

"I meant the ... thing. The whatever's going on. Maybe they're just covering up for lax security, afraid the insurers won't pay out for ... whatever's gone missing. I don't know who's in on it." A thought crossed her mind. "Kiki Harris."

"What of her?" he said, running the tap to start washing up.

"I mentioned you and she spoke favourably of you."

"We don't know each other."

"She was more interested in your ... celebrity appeal."

"Oh?"

"I think she's quite a lonely woman."

"Oh?" he said again, although this 'Oh' was half an octave higher.

"Maybe I could give her your phone number and you two could meet up some time."

He swirled the water for long moments before turning to look at her. "Are you suggesting I reach out to the extremely wealthy former model and actress Kiki Harris? Perhaps even impress her with my showbiz connections and repartee? At the same time grill her for information regarding dodgy doings at Candlebroke Hall?"

She relented. "Sorry. That was crass. I don't want to feel like I'm abusing you."

"Are you kidding?" he said. "I get to take a beautiful celebrity to dinner and go on an undercover mission at the same time? Sounds amazing!"

"Oh. Right. I see."

He bit his lower lip in anticipation. "Maybe I should wear a dinner jacket and bow tie. Bit of a James Bond look."

Sam half smiled. "Actually, I think Kiki would like that."

32

R agnar grinned, his arms opened wide in welcome as his potential saviour crossed the floor of the Beachcomber chippy and bar to his table. "Always good to see thee, Runesplicer."

With his spectacles and suit Runesplicer looked more like he worked in an office, but Ragnar had known him for years. The man was like an undercover Viking. "Ragnar. Surprised to find you in this setting."

Ragnar glanced around at the restaurant bar. It was squashed among the arcades and shops between the Scarborough Esplanade car park and the fairground. In the height of summer the place would be stuffed to the rafters with families chowing down on fish and chips, and reasonably priced beer. It was far from the Odinson compound and too light and cheery for Ragnar's tastes.

"Chip?" he said, pushing a plate towards Runesplicer.

"An offer of food is never refused."

Ragnar waved at the barmaid. "Beer for Runesplicer here."

"Lime and soda, please," said the suited man and sat down. "You know, you could use my name. Runesplicer is more like my brand."

Ragnar pulled a face. "I can't call you Nigel, it's too Saxon. Runesplicer is a fine name."

Runesplicer ran *Enchanted Glade*, a shop on Steep Hill in Lincoln, Ragnar's go-to place for amulets, jewellery, clothes and other essential Viking accoutrements for several years. The man also catered to the crystal-swingers, joss-stick sniffers, unicorn fans, white witches and other general weirdos.

"So, let's talk," said Runesplicer. "You mentioned a bit of a crisis. I've brought something guaranteed to cheer you all up. But first, tell me what's happened."

Ragnar blew out a heartfelt sigh. "This tale starts, as so many do, with the small-minded and jealous nature of the Saxons pitted against the mighty—"

Runesplicer held up a hand. "Ragnar, it's me. You don't need to spin me a ballad. Just the bullet points will do."

Ragnar grunted. He'd been building up a decent head of steam with his storytelling. He should note it down before he lost the thread. "Aye, well there's been some ... difficulties with the longship."

Runesplicer pulled a face. "I can't believe there's a problem you can't overcome. Building it was the hard part, after all. I was pretty impressed to hear about it. What's happened?"

"It's been confiscated," said Ragnar.

"What?"

"Confiscated. A misunderstanding about us using an oak tree as weren't ours."

Runesplicer looked horrified. "As if an oak tree can be owned!"

"That's what I said!"

"You should get the police onto—"

Ragnar felt his facial muscles tighten.

"Oh." Runesplicer understood. "The police took it?"

The barwoman brought Runesplicer's drink over. Ragnar wasn't sure a man with such intimate understanding of the Viking way should be drinking something that shade of green, but he said nothing.

"The police had a warrant?" said Runesplicer.

Ragnar paused for a moment, trying to think if he'd seen any paperwork. "Not sure as they did, now tha comes to mention it. They got a local contractor for the job. She paid us to do it in the end."

"No!" Runesplicer pulled a face. "This is sensational stuff. We can work this up into a really compelling sympathy piece."

"A what?"

Runesplicer pulled out his phone. "Let's start now. A few photos first. Pull a sad face for me, Ragnar."

"Eh? I was only going to ask thee, since tha knows a lot about these things, if tha knows a Viking lawyer who could fight our case for us."

"Well, maybe. But this is a social issue, an issue of faith and discrimination, best tackled via a social media campaign."

"Like on the web?"

"Oh Ragnar, you do make me smile."

Ragnar gave a dismissive grunt, not sure if he was being complimented or not.

"How do you think I got where I am?" said Runesplicer. "I don't just have the shop you know. I'm the biggest online retailer catering to the Pagan, Wicca and Asatru communities in the UK."

Ragnar blew out his lips. "Hipster Vikings."

"There's never any call for name-calling. Whatever your Heathen or Pagan perspective, all deserve respect."

Ragnar sniffed. He was about to say there'd been none of that nonsense when he was a lad, but he couldn't be certain. "I've seen the stuff tha peddles in tha shop."

Runesplicer grinned, amused. "Well, maybe there's some other stuff I could be peddling. Here's what I wanted to show you." He pulled a bottle from his bag and held it up.

"What's this? *Odinson Mead.* Champion! That'll put a smile on their faces." He held it up to look at the label properly. "Is that supposed to be me?" There was a cartoon bearded character swigging heartily. It had a wild-eyed madness he wasn't sure about.

"It's a caricature," said Runesplicer, hastily. "Listen Ragnar, this could come together nicely. Let me come over and have a chat with your kin; get to the heart of the problem. I'll get you trending on social media so we can shine a light on the prejudice you're facing. This stuff will just sell itself."

"It's prejudice then, is it? The business with the ship."

"Yes, of course. This is a direct attack on your beliefs."

"Yes," said Ragnar slowly, testing the idea. "I reckon it is."

33

"Knock knock!" shouted Antoine into Kiki's open doorway.

"Come in," she said.

He slipped inside, nearly getting a door in the face when it rebounded off a snag in the mouldering carpet.

She was in the kitchen, gazing out of the tiny window.

"I have some wonderful news," he said, waggling the bottle of champagne he'd brought with him.

"Is that so?" she said, flatly, not looking round.

"Something bothering you, my dear?"

She made a childish and derisory sound. "I'm worried. And miserable."

"Oh, well then..." He waggled the champagne once more.

"This inventory thing has me on edge. Sam Applewhite snooping round Hugh's enclosure, where I know you've got a whole treasure trove of relocated items. She seems very efficient. I don't like that quality, especially in the young. I'm sure she's going to turn up something. And I seem to have acquired a layer of soil in the apartment. Crumbs here, crumbs there. I'd say I had an infestation of moles, but we're on the third floor and—" She stopped at the sight of the champagne. "What's that for?"

"The good news!" he said.

"I'm not seeing much bloody good news." She eyed the bottle critically.

Antoine knew if there was champagne, she'd be hoping for Krug non-vintage. Not to worry, she would put up with supermarket champagne at a pinch. She wasn't that fussy.

"I brought glasses too."

"What's the occasion?"

"I was going to give you a surprise gift, but since you're so down, I suppose I will have to share my entire three part plan to cheer you up and put your mind at ease."

"Well?" she said, sourly.

Antoine fixedly kept the cheery smile on his face. Old people could be such grumpy stick-in-the-muds. Sometimes you had to win them round slowly.

"Come," he beckoned. "First the surprise gift. I know you crave your little seaside bungalow in Blackpool—"

"Lytham St Anne's."

"Exactly. So, I got my thinking cap on. How could we make this place of yours more like that dream house?"

"You got me a bulldozer?"

"Not quite," he said. "Up to the roof!"

She gave him a strange look, but turned to the ladder. Moments later they both stood in the cool evening breeze.

The rooftops of Candlebroke Hall were a hodgepodge of

felt, asphalt, lead sheet and bare concrete. It was a landscape all to itself, and a world away from the hall below. Kiki walked to a screened off area in the centre of the flat roof that had not been there the week before.

"Oh, my goodness," she said. She touched a planter filled with lavender that was both decorative and acting as a support for one of the screens. She ran her fingers through the soil.

"How on earth did all of this get up here?" she asked, suspiciously.

"Um, the power of magic," he said.

"I don't have moles in my apartment, do I?"

"...Which is good news in itself. I did try to get the lads to not spill any dirt. It was a devil of a job making sure it was a surprise, I can tell you."

"I'll say." There was the briefest of smiles.

"Here," he said, passing her the champagne glasses and popping the champagne cork like the showman he was: making sure it flew across the roof in a neat arc and vanishing over the side. Kiki made the correct whooping noise of surprise and delight.

"Delightful." She smiled coyly as he poured her a glass.

"Let me take you on a tour of your charming rooftop haven." He ushered her forward. "First of all, there are these fragrant pots of lavender, so it will always smell nice out here. And they add a nice splash of colour too, don't you think? You will see I have arranged a chair for relaxing. You can read a book, or just sit and enjoy a drop of the good stuff. Speaking of which..." He clinked his glass against hers.

"Is that a patio heater?" said Kiki, incredulous.

"It is indeed. You might want to use this space when it's chilly, and that makes it possible. Shall I show you a really neat feature? You see this gorgeous trellis enclosing your space, here? We can stretch a canopy across this part and keep the rain off."

"Oh, that is rather good!"

"And that is not all. Now, what is the number one thing you dislike about your present living quarters?" He did not give her a chance to answer, just in case she came up with something new. "The damp! I'm right aren't I?"

"Yes, it's a hard-fought battle for that top spot, but damp is always in the top three," said Kiki with a sniff.

"Well then, this might interest you," said Antoine, and he went over to a large beam. It was a piece of wood around twelve feet long which pivoted as he pushed it, swinging in a horizontal arc, so that the end moved over the parapet wall and was suspended in mid-air. The beam formed the bottom part of a frame that had lines running along the top.

"It's a heavy duty clothes airer!" he declared, in case it wasn't obvious. In fact it looked more like the boom of a rudimentary crane, with plastic washing lines strung across it. "You can keep it on top of the roof during the day when visitors are around, but you can hang it out further and catch that breeze."

He watched as Kiki tried the mechanism for herself. He could tell she was delighted by the rule-breaking element of it. In the same way she enjoyed drinking a cup of coffee underneath the sign forbidding it. Now she could flout Phoebe's 'no hanging of washing' rule too.

"It's rather magnificent," she said. "So thoughtful."

He smiled at her. "I know we've hit a bit of a bump in the road vis-à-vis our business enterprise..."

She pouted and knocked back a huge gulp of champagne. "It's trying, Antoine. Honestly, the whole thing makes me wonder if I'll ever be free of this place."

"You will," crooned Antoine. "Let this rooftop haven soothe your mind and ease your frustration." He waved his hand towards the rear gardens and the menagerie. "I'm moving the valuables in Hugh's enclosure to a new safe space. Somewhere Sam will never find them."

"Where?"

He tapped his nose and smiled. "Loose lips sink ships, my sweet. Let the magician keep some secrets."

She sipped the champagne and hugged herself against the cold. "And what's the third part?"

"Pardon?"

"Of the plan to cheer me up. Rooftop haven, move the goods..."

"Ah ha! I am going to interrogate one of the thorns in our side. Miss Applewhite. Interrogate, subvert and throw her completely off track." He topped up Kiki's glass. "We have a dinner date on Friday. She doesn't suspect a thing."

Kiki stared at him. "A date?"

"A dinner date."

All joy dropped from her face. She threw the contents of the glass aside. "You bring me up here, butter me up with a deckchair and a trellis and a ... a fucking washing line, just so you can tell me you've started dating Sam Applewhite?"

"One date. And we haven't had it yet."

"You're old enough to be her dad!"

"Hardly! And I'm closer to her age than—" He bit down hard on the end of that sentence. "I'm doing it for us, Kiki!"

"Of course, you are," she said. Her face, puckered with anger, looked older than ever. "A serial wooer of women. I told you!"

"It's just business!"

She stalked away, ferreting around for her mobile phone. She stood at the top of the ladder hatch and dialled. When it connected she spoke loud enough for Antoine to hear.

"Hello, is that Marvin? Hello, Marvin. It's Kiki Harris here. Your daughter gave me your number and—" She paused. "Oh, you are too kind. Too, *too* kind!" As she spoke she glared at Antoine, making sure he was watching.

34

Ragnar welcomed Runesplicer back to the compound. He wasn't a houseproud Viking, but with a respected outsider at his side, Ragnar felt a peculiar embarrassment at the muddy compound and the generally shabbiness that afflicted the caravans and shed. He strode through telling mothers to get their kids washed and dressed, shouting at the more obviously lazy loafers to be about their business.

"Do excuse the place," he said to Runesplicer. "It's been a, er, tough winter."

"Not a problem," said Runesplicer, cheerfully. "I'll just wander around and get a few background shots, talk to a few people to get some colour."

Ragnar nodded. "Tha'll want to share some sagas. I can talk into yer dictation machine if—"

"Maybe later," said Runesplicer, a little too hastily. "We'll see,"

Ragnar accompanied Runesplicer as he walked around the camp.

"The sea's just beyond those dunes we saw as we came in?" said Runesplicer. "Maybe we'll go up there and get some nice atmospheric shots later."

"Right you are." Ragnar ran through a mental list of accessories he might grab to look like a proper warrior for Runesplicer's photos. He would need an axe, obviously. He'd pop on the leather tunic that Astrid had made for him out of an old sofa. Would a horned helmet be too much?

"Is that young Yngve over there?" said Runesplicer. "I'll get some quotes from him."

Yngve was on the phone. He muttered something and terminated the call.

"Hi, Yngve," said Runesplicer.

Yngve looked blank.

"It's Runesplicer," said Ragnar. "The one as sells the amulets and whatnot in his shop in Lincoln."

"Oh, aye!" Yngve grinned, offering Runesplicer a fist bump.

"I'm documenting the outrage of your ship being confiscated," said Runesplicer. "It's a terrible injustice. The public needs to be told. Can I get some pictures and quotes from you?"

"Why do you need pictures of me to tell the public about our ship?" asked Yngve.

"We need people to *care* about you as individuals. They need to see your way of life."

"I'm not sure as they do," said Yngve, glancing nervously at Ragnar.

"They don't need to see *everything* about our way of life," said Ragnar. He reached across and tucked a roll-up deeper into Yngve's top pocket, so it wouldn't feature in the pictures.

"You've got a bit of a rock'n'roll vibe going on with the bandana and hair," said Runesplicer. "We should make the most of that in the pictures. Contemporary, but cultural."

"Cool." Yngve preened and strutted like a rock star while Runesplicer took pictures. Ragnar rolled his eyes at the sight of his son acting like a cock.

"Let me get some quotes to go with that," said Runesplicer. "Tell me what it means to you to be a Viking. What are the things that mean a lot to you?"

Yngve thought for a moment. "The drinking and the raiding would be the main things. I mean I like the clothes as well, but it's mainly that."

"Uh huh," said Runesplicer, his pen hovering over the page of his notebook. "So, I understand the drinking. What do you mean by raiding, exactly?"

"Well, er, you know..." Yngve looked uncomfortable.

"I reckon," said Ragnar, throwing an arm around Yngve's shoulders, "what Yngve means to say is that raiding can tek many forms."

"Aye," said Yngve with a nod. "But it's always nicking stuff."

35

S am was ready for her evening out, having showered and changed into jeans and a sparkly top. Marvin was taking much longer than usual.

"How about a cravat?" he called.

Sam frowned. "I thought you were going for the bow-tie. Have you even got a cravat?"

"Of course. Don't get to wear them all that often. I wondered if this might be the time?"

"It probably isn't," said Sam. "Why don't you just wear something you'll be comfortable in?"

"Because," said Marvin, "I spend all day, every day wearing things I'm comfortable in. This is a genuine chance to dress up – except I think I might have forgotten how to do that. What do you think?" He stood in the doorway in a smart black dinner jacket and bow tie.

Sam wanted to be charitable because there was nothing

specifically wrong with the outfit, and yet... "Maybe it's because I know you..." she began.

"What is it?" he said.

"The only things you're missing are a top hat, white gloves and a dove stuffed up your sleeve."

"I look like a magician?"

"A magician's magician."

He sighed, fiddled in his cuff, then put his hand to his mouth to cough. A small storm of feathers flew out of his fist. "I'll get changed then."

He returned ten minutes later, wearing a rust-coloured shirt under a navy blue jacket, with a pair of dark grey trousers.

"You look great, dad," said Sam, genuinely impressed. "It looks like something you'd normally wear, only better."

Marvin grimaced. "Well, I think that's a compliment." There was a horn toot from outside. "That's me. Where are you taking that scoundrel, Winters?"

"Just going out for an Italian."

"As long as it's somewhere public and brightly lit," said Marvin. "I'm serious."

Sam held back the sigh and just smiled. The car outside beeped again.

"For me, it's a chauffeur-driven Mercedes to Candlebroke Hall—"

"A taxi."

"A Mercedes."

"All taxi drivers drive Mercs now."

"Regardless, I'm going over to Candlebroke Hall to collect Kiki. Where we go from there..."

"Dining options in Skegness can be limited."

Marvin put on a superior air. "Maybe she'll have the kitchens rustle something up and Willikins the butler will serve it to us in the grand dining room."

"I don't think anyone's buttled at Candlebroke Hall for years."

"Then it sounds like her ladyship is a rich but lonely celebrity and needs a gentleman to show her a good time."

"And maybe find out what mysteries the place holds, eh?"

He threw her a silly salute and went outside to his taxi.

KIKI STEPPED out of the front door of Candlebroke Hall in her floor length faux furs. On the driveway, Marvin Applewhite stood by the rear open door of a silver prestige car.

"Lady Lettuces," he said with a friendly nod of greeting.

She came down to him and held out her hand. He took it in his firm grasp. Kiki's keen gaze scanned Marvin's outfit. It was quietly smart, if provincial. She approved. Marvin looked greyer and more wrinkled than she remembered from his television appearances, but he still had that easy smile.

"It's Kiki," she said. "Everyone calls me Kiki."

"Then our carriage awaits, Kiki. You said I shouldn't book..."

"I have somewhere in mind."

He held the door for her and then went round to the other side to get in. She was struggling with the folds of her fur coat as he climbed in.

"I bet that keeps you warm," he said.

"*Giuliani's* on Roman Bank," she said to the driver. Marvin was looking at her. "Don't worry. It's not real."

"The restaurant?"

"The furs. I don't believe in hurting dumb animals."

"Nice to know I'll be safe," he smiled.

She tugged at a slightly distressed edge. "I wore it for a Cinzano advert in the seventies."

"Leonard Rossiter and Joan Collins?"

"The very same."

Kiki decided not to mention that her appearance in the commercial had been cut. She'd been furious at the time. Her agent, Barcroft Leaning, had persuaded the wardrobe people to let her keep the coat as a consolation. And it was a piece that never failed to get noticed.

The lights of the town strobed over the car as they drove towards the seafront. Kiki couldn't recall the last time she'd been out for the evening, let alone the last time she'd been taken out for dinner by a man – other than that insufferable schemer, Antoine.

"The last thing I saw you in was a horror movie," said Marvin. "I can't recall the name. Something about a pumpkin monster that comes to life."

"*Pumpkinhead*," said Kiki. "Oh, that was a hoot. Four weeks filming in LA. My character was dragged into the bushes and brutally murdered."

"I remember. Can't have been much fun."

"Oh, it was a delight. I was put up in a nice hotel. The effects guys were lovely. Even covered in five pints of fake blood, they treated me like royalty. Oh, Italian horror directors are a *very* different story. Some of them were a touch ... 'hands on'. Not that I have anything against Italians, generally."

Giuliani's was on Roman Bank, parallel with the seafront but one road back. There was space to pull up outside and Marvin, greyer and wrinkled though he might be, scurried round to get the door for her. She liked that.

He held out his arm for her to take. They would have walked in together, arm on arm, if the door was wide enough. Kiki put in an extra sashay to make sure her coat's glorious length swished around her ankles to best effect. She paused while a member of staff took care of her coat, then followed the waiter to their table.

Giuliani's was small, but delightful. Cosy and bijou. She had discovered it years ago, even introduced Antoine to it. The staff, though possibly not authentically Italian, certainly worked hard to generate the air of a corner of rustic Italy transported to dark and dreary England.

Kiki, seated, regarded their environs. "I am surprised at the seats we've been given," she said.

"Really?" said Marvin, picking up his napkin.

"We are, without a doubt, the A-listers of Skegness."

"Nice of you to include me in that."

"Now I don't need all of the endless fawning I would get in London, as it just draws in the paparazzi, but I would not have expected to be seated by the toilets."

Marvin laughed, leaned forward and beckoned Kiki closer. In spite of herself, she found herself intrigued. She leaned in.

"At our age," he whispered, "being near to the toilets can be a good thing."

"At our age?"

"Now the question is this. Silver lining, or special celebrity treatment? What do we think?"

She laughed. If anyone else had made such an overt reference to ageing and the possibility of failing bodily functions she would have treated them with her trademark haughty disdain, but Marvin had an earthy charm that was easy to enjoy.

She straightened up. "Silver linings, eh? Well, I'm going to put myself in your capable hands for a good old fashioned cheering up. I don't know about you, Marvin, but I've had the devil of a week and I'm in the mood for getting tiddly. Shall we order some bubbles?"

"Or what about a Cinzano aperitif?" he suggested.

"Or both?" she countered.

"Or both," he agreed.

Over their starters, insalata caprese for her, king prawns for him, they enjoyed a good-natured game of name-dropping one-upmanship.

"Russell Harty? I once stole his buttonhole for a dare at an awards ceremony!" declared Kiki with a laugh.

"Ah, the old, old story of a pretty woman getting away with things that would get most of us a thump on the nose!" said Marvin. "Speaking of awards, I did once accidentally get my specs mixed up with Michael Caine's just before he went on stage at the London Palladium. He wasn't best pleased, I can tell you."

"Oh, Michael! He was a character! I worked with him on

that *Jaws* film. I didn't die in that one. I can't remember the last time I saw Michael."

"Well if he was still wearing my glasses then he won't have seen you," said Marvin.

Kiki roared with laughter. "Marvin, you're hilarious! You've still got that star quality." She raised a glass.

"You too, Kiki," said Marvin, clinking his glass with hers. "What a shame it doesn't pay the bills, eh?"

Kiki saw an opportunity to probe a key area. "Goodness me, Marvin, don't tell me you blew it all on fast cars and drugs back in the day!"

"You know what? I think I moved in the wrong circles for all of that. Strongest drugs I was ever offered was a Beechams Powder. We all needed that to get us through panto season." He thought for a moment. "I do remember one of the dancers trying to snort it, though."

"A man who's prudent with his earnings," said Kiki. "Always better off in the long run, eh?"

"Says the woman who lives in an enormous stately home."

Her mind was abruptly thrown back to her dreary existence in those damp and miserable apartments. "It's not the fairy tale existence one might imagine," she said.

"It can be lonely sometimes, I imagine. You, rattling around that huge house all by yourself."

He had failed to grasp the root of her sadness. Yet how would he know? Perhaps she should be grateful she gave off the air of a fabulously wealthy lady with a castle-sized house to call her own.

"Here's to rattling around in huge houses," she said. "And getting out of them every once in a while."

She drank the champagne. At least Marvin was willing to splash out on the proper stuff, not that supermarket plonk Antoine propositioned her with.

36

Antoine watched the silly little DefCon4 van pull up on Roman Bank and Sam Applewhite get out. She was wearing jeans and a top. Hardly made any effort at all. But then again, he thought, she had youth on her side and they seemed to get away with wearing whatever they wished. It was he, closer to fifty than forty, who needed to put the effort in here.

He looked at his watch as she approached. "Late for our date. But I suppose it is a woman's prerogative."

She checked her phone. "I'm not late."

"She says," he grinned.

Antoine opened his arms wide. Sam avoided the embrace and clasped one of his outstretched hands, shaking it firmly. His smile didn't falter.

"And," she said, finger raised, "this isn't a date, is it? Just a meal and a chance to chat, you said."

"Po-tay-to, po-tah-to." He opened the door to *Giuliani's* restaurant for her.

Antoine made a point of rejecting the first table they were offered, insisting they be given a table by the window. The view consisted of a car park and a Co-op supermarket, but that wasn't the point. A table with a view, whatever the view, was the best table in the house.

"You look so charming, my dear," he said. "I might have mentioned my interest in observing and creating interesting visual effects, and the way the sequins on your top illuminate your face is fascinating. I could study it for hours."

Sam glanced down at her top, then back at him. Her expression hadn't softened. "So, how was your day?" She picked up her menu.

"My day? Well, I thrive on variety, so a day in the life of Antoine de Winter is a rich and complex dish, comprised of many exotic ingredients." He accompanied this with much eyebrow waggling. "How about you Sam, how was your day?"

"Mainly filled with the inventory at Candlebroke Hall."

"Oh, I want to hear all about how that's going," said Antoine. He plucked the menu from her hands. "I'll save you the bother of studying the menu, if I may, and order for both of us? I know the chef and what's best." Antoine clicked his fingers to get the attention of the serving staff.

"Do people really do that?" she asked.

"Do what?"

"Click their fingers for waiting staff. Or maybe what I meant to ask is, do people do that and not make the waiting staff really, really angry?"

He laughed at her cute naivety. "Oh, you are a funny kitten."

Sam fixed him with a gaze – a confused pout, Antoine decided – and he raised a hand to click his fingers again. Sam reached out and grabbed his outstretched hand.

"Tactile," he said.

"How about you wait until they're ready?"

"Humble."

"Just polite."

He rolled his eyes and made a goofy face. He could see he would have to go slow with this one. Being a stage psychic, and before that a stage magician, had taught him a lot about people. People lived in boxes of their own making. Class played a large part in that. Even now, when people thought the barriers between social classes had faded to indistinction, there were codes and rules for the various strata of society. Regional differences played a part too. What worked in a Lancashire working men's club probably wouldn't work in a regional theatre in Surrey.

Here was Sam Applewhite. Sure, she seemed educated and articulate, but clearly she had the lowly mannerisms of the working classes. Class consciousness they called it. Antoine had read up on it. Class consciousness was the concept the working class held about themselves, ideas that they held up as virtues but which only existed to keep them in their place.

When Antoine clicked his fingers for a waiter, he was playing his part in the client-servant relationship between restaurant and customer. He had come, with his money, to buy food and drink and quality service, and was exercising his right to be treated as that valued customer. However, poor Sam Applewhite, who had no grasp of that relationship, thought his behaviour was rude. It was funny, really.

She was probably in awe of him. How often did she get treated to dinner by a confident man of the world? She hid it well enough, but she was clearly out of her depth: a rabbit in the headlights, hiding her fear (and almost certainly her base desire for him) behind snappy behaviour and formal language.

But, point was, he needed to get inside her little box; step inside her world.

He turned his hand round in hers so he was holding her fingertips. "You were telling me about your day," he said.

"I was," she said. "Then someone stole my menu from me." She snatched it back and opened it again.

She began to talk about her work, which sounded deathly dull. Strip away the hi-tech trimmings and it boiled down to finding things and writing them down. She had spent her days counting plates and jugs and silverware. It was menial work in the extreme; the kind that might just as easily be done by a robot, or an immigrant labourer if a suitable one could be found. Listening, Antoine might well have fallen asleep if her work didn't have a direct impact on him.

There was a cat and mouse aspect to it all, he mused. Candlebroke Hall was a treasure trove of vast size, ten thousand antiques large and small, stuffed into thirty-plus rooms. Over the past year or more, he'd been discreetly removing items and passing them to Vance to sell on the black market, splitting the proceeds with pathetically cash-strapped Kiki. Into the game comes Sam from DefCon4, with an impossible list of items to catalogue. He steals and sells. She searches and records. The business with the burglar girl was just a minor aside, a wild card to be played by either side. If a few items were missing, their disappearance could be blamed on the burglar. If the true scale of Antoine's enterprise was uncovered, the burglar theory wouldn't hold.

Sam pulled a face. "All told, it's going to be a while before the job is done. The old inventory is of no help. The language is arcane, the abbreviations are bizarre, and there's no order. Matching one set of things to the other has been almost impossible. There are some things I can't wait to find, though. At some point, I should come across a pair of ancient Greek drinking vessels showing erotic scenes – if I've correctly understood what 'Grk', *'kylix'* and 'scns' mean."

"Goodness me, I had no idea Candlebroke Hall housed such things," he said, recalling the pornographic Greek pot he'd passed to Vance several months ago.

A waiter appeared. He smiled at both of them and Antoine felt vindicated that his finger-clicking had evidently done nothing to offend or depress this willing servant. They ordered drinks, starters and mains.

"Are you sure I can't tempt you to the ravioli lobster?" said Antoine.

"The steak," Sam told the waiter. "Definitely the steak."

She was making a point. No doubt she would look at his ravioli with jealousy when it came, but she had her pride to maintain. She had little else.

"What a shame the job is proving such a difficult one," Antoine said once the waiter had gone. "But, between you and me, I am happy to sign off on your work whenever you like."

"Meaning?" she said.

"I am saying that, in my capacity, I could simply put my name on the dotted line. When you have done the bulk of the counting and recording, just pass it to me. No need to dot all the 'i's or cross all the 't's. I'll put my name on your chits."

There was a loud woman's laugh from somewhere near the back of the restaurant. It was raucous and disruptive. Antoine tried to ignore it.

"What is your capacity?" asked Sam.

"Pardon, dear?" said Antoine, refocusing his attention.

"You said 'in your capacity'. As what? I'm not clear what your role or function is at Candlebroke Hall. Are you staff?"

He laughed heartily. It was very funny. The young woman, with her fresh looks and youthful body, was now getting to the nub of the matter. She was interested in him – of course she was – and wanted to know exactly what status he had. She wanted to know how loaded he was. Wealth and power were magnetic attractors.

"Do I look like staff?" he said, with a sly smile. "I have the run of the place."

"Do you?"

"Day. And night."

She nodded. "Because your security is lax."

That threw him. "What?"

"The house is clearly not secure. Some alarms not set. Some windows without alarms at all."

"Ah," he nodded, thinking he understood. He wasn't

averse to talking in code or a little roleplay. "And you, my security gal, you want to come 'check my alarms'."

"What?" There was a horrified scowl on her face. "Oh, God—! Here come our starters."

The waiter arrived with the first courses. Sam gulped down some wine and stared at her soup. She should have gone for the goats cheese starter and lobster ravioli like him. She sighed. Yes, she was regretting it already. He smiled at the impetuous wrong-headedness of the young.

"This is not what I wanted," she said. Antoine waved a forgiving hand. She looked him in the eye. "I'm not interested in you."

"Just what I have to offer, eh?" he nodded. "No names. Two human beings. Ships passing in the night. You don't want ties. I understand. We should be free, yes?"

"What? No! I mean I'm not interested – in-ter-est-ed – in you. In that way?"

He smiled. "I get it. I get it."

"You do? Great."

"This is all part of the routine, you know?"

"No. No, I don't know. What routine?"

"You know, that thing." He made a playful pedalling hand gesture, as if he was bouncing a pair of tennis balls off his chest. "The back and forth banter thing where you like me, then you hate me, then you want me, but most of all you want me to like you. It's nature, it's the way we're all hard wired. That thing."

Sam shook her head. "Where are you getting this from? Have you analysed a load of bad romcom films, or something?"

"Romcoms? Do I look like a man who watches romcoms? No, I do my research, The facts are out there."

"You mean on the internet? I'm going to take a punt and guess you've been listening to the nonsense from those pick up artists."

Antoine sucked his teeth. "You're cynical, I can tell. You've got to ask yourself how they're so successful if their ideas are wrong?"

"Cynical? That is one word for it." Sam shifted in her seat. Her skin was flushed. She was either angry or excited. Antoine suspected the latter. "Listen, Antoine," she said, "the only reason I'm here is because I'm hungry. For *food*. Nothing else. Now, you can tell me your crackpot theories, by all means, I'm sort of curious, but you can stop trying to pick me up with this macho man nonsense."

"Are you sure? There is a certain type of unreconstructed, rugged man many people believe is missing in the modern landscape of bland desexualised political correctness. The alpha male is unafraid of showing his dominance." He accompanied his words with a lascivious wiggle of his moustache. His hands went to his chest and touched his curly chest hairs.

Sam shook her head as Antoine held her gaze. Clearly trying to resist. He licked his lips and circled a finger on his chest.

"You feel it, don't you? There's a part of your brain that responds to the alpha male. Don't be afraid to tune into it, Sam."

"Right!" Sam picked up a spoon and rapped the table sharply. "I'm introducing a new system. Every time you say something sleazy, fake or weird I'm going to bang this spoon. I'd like to enjoy this meal, so can you converse with me as if I'm another human, and we're having a normal conversation, do you think?"

"Yes?" said Antoine, his voice a little squeaky with shock. He coughed. "Yes."

There was a long moment of slightly awkward silence.

"Tell me about your work on the stage," said Sam. "Let's pretend you already tried to peddle the woo-woo stuff and I showed polite cynicism. You're a medium, yes? What I'm curious about is how people react to your show. Does it bring them comfort when they've lost a loved one?"

Antoine paused for a moment. "Are you asking if I'm a combination between a therapist and an improv performer?"

Sam nodded.

Antoine speared a chunk of cheese with his fork. "Yes, I'd say I am. You can be cynical about it, but it takes a good deal of skill."

"Is it lucrative?"

"You are very direct, Sam."

"I think bluntness is the way forward with you."

He chewed. "The live arts do not pay as much as they used to. The skill of the performer isn't recognised as it used to be."

"I understand."

"In my heyday I invested my money. Big projects. Some didn't pay off. That 'Magic' Kingdom fiasco."

"Magic Kingdom? As in D—"

"No, not the theme park. That was part of the problem. Turns out they can be quite litigious. 'Magic' Kingdom is a man. Was a man. Past tense, I hope." He realised he had got distracted and had waffled on for a moment. "Where was I?"

"Actually having a genuine human conversation without trying to hit on me," she said and smiled. It was an authentic, warm smile, and Antoine felt something quiver inside him like a lovestruck teenager.

Maybe this would be a pleasant meal after all. They finished off their starters, discussing a little of this and a little of that. The plates were cleared and the mains brought out.

He looked at the medium rare steak placed before Sam.

"A woman who is unafraid to enjoy red meat," noted Antoine, with a lascivious smile. "You know, that usually indicates—"

Sam slammed down her spoon to cut him off. Unfortunately, she had forgotten to check that Antoine's hand wasn't resting on the table. She'd also forgotten that she'd swapped her soup spoon for a steak knife.

Antoine gave a restrained gurgling scream of pain and clutched his hand. She'd only grazed it with a line of serrated points, but it was still bloody painful.

"I'm sorry!" she said. "Let me take a look."

37

Kiki looked up at the sound of a peculiar strangled scream.

"Someone hurt?" said Marvin, pausing in the difficult deconstruction of the calzone pizza he'd ordered.

Kiki glanced over towards the better tables near to the window. She was shocked to see Antoine there with Sam Applewhite. Sam was holding Antoine's hand tenderly in hers. Hurried and impassioned conversation was flowing back and forth between them.

"Interrogation, indeed!" she sniffed.

"Anything wrong?" said Marvin.

"Nothing," Kiki said decisively, wondering if Marvin knew his daughter was currently making googly eyes at an older man who should know better than to chase young skirt. "It's just someone I'd rather not see."

"Oh?"

"And it was I who introduced him to this place! But we won't let it spoil our fun, will we?"

"Absolutely not," said Marvin, oblivious to what was going on and happy to be so.

"So, you were telling me about retiring on a fat and healthy nest egg," she said.

"I was saying that I *should* have had a decent nest egg from my career, but I was led into some unwise financial choices and—" He gave a dismissive shrug. "*C'est la vie.*"

Kiki admonished herself for feeling disappointment at this news. If he'd been fabulously wealthy, he wasn't necessarily going to whisk her away from her miserable and increasingly risky existence. She'd just met the man. However, she had to admit to herself, from the moment they'd met her mind had turned to fantasies of an easy way out. She glanced over at Antoine, who was still staring at Sam Applewhite.

Kiki raised her glass. "Then here's to being broke but fabulous!"

Marvin quickly joined her. "And maybe just a little bit drunk," he added. He looked at his half-eaten dinner as though preparing to admit defeat. "Naturally, it is entirely possible to be broke and happy. Money doesn't provide us with all the answers."

Kiki scrunched up her face. "I find it does help, though."

"Of course. The sense of security it provides."

"I don't want much," she said. "I don't want diamonds and pearls. I certainly don't need that big haunted house."

"What do you need?" he asked.

She thought about it. She knew the answer, but had so

rarely discussed it with anyone apart from Antoine and, with him, her answers had always been guarded, carefully phrased.

"What I want ... a bungalow by the sea I can call my own. A quiet life but a comfortable one. A bit of adulation now and then. You know, some recognition. I don't want to be forgotten."

Marvin shook his head slowly, eyes on her. "How can anyone forget you?"

She laughed. As she did so, she realised there was a real danger of it turning into a sob. The ridiculousness of that made her laugh even more.

Marvin waved his hand and a man appeared: one of those hawkers selling individually wrapped roses table by table.

"Rose for the lady?"

"Please," said Marvin.

As a flower in a cellophane tube was taken from the man's basket, Marvin produced a tenner from his wallet.

"You don't have to," said Kiki.

"I want to," said Marvin.

It was a cheap and tacky gesture, the dark rose already drying and curling up, but Kiki found herself disproportionately touched by it. "You shouldn't have."

"The least I can do, from a man who apparently has everything one could need."

She looked at him. There was a playful look on his face.

"I have a bungalow by the sea. A quiet and mostly comfortable life. I'm not sure I get much in the way of adulation, though. Having an adult daughter living with me and groaning at my jokes isn't quite the same thing."

"You have a bungalow?"

"Well, not so much a bungalow as a sprawling rabbit warren. And the debt collectors may yet come calling and force me to sell up. But, yes, a bungalow."

As Marvin spoke about his house and living arrangements, Kiki sniffed the rose. It didn't smell of anything. But the act of sniffing it had significance. She leaned back and looked across to Antoine and the girl, Sam. Kiki twirled her rose and – ah-ha! – Antoine looked her way. The surprise on his face was an absolute picture. He saw her and her rose and, although Marvin was out of sight behind the pillar, must realise Kiki was being treated to a romantic meal of her own.

How would he react? she wondered.

She giggled as the predictable little man raised his hand, clicking his fingers for the rose-seller to come over. Two fingers held out for two roses . Unimaginative levels of competitiveness.

She returned her attention to her own date.

"But, you know," Marvin was saying, "in a modest place, two can live as cheaply as one."

Kiki blinked. She had tuned out what he'd been saying, but now he'd dropped that line into the conversation. "I'm sorry?"

"What I mean is, I'm not saying my place is overly modest but it is a nice place for two people to ... rattle around together." He smiled, wistfully.

Was he asking her to move in with him? They'd not even

moved onto desserts yet! It was impertinent and far too forward... Yet was that a thrill of excitement Kiki felt running through her?

"Gosh, I suppose so," she managed to say, then felt something more was required. "Do you mind me asking how long it's been since...?" She hesitated, not sure where that sentence was going. "Sam's mother? She not been in the picture for a while?"

"No," said Marvin. "Quite a few years now. She lives in Paris, I believe. Or certainly some European city. I don't mean to be blasé. I'm sure I do know where she is living. I mean, I don't keep track."

"I understand," she said. "It's hard to let go of the past."

"There seems to be so much of it," he agreed.

There was movement behind her. She turned to see Sam Applewhite sliding by to go to the toilets. Antoine was hot on her heels. Hasty even.

Kiki looked up at him, but their eyes didn't meet. She looked back to Marvin. He hadn't noticed at all. He was looking at his food.

"Whilst I admire the Italians," he said. "A mostly wheat-based diet fills me up very quickly. I think I might need to stop and leave some room for dessert." He regarded the empty champagne bottle. "Maybe another drink?"

Kiki was watching the swinging door that led down the short corridor to the toilets. She was thinking.

"Yes, yes," she murmured. "Let me think. Will you excuse me, Marvin?" She put her napkin on the table and got up to go to the toilets.

38

There were two unisex toilets at the rear of *Giuliani's*, each with a toilet and sink. They were large, but not necessarily enough for two people together.

As Sam tried to run her bleeding finger under the cold water, Antoine fussed over her.

"It's fine. It's fine," she said, but it was surprising how much blood one little rose thorn could produce.

"More cold to numb it," he said and turned the tap up. The water spurted erratically and sprayed her.

"Too much!" She grabbed for the paper towels. "You really don't need to be here."

She meant that in more ways than one. She didn't need his assistance to deal with a minor cut. She also didn't need to be in a confined space with this man. She had nothing to fear from him, was confident she had dampened any misplaced passions he might have felt, but privacy and seclusion might give him other ideas.

There was nothing romantic or erotic about white porcelain and the smell of drain cleaner, but Sam wasn't sure Antoine picked up on the same cues as normal humans. Besides, if she'd put the dampeners on his ardour, why had he insisted on buying her roses? She did not like roses, didn't know any women who did. They were austere and fusty, the floral equivalent of a bitter maiden aunt. Surely the ones sold in florists were thornless? Had the vendor cut them from a local garden? But there had been no opportunity for Sam to say no, and so here she was, nursing a cut in a restaurant loo.

"Is this karma?" she said.

"How so?" he said.

"I stabbed you with a knife. You pricked me with a rose."

"*I* pricked you?"

"I meant the universe."

"I don't think the universe does me any favours," he said.

There was a rap at the door. "What's going on in there?" said a woman's voice.

"We're just finishing up," said Sam.

The door opened an inch but jammed against the back of Antoine's legs.

"Not enough room," said Sam. She bunched paper towels in her hand and pressed her injured finger to it. "Go on. Get out."

Reluctantly, he levered himself around the door. "If you're sure?"

"It's a small prick," she said. "No big deal. I've had worse."

The door swung in. It was Kiki Lettuces in the corridor.

"Lady Lettuces," said Sam. "This is a coincidence!"

"Well, isn't it!" she snapped in a harsh tone that seemed utterly unjustified.

"Are you with my dad? Having a nice time?"

Antoine seemed deeply uncomfortable. "Everyone's having a nice time, aren't they?" he said. "Just a nice dinner. No need to make a scene."

"Not at all," said Kiki. "Apparently it's 'no big deal'."

Antoine backed away down the corridor. Sam smiled politely and moved past Kiki. The older woman looked pointedly at Sam's jeans. There were water marks across her upper legs.

"It'll dry," said Sam.

Kiki scowled. "But you've had worse."

"Um. Yeah." She moved off, still trying to decode Kiki's weird mood.

In the restaurant she saw her dad, parked between a column and a potted plant at the table nearest the toilets. "You decided to come here too?" she said.

"Lady's choice," he said. He put his hand to his mouth as though to make a stage whisper. "Nothing to report on the secret mission front."

"Yes." Sam looked over to Antoine, back at the window table. "A strange pair though, and no mistake. Are you enjoying your evening?"

He looked down at the table. "I am. I really am. But I think I'm done with this. Ready to move on."

"Move on?"

He chuckled to himself. "None of us as young as we used to be. The hour grows late. I asked Kiki."

"About moving on?"

He looked momentarily worried. "I hope I'm not rushing her. I forget how these things are done."

The purse on the table began to vibrate. There was the sound of a distant flush.

"Wow," said Sam. "Well, whatever makes you happy. I'd best get back to my definitely not a date."

She removed herself to her own table. Antoine watched her approach. No, more specifically, he looked beyond her, to the toilet door.

She slid into her seat. "Are you okay, Mr de Winter?" she said.

"What? Yes. *Naturellement, mademoiselle.*"

She studied his face. "And what is the relationship between you and her ladyship? Seeing you two back there..."

He looked surprised, as though suddenly caught out in a lie. "Er, purely platonic. I would even go so far as to— What did she say?"

"She?" Sam sipped her wine. "Nothing. I was just wondering what you might do for her, if asked."

"For her?"

Sam shrugged, keeping it casual. "Someone jemmied that window you were so eager to show me the other night, and I would bet a million pounds that that person was you. You or Kiki."

"What?" he blustered. "You have no basis for such an accusation!"

"Oh, it's true then," she said with a half-smile. "I assume there was something amiss at the house. Worried the insurers won't pay out?"

"I think you've had too much drink to think straight."

"I do all my best drinking while I'm thinking," she said.

Kᴜᴋɪ ᴀɪᴍᴇᴅ for her seat and mostly missed.

Cinzano and champagne very much agreed with her, but her legs might have had a different opinion. She clung to her chair back and swung herself into position.

"You're vibrating," said Marvin.

"I'm certainly doing something," she agreed.

He pointed to her purse. She grabbed for it and accidentally punted it off the side of the table. Bank cards, emergency make up and various random objects spilled out. Marvin came forward and crouched to retrieve the ringing phone.

"No one ever calls me," she said as he passed it to her.

One of the things she liked about the phone was the big green button for answering calls. None of that fiddly smartphone stuff. "Hello? Yes?"

Barcroft Leaning spoke for a full fifteen seconds before Kiki recognised him. Barcroft Leaning, her agent. It had been at least two years since she'd last spoken to his PA, and a further three since she'd spoken to him in person. Both conversations had been to impart disappointing news. Right now, the man was positively gabbling.

"—and they'd been shockingly let down by Howard and were going to have to delay shooting and then they saw the pictures of you and the house in that magazine, er..."

"*British Sights and Scenes,*" she said.

"That's the fellow and – Kalamazoo! – they said they were interested. Period piece. Right up your alley."

Kiki was suddenly dizzy with excitement. They wanted her. *Someone* wanted her!

"—very regal aspect, absolutely perfect for this picture."

"A movie?"

"A fully financed feature film, already in the pipeline for a theatrical release, Kiki dearest. I know it's not the usual thing I might come to you about but—"

"No, no," she whispered. "I fully understand."

"Then I should give them your details and ask them to send a script?"

"Oh, yes! Yes!" she said with unrestrained joy. Marvin, still picking up lipsticks and compact off the floor looked up at her. She grinned at him. "Oh, definitely yes!"

39

Sam and Antoine looked across at the outburst from Kiki.

Kiki had her hands to her face, nearly weeping with ecstasy. Marvin— Sam craned to see. Was Marvin kneeling on the floor in front of her? There was certainly something shiny in his hand.

"No," whispered Antoine. "That's not ... they're not ... are they?"

"He said he was going to ask her," said Sam.

"No!" gasped Antoine.

Sam wasn't sure how she felt about it either.

"I think I've lost my appetite," said Antoine.

"Me too." She raised a hand to signal a waiter to fetch the bill. "Antoine, I have to say that of all the dinners I've had this has been the most recent."

"Hmmm?" He was still lost in the goings on at the other table.

"I'm saying it was a nice try. We'll split the bill."

She had already paid for her half by contactless before Antoine's attention finally circled back to his own table and the woman who was preparing to leave.

"That thing you said."

"What thing?"

"You said I had broken that window."

"An amateurish effort, to be frank."

He didn't move his head, no attempt to confirm or deny. "What are you going to do about it?"

"Remove it from the equation. If you're trying to hide your security failings from the insurers, that's between you and them. I'm not going to try to stop you. But I need to know what happened with Hilde Odinson."

"The burglar?"

"If you've got anything you need to get off your chest—" The words made her eyes go to his unbuttoned shirt and the unappealing curls of hair poking through. "—then you can tell me."

She stood. A waiter was already waiting with her coat.

She looked to her dad's table, but he and his date were chatting back and forth excitedly and she didn't want to interrupt. Instead, she raised her hand in simple farewell to Antoine and headed out into the night.

SAM WAS DRINKING a long glass of water at the kitchen counter when her dad came in an hour or more later. He was humming a show tune of some sort as he clumsily entered.

"You seem in a good mood," she said.

He gave a start. "You surprised me."

"Nice evening?"

"Quite delightful," he said. "I may have drunk more than I would usually. I'm positively giddy."

Sam paused to find the right words, opting for wrong ones instead. "I'm not going to call her 'mum', you know."

"Huh?"

"Just in case you thought I should."

He looked at her with the wide-eyed scrutiny of the drunk. "It was a lovely evening. That was all. We might do it again but..."

"You said you'd ask her but was worried you were rushing into it."

He blinked and blinked as the cogs in his brain turned. "Dessert! Ask her if she wanted to move onto dessert! I was stuffed. Hell's bells, Sam!"

She could have asked him what the business with the proposal on one knee was about, but didn't have the energy.

He went to get himself a glass of water. He let the tap run until it went cold. "She's a very lonely woman," he said, reflectively.

"She's got Antoine de Winter for company."

He filled the glass and turned off the tap. "In her head. She's not just rattling around in that old house. She's rattling around inside her skull. I don't know if it's the aristocratic title, or the fading fame, or I don't know ... but something's insulated her from reality and the rest of the world." He took a gulp. "Very, very lonely."

Sam gave a half-laugh. "So what about you? Has fame insulated you from reality and made you all sad and lonely?"

His laugh was a full one. "How could it? When I've got you to keep me company and grounded." He shuffled in the direction of the hallway and his bedroom. He stopped in the doorway. "And I talked about you. I told her about you living with me. In positive terms, I assure you. And I said it made financial sense. You and me, here. Two of us able to live as cheaply as one. And that's when I saw it in her eyes."

"What?"

"The sadness. The complete sadness." He gazed at nothing for a long moment. "Never get lonely, Sam. It's not worth it."

"Some people are happy on their own."

"There's a difference between alone and lonely, my love. Goodnight."

40

R agnar waited for quiet in the mead hall. There was much chatter in the room, because he had been deliberately vague about Runesplicer's return visit that evening.

"Right, now I want you all to listen. You know Runesplicer, yeah? You know he's been working to get our ship back for us, and all?" There was a cheer at this. "Well, he tells me that we might need to fine tune some of the things that we say to people, if we're asked."

"Like what?" shouted someone from the back.

"Mostly stuff about being a true Viking. Think of it as an education on how to talk to Saxons." Ragnar stepped back and waved Runesplicer forward.

"Good morning to you all!" he said. "Now I want this to be a fun and interactive session. A workshop, really. Hopefully we'll all learn something about ourselves." Runesplicer dragged a flipchart stand forward. "Now, I'm just going to capture some initial ideas from the room. An open question to you all. What are you?"

There was a confused silence, some covert glances and shrugs.

"We're Vikings!" shouted Ragnar, to get the ball rolling.

Runesplicer wrote _VIKINGS_ at the top of the flipchart, underlining it. "Very good. Now I want to dig into what that means. Who wants to start? What does it mean to be a Viking?"

There was more silence.

"If it helps," said Runesplicer, "we can capture what it doesn't mean. Or what you reject."

"We reject the Saxons!" Ragnar couldn't help himself.

Runesplicer nodded. "What does that mean, exactly? How do you know a Saxon when you see one?"

As Ragnar thought on that, Yngve raised a tentative hand. "Mostly it's folk who's not us," he said.

Runesplicer nodded. "Does anyone have a more nuanced definition?"

Ragnar looked around, only seeing faces which didn't know what 'nuanced' meant.

Freyella raised a hand. Of course Freyella would know what it meant. "I believe, in this room, authority figures of any kind would embody what's thought of as Saxon."

Ragnar nodded. She was a bright one, Freyella. "Aye, 'the man'."

Runesplicer added that to the flipchart. "So as Vikings, you reject the authority of the Saxon. What else do you believe in, or do?"

"We tek what's ours by getting one over on the Saxons!" shouted Ogendus. This was met with chortles of approval.

"I will capture that as 'theft'," said Runesplicer.

"What? No!" Ogendus was crestfallen. "It's getting one over on—"

"It's one of the things that we'll be taking a closer look at," said Runesplicer, circling it in red on the flipchart.

"We love sagas!" shouted Sigurd. Ragnar glowed with pleasure at this.

"Great!" Runesplicer wrote it down. "Who here has read any of the classic Icelandic sagas?"

Sigurd looked at the others, his brow wrinkled. "Mostly it's Ragnar's sagas we like."

"Which is fine," said Runesplicer smoothly. "While we're on the subject of literature, have any of you studied the Eddas?"

"Eddie who?" said a quiet voice at the dark.

"Okay. Anything more for me to write down?" said Runesplicer. "What it means to you to be a Viking?"

"It's like a cool club," said Gunnolf.

"Yeah!" said Hermod at his side. "We wear leather and have axes. I got a Thor's hammer necklace, Runesplicer."

Runesplicer wrote down some of Gunnolf and Hermod's words. Ragnar thought he saw him shaking his head.

"I want to add something," said Astrid. "We've heard a lot from the boys and the things that excite them, but I'm surprised nobody's mentioned hospitality and the sharing of food, drink and hearth."

"Oh, this is very good, Astrid," said Runesplicer, writing on the flip chart.

"How come you've written down Astrid's without changing it!" complained Ogendus.

"Very good question," said Runesplicer, pointing for emphasis. "Now, if we've captured all the thoughts in the room, perhaps it's time to take a closer look at some of the things we have. We are going to think just a bit more deeply about some of the ideas that we've uncovered, and whether they really represent the people you aspire to be." He moved away from the flip chart and fixed everyone with a commanding look. "I have something I am prepared to award at the end of this session: a prize to the person who I think has thought really hard."

There was some straightening of spines. The Odinsons were nothing if not competitive.

Runesplicer reached under a chair and pulled out a bottle of mead. "Special edition cherry mead. Even the purists love this one. It's something a bit different."

There was a shuffling of excitement. Ragnar did not approve of flavoured mead, but it had grabbed the attention of the audience.

"Now, we are going to do a thought experiment." Runesplicer looked around at several blank faces. "A thought experiment is where we use our imaginations for a moment to work through a scenario. I want you all to imagine there is another compound nearby. Someone has sold an area of the caravan park to a group of people and you haven't met them yet. You're just hearing things about them." He paused. "Is everyone with me so far?"

There was a chorus of 'yes'.

"Good!" Runesplicer pointed at the flip chart as he spoke.

"So, this new group that has moved in. They are known as thieves who like to wear leather and other finery. They glory in subverting the law of the land. How do you like the sound of them so far?"

Ragnar didn't much like where this was going, but he kept quiet for a moment.

Torsten stood up. "You know what this reminds me of?" he said. "It's like what them lawyers do when you're in court. They take yer words and make you sound like an idiot."

Rumblings of agreement filled the room.

"Torsten, I thank you for pointing this out!" said Runesplicer with a triumphant smile. He held his arms wide. "That is exactly the problem you all face. Being in the public eye, especially on the internet, is like being in court, only much worse. People will be judgemental. What do you think you need to do about it?" There were dark mutterings and Runesplicer held up his hands. "Let me tell you now that violence is definitely not the answer. I think you've got some of the answers on the board already. Which things didn't we mention yet? Ah yes, hospitality. The sharing of food and drink. What if I'd mentioned that first about the new group of people, eh? If I'd said that they always offer hospitality to friends and strangers? That you will be warmly welcomed if you pay them a visit?"

Ragnar watched Freyella's face. She was looking at the rest of the family with hopeful interest: the sort of look you'd give a dog if you were trying to teach it a trick.

"So, we'm got to talk like them bluddy lawyers?" Torsten asked.

"No. Nobody wants to turn you into a lawyer, Torsten, or

put words in your mouth. It's just thinking through how your family is perceived."

"I reckon I've got it," Ogendus said, holding up his phone. "I just posted a picture of your home-made pork pie, Astrid, with a caption that says '*Our women will always mek you welcome when you visit*'. How's that then?"

Freyella buried her face in her hands.

Runesplicer hesitated before speaking. "Good job in taking on new ideas so quickly, Ogendus. Well done. One step at a time though. I think we now need to talk about how a modern audience reacts to gender stereotypes and sexism."

41

Antoine watched Kiki descend the grand staircase of Candlebroke Hall. She walked slowly, not like the ageing old baggage she was, but as a princess bride stepping down the aisle. Her hand swung gently at hip level as though holding the skirt of a glamorous ballgown, although she was wearing nothing so delightful. She stopped to admire herself in the full length mirror on the second turn, lit by the morning light from the domed skylight high above. There were bags under her eyes, which was unfair as it had hardly been a late night. She smoothed them with her fingertips and lifted her chin to hide her sagging neck before continuing down.

"Someone looks like the cat who got the cream," said Antoine.

Kiki saw him and her serene manner instantly vanished. "Whereas you're something the cat dragged in. That was a shameless – and shameful! – display last night."

He scratched the edge of his moustache. "Who are we talking about? You?"

She touched her decolletage innocently. "I had the most wonderful evening and I have some good news to share."

"Oh, I know," he scoffed. "You screamed 'Yes!'" loud enough. The desperation was positively oozing out of you."

"A woman can't enjoy a change in her fortunes? At least, I didn't behave like a filthy hound."

"Who told you that?"

"Told? Told?" She stomped down the final steps and came towards him. "I was there! I knew you were from the sleazier end of the entertainment business, but *really*! Taking the young woman into the toilets to ... to..." She ran out of words and gestured with both hands at his groin.

Antoine frowned, but there was something so absurd in her accusations that he could feel a smile breaking through. "I went in there to help her!"

"Please!" she spat. "I saw it! In *Giuliani's* of all places! It's unhygienic! And I don't think you made much impression on her with your 'little prick'!"

The laughter exploded out of him. "Rose prick! A thorn, Kiki. She'd cut her finger on one of those overpriced roses and I went to help her clean up."

Kiki's face ran through several changes of expression. "It certainly didn't come across that way." Her fiery tone was extinguished. "So, you didn't ... proposition her?"

"Not in the toilet or anywhere else," he said smoothly. "The girl was smitten, maybe, but she's not my type. She's no more than a child and has no class, no élan. She's a drudge, fit for counting and cataloguing treasures that belong to others." He felt his smile fade. "Although she outright told me that she believed I had broken the cellar window."

It was Kiki's turn to frown. "She was speculating."

"She didn't think there was any doubt."

"You said it would throw them off the scent."

"But she also said she wasn't going to tell anyone."

"Why not?"

"Seems she has some interest in that burglar girl."

"In what way?"

Antoine shook his head and then took a deep breath. Time for a change of subject. "So tell me, are you planning on leaving us any time soon?"

"What do you mean?"

"You and your new lover. Is he going to whisk you away from this sordid hovel?" He raised his hands to the high ceilings of the hallway.

Kiki smiled with coy embarrassment. "We talked about living arrangements. He has a bungalow by the sea."

"In Blackpool?"

"You mean Lytham St Anne's. And no, here in Skegness. We chatted and, yes, he did say two of us could live together as cheaply as one. But it was just chat, a bit of fantasy. He's a sweet and funny man and – you know what, Antoine – he *gets* me. He really does." She reached out and smoothed down Antoine's wide jacket lapels. "But he's too old for my tastes, and he's poor, which is not an attractive feature in a man."

"But he proposed," said Antoine.

"He did not."

"He told Sam he was going to pop the question."

"Did he now? Christ. These Applewhites, so easily smitten."

"And then he went down on one knee and you started shrieking."

She froze, then laughed. "Oh, that's rich! You thought—? Oh, my dear sweet stupid Antoine. I was saying yes to my agent." Her face was alight with excitement. "You will never guess, it's just too fabulous."

"What is it?"

She linked her arm through his and steered him toward the doors onto the rear terrace. "Fearful Symmetry Productions – a film company apparently – are coming here to film *The Scarlet Pimpernel.*"

"Here?"

"They want me and the house. The perfect package. They're putting together the filming schedule as we speak and we'll know more shortly."

"Oh my, that's amazing! Who will you play?"

"They haven't sent me the details yet. Of course, I expect to be Marguerite. I'll be perfect. It's the role of a lifetime! They say this could be as big as Downton."

"Marguerite is the wife of the Scarlet Pimpernel, yes? A ravishing beauty?" Antoine could have kicked himself for the slight questioning tone to his voice, but Kiki didn't notice as she was so wrapped up in the idea.

"I can only assume that's the case. My agent said they had been badly let down by Howard, and I wracked my brains as to who that might be. Of course, he meant Bryce Dallas Howard. American actress. Statuesque like myself. Well, if I'm to step in – I'm a professional and not afraid to step into someone else's shoes – then it must clearly be in the role of Marguerite. Beautiful of course, but also a woman of great character. A well-loved and stylish lady, known for her cleverness." Kiki twirled about the terrace as she stepped into the role in her mind.

Antoine was not going to question any possible age discrepancy, nor any other shortcomings. He hoped this would distract Kiki from any problems in their criminal enterprise.

"Such fantastic news, my darling," he managed to say. "I'm so happy for you. Do you need to practise breathing in a corset or fanning yourself in a coquettish manner?"

42

Sam placed the paper inventory and a cardboard box next to the plan of Candlebroke House on the table serving as Phoebe's desk. Storm winds outside rattled the wooden sash windows and a draught from somewhere rustled the papers. The National Heritage woman's office was barely an office at all. It might once have been a larder, or a very small sitting room. It was hard to tell. It was a boxy room, possibly taller than it was wide, and furnished not with contemporary office furniture but items from the house that were neither ostentatious enough nor valuable enough to put on display.

Phoebe's desk was a bulky, deeply scratched dining table with scalloped edges and a damaged leg. A rolltop bureau with a broken rolltop sat in one corner, serving as a secondary desk. A highly varnished wardrobe sat in the opposite corner, its interior stacked with filing boxes. The only new items in the cramped space were Phoebe's laptop computer and a cork noticeboard, which was covered in a dense collage of notes and leaflets.

Sam could not imagine how anyone ran a stately home from such an unsuitable office, but it seemed Phoebe was able to.

"Oh, I know," said Phoebe cheerily, seeing Sam looking round. "It's far from ideal. But, as they say, *wir können nicht alle leben wie Gott in Frankreich.*"

"Who says that?" said Sam.

"Germans. I'm learning the language. For fun."

"Nice to have a hobby. So..." Sam spread out a number of inventory pages. "There are a large number of items I cannot find."

"How large?"

"More than fifty. And I would say I've only covered twenty-five, thirty percent of the house."

"Oh, dear."

"I've also been through the storage shelves in the cellar. There are quite a few empty boxes like this." She tapped the sturdy box she'd brought with her. "There should be an ancient Greek drinking vessel in here. In fact, there should be two." She rummaged through the tissue paper and pulled out a typed note. "Attic Greek *kylixes* (pair). Gifted to the Lettuces by the Ottoman government in 1802. Currently on display'. And yet there are no Greek bowls anywhere on display."

"Ah," said Phoebe. "They were on display. The 'History of Drink' exhibition. They caused a mild stir due to the erotic nature of their decorations. There were a lot of giggling schoolchildren, I recall."

"The history of drink?"

"Wine glasses, chalices, the jewelled drinking horn the burglar tried to steal. A very exciting exhibition."

Sam tried to imagine how exciting an exhibition of what amounted to differently shaped cups could be. She struggled. "Giggling schoolchildren, huh? Listen, these *kylixes* were extremely valuable. According to an auction house website I checked out, they could be worth four to five thousand pounds apiece."

"Apiece?" said Kiki, in the doorway.

"Oh, I'm sorry," said Phoebe. "Didn't see you there."

Kiki had the manner of someone who was merely idling, eavesdropping one might even think. She carried a bulging handbag in her arms.

"I didn't mean to intrude," said Kiki. "Sorry? You said they were worth five thousand each?"

"We shouldn't take what the internet says at face value, Kiki," said Phoebe. "Sorry, was there something I could help you with?"

Kiki shifted guiltily, then dipped her huge bag. There were many things women, particularly older women, carried around in their handbags. Flintlock pistols were a new one on Sam.

"I wondered if I could borrow this?" she said

"That's the flintlock holster pistol," said Sam automatically. "One of a pair. On display in the Winter dining hall."

"Yes," agreed Kiki. With some difficulty she extracted the second pistol from her bag.

"I hesitate to ask," said Phoebe.

"Props," said Kiki. "Pretend shooting practice. For a role. I mentioned the film company…"

"Oh, yes," said Phoebe, shuffling papers. "Frightening Symbols production company, or something. I saw an e-mail somewhere."

"Fearful Symmetry Productions, and why are you looking on your desk if it was an e-mail?"

Phoebe pulled an embarrassed face. "To show you I was looking and hadn't forgotten? Yes, they're looking to film in few weeks. A film version of *The Scarlet Pimpernel*, isn't it? Hence the era-appropriate weapons. You fancy yourself for a part?"

"They called. I answered," Kiki sniffed and walked off.

"Those guns are valuable antiques!" Phoebe shouted after her.

Sam jigged her head. "A few hundred each. Not the same league as those *kylix* bowls. This might be a far greater issue than the drinking horn."

"Oh, let's not exaggerate," said Phoebe. "The Thunderhorn is unique. Although I'm not interested in the price of things, unless it's the deluxe cream tea at our delightful café, I would imagine an aurochs drinking horn is beyond value."

Unique. The word struck Sam. She wanted to say she had seen another elsewhere, and it took her a moment to recall where.

"I might need to check something out," she said.

"Are you saying this might be a criminal matter?" Phoebe asked. "Do we need to call the police again?"

Sam made an uncertain gesture and headed for the door. "Let me just look into things a little more..."

"I can call the police if we need to," Phoebe called to her as she left.

Sam was suddenly fired up, both happy and unhappy. A line of enquiry had popped into her head, but she didn't see where it could possibly lead. She stood in the hallway, searching the internet on her mobile. The search terms VIKING SHIP RESCUE brought up a local news page and photograph.

Sam had a copy of the photo pinned to her office wall as part of her Odinson family tree. The Odinsons on Skegness beach, their ship, *Sandraker*, drawn up onto the sand behind them following their first sea trial and coincidental rescue of Sam from drowning. Ragnar and his children and his grandchildren, sea-soaked and full of adrenaline, toasting their own success.

At the centre of the diorama was Ragnar Odinson himself, laughing at something just said and holding his drinking horn aloft. It was nearly as long as his arm and banded in yellow and, although the digital image wouldn't allow a better resolution when she zoomed in, Sam would have said it was the absolute twin of the horn Hilde had tried to steal.

"Ah, Ragnar," she sighed.

She went out to her Piaggio Ape parked out front, getting battered from one side and then the other by the winds as she crossed the gravel drive.

A trip to the Odinson compound was called for.

43

Kiki sat on her rooftop patio watching the clouds scud across the sky. The winds blew unrelentingly across the roof, shaking the anchored screens around her. She wore coat, hat and gloves against the chill. The view of the surrounding lands – lines of trees bisecting fields and the distant grey of the seaward horizon – was beautiful. In the warmer months it would be delightful. Right now, she relished the cold and the howl of the wind and the solitude. She was hiding in her private cave with her thoughts. Thoughts that were intruded upon by a muffled bang from below. She realised it was her door.

"Kiki? You in?"

"Up here, Antoine!"

He emerged from the ladder hatch. A gust of wind inverted his droopy moustache for a moment. "Breezy," he said, stepping out. "So, the rooftop space is proving its worth, eh?"

"Very much so. Roll on the warmer weather."

"Oh yes, you'll get more value from the airer as well." Antoine swung the beam back and forth as he spoke. "Any idea why Phoebe was thinking of calling the police?"

"Is she?" said Kiki, disinterested.

"I heard her shout at Sam."

Kiki let this sink in. "Those *kylix* drinking cups..."

"Yeah?"

"Did you sell them?"

Antoine hugged himself against the cold. "One of them, I think. Why?"

"Five thousand pounds."

"What is?"

"The amount they're worth."

"Is that so?"

"That's what Sam said. And I'm thinking, I haven't seen five thousand pounds."

"I have given you far more than that, my dear," he insisted.

"In dribs and drabs. For everything you've siphoned away." She looked into the distance. "I'm wondering if I've been left somewhat short."

He attempted a laugh. It was a sharp clap of noise in the cold air. "Black market prices. My dealer takes his cut. I barely take anything."

"Not holding back on me, sweetie?" she suggested.

"Heaven forfend! I am as honest as the day is long."

"In winter, perhaps. Where's the other?"

"In my little stash."

She looked across the gardens to where the menagerie

lay surrounded by walls and hedges. From this angle only the tallest hedges were visible. "You moved them from Hugh's enclosure?"

"I did."

"Where to?"

"Do you need to know the details?"

"In the mood I'm in?" she mused. "Yes. Where's my fucking expensive Greek cup, Antoine?"

He pointed through the gap in the screens and down the lawns to the distant trees. It told her nothing. She leaned across and sighted along the length of his arm. He was pointing to the cedars and the eyesore of the recently arrived longship.

"You put them in the boat?" said Kiki.

"Sam Applewhite is not going to do an inventory there. But those *kylixes* could be a potential bother. She might draw certain conclusions when she finds they're missing."

"You weren't able to throw her off the scent with your dazzling charm, then?" Kiki heard the barb in her own voice and hated herself for sounding bothered.

"The girl lacks our sense of poetry and style," said Antoine. "As emotionally unmoveable as a cow. We need to do something."

"Yes," Kiki agreed. "What would happen to poor Antoine if the police found out he was selling off antiques he didn't own?"

"We're in this together, Kiki."

She hesitated. It was a delicious moment. "Yes. Yes, of course. In it together," she agreed softly.

He turned towards the ladder hatch. The wind swept his

hair up. "Keep an eye on things here. I will see if my contacts have sold the other *kylix*."

"And see if he has my four thousand pounds while you're at it."

"Oh, you'll be the death of me."

She could tell he was trying to inject some levity, but his tone failed to hide the bitter irritation.

ANTOINE HURRIED to the *Who Do You Ink You Are?* studio, arms huddled against the wind. He glanced at the door to the DefCon4 office next to the tattoo parlour. Sam's company. He momentarily wondered if Sam's boss was up there. Could he put in a discreet word and have her fired or shifted to another job? It was worth looking into.

He went inside the tattoo studio and closed the door against the elements.

Vance was at the counter, idly flicking through a magazine. "Ah, happy fate has brought you to my door once more."

Antoine pointed directly up. "DefCon4. The company upstairs. What do you know about them?"

"You mean Sam?"

"And the rest of them."

Vance made a doubtful noise. "I only ever see Sam. There's another guy, Doug, I think. What about them?"

Antoine considered pursuing that line of conversation but it wasn't why he was here. "What happened to that *kylix*?"

Vance gave him a blank look. "Our playlist in here tends to be your classic rock. It's what most of the clients want—"

"—I'm talking about a Greek drinking vessel, not a pop star, you idiot!"

"Oh. Of course. Yeah. I kid."

"I thought you knew about this stuff?"

"Oh, I do. I do. but you weren't clear. Now, let's make sure we're talking about the same thing." He pulled out his phone and scrolled through photos. "This one, yeah?"

Antoine peered at the screen. Vance had gone to some trouble with the composition of the photo, putting the drinking vessel against a background of crushed velvet, with a pair of peaches positioned artfully in the foreground.

"That's the one." He pointed at the photo. "You've made it look sort of kinky."

Vance laughed, making the mermaid tattoo on his neck do something like a belly dance. "Sort of kinky? Did you see what they're up to in those pictures? Seriously, that's what sells it."

Antoine suddenly gripped Vance's wrist. He'd realised what he was looking at. "eBay?" he said. "e-bloody-Bay?!"

"Yeah?" said Vance.

Antoine gripped tighter. "You're selling our bloody antiques on eBay?"

"Huge market. There's some really eager customers out there."

"You said – Jesus wept! You said selling these things wasn't as simple as putting them on eBay or car-booting them down at Skegness Fields."

Vance's eyes were wide, his forehead studs arched

clownishly. "I said it wasn't *just* about putting them on eBay or selling them at the car boot."

"You mean you do sell our things at car boot sales?" Antoine was reeling. "Our antiques? I thought they were going off to Tokyo and Amsterdam and – fuck!"

"Sure, sure," said Vance. "They end up all over the globe. It's an international trade, man. It flows wherever it flows. And I'm not talking about selling it out of a car boot to regular folk. Nah, I mean the secret trading that goes on before the car boot starts. You know how that is. If the car boot sale opens at ten then all the important deals are done by nine."

"This ... this is crapping on our own doorstep. I thought you were a professional! I told Kiki—"

"A professional succeeds. This stuff is selling."

Antoine saw the *kylix* had a current bid of over nine hundred pounds. "Nine hundred?"

"And it's got a way to go yet. We'll double that before it's done."

Realisation dropped. "You've not sold it yet?"

"Another two days still to go," said Vance.

Antoine let go of Vance's wrist. There were white depression marks in the skin. "You've still got it."

"In my lock-up. But it's up for auction. As a seller, it would be morally wrong of—"

"Don't even think about invoking some fence's code of ethics! Jesus, you're not a fence. You're shifting my stuff at jumble sales! I need that *kylix* back. Now. I'm telling you your position is in as much peril as mine if I can't make this problem shut up and go away."

Vance gave him a long look and sucked his teeth. "I might know someone who can help with that. You know, making problems go away." The eyebrow studs converged, making Vance look suddenly menacing.

Antoine was taken aback. "What? No. I just need to get the *kylix* back. Take me to it. Now!"

44

Ragnar heard raised voices and went to investigate. He found Freyella and her uncle, Ogendus poring over a laptop screen and shouting at each other.

"I didn't set you up on Instagram so that you could undermine our entire campaign!" Freyella said with a shake of her head.

"Tha should have some respect, lass! Who's in charge around here, eh?"

Freyella ignored the question and pressed more buttons. "You've posted regularly, which maintains engagement. That part is good."

Ragnar recognised the sound of a 'but' travelling towards the conversation, like an approaching storm cloud. He decided he wanted to know what was going on.

"What's all t'shouting?" he asked.

Ogendus turned to him. "Young Freyella is taking

exception to me helping with social media. Seems to think she's queen of t'internet or summat."

"That's not it," Freyella said. "Helping with social media would mean sticking to the narrative, but your posts are off-brand."

"Off-brand?"

"Let's take a look, shall we?"

She brought up a picture that showed Ogendus sitting astride a motorbike wearing a horned helmet.

"Nice picture of you, that," said Ragnar.

"See!" said Ogendus triumphantly. "Yer grandad thinks it's a good 'un!"

"It's not the picture that's a problem," said Freyella. "It's the caption."

Ragnar leaned in. "'If it was a turban, it would be fine'," he read. "That one?"

"Yes, that one."

"Now lass," said Ragnar. "I can help out here. Runesplicer hisself said those very words, dint he? Why shouldn't Ogendus say so on yer blummin' social media?"

Freyella pulled a face that Ragnar wasn't sure was respectful. Did the lass just roll her eyes at him? "Runesplicer mentioned Sikhs and their turbans as an example of indirect discrimination," said Freyella.

"Indirect—?" How a little girl knew such words was beyond him.

"In other words, making it compulsory to wear a crash helmet would discriminate indirectly against Sikhs, because it's an important part of their faith to always be seen in a turban."

"Aye, that's what it says," said Ogendus, waving his arm at the screen, confused.

"No! It doesn't," said Freyella. "It sounds like you're having a pop at Sikhs because they're allowed and you're not. The tone is sulky at best, but most people would read it as racist."

"Oh. Well, I can mebbe change the words around a bit," said Ogendus.

"It's not the only problem, dad. You've mentioned robbing, creating cut 'n' shut cars and loads of other things that will turn public sympathy away from our cause."

Ogendus pouted. "But look! I've got all these followers!"

Freyella gave him a frank look. "That's because everyone loves to watch a car crash on social media."

There was the splash of tyres in puddles over by the compound entrance. Ragnar looked up to see Sam Applewhite's little van.

"What's she want now?" he muttered.

He started to walk over, but Freyella grabbed the tails of his leather jerkin.

"This is an opportunity to demonstrate some of those 'respected Viking qualities' Runesplicer talked about."

"Why? Is he still filming us?"

The girl huffed. "We need to be the kind of Vikings that deserve to get their ship back. Uncle Ogendus, you could even do a bit of video, and we'll see what's worth putting on social media later."

Both men sighed irritably.

. . .

THE OFFSHORE WINDS brought a sharp briny smell to the Elysian Fields Caravan Park. It filled the lungs and cleared the head. Sam parked her van outside the chain barrier. The Odinsons had clearly seen her coming: Ragnar was walking over.

"Oh, welcome stranger to our humble home!" he called loudly, arms spread wide. Then, as he reached the barrier, lowered his voice and whispered. "What's tha doing here? Come to steal more of our cultural artefacts?"

"I need to chat with you," said Sam. "I haven't finished with this business with the horn."

"Oh, it gladdens my heart to see thee. Our home is your home," he declared loudly before whispering. "Piss off, Saxon. We're busy at the moment."

The fact that Ragnar seemed to be doing some sort of one-man theatre performance for an unseen audience was somewhat confusing.

"What's going on?" she said.

"Oh, this is just an average day in t'life of us decent heathen folk. Come! We have mead and bread!" he shouted and then leaned in real close. "Listen, I've got enough on my plate, right now," he hissed. "Do me a favour and forget whatever flamin' foolish Saxon mission tha thinks tha's on."

"I'm not going to let Hilde go to prison for something she didn't do!" she hissed back, then called out in a loud voice of her own. "Mead? Bread? Why, I'd love to partake of your hospitality! Lead on, dear friend!"

The look Ragnar gave her could have curdled milk. "Oh, good! Come in! Come in!"

Sam walked with him across to his caravan.

Ragnar ushered her inside, turning at the door to address the outside world with a bellowed, "Come! Sit at my hearth! Never let it be said that an Odinson does not show fraternity and hospitality to his visitors!" He shut the door.

"You don't have a hearth," said Sam.

He scowled at her. "Say tha piece then bugger off."

Sam plonked herself on one of the banquette seats by the dining table. "I need to ask you about horns."

Astrid bustled in with a tray laden with tea things and hot scone-like cakes.

"She's having nowt from us," said Ragnar. "That's just for show in front of Runesplicer."

"Don't be daft," said Astrid. "A proper brew and a cake. Now answer her questions, dear."

Astrid bustled off again. Ragnar glared at the teapot. "Guess I'll be flamin' mother then, eh?"

Sam took out her phone. "Hilde was arrested with a huge decorated horn she'd taken from Candlebroke Hall. Priceless, the woman who runs the place thinks."

"Aye. That's what they claim."

"And yet here—" She presented her phone and zoomed in as best she could on the beach photo of the Odinsons with their ship. "That's a mighty similar drinking horn in your hand."

"We've all got drinking horns," he said.

"It's two feet long. Do you know how many aurochs drinking horns there are in this country?"

"Aurochs?"

"Monster cow."

He stared at for a long time, so long that Sam wondered if

this senior Viking actually needed glasses but was just too proud to wear them.

"Aye," he said, and as if that was that, topped off their teas with a splash of milk and began spooning sugar into his.

"You don't think it's a coincidence that you happen to have a monster cow drinking horn and then, not a few months later, Hilde is caught trying to steal another."

His barrel chest heaved as he sighed. "I didn't ask her to."

"I didn't say you—"

He held up a hand. "Though I might have said how pleased I were with that one and that I would love to have another like it." He shook his head, filled with rare self-recrimination.

"Hilde wanted to impress you," said Sam.

"What grandchild doesn't want to make their Farfar happy?"

"So, where did you get this one?"

"Torsten gave it to me."

Her brow furrowed. "Torsten?"

"Ogendus's lad."

"I know who he is, Ragnar. I was his community payback supervisor all last summer. Where would he get a horn like that?"

Ragnar shrugged.

Sam took a quick, mouth-scalding slurp of tea. "I'd best go talk to him, then."

45

K iki kept her head down as she walked along the lawns to where the stupid Viking longship had been placed. Even on a blustery day like this, there were still a number of visitors to the Hall. She had no idea what kept them coming in droves. Something about an old house and a gift shop was like catnip to the retired middle classes. One would have thought that after a lifetime of dull work as office managers, teachers and bean counters, they'd crave some excitement in their twilight years. But, no, it seemed they wanted nothing more than to poke around someone else's ornamental rose gardens and buy a souvenir tea towel or soporific history book.

She ignored the polite greetings of those she passed and strode determinedly up to the longship. "Right. Where has he put the loot?" she mused to herself as she slipped through the barrier placed around it.

The vessel was essentially a glorified rowing boat, with a

mast and a carved dragon figurehead. She ran her fingers across the sharp runic carvings along the side.

"*Sandraker*, huh?"

The stashed goods would have to be inside. A rockery stone provided her with a step-up, although climbing in heels wasn't easy. Kiki reminded herself she'd done it before, in one of her first big screen roles. She wasn't sure why the production designer had thought the sexy but deadly Amazon women in *Star Crash* should be kitted out in high heels, but at the tender age of twenty-three she'd been young and keen to please.

At the less-than-tender age of sixty-five, things were trickier. She pulled herself over the side, narrowly avoiding falling hard onto the deck. She looked around to see if anyone had noticed. Apparently not.

The deck was open to the elements. There was no cabin or steps to a lower deck. However, it did not take Kiki long to find the storage compartments. There were bundles of various shapes and sizes, all neatly wrapped in black plastic.

She crouched and tried to see how much was down there. There were at least a dozen bundles of considerable size: the stacked spoils from a ransacked house. Kiki had assisted Antoine – pointing out some items and helping with a little light lifting – but she hadn't realised how much stuff they'd taken. And more had been sold! She'd not kept a full record of what they'd achieved since setting themselves on this course. It had been a shared idea, to fund their dreams, but Antoine had picked it up and run with it.

It occurred to Kiki that Antoine did not actually need her anymore. He had her wealth at his disposal and was obviously keeping her in the dark, excluding her from the details. He could move on any time he liked.

Simultaneously feeling a bitter dread and a tense sense of purpose, she pulled out the first wrapped package and began looking for the *kylix*. While Antoine was on his wild goose chase for the other cup, she could at least put the second back on display.

Vance pulled up outside a bungalow in Burgh le Marsh, a large village halfway between Skegness town and Candlebroke Hall.

"This is your lock up?" said Antoine. "It could be your granny's house."

"Yeah, funny that," said Vance.

They walked to the front door and Vance rang the bell. A short elderly woman opened the door.

"Ay up, grandma," said Vance. "Me and my mate just need to get in the garage."

"Oh, look who it is," said the woman, unexcited. "Does a member of my family want something from me?"

"I just need to get in the garage. You got the keys?"

"Here, there, everywhere. Not given a moment's peace." She looked at Antoine. "I used to be six foot two, you know. Now look at me."

"The keys, grandma."

Antoine took the woman's hand in his. "Afternoon, madam. I'm Antoine. I didn't catch your name."

The look she gave him was a delight. He could see her

thinking, 'This one's a rum bugger and up to no good', while simultaneously charmed by attention from a younger man.

"Terry," she said cautiously.

"Terry. You don't get to meet many female Terrys."

"We're a rare breed."

"Indeed."

"You're a strong specimen, aren't you?"

"A man tries," said Antoine.

"Could you two stop buttering each other up?" said Vance. "Keys, grandma. It's a bit urgent."

She gave him a curt look. "Shush, boy. The adults are talking. Antoine here is the kind of man I've been waiting for. You don't mind me saying that, Antoine?"

"Not at all," he breathed huskily. "Perhaps you and I could get to know each other a little better while Vance gets on with—" he grinned confidentially "—whatever silly thing he needs to do in the garage."

"Oh, I think I want to do more than get to know you," she said. "I think I'd like to put that muscly body to some good use." She took a set of keys from a hook beneath the hall mirror and passed them to Vance. "Don't go breaking nothing in there. And don't be disturbing me and Anthony here until you're done."

Antoine looked at Vance before sliding into the house. It was hard to know which of them was more embarrassed: Vance for having a sexually brazen grandmother, or Antoine for being willing to entertain her while Vance went to the garage. Antoine tried to convey that any and all embarrassment was Vance's problem.

Vance's grandma shut the door and checked the latch. "Follow me," she said, leading him by the hand.

Antoine felt pride swelling inside him. It didn't matter that this woman was probably a good ten years older than any woman he'd seduced. The fact was, he hadn't lost his touch! He was about to climb back on the horse, so to speak. Particularly ego-boosting after that less-than-successful dinner with Sam Applewhite.

Terry led him through the house. They stepped through a patio door leading to a secluded area at the rear.

"Do you see all of these paving slabs?" she said. "I need them to be taken up and stacked carefully over there, by the garage. It won't take you more than an hour, a man with your physique." She winked at him. "I'll put the kettle on."

Torsten Odinson was in one of the rough lean-tos that surrounded the hall-like sheds dominating the compound. With sheds, lean-tos, caravans, polytunnels and greenhouses, the place was just a pub and church away from being a full-blown village. With Ragnar's mead hall sort of filling both those functions, maybe it had already achieved that status.

Torsten was spray painting an old Opel. The windows and chrome trimmings were covered in masking tape as he gave the vehicle a shiny midnight black finish. Powerful paint fumes filled the place, despite the front and back doors being open.

"Torsten!" Sam shouted over the industrial metal blasting

from the music player on a shelf. She had to shout again before he heard.

The muscly young man turned off the music and lifted his goggles. There was a shadowy paint outline around his eyes and the protective mask he wore.

"How's things?" said Sam.

Torsten started to speak, a mumble of words through the mask. Sam gestured for him to take it off.

"You checking up on me?" he said. Then he seemed to remember himself, looking to the door and shouting, "Oh, hello! I would like to offer you hospitality like a proper Viking!"

Sam had no idea what he was banging on about. "What are you meant to be doing?" she said.

"Offering you hospitality!" he shouted. "Would you like a —" he cast about and picked up a socket wrench "—a tool?"

Sam shook her head. "I meant generally. What're you up to?"

He gestured at the car. "Keeping busy. I ain't done nothing wrong."

"No, I see. In fact, Ragnar was telling me you're a very generous young man."

He frowned. Torsten was blond-haired and generally did nothing in life to counter the stereotype that blonds were thick. When Torsten looked confused, he was like a little dog trying to carry a long stick through a narrow door. It didn't take much to flummox him.

"The big drinking horn you gave your granddad," said Sam.

"Oh," he said and his face shut down.

"A nice gift," she said. "I was wondering where you got it from."

"I got things to do," he said, gesturing at the car.

"Because it's rather like the one Hilde was caught stealing from Candlebroke Hall. You think she was jealous?"

"I don't know nothing about that."

"Where did you get yours from?"

"Freyella said—" He stopped himself and put the mask back on his face.

"What did Freyella say?"

He making loud mumbling sounds and pointed to his ears, indicating he couldn't hear.

"That's a mask, not ear muffs, you fool," she said. "Oh, and another thing." She stepped forward. The fug of paint fumes was dizzying. "A little bird told me something. I found it hard to believe, and I'm hoping it isn't true."

There was that frown again.

"Someone told me you belonged to one of those alt-right, neo-Nazi groups or something. 'Torsten?' I said. 'A white supremacist?'." She turned and walked swiftly to the door, where she could gulp in fresh air. "Freyella, you say?"

"Miss Applewhite," he called after her. She turned. He'd taken the mask off again. "I ain't a Nazi. We're not like that." He spoke sorrowfully. From confused puppy to kicked puppy.

"Well, that's what I thought," she said and went off to find young Freyella Odinson.

46

I t had taken the careful unwrapping, searching and rewrapping of six bundles of goods to locate it. Six bundles of crockery and silverware and pottery and pictures. And all the time, while she'd hunkered down low and searched, the wind howling about her, she kept a rough tally of everything she'd found.

A stack of five bowls, surely worth twenty quid each. An oil painting in a gilt frame – the frame alone would have been worth at least a couple of hundred. An ivory shaving set. A bronze statuette. She valued everything modestly, still pretty certain that several thousand pounds had passed through her hands before she found the ancient Greek bowl.

Words would be had, she decided. For too long she had let Antoine keep the numbers to himself. That dishonest philanderer needed to start paying up properly, or there would be a reckoning.

Kiki repacked all the antiques securely, then scurried

back to the house. She moved through Candlebroke Hall with the remaining *kylix* in her handbag, trying to work out the safest place to put it. If, against all odds, Antoine managed to locate the other, then they could hide the pair in some place Sam could find them. If Antoine hadn't, then they needed to work out what to do with this one.

Kiki was halfway up the stairs when she realised Phoebe was coming down them.

The insufferable woman smiled. "Been out for a walk, Kiki?"

Kiki froze, hands clutched around the handbag. "Um. Yes."

Phoebe eyed the bag and the way Kiki was holding it. Kiki felt an instinctive urge to change her pose, but that would just compound her guilt.

"You haven't been taking items from the collection again, have you?" said Phoebe.

Kiki's guts lurched. "What?"

Phoebe arched an eyebrow. "Like the flintlock pistols?"

"Oh. Like that. No. Not at all." She took a step up to go past, but Phoebe gently blocked her.

"Nothing hidden at the bottom of that bag?"

"No. Definitely not."

"Sure?"

"Sure."

Phoebe smiled. "Well you could always empty it out here just to check."

Kiki held her bag close to her, fearing Phoebe might make a grab for it and send the *kylix* tumbling to the floor. "A lady does not like to expose the contents of her bag," she said primly.

"Of course," said Phoebe, moving aside. "But I would ask you to be mindful in future."

"Yes. Yes."

Kiki was almost at the top of the stairs when Phoebe called, "Oh, and Kiki?"

"Yes?"

"Those lovely people at Fearful Symmetry are coming over next week to do some location scouting. They said it's just a formality. I think they're entirely dependent on us."

"I'm always dependable," said Kiki. "Did they mention the role at all?"

"Role?"

"Or the fee?"

"I believe ten thousand pounds was mentioned."

It hardly seemed much. Kiki had picked up a larger cheque for her last film role, *One Grave, Two Bodies*, and that was for just a single scene with Eric Roberts and Connie Nielsen. Two scenes, if one also counted the funeral. But all she had to do was lie still for that one. The director had said her performance as a beautiful corpse was the highlight of her career. Despite the sniggers of the Assistant Director, Kiki had taken it as the compliment it was no doubt meant to be.

"Ten thousand? Well, better than a poke in the eye."

She stepped through the clutter of the first floor hallway exhibits. One of the comments turning up regularly in TripAdvisor reviews, much to Phoebe's chagrin, was that

Candlebroke Hall was cluttered. Not like a house with too many books was cluttered, the sort you could only achieve when many generations of eccentrics had piled their accumulated collections into one place. It was the reason why Sam's job was so difficult. Frankly, Kiki could slip the *kylix* down among the ornaments on that French-polished table, or hide it behind that huge ormolu clock. No matter how meticulous Sam had been, she couldn't possibly prove it hadn't been there all along.

Kiki could hide it among any of the amassed antiques in these rooms. Better still, if there was an accident, and the exhibits were all dropped together in a single pile, who would be able to tell this from that?

Then Kiki had a better idea. *"One Grave, Two Bodies."* Strange how the mind worked.

In that TV movie, an old mobster family owned a funeral parlour. They would put murder victims in a double decker coffin, below the legitimate corpse. It was such an elegant solution to a messy problem. They would have gotten away with it too, if not for Eric Robert's tenacious New York cop character.

Kiki realised she could do something similar here. There was a sizeable space on the first floor landing, an even larger one on the second. The second floor landing contained a bookcase, a chair and a small table. Kiki decided the bookcase would suit her purpose. She dragged it out from its position of relative safety and put it close to the top of the stairs. After a few minutes' work, moving things around, she had arranged several weighty books at the lower end of it, and tilted it slightly off the ground by kicking the loose carpet into heavy ripples. Finally she put several vases and figurines on the top shelf of the bookcase, adding the *kylix* as the finishing touch.

When Phoebe went around checking the house, as she always did at the end of the day, she never, ever looked down. Kiki knew this from the *Barfusswalk*. Phoebe just trotted through it all, as if she didn't even know she had feet. Kiki was confident the woman would trip on the loose carpet, create a massive landslide, and lots of smashed crockery. That embarrassing single *kylix* would be out of Kiki and Antoine's lives. Kiki might even point out the shards to Sam, if the opportunity arose. After all, who would be able to tell whether the remains contained one *kylix* or two?

"One Grave, Two Bodies," she said. "Perfect."

It was clearly time for a celebratory drink.

SAM FOLLOWED the sound of children's voices into the shed area given over to Hilde Odinson's workshops. She was aware that Torsten, Ragnar and a few other folks were watching her from a distance. Sam stood in the open door and saw the mass of Ragnar Odinson's grandkids and great-grandkids gathered around the work benches. There was chatter, and the low-level arguing that children seemed to just magically generate, but Hilde held their attention throughout.

"Now, has everyone got their drinking horn?"

The children all held various mucky cow and sheep horns aloft.

"Right. Now, we're going to be coating them with a polyurethane resin. Can everyone say polyurethane?"

The children chorused it back faithfully.

"Grand. Now, tha has to do it properly, or the resin won't set. Does everyone remember what happened to Ogendus because he didn't apply the resin on his correctly?"

"He shit the bed!" yelled a child excitedly.

"He came down with a gippy tummy, aye," said Hilde.

"Whilst it was a bit vulgar, I would say that 'shit the bed' was entirely accurate," offered one of the taller girls to much giggling from the others. It was Freyella.

"For better protection, we are also going to line ours with beeswax from Bjorn's bees," said Hilde, then stopped when she saw Sam.

There was a peculiar look on Hilde's face. She had known Sam for a while now, and for the past few weeks Sam had done nothing but work for the young woman's best interests. But now there was frostiness, a wall between them. Had recent events reminded Hilde the world would always treat Odinsons and 'Saxons' differently.

"Good day, everyone," Sam said brightly. "Is no one going to be weird like the rest of your family and loudly say something about your Viking hospitality?"

Hilde's eyes narrowed. *"All the doorways, before one enters, should be looked around, should be spied out. It can't be known for certain where enemies are sitting in the hall ahead,"* she said. "And that's a proper quote, that is."

Sam took it on the chin. Whatever grudges Hilde had against the world, Sam wasn't going to argue with them. "Actually, I wondered if I could have a word with Freyella."

The younger girl frowned, then shrugged. She put her horn down and made to come forward.

Hilde put a hand on her chest. "You shouldn't be talking to Saxons."

Freyella gave her sister a tart look. "Are you saying a young woman can't make decisions for herself?"

"I'm just saying—"

"Being ageist and upholding the patriarchy?" Freyella shrugged out of Hilde's restraining hand and came out to meet Sam. She looked back at the children and Hilde watching. "Go on. Get on with your beeswax."

Freyella scrutinised Sam's face. "Dun't mean I trust you just cos I'm talking to you. What do you want?"

"I'm impressed with all the horn-making stuff," said Sam.

"Why do adults do that?" said Freyella.

"What?"

"Start a conversation about one thing when everyone knows they want to talk about something else?"

"Do they?"

"Is that why people talk about the weather all the time, as something to talk about before they talk about the real thing? People would save a lot of time if they just went up to each other and said the things they wanted to say."

"You're a very honest and forthright young woman."

"You're still doing it. Was there something you wanted to say?"

Sam opened her mouth, rejected the first thing she was about to say, and the second. She opted for straightforward honesty. "What did you tell Torsten?"

"When?"

"I don't know when."

"I say lots of things to Torsten, mostly when he's being an idiot."

"Anything particularly idiotic spring to mind?"

"There was that time when he was making toast on an upturned three-bar fire and when his toast fell through, he tried to get it out with metal tongs."

"Probably not. Something to do with the horn."

Freyella frowned, glancing back at the children and Hilde. "We're not horn crazy, you know. It's just a thing we're doing. Me and Erik and Gosta saw some when we went on a school trip in year five."

"Uh-huh."

"And they're dead easy to make. I paid attention to the horns. Erik and Gosta were just giggling at these rude cups painted with pictures of people doing sex on them."

The revelation struck Sam as a soft blow. " You went to Candlebroke Hall? The History of Drink. And you saw the horn."

"*A* horn."

"And you told Torsten it was just like the one he'd given to your grandfather."

"I did."

"That was what you told him."

Freyella gave her a suspicious look. "You're doing that other thing adults do."

"What thing?"

"Where I'm telling you one thing but you're thinking about another thing."

"Yes. Possibly."

"Are all Saxons like that?"

Sam pushed out her bottom lip in thought. "Mostly."

"Ah," said Freyella, disappointed. "Life would be better if people just said and thought what they meant."

"It would."

Freyella ran back to join the other children. Sam turned away. She was sure she had just learned something very important indeed, but couldn't work out what or why.

She walked back across to the chain barrier and her van. Conflicting gusts of wind twisted her clothing. She waved her thanks to Torsten and Ragnar, then remembered.

"Thank you for your exceptional Viking hospitality!" she shouted, for the benefit of whoever needed to hear.

47

ntoine's body ached as he hauled himself out of his car at Candlebroke Hall. He had never worked so physically hard in his life and had torn one of his favourite casual shirts. He had hauled paving slabs from one end of Terry's garden to the other. When she had pointed at the first pile, Antoine hadn't realised there was another, much larger pile just around the corner.

Still, she had been grateful and Vance had found the *kylix*. Now Sam's suspicions could be assuaged. He leaned against the car, tried to stretch the ache out of his back and put a call through to Kiki. He'd tell her to crack open the champers. He'd saved the day, and maybe she could rub some soothing oils into his back. Getting her to massage his back had the twin benefits of him not looking at her face, while he imagined it was a younger, more palatable woman's hands caressing him.

Wind hissed on the line. she was outside somewhere.

"*Antoine?*"

"Sam – I mean, Kiki. Good news about the *kylix*."

"*Yes. I found it and – loaded it up – the stairs.*" Windy interference cut through what she was saying.

"What? Where are you? I can't hear."

"*Up here!*"

He looked up to see her waving over the roof edge.

"*—it's not safe – the stairs—*"

"You're upstairs," he shouted. "Bit windy up there but I'm sure it's fine."

She said something again that sounded like '*stairs*', but the wind whipped her voice away. Antoine decided it would be quicker to pop upstairs and show her. He couldn't wait to see her face when he produced the second *kylix*. She needed to see how much she relied on him.

K<small>IKI</small> <small>COULDN'T</small> <small>BE</small> sure if Antoine had understood her warning about using the grand staircase. She leaned further forward. "Antoine!"

Had he entered the building already? She edged closer, unable to see. "Antoine!"

No, she'd missed him. She straightened, suddenly conscious it wasn't safe to be so close to the edge. She turned to walk back and was hit full in the chest by the washing line beam, swinging in the wind. It knocked her straight over the edge.

Kiki flailed, all thought fleeing from her mind. She could see, without seeing, the drop below. Three storeys to the lawns and paths, each as hard as concrete from this height.

And not three regular storeys either, three lofty-ceilinged storeys. Images of her head splattering against hard ground drowned her thoughts as her arms whirled.

Something snagged her wrist. Something else caught around her ear and throat, tightening abruptly. Washing line! The sudden constriction around her neck made her yelp. There was no way for the yelp to escape her throat. She produced a harsh, quacking bark instead.

She could only see grey shifting skies, but could picture herself dangling – her hand trapped in wire, her neck caught in a noose. She kicked her leg, raging inwardly at the pain in her neck. The absolutely bloody injustice of the situation made her blood boil. She didn't deserve to die in some stupid washing-line related incident. She was Kiki sodding Lettuces! – née Harris! She was owed a glamorous existence and a dignified death, surrounded by riches and admirers.

Her shoe heel caught against the parapet wall and she tried to haul herself in. She could feel the blood swelling her face. Her lungs burned. Her eyes felt like they were going to pop from their sockets.

She swung her other foot round in search of purchase. The washing line sawed more deeply into her neck. She felt heat. Had she cut herself? Was it possible to decapitate oneself with a washing line? She hauled with her trapped arm, clawed with her feet, pulled herself against the clothes airer swinging unhelpfully in the wind.

She could feel her vision dimming. The pain in her chest reached unbearable levels and she wanted to scream. She so very much wanted to scream, yet nothing came.

. . .

ANTOINE JOGGED up the grand staircase, the *kylix* in his hand. He tutted as he approached the half landing. The clutter in this place was getting worse. Still, it would keep Sam Applewhite off their backs while she tried to figure out where and what everything was. He would pair his *kylix* with the one in his stash and put them where they could be found. Sam would be happy and perhaps could be made to go away.

His foot slipped as he reached the top step. The carpet just seemed to move beneath him, like leaves on a wet path. His legs shot back and he fell, feet first, down the stairs. Momentum kept him going in what seemed like slow motion, jarring his chest against every step as he slid. His knees knocked, his groin squished. On a couple of stairs he hit his jaw so hard he nearly bit his tongue off. He came to a stop at the turn in the stair, amazed at the astonishing array of pains awakening in his body. He panted with agony.

He turned over and thrust himself into a seated position, gasping. Three over-riding concerns filled his mind. His spine, his face and the *kylix*.

He didn't have time to dwell on them. His eyes were caught by movement at the top of the stairs. The loose carpet which had thrown him downstairs, now pulled taut at the top like a slide, had dislodged a bookcase. It had already pitched forward, hanging at an angle, and sheared away a strip of wallpaper before halting. But something heavy shifted audibly inside it. The bookcase broke away from the wall and tumbled down the stairs. End over end, banging towards him.

He had time to raise his arms and begin screaming.

48

There was a pile of post on the doormat of DefCon4 when Sam returned. It included the usual selection of missed parcel delivery cards. Head office sent through equipment and other random items with such frequency that Sam was rarely in the office when anything arrived. She had adopted a personal policy of ignoring any and all such cards. The cryptic warnings of *You MUST COLLECT THIS PARCEL FROM SUCH-AND-SUCH DEPOT WITHIN X NUMBER OF HOURS OR IT WILL BE RETURNED TO SENDER* held no terror for her. She'd actually found that, given enough time, couriers would contact her and beg to be allowed to deliver it again, just to get it off their shelves.

She took the post upstairs and determined she had accumulated enough of it over the preceding days to justify opening it and doing a bit of filing. Filing was a simple process. There were things that were clearly important (usually relating to her own income and job security). There were things that were clearly not important, and went into a paper recycling bin. Then there were things that might be important, but didn't seem important, which went into a drawer section all by themselves. She had marked the drawer section with the year, in black marker. If she was still here next year, she would start another section. She had four drawers in her filing cabinet, and room for several folder sections in each. Her current filing system would suffice for the next twenty years. If she was still working for DefCon4 by the time she ran out of filing space, then she would know she had made some disastrous life choices somewhere.

The recycling bin was overflowing by the time she was done, but it felt good to know her office admin was complete.

Thoughts of files and records prompted her to turn to her computer and go to the web-based interface for the community payback. She looked up Torsten Odinson and read his record. Naturally, legally, DefCon4's records did not give her access to her client's criminal records, but she was provided with such information as was necessary to risk assess her work with him. There were scant details. References to categories of severity led her down an internet wormhole that led her through the Crime and Disorder Act, the Criminal Justice Act and the Equality Act. In the end, she gave up and phoned DC Camara.

"Tell me," she said. "What links does Torsten have with neo-Nazi groups?"

"You want me to give out personal information regarding a convicted criminal? Over the phone? To a company that has no need of the information?" There might have been a humorous tone to his voice but Sam wasn't having any of it.

"You told me before. You did more than hint at it. Lucas, you want me to know."

Camara sniffed. *"Just look at his tattoos."*

"What do you mean?"

"There's long been a crossover between Norse symbols and fascism, going back to the Second World War. Several Nazi organisations used runes as their symbols."

"Yeah, but the Odinsons are just ordinary stupid wannabe Vikings."

"Yeah?" said Camara. *"And Torsten having 'Heil Hitler' tattooed round his arm in rune letters. That's ordinary, is it?"*

"Shit."

"Exactly. I mean the boy's hardly a prime example of the master-race. That fight he had wouldn't have happened if some undergrad history student hadn't been able to read runes, or if Torsten had worn a long sleeve shirt."

"And if he wasn't a fascist," she said, stunned.

"Yeah. That too."

She stared blankly long enough for Camara to have to say her name to check she was still on the call.

"There's no chance he didn't know what it was when he got it?" she said.

"Didn't know he'd asked for a Nazi tattoo? Pfff."

"I've seen enough 'no regerts' tattoos."

"No. Most tattooists know their fascist and racist symbols pretty well. They know to turn those people away. They actually have a decent code of ethics."

"But someone gave it to him."

"Yep. I've seen it. Too professional for a homemade tattoo."

"Someone will know. Thanks." She hung up and went

over to the Odinson photographic family tree. The headshot she had for Torsten was just that, a headshot. On the family picture on the beach with *Sandraker*, Torsten had his arm raised in a toast. There were tattoos across his forearm and upper arm, too blurry to make out. His raised arm was exposed to the shoulder and there was a white rectangle around his arm.

"A bandage?" she mused. She looked to Doug Junior. "You think he had the tattoo covered or removed?"

Doug didn't have opinions on the matter.

49

Antoine was in a unique situation. He sat at the bottom of the steps. He had the base of a bookcase directly between his spread legs. The feet of the bookcase had snapped off. The top of the bookcase was buried in the wall above his head, showering flakes of plaster and vintage wallpaper onto his face. Antoine was wedged in the right angle triangle formed by the bookcase, wall and floor.

Antoine believed in an afterlife. He might have been a fraudulent psychic (or psychic impressionist as he liked to think of it), but he did believe there was a place where spirits went after they had moved on from this earthly life. Nonetheless, he didn't put much thought into his own death. Death was like nursing homes and prostate problems – an almost inevitable part of his future, but not worth dwelling on while he still had life and vigour.

This bookcase, he realised, was as close to death as he'd

come in a very long time. And to nearly be killed by a bookcase! The indignity of it! It was like that Indiana Jones thing with the rolling ball, but a Queen Anne bookcase instead! Laughable!

But he was alive and that was a pleasant surprise. And the *kylix* had survived too. It had rolled down the steps, one by one, avoiding being crushed by the bookcase and now rested just out of reach. More than could be said for the numerous things that had crashed down the stairs after him. He looked at the smashed fragments, freezing as he saw the broken remains. The distinctive colour of the glaze drew his eye, and he saw a fragment depicting unlikely sexual exploits, the twin of the one by his hand.

"No, no, no!" he moaned. "Kiki, what the hell have you done?"

There was a clattering on the stairs and there was Phoebe and a pair of National Heritage volunteers, no doubt brought running by the crashing sounds.

"Oh, Antoine!" cried Phoebe, horrified by the sight of him (which was by no means reassuring).

"The Chinoiserie wallpaper!" said one of the volunteers, apparently more concerned by the damage to the décor than Antoine's near death experience.

"The *kylix*," Antoine grunted. He gestured to the one intact bowl. He let the fragments speak for themselves.

"Can you move?" asked Phoebe, assisting in hauling Antoine from his awkward position. "Here. Let's find you a seat. Mr Montamoor, could you phone for an ambulance?"

"Really..." said Antoine, about to suggest it wasn't necessary. He lost the energy after the first word.

Phoebe helped him (his legs screaming in agony at every step) down to the first floor. "Where does it hurt?" she asked.

"Uh. Here. Legs. My back. Although that might be the paving slabs."

A ravaged zombie figure staggered onto the landing.

"Oh, my goodness!" Phoebe exclaimed. "Kiki! What happened?"

Antoine looked up at Kiki. Her clothes were twisted, her hair was wild and her face— It looked like she'd been nearly whipped to death. Red scores circled her upper body, neck and face. Straight red lines, glistening and oozing. And where the marks crossed her face, one of her eyes was bloodshot.

"Your damned washing line!" she croaked with fury.

"Washing line?" said Phoebe. "Come."

She swiftly helped the wobbly Kiki into an armchair, plonking her straight down on the Do Not Sit on this Chair sign, and told the woman volunteer to go tell Mr Montamoor that two ambulances might be required.

Kiki coughed and gargled.

"You need water," Phoebe decided and hurried off to get it.

"What did you do?" Antoine grunted.

"I just fell off the roof after your death trap swept me off my feet," Kiki spat. "Bloody garrotted me."

Antoine turned with an agonised groan. "No. What did you do? I got the *kylix* and you..."

Kiki tried to shake her head, winced at the pain and immediately stopped. "One grave, two bodies."

"What?" he said, scowling at her nonsense. Was this some mafia lingo she was using?

"Kill two problems at once," she managed to say.

Two problems? Was she talking about him?

"Why did you put ... clothes airer so close the edge?" she said.

He frowned at her question. Why was she blathering about clothes airers when the big issue was the pair of *kylixes*? And the bookcase she'd apparently tried to kill him with. "You destroyed the *kylix*! I get the first one, and I come back to find you've smashed the second!"

"Trying to cover up your tracks."

"My tracks?" he snarled.

"Were you trying to kill me with that contraption?"

He could have screamed, if he'd had the energy. It was enraging that she couldn't see the rooftop garden and clothes airer were meant to make her happy, divert her from dwelling on their criminal endeavours, and to stop her nagging him.

"Just wanted to keep you quiet," he said.

Her mouth dropped open in an O of surprise. "You owe me thousands," she said. "I saw all the stuff in the boat. You owe me."

"I'll take care of you."

"You? Take care of me?"

"That was always the plan."

She raised her good arm to point. "Just remember I am your only source of income."

He tried to laugh, but it turned into a wracking cough. "You? You're the biggest barrier to this whole enterprise."

She breathed heavily, with difficulty. "Maybe I don't want to do this anymore. I've got options."

His eyes flicked upwards. He could only see the sculpted ceiling, but he was thinking of the bookcase trap she'd left for him. "Kill the golden goose and make a clean break, eh?" He was about to say more when Phoebe reappeared with a glass of water for Kiki.

"Ambulance is on the way. I don't know if they're sending one or two. Maybe you could ride together. Ambulance buddies, eh?"

50

Sam believed in the miracles that were often worked by the subconscious mind. There had been many occasions when she'd been thinking hard about something and failed to bring forth the goods from her conscious mind; then later, when she was stepping out of the shower or just dropping off to sleep, the answer would present itself in an unexpected flash of clarity. For that reason, she opened up her laptop while she ate her breakfast croissant, knowing that a fresh look at some of the last tricky parts of the inventory might help to resolve some of the outstanding niggles.

The job had been a long, hard, horrible slog, filled with pointless irritations, frustrating dead ends, and seemingly no reward or conclusion in sight. In that, it had been a classic DefCon4 assignment. She hoped, however, once out of the woods (a woods composed of antique clutter and bad record-keeping) she would be able to see the big picture and even comprehend Hilde's role in it. Close to the end, there were a few outstanding unmatched items that Sam was certain were simply eluding her because of the arcane wording in the older inventory. She scanned the new and old documents as she ate, hoping to find something to help her match the last few items.

Marvin came into the kitchen, swishing the hem of his dressing gown as he danced to some tune playing in his head.

"What's today's earworm?" she asked.

"I wish I knew," he said. "Sometimes I think I'm a master composer because I made up a brand new melody, then I realise it's a Hollies B-side I just forgot about."

Sam was about to ask him to hum it for her, to see if she recognised it, but the phone rang. Marvin picked up, and Sam saw something change in his body language, the way he stood more upright.

"Kiki, how nice to hear from you!"

Sam smiled to herself. Was her dad truly smitten?

"The roof? Oh no! Oh goodness me!" Concern etched Marvin's face, and Sam wondered what had happened. "Your neck? Poor you. Do you need me to come and bring you anything?"

Sam looked up. Her dad no longer had a car, so did this mean she was needed to drive him somewhere?

"Well you're being extremely brave about it, Kiki. I can't say I'd show such fortitude in the face of injuries like that. I understand that you need to rest, but call me any time you fancy a chat, won't you? No, I love a chat. There doesn't have to be a reason. We can just chew the fat, as they say." He hung up the phone. "Kiki was in an accident."

"Really?"

"She fell off the roof."

Sam was incredulous. "The roof of Candlebroke Hall? That's got to be ... well, high. She's lucky to be alive." Her mind was racing. Another odd occurrence at Candlebroke Hall. It couldn't be a coincidence.

"She got caught in a washing line which saved her life whilst simultaneously nearly strangling her. She's at the Pilgrim Hospital. I'm going to take a taxi over there later. Maybe I could take her some flowers. Would that cheer her up? Or are flowers not de rigueur anymore?

"Maybe some fruit and a book or something? Whatever you take I'm sure she'll be happy." Sam dabbed at the croissant crumbs on her plate, licked her finger and stood up. "I'm off to see Delia. If she's got an ideal gift for a poorly patient, I'll let you know."

"Off to Delia's again?"

"I want to see if she can help me with some of the strange terms in the old inventory."

"You could always try me with some of them," said Marvin. "I'm from the actual olden days, you know."

"Go on then. What's a *pouter*?"

"One who pouts. Next!"

"My first thought as well, but I haven't found anything at Candlebroke Hall that sounds like that. Try this one then, what about *nepken*?"

"Napkin?" Marvin gave her a look. "I know we don't

always dine formally, but I thought you might have a passing familiarity with what one of them is."

"Maybe. Now that I've said it out loud it seems so obvious. When it's on the page it just looks like a made-up word. All right then smarty-pants, what about *glinarium*?"

"Glinarium." Marvin said it out loud as he stared into the middle distance. "Glinarium. No, I've got nothing."

"Aren't old people filled with wisdom?" said Sam in mock astonishment.

"It's a selective kind of wisdom. I could probably still whip up Petula Clark's favourite omelette, but that's not much use unless Petula Clark comes calling."

51

Sam called into *Back to Life*. There was a customer in there. An actual customer. They were such an uncommon event that Sam didn't mention it in case the rare creature was spooked and fled the shop. Sam put the kettle on while Delia fished some linens out of a bucket of dye and rinsed them in the sink.

"I'm glad you dropped by. We've got the final reveal for these coming up right now," said Delia as she slopped the material up and down in the water.

"If this is a pitch for a new TV reality show, you need to up your game," said Sam, "I want to see seriously manic levels of excitement at the potential in that glooping mess."

"Yup, gotcha," said Delia, fixing a zealous grin onto her face.

"Then I need to hear the back story. I need to know why this matters so much."

"Oh right. Like these are my granny's bloomers and I

want to make them a part of my own life, reaching back across the years and feeling that family connection?"

Sam was taken aback. "Is that true?"

"No," sighed Delia, "I was just building up my part. I'm not sure a TV audience wants to hear the truth about covering stains. Antique linen is always popular, but nobody will buy it if it's stained or discoloured. I'm having a go at tie-dying some, try and appeal to a younger market."

"A younger market? You do know that you're in Skegness, don't you?"

"There *are* young people here," said Delia. "And they deserve nice things." She held up an antimacassar that was striped in purple and turquoise.

Sam looked first at the antimacassar, then Delia's face. "You are my friend, and I support all of the marvellous creative things you do. But I have questions."

"Yes," said Delia with a slow nod. "I can see you might. Let's work through them."

"First question. I now know, because you told me, that antimacassars were to put on chair backs when men wore messy hair products. I think they slipped out of fashion a few decades before I was born, so what are millennials going to do with them?"

"Hm." Sam could tell that Delia was thinking on her feet. "I mean, have you seen the amount of hair product and beard oil some of them wear? It's only a matter of time before they realise that they need to protect their upholstery."

"Really?"

"Or," Delia was concentrating hard now, "I could see them being used in an ironic way."

"Seriously?"

Delia pulled a face and sighed. "No. I'll put them on the pile of things that I might make into a bag one day."

"What pile is that?"

Delia pointed to a towering pile of textiles. "It will be perfect for a rainy afternoon."

"Or a rainy fortnight," Sam suggested.

"Hey, did you see that the Odinsons are trending on Instagram?" asked Delia.

"No, how on earth did that happen?" Sam asked.

She jerked her head back towards the rear workshop. "Hilde pointed it out to me. There's a guy with a new age shop in Lincoln who's been shouting about the injustice of their boat being taken. He's talking about it being an attack on their religious beliefs."

"Do the Odinsons have religious beliefs?"

"It seems they do now." Delia fished in her pocket for her phone. "The young girl, Freyella, she's a regular Greta Thunberg."

Delia showed Sam a video of Freyella earnestly describing a set of core beliefs based on equality, respect and hospitality. She insisted the Odinsons simply wanted to be allowed to practise their religion in peace, all the while meeting the viewer's eye: a wholesome young girl speaking up for her family.

"Wow!" said Sam.

"There are several videos of this one. There's one of her nan as well, talking about the meaning of home, hearth and big family meals."

"Astrid?"

"Yeah, that's her. The ones with the men in are mostly them posing with axes while someone else does a voiceover."

"Figures." Sam suspected the Odinson men would need heavy editing. "I'm heading over to Candlebroke Hall in a bit. Would you believe Lady Kiki fell off the roof?"

"What?"

"It's true. She rang dad to tell him."

"Wouldn't it have been better to ring an ambulance?"

"Smarty-pants. I'm going up there to finish this inventory job. I'm on the last part and I wanted to pick your brains about a couple of things, if you're up for it?"

"Ooh yes, always!" said Delia, sitting up to attention. "Hit me!"

"Sam opened the laptop. "One I remember is *pouter*. What do you reckon that might be?"

"I believe I've seen that used to mean pewter. So it would be a pewter charger."

"Ah – big plate made from pewter, yes?"

"Yes! Score one for Delia." She punched the air. "Ask me another."

"*Glinarium*," said Sam.

Delia gave her a look. "Glinarium. Doesn't even sound like a word."

Sam shrugged. "Internet doesn't think it's a word, either."

"Can I see it in the old document?"

Sam found the reference and they both stared at the screen. Sam zoomed in until the image was large and grainy, but it didn't look any clearer.

"Do you think that might be an 'r' instead of an 'n'?"

asked Delia. "The handwriting is beautiful, but it's not that consistent."

"So it would be *glirarium*?" Sam typed it into a search. "Wow! Yes, this must be it!" She laughed and hid the screen. "You could have a lifetime of guesses and never, ever come up with the answer."

Delia raised her eyebrows. "In that case I won't waste my breath. What is it?"

Sam spun the laptop round. "It's a large terracotta jar that Romans used to raise dormice, to eat."

"Were they into dormouse cuisine?"

"Big time. It's like an old-fashioned hamster cage, really. Look, it's got galleries for them to, I don't know, scamper round."

"Oh yeah! You'd look at that and think it was for the garden, wouldn't you? For growing strawberries or something. So, did you see one in Candlebroke Hall?"

"Most definitely not. So, it's another thing that's gone missing."

Delia pointed at the image on Sam's search. "Is that one for sale? Surely not! They should all be in museums, or something. Shouldn't they?"

"Well this one isn't."

"Let's see how much it's going for."

They clicked through and found a listing on an auction site. "They're asking five hundred pounds, or nearest offer," said Delia. "Crazy. These things are rare."

"It's local," said Sam. "Says it's in Skegness."

"No way! What are the odds?"

"Well exactly," said Sam. "What *are* the odds?"

"You think this is the actual one that's missing from Candlebroke Hall?"

Sam nodded, beginning to scroll. "The seller has loads of things up for sale."

"They all sound valuable," said Delia after a few moments. "Not your usual internet tat."

Sam gave Delia a look.

"I sell the usual internet tat. Trust me. It would be interesting to compare this list with yours."

"I've recognised a few things just by looking," said Sam, her excitement growing. "I wonder where this seller is?"

"Yeah, we can't see that on here. Or can we...?" Delia pointed and gave a muted squeak.

"What?"

"See how all the items for sale are arranged on a trestle table. Like the seller just did a massive photo shoot outside, yeah? You can even see the same garden gnome in the background of most of them."

"I guess the light is better outside. We can't tell where it is, though. That garden could be anywhere in Lincolnshire."

"Except for that," said Delia, tapping a blurry shape in the background.

"What? It's another house or something. No – I see what you're saying! The way the sides slope in. That's a windmill."

There were many traditional windmills in Lincolnshire, but there was only one that could be described as near Skegness.

"Burgh le Marsh," said Delia.

"That's amazing," said Sam. "It's a starting point, anyway.

Burgh le Marsh isn't an enormous place, but where would I start looking?"

Delia pulled a face, stared at the ceiling, and wagged a finger to indicate an important thought was coming. "We need ... that thing."

"What thing?"

Delia flapped her hands in frustration. "At school, the thing we all swore we'd never have any practical use for..."

"Fronted adverbials?" Sam tried.

"No."

"Latin declensions?"

"What? Where did you go to school? No. Trigonometry! That's what you need, you need trigonometry."

"The thing with triangles? All right, so we're going to use the height of the windmill to erm, do something?"

Delia stabbed the screen with a finger. "We know a bunch of things here. We know the height of the windmill, or we will when we've looked it up. We know the height of the gnome. We know the angle we're looking up at—"

"Do we? Really?"

"Pretty sure we can estimate it. Or work it out from the gnome."

Sam wasn't convinced. "Not sure how the gnome is helping."

"The gnome appears in several photos, taken from different places." Delia ran out of steam. "I don't know either, but I'm sure it does. Let's sketch it out."

After an hour Sam and Delia had filled several pages with sketches of triangles. Sam's were carefully annotated with arrows and captions, whereas Delia's had questions scrawled wildly across them in different colours. Some of them hung off the edge of the page or encroached onto Sam's diagrams. They were no closer to the answer.

"I might have another idea," said Delia.

"That's good, because I'm late for work."

"There's this online parenting forum where we get help with the kids' homework and revision. If I pretend this is a homework question, I can get help with it."

Hilde came through from the back room and looked at their diagrams, and their gnome and windmill drawings. "Saxons are mad," she said.

"Possibly," said Sam.

Hilde hefted the slightly wonky cockerel-topped weathervane in her hand. "Delia, I'm taking this back to mine. I'm going to need the welder."

"Okay."

"Also, Runesplicer wants to film me engaged in what he calls—" she closed her eyes to concentrate "—authentic cultural crafts."

"How goes the social media campaign to win your ship back?" asked Delia.

Hilde shook her head. "Maybe Saxons don't have a monopoly on madness." She raised her eyebrows. "Then again, we don't need to stick a big metal cock on our roofs to know which way the wind's blowing."

52

S am drove to Candlebroke Hall. It was time to hand in as complete an inventory as she could possibly give. The A158 road to Candlebroke Hall bypassed the village of Burgh le Marsh. Sam looked over, hoping to catch a glimpse of the windmill, knowing full well the trees along the roadside hid it almost completely.

She parked and went in search of Phoebe. The office was empty, but she found her halfway up a staircase, discussing a nasty series of rips in the wallpaper with an earnest-looking man.

"Bit of an accident?" said Sam.

"Accidents, plural. Problems pop up all the time on a site this size, I'm sure you can imagine," said Phoebe.

Sam could. She held up her laptop. "It's all finished."

"The inventory?" Phoebe managed to look excited at this news.

"Yes. It was quite a task. It's formatted as a searchable

database now, so you can look things up more easily in future. I could show you."

Phoebe led the way back to her office, moving some papers so Sam could sit. Sam opened the laptop.

"I'm so glad that it's all in hand," said Phoebe.

"I wouldn't call it 'in hand'," said Sam. "You have some serious problems. A great many items are missing."

"Ah, breakages and so on," said Phoebe.

"No," said Sam firmly. "Not that. I made some charts to show you the numbers." She clicked through to the visualisations she'd created. "Here. Do you see this pie chart?"

"Oh this is so organised! I love it," said Phoebe. "What's it showing?"

"This portion here is what I matched to the old inventory. This portion here is where I found items I couldn't match to the old inventory. This very slim portion is where I was mostly successful in eventually finding a match."

"I admire your determination," said Phoebe. "So what's this portion here?"

"The items which appeared on the old inventory, but there's no sign of them in the house now."

Phoebe stared at the screen, her mouth agape. "That can't be right. It's nearly a third of the pie."

Sam nodded. "That's why I wanted you to see it like this."

ANTOINE HAD MIXED views on scars. There was the old idea that women loved men with scars, but Antoine felt his stage and YouTube persona was best served by having unblemished, smouldering good looks. As he slowly sank into middle age, he wanted one of those faces which looked wise and lived in, rather than the jowly, double-chinned and foolish facial flab most men seemed to get.

Yet, as he sat in a taxi taking him back to Candlebroke from Boston's Pilgrim Hospital A&E department, he wished he had some outward signs of his calamitous accident. His chest ached, though the X-rays showed no broken ribs. His back was a dozen individual points of sharp pain, though there was no visible damage there either. His chin was sore, his knees creaked painfully, and his inner thighs chafed from where the bookcase had pressed intimately against him. There was not a single part of him that had not been hurt in his ignoble tumble. Yet, after the accident and a sleepless night being shunted from one place to another, he had nothing on his body – not one thing! – he could point to and say, "See that? Looks painful, doesn't it?" It was unfair.

One of the few consolations was the knowledge that Kiki Harris, that demented and deluded starlet of yesteryear, had been admitted with more significant and unsightly injuries. She was still in hospital, and from what he could glean, would be there a while longer. That gave Antoine a bit of a head start. He was sure he needed one.

Kiki had tried to kill him. While he had been racing round Skegness in search of the *kylix*, she had been concocting some cartoonish 'accident' to kill him. She had told him to come straight upstairs just so he could run into that loose carpet and bring the bookcase tumbling down. He shuddered at the intense memory. It was a stupid plot, but it had almost succeeded.

And what had she said? Something about graves? *"Kill two problems at once."*

Get rid of Antoine and the incriminating *kylixes*?

"I don't want to do this anymore. I've got options."

She planned to kill him, ride out any speculation about his death and maybe try to sell off the concealed valuables herself.

"This place here, mate?" said the taxi driver.

Antoine rankled at the man's chummy use of the word, 'mate', but he hurt too much to care. "Yes. Here. Down to the end. Park in front of the house."

"Nice place this. Can't imagine what it must be like to live in an old place like that."

Antoine glared as Candlebroke Hall slid into view. "Hell," he muttered.

The driver pulled up on the driveway. A volunteer came over to complain, pausing when he saw it was Antoine. When the volunteer tried to help Antoine out of the car, he batted the man away. He wasn't about to be treated as an invalid by these clots. Antoine gave the driver a twenty pound note.

"Keep the change."

"It's twenty-three quid, mate."

Antoine hid his embarrassed revulsion, rifled through his wallet – Gods! Even his fingers ached! – and flung the man an additional fiver, before taking a slow but dignified walk into the hall.

Antoine's mind whirled over the possible courses of action lying ahead of him. Kiki had betrayed him and now, with her stuck in hospital, he had to prepare for the trials to come. He had no intention of any of them being a criminal trial, with poor innocent Antoine de Winter in the dock.

As he hobbled through the hall, he concluded his plans had two main strands. Number one was to protect his wealth and future income. He would go to the stash of treasures, currently hidden inside that stupid Viking longship and remove the most valuable and most transportable. There were some small bronzes, some horse sketches by Stubbs, and a whole casket of jewellery that, to the right buyer, should be worth hundreds of thousands. He would hide them elsewhere, off-site. The second strand entailed the silencing of his now unreliable partner, Lady Kiki Lettuces *née* Harris. Silencing the old bat didn't have to mean killing her, but right now, while his hips groaned and his back ached and his chest burned, he could think of nothing but killing her.

An accidental overdose of sleeping pills? Kiki might appreciate going out like Marilyn Monroe. Maybe he could engineer a gas leak or carbon monoxide poisoning in her flat? She had often said the squalid little place would be the death of her. There were many options. Antoine just needed to devise one that would play to his strengths.

He stopped at the sound of voices, specifically at the sound of Phoebe's voice, high and querulous, wondering if there might be some other explanation for 'missing items'. Antoine moved towards the open door of Phoebe's office.

"You must have made a mistake," said Phoebe.

"No," said another voice – Sam Applewhite. "Every step I have taken has been transparent. The only place the missing items could be is here." From his angle of approach, Antoine could just see Sam's arm pointing to something on a computer screen. "You can see even if we assume all of these items were in the old inventory, it doesn't change the overall story. Too many of them are missing."

Phoebe sighed. It was more of a piteous mewling sound.

"Are there any locations that I haven't checked?" Sam asked.

Inside the Viking longship, thought Antoine, automatically.

"No," said Phoebe. "You checked everywhere." Antoine approached the edge of the door, still unseen. Phoebe was staring at a pie chart on a laptop screen. Evidently one of the slices of pie was causing her great consternation. "I need to report this, don't I?" she said wearily.

"I think you do, yes," said Sam. "Although how they'll investigate a crime that's been committed some time in the last twenty years or so is going to be a challenge. I'll talk to the police myself once you've reported it to them. I might have some ideas."

Sam reached for the laptop. In moving she saw Antoine peering round the doorway. She blinked. Was that a momentary look of terror in her eyes?

"Bear with me. Nearly with you," he said, grunting as he shuffled painfully into the office. He didn't need to pretend to be in pain, but he needed to make them think he hadn't been loitering, just moving with incredible slowness.

"Antoine," said Phoebe. "They discharged you?"

He grunted. "Nothing they can do for me. I was saved permanent injury by my cat-like agility. But there are various aches and bruises."

"The bookcase on the stairs?" said Sam. There was now a look of genuine concern in her eyes.

Antoine found himself unaccountably aroused. They'd only had one dinner date together, and whilst not exactly a rip-roaring success, he could see his charms had finally begun to work. She might not be as classy a woman as he would normally go for, but if this doe-eyed girl wanted a roll in the hay with Antoine de Winter, then who was he to say no. If only poking her nose into the affairs of Candlebroke Hall wasn't as insufferable as Kiki's treachery, he might have given it some serious thought.

"We had a couple of nasty accidents here yesterday," said Phoebe.

"Accidents," agreed Antoine. "I'm sure I'll pull through." He stretched to show his improving health. As punishment, a lightning bolt of pain shot up through his spine. He gave a groaning squeak. "That's not from the fall," he assured them. "I was helping an old lady move some paving slabs yesterday. Bit of community spirit, and all that."

Sam nodded, uncertain. She closed her laptop and addressed Phoebe. "I've emailed you a copy of what we just looked through, with a covering letter."

"Thank you. You've done a great job."

"A quick question, though," said Sam. "Do you know what a glirarium is?"

"A dormouse pot," said Antoine automatically, always happy to share his knowledge.

The look Sam gave him was suddenly suspicious. From alarmed, to loving, to suspicious. The girl was a bloody tease.

"The dormouse pot, oh yes!" Phoebe clapped her hands. "It was such a hit with the children."

"You remember it, then?" said Sam.

"Of course. It's about this high, and hardly damaged, apart from a chip on the rim, which is incredible for something so old, don't you think?" She paused. "Is that missing too?"

"Yes."

"I can't remember when I last saw it, but it was within the last couple of years. It was part of an exhibition celebrating the antiquities collected by the fifth baronet."

"It's missing," said Sam and, with her laptop under her arm and a final look at Antoine, left.

53

Hilde made a shooing motion at Runesplicer. "You're getting in my way with your filming. Back off a bit, can't you?"

Runesplicer backed away slightly, not enough to be useful. Normally, Hilde found comfort in the intense heat and glow from her forge, but right now she felt hot, stuffy and claustrophobic. Runesplicer peered intently at his phone as he filmed. "So, tell me Hilde. What is this that you're working on?"

"I told you already."

He tutted. "It's for me to edit into the finished piece, Hilde. This is going to be brilliant for getting some public interest. The right kind of public interest."

"Oh yes? What is the right kind of public interest, exactly?" Hilde had experienced enough people interested in her activities of late.

"The kind that portrays the Odinson brand as something

to be admired. We need to build on the idea that your family is different, but in a good way. The Odinsons have yet to show the outside world their contributions to the fabric of society. Odinson Mead is one way they're doing that. Ragnar has agreed to sponsor a roundabout in the local area, too."

"To do what?" said Hilde.

"Sponsor a roundabout."

"Like in a playground?"

"A traffic island."

"Sponsor it?"

"It's a form of advertising. Shows the Odinsons have something to give." He waved a hand to indicate the surroundings. "Your activities, your workshop, is a perfect example of that. You're doing good work, creative work. Recycling as well. It's perfect. Now, can we take it from the top?"

Hilde grunted in agreement.

"So tell me, Hilde. What is this that you're working on?"

Hilde decided she needed to accept her role as some sort of cheesy ambassador. She smiled at the camera. "It's a refurbishment project. I'm working with a local business to restore antiques and other pieces of history. This is a weathervane, made from cast iron, which once stood on a farm building out by Slackholme. It's fallen into disrepair, but with a straightened rod and bit of welding, it could be put up again."

"You're doing a thorough job," said Runesplicer. "And one that calls for a good deal of expertise. How would you describe your role in the family?"

Hilde was momentarily thrown by the question. Her

role? "I would describe myself as the maker of things," she said.

"Maker, refurbisher and designer as well," said Runesplicer.

Hilde nodded.

"What would you say is your most impressive achievement to date?" he asked.

She unbent from the task at hand and looked straight at the camera. "That's easy. I designed and built a Viking longship, with the help of my family. The *Sandraker*. It sails like a dream as well. Fabulous piece of work."

"What did you base the design on?"

"The ships the old Vikings built. Ragnar was the one with the vision." She chose not to mention that Ragnar's vision also included putting outboard motors on the end of each oar.

"Based on the ships of your Viking forefathers," nodded Runesplicer earnestly. "How did it make you feel when you were out on the sea, sailing the ship you built from scratch?"

"I was very proud," said Hilde honestly.

"I bet you felt a strong connection to your forefathers as well, didn't you? You imagined the way they would have felt when they set sail upon lonely seas, putting all of their faith in the sturdiness of the ship they'd built?"

"Oh right. Yeah that too," she said and turned the glowing metal rod.

54

The doctors kept Kiki in overnight to monitor her. Apparently, accidentally garrotting yourself with a washing line, warranted one day and one night of hospitalisation, nothing more. She had appreciated it at first, being in a place where things like adequate plumbing and regular hot meals would be the norm. Then the loneliness and paranoia kicked in.

Hospitalisation was a true barometer of how loved you were. If she had been a regular sixty-something woman, she'd have children, grandchildren even. They'd be visiting her right now, in shifts. Not that children were essential. Even if she was an ordinary woman, living in her little bungalow – oh, it could be Lytham St Annes, or Scarborough, or even bloody Skegness – she'd have neighbours and friends. Folks who'd pop in for a chat and send her flowers and grapes as soon as they discovered she was in hospital.

"Who's going to bring you grapes, huh?" she asked herself in the mirror as she hobbled around the toilet cubicle and washed her hands.

Kiki had been on her own for a long time. She'd allowed herself to believe Antoine was some sort of a partner, a rock in her life. She'd fallen to her senses with a dramatic bump.

"Hah!" She jabbed a finger at her reflection in triumph at the sharpness of her wit, even in the face of adversity. "Fallen to my senses indeed!"

She hobbled back to her bed gingerly, each movement a reliving of that near-fall from the roof, and thought about the injuries underneath her dressings. Surely the person responsible for scarring a Hollywood A-lister should be liable for damages?

She had to face facts. She had solid evidence that Antoine had tried to kill her. He'd built a death trap and encouraged her to use it, for crying out loud! And then, when he'd seen she'd survived her encounter with his washing line death machine, what had he said?

"I'll take care of you."

Oh, yes. She had read between the lines of that unsubtle comment.

"I'll take care of you. That was always the plan."

God! The man had said it out loud, and in front of witnesses too. He intended to kill her and didn't care if she knew.

The trouble was, if she involved the police, there was no way of knowing what he might say to them. He meant her harm, there was no doubt about that, but she was powerless to do anything about it. If she had anything like the money she needed to set up home elsewhere, she would make a run for it. But then she would be leaving all of the profits behind for him. She seethed at the thought. The house and its valuable contents were hers – morally, if not legally. The thought of him plundering her wealth and chasing her off as an inconvenience lit a fire of righteous anger in her.

The arrival of Marvin Applewhite at her hospital bedside brought painfully mixed feelings to Kiki. Having one unambiguously friendly face show up was an absolute delight. The rush of tear-inducing happiness it brought was, however, testament to how pathetically lacking the rest of her life was. Here came the grey-haired light entertainer in his button-up cardigan, carrying a book of wordsearch puzzles and – ha! – a punnet of grapes.

"Kiki," he said, dismayed. "How are you?"

"Don't look at me, Marvin," she said, holding out her hands as though to fend him off.

If this had been a film role with fake injuries, they would have taken more care. A modest cut at the top of her cheekbone might have rendered her heroic, and perhaps a little cruel. Whereas the untidy, messily-weeping abrasions all over her neck and face were just plain ugly. When the film crew turned up at Candlebroke Hall to film *The Scarlet Pimpernel*, she would need to get busy with her Pan Stik fast fix foundation.

He sat at her bedside and asked her, if it wasn't too painful, to recount what had happened.

Kiki demurred for maybe a second before rushing in to tell him everything of that fateful day, leaving out any reference to antiques being sold on the international black market. Hers was a tale of a lonely wealthy woman, wronged and harassed by a smarmy charming con-man with a stupid moustache and a penchant for the good things in life.

"Tony bloody Winters," said Marvin bitterly.

"You know, Antoine?" she said and then thought. "Fellow magicians."

"Nothing fellow about it," said Marvin. "Showy magic sets and no finesse. You know what happened to his stage assistant."

Kiki nodded as much as her injuries would allow. "Mauled to death by a tiger. That same tiger's living in my back garden right now."

Just saying it made the rancour rise in her like bile. *Her* house! *Her* home! And Antoine's precious bloody tiger had the run of her late husband's menagerie.

"I didn't meet him until years later," said Marvin. "He was casting about for people to invest in a new performance magic project. Not his idea. Based in America. I was a fool to listen to him."

Kiki put her hand on his on the bedsheet. His hand was warm, the touch intimate.

He smiled at her, but it was not a happy smile. "I've lost a lot of money. I had to sell my car last year to cover some debts. If you believe my daughter, I might have to sell my house before long."

She grunted. "At least you own a house."

He was confused. "I've seen that enormous pile you live in."

"Belongs to National Heritage," she said. "All of it. I'm permitted to live in a poky apartment. Why do you think I've got a death-trap clothes airer on the roof? I'm reduced to living up there with the pigeons."

"I had no idea. You seemed so happy. I pictured you surrounded by luxuries."

"Like a mouse in the skirting boards of Buckingham Palace."

"Then we should have you out of there as soon as possible."

"And give them the satisfaction of seeing me running away from my ancestral home?"

Marvin couldn't understand. They barely knew each other, except by reputation. One dinner date and a couple of phone calls was all they'd had. And yet, here he was, the only person to visit her bedside.

"This is very sweet of you," she said and peeled back the lid on the tub of grapes.

"I never know what the right thing is these days," said Marvin. "I always remember, when I was starting out in the business, going to visit Diana Dors in hospital. She'd had a fall on the set of *Queenie's Castle*. I took a posey with me. Well, her room was absolutely awash with flowers. Hundreds of them, there were. You couldn't move for them."

"A popular woman," said Kiki.

"Now, they don't want you to bring flowers in. Too much pollen dust, or something."

"The grapes are lovely," said Kiki and popped one into her mouth. Even the act of chewing made her face ache. "Tell me another story."

"What story?" he said.

She let her head sink further into her pillow. "Any. Stories of the stage. Stories of your glory days. Tell me them all."

Marvin chuckled and began one about someone stealing Bernie Clifton's ostrich at the Royal Variety Performance in 1979. Kiki smiled and let the soothing words wash over her.

55

Antoine sat on the stool outside Hugh's enclosure. He wanted to think through the problems he faced. By his side on the ground was a carpet bag filled with choice items from the Viking longship. Enough to keep him going while he contemplated what he could do about the incriminating inventory and the deranged Kiki Lettuces.

The gardeners were cutting back and chipping some bushes, and the sound of their whining, stuttering machine was a constant background noise. It was almost drowned out by the cold wind that blew in over the menagerie wall. Antoine wrapped his arms around himself and gazed into Hugh's eyes. He focused on the spiritual connection between them, tried to draw warmth and wisdom from the furry beast.

The tiger was one of the mythical super-intelligent creatures of Chinese myth. Antoine wasn't getting any particularly super-intelligent vibes off Hugh today. Sometimes he suspected he'd bought a duff tiger, or maybe just a non-Chinese one.

"The inventory," Antoine mused. "You'll be familiar with the notion that information is a combination of data and its context in the world?"

Hugh lay on his wooden platform and licked his own nose. The mildly hypnotic effect of the tiger's gaze was like a window into his mind. Hugh didn't need to answer for Antoine to know his thoughts.

"So I need to destroy or discredit the inventory data, that much is clear. But the context. That's in Sam's head. She knows enough to cause a lot of trouble."

Hugh blinked sleepily.

"The most elegant solution would be to tackle both of those things together. Discredit the data. Discredit Sam Applewhite."

Hugh yawned, his massive mouth obscuring the rest of his head for a moment.

"Disruption would come fairly easily with a strong complaint to head office. If I create enough stink it could tie things up for a good long while. Best of all, it's zero risk."

The tiger closed its eyes.

"Good idea, Hugh." Antoine stood, grunting loudly at the pain in his joints.

As he walked to his car, Antoine took out his phone, googled the contact details for DefCon4 and phoned them. The automated answer system kicked in instantly.

"*If you are interested in our services, press one. For partner companies, press two. For agencies and client, press three. For any other business, including pest control, press four."*

Antoine pressed four.

"If you have a problem with rats or mice, press one. For insect control, press two. Pigeons, press three. If you wish to speak to our border patrol team, press four."

"What?" said Antoine and pressed zero. That sometimes worked.

"You have made an incorrect choice," said the automated voice. *"If you would like to hear more about option selection, press one. Press two to return to the previous menu."*

He pressed one. He had now reached his car and placed the carpet bag on the ground while he searched for his keys.

"Option selection is the process by which you select the options you want from our automated answer service," said the voice. *"The numbers selection options correspond to the numbers on your telephone keypad. If, for example, you wish to select option one—"*

Antoine stabbed the number one.

"Well done, you have pressed the number one. Try another key."

Antoine pressed the hash key.

"Well done, you have pressed the hash key. Learning how to use our option selection system is both fun and easy."

Antoine gargled in annoyance, unlocked the car, put the bag inside and threw himself angrily into the driving seat, forgetting his injuries. He swore at the pain.

As he calmed himself, he put the phone back to his ear.

"If you are happy with option selection and wish to return to the main menu, press one. Or press any other key to continue."

He didn't want to go right back to the original menu. He pressed the number two.

"*Well done, you have pressed the number two. Try another key.*"

"Oh, for fuck's sake," he said and started the engine.

He would get through to DefCon4's complaints department if it killed him. Then, after complaining about Sam Applewhite, he might lodge a complaint about their telephone system, and if that didn't yield results, complain about the complaints department as well.

He drove into Skegness. He would swing by his own measly little house later on, a place he'd foolishly bought last year with money he'd borrowed on the assumption that the Candlebroke Hall racket would be bringing him in a pretty penny for years to come. It had seemed like a bargain at the time. The new-build had been reduced in price after the owner of the building company had been arrested for conspiracy to murder. The builder who'd picked up the pieces of the project and finished the houses off, then died in a freak hot tub accident. Maybe the whole building site was cursed. It was built on the edges of a cemetery after all. Not quite a cursed Indian burial ground, but maybe the area would be worth exploring in a future Antoine de Winter ghost hunt video?

He parked on the pavement outside the *Who Do You Ink You Are?* tattoo parlour.

Before going into the tattooists, he stood outside the narrow door to the DefCon4 office. He could just go right on up there and make a personal complaint about Sam. Inappropriate behaviour, perhaps? No, he needed to make an anonymous complaint, draw scrutinising eyes away from himself and towards Sam.

He left the DefCon4 doorway and went into the tattoo parlour. Vance was at the counter, sorting through vacuum sealed packs of sterilised equipment.

"Ah, happy fate," said Vance as greeting. "I've got a buyer for that pornographic Greek pot of yours."

Antoine scowled. "What? I'm not here about that."

"Fifteen hundred pound is the current bid and there's still a few hours to go."

Fifteen hundred pounds? It might not have been retire and run away to Vegas money, but one and a half thousand quid wasn't chickenfeed, either.

Antoine swallowed his pain. "Take it down, Vance."

"What?"

"Remove it from sale. And that glirarium too."

"The what?"

"The ancient pottery mouse thing. Take it down. Take them all down."

Vance looked stricken. His studded eyebrows rose in incomprehension.

Antoine sighed miserably. "The authorities are closing in."

"The police?"

"Mostly it's bloody Sam Applewhite. She's completed her damnable inventory and has a list of missing items to show the police."

"Fuck," said Vance, then sought out composure. "No. Karma will provide shelter for those who have lived honest lives."

"Honest lives?" Antoine almost laughed. "Karma is about to piss all over us, sunshine."

"You've read that in the cards?"

"Remove from sale every item you've put up there. Delete old listings too. No car boot sales. No black market deals. Get rid of your receipts. Burn the evidence."

"Burn, right."

Antoine pointed directly up at the DefCon4 offices above them. "I need to get Sam Applewhite off our backs. Permanently." He waggled his phone. "It's Sam Applewhite and that Doug character, right?"

"Doug's the boss, I think."

"Right. Then it's probably best to make sure neither of them can do us any harm."

He backed out of the shop, hoping he'd put the fear of God – or at least fear of the law – into Vance, and that the man would swiftly and silently wind down his black market operation.

56

On her first night back at Candlebroke Hall, Kiki woke in the early hours, thinking she'd heard a noise in her apartment. She couldn't rightly say what had spooked her – a bang? A scrape? – but she'd definitely heard something.

It was not like her to be afraid of bumps in the night. She'd lived alone since her dearly departed husband's death and not worried a jot about night-time attackers. She was not afraid of thieves and burglars. There'd been that time, back in the eighties, when she had been accosted by muggers in the streets of Paris while filming *Fall of the Eagles* with darling Christopher Lee. The pair of them had sent the muggers packing in no time, and laughed as they did so.

No, Kiki was not easily frightened, but she was frightened now. She got up from her creaking and mouldering bed and turned the light on. Her apartment, depressing by day, looked squalid and pathetic by night. The nurses at the hospital had said she must be looking forward to going home, laughing when she said she wished she could stay in hospital forever. They thought she'd been joking.

She was abruptly aware of how vulnerable she was. She turned over in her mind just how many people had accessed her rooms without her permission. Antoine had invited those gardeners to trample through with their muddy boots, for goodness sake!

She toured her apartment and made a list of vulnerabilities and possible fixes.

Door: too many people have access. Where are all the keys? Change locks. Needs peephole.

Windows: completely unsecured (intruders may gain access from roof or ladder). Need double glazing and locks

Roof hatch: unsecured against intruders on roof. Needs lock.

She felt better for writing them down.

Kiki enjoyed quality stationery. She loved the feel of a fountain pen as it flowed across cartridge paper. Her handwriting had been admired by many, but of course so few people wrote letters nowadays. A pity. She sometimes thought she might have been a writer if her career in acting hadn't taken off. The tawdry word 'bonkbuster' was beneath contempt, but she could definitely have written something racy, devoured by millions. She could have been a Jackie Collins or Judith Krantz if she had so desired.

By the yellow light of a lamp, Kiki sat at her dressing table and composed something entirely different. Initially hesitant and unsure, she wrote an account of what she and Antoine had been doing.

I, Lady Kiki Lettuces, and Mr Antoine de Winter, have removed and sold on hundreds of items from Candlebroke Hall...

It was, though she didn't acknowledge it at first, very much an 'In case of my death' letter, something to be left with a solicitor, or other trusted individual. If Antoine did succeed in killing her, as he no doubt intended, she needed to ensure he would not get to reap the financial benefit. She jotted several pages, adding what details and dates she could recall.

By the time the first pre-light of dawn was visible through her window, she had composed a considerable document which she folded and sealed in an envelope.

"Try wriggling out of that damning evidence, Antoine," she said.

The letter complete, she tucked it for safekeeping into the pocket of her brown leatherette jacket by the door, then regarded herself in the dressing table mirror. She studied the landscape of her face, a mixture of the fine bone structure which had given her a career, along with lines, wrinkles and now the wounds of her current campaign. She stared at the eyes most of all. Eyes which had seen travel, luxury and adoring fans, but now glared back at her like an angry old woman. Yes, it was a face that was prepared to take the necessary steps to rid her of the dangerous menace that was Antoine de Winter.

She phoned Phoebe. The woman picked up after several rings.

"Morning, Kiki," she yawned.

"Phoebe, it's Kiki."

"Yes, I know. I, er, said"

Why were young people so insufferable about technology? Everyone with a decent upbringing knew that you introduced yourself on a phone call.

"I need you to come and see me, I have some jobs that need doing."

"Sorry, Kiki. It's only – it's five in the morning! Why don't you pop down and see me when I get into my office? Come see me during office hours."

"Have you forgotten I was injured on the premises?" thundered Kiki. "I'm taking bed rest as advised by the doctor." That was a lie, but Phoebe wasn't to know. "I'm having some trouble though, because my apartment is not secure. You do realise that my current situation makes me extremely vulnerable?"

Phoebe sighed. *"I'll be over."*

"Right away."

"In a bit." Phoebe yawned again. *"In a bit, Kiki."*

57

Antoine breezed into Phoebe's office. It was a bright new day, he had successfully lodged his anonymous complaint about the Skegness DefCon4 staff and had slept off most of the aches and pains of his accident. It was time to go on the charm offensive with Phoebe, find out what was going on with this blasted inventory, and get it all shelved before any real damage could be done.

"Well, hello beautiful," he said.

She looked up at him. He couldn't read her expression. Normally the girl was dazzled and a little bashful when he made an entrance like that. But not today. She looked worried or fearful, he couldn't decide.

"I am detecting a lack of joy in this office. I will do whatever is needed to fix it. Tell me!" he declared. "A fancy coffee? A cupcake? Or something else sweet and chocolatey?"

"Sorry Antoine, I've a lot on my mind," said Phoebe. "And I've got to go see Kiki about some problem she allegedly has."

"Let me guess. Is Lady Kiki being an insufferable diva?"

"Haven't you spoken to her yourself?"

"Ah," he said with heavy regret. "My dear lady friend appears to be in one of her reclusive phases." And downright murderous too, he added mentally.

"You two had a falling out?" Phoebe shook her head. "I don't have time. The film company are sending location producers, or directors, or whatever it is in the next few days, and the gardeners haven't finished tidying the grounds to the agreed specification. I'd have thought having a film crew on site would be a positive thing, but it's just creating work. And —" She closed her eyes and massaged her temple. "This inventory! *Ich glaube ich spinne.*"

"Pardon?"

"It's driving me crazy."

"Oh, is there a problem?" asked Antoine innocently.

"There certainly is," said Phoebe. "Either Sam Applewhite has made some serious errors, or a great many things have been stolen from this house. I've been through everything and I don't think Sam's wrong." She gave a huge sigh. "This has happened on my watch, and I have no idea how. Just today I've found some things were missing from the armoury. I will have to resign, of course."

"Phoebe, darling girl, I can't bear to see you so distraught!" said Antoine, approaching her around the desk. He raised his arms for a hug, but she looked so alarmed he turned it into an exaggerated shrug at the last moment. "This place could not possibly operate without you, and don't you dare forget that."

"Thank you, Antoine. Now, I really must go and see what Kiki wants."

It would have been handy if Phoebe had simply left the door open, so Antoine could take a look at this inventory himself. But she ushered him out and locked the door behind her. Apparently, the cumulative stresses of recent events had brought out her security conscious side.

He watched her hurry towards the stairs, then he strolled out via the terrace to the tea rooms to collect his complimentary morning coffee.

The gardeners were working along the side hedges, lopping them back severely. Branches were being fed into the trailer-mounted woodchipper they'd been using all week. Thick branches went in and a spray of fine chips came out.

The noise might have been irritating, but it was therapeutic to watch. Large things went in. Inconsequential dust came out. If only Antoine could solve all his problems that way. His cashflow problems. That damned inventory. Kiki bloody Lettuces.

"Hmmm..."

Oh, how to engineer an accident in which the tottering and clearly accident prone Kiki took a tumble into a woodchipper? Such an interesting and delightful conundrum. He would think of it while enjoying his coffee.

58

There was knock at the apartment door. Kiki already had the sharpest knife from the kitchenette in her hand. She opened the door a crack.

"Morning, Kiki," said Phoebe. "I'm in a bit of a rush. Lots to do and—"

"Took your time coming to see me," said Kiki curtly and, knife folded flat against her wrist, hobbled to her armchair. She didn't need to hobble, but it was important to get a message across.

Phoebe's expression was less one of concern and more one of patient tolerance. "How can I help, Kiki?"

"Well, you could put the kettle on while you're here." Kiki didn't especially want a cup of tea, but it never hurt to remind the damned girl how primitive the arrangements were up here. "Don't forget you can't use the water out of the tap."

Phoebe bustled in the kitchen for a few minutes and

came out with two cups of tea. She'd given Kiki the wrong cup, but she wasn't to know.

"I have prepared a list for you, to take away and action appropriately," said Kiki, handing Phoebe the paper.

"List?"

"Of security measures. Protection."

Phoebe scanned the list, her face becoming more incredulous. "Oh my, Kiki! You know we can't stretch to all of these, don't you?"

"Am I to be murdered in my bed then? Do you want that on your conscience? Do National Heritage want the reputational damage?"

"Kiki, come on! Think of the rules we have to live by. You can't have double glazing on these windows, it will spoil the facade. Don't forget this is a grade one listed building. The film people will be here before we know it."

"What?"

"We're preparing the grounds now. The location something-or-other, Imogen someone is coming over in the next few days."

"So soon?" Kiki flew to her dressing table and stared at her ghastly reflection. "And that's another thing! How can I be expected to recuperate in this environment! The film people don't want to see me in this state, yet how can I relax?"

"I'm sure they won't mind."

"You're an expert now, I suppose? Made a lot of films, have you?"

Phoebe handed the list back to Kiki. "I'll get one of the handymen to see about changing the lock, and perhaps he can install a peephole as well. That's the best I can do right now, Kiki. You know I'm working with a lot of constraints – budgetary and otherwise."

Kiki clutched at her wrist as she made to go. Phoebe had the plump wrists of a farmer's wife. Kiki could have screamed at the woman's undeserved youth and doughy vitality.

"You can't leave me like this."

"I'll have someone come up with some food at lunchtime too," said Phoebe, extricating herself from Kiki's grip. "That will be nice, won't it?"

And with that, Phoebe had gone.

Kiki stared at the closed door. She stared at the two cups of tea and refused to drink either of them. She did not know how long she simply stood there, staring. Eventually, she decided to take her mind off her injuries by preparing for her film role.

She spent some time accessing the internet on her phone, researching the outfits and hairstyles that would be appropriate for Lady Marguerite Blakeney, wife of the Scarlet Pimpernel.

"Oh, and hats!" she exclaimed to no one at all.

Huge bonnets. Or perhaps something a little more modest and compact that could be worn at a slightly rakish angle.

Kiki went hunting through her collection of clothes. There was so little left of her magnificent wardrobe. A lesser person might be laid low in a fit of depression, but Kiki on a mission was made of sterner stuff. She pulled on a dress with a low-cut collar. Obviously it needed a push-up bra to create the eye-popping decolletage that would be part of the role. She had a number of diaphanous wraps, so she formed one of the lacier ones into a fetching collar.

She took another sheer wrap and slipped it around a paper plate. It was a reasonable substitute for a bonnet of the time, especially if she scrunched the wrap's tail ends up on top, as decoration. She created an updo with her hair, pinning her hat into place. She was already feeling very much Marguerite.

She swept around her apartment muttering "Oh, Sir Percy!" as she pictured the scenes she'd be playing. Who would be her leading man? She allowed her imagination to go wandering for a moment, but stopped when she realised several of her possible candidates were already dead.

She spent some time sitting in her boudoir, in front of her mirror. In her mind's eye it was one of the glorious bedrooms in the public part of the house, furnished in silks, with the latest fashions arrayed for her in a nearby dressing room. She sat at her mirror, dabbing powder on top of the Pan Stik covering her weeping scratches.

She thought about how she could mentally prepare the upcoming role. Her life as Marguerite was split between several personas. There was Marguerite St Just, the beautiful and witty actress, much-loved by the French. She was also the wife of Sir Percy Blakeney, who would ultimately prove to be the Scarlet Pimpernel, but who was initially the Georgian fop she married. She would need to practise the haughty smugness of believing herself his moral and intellectual superior. Kiki knew she could readily summon that sort of feeling: it very much reflected her day-to-day existence.

What would be challenging and exciting was the third incarnation of Marguerite, where she used all of her cleverness to become an eighteenth century action hero. When it came to anything more energetic than brief interludes of jogging Kiki knew she wasn't up to it, but that's what stunt doubles were for. This would be her opportunity to show what she could have done if she'd been selected for *Dempsey and Makepeace*.

"Eat your heart out, Glynnis!"

She stood up and struck a couple of poses, making sure that she could see herself in the mirror.

Nonchalant, yet deadly with a pistol.

Beguiling and innocent as she tricked the guards.

Giddy and wild as she escaped on the ship with her dashing husband (who was clearly aroused by her courage and resourcefulness).

She smiled at her reflection, pleased with her performance. This film production was going to be her moment to shine!

RUNESPLICER RAPPED on Ragnar's caravan door. "Is there anyone in?"

Ragnar was up on his feet at once. "Come in, honoured guest. Sit by my hearth and let me offer thee the hospitality of—"

"Yes, yes." Runesplicer waved the effusive pleasantries away. "I'm not filming at the moment."

"Oh. Right then," said Ragnar, letting the man inside. "And how's that going, then?"

"I came to tell you I've finished."

"Champion. Got everything you need, right?"

Runesplicer sighed and slid onto the banquette seating by the dining table.

"Mead?" suggested Ragnar, ill at ease with the man's downcast expression.

"I think I'd rather have a cup of tea," said Runesplicer with a weak smile.

As if by magic, Astrid appeared with a mug of tea and a packet of Jammie Dodger biscuits.

"I have taken hours of footage," said Runesplicer. "I have edited and packaged much of it, sharing it on a range of platforms. Instagram, Facebook, TikTok, Twitter."

The man could have been listing ice cream flavours for all the words meant to Ragnar. "Aye? And?"

"You've definitely built up something of a cult following."

"And that's a good thing?"

Runesplicer pulled a face. Again, it wasn't a particularly positive one.

"The video of Ogendus and Torsten jousting against one another on mobility scooters, while wearing horned helmets and carrying shields, has arguably gone viral. Hundreds of thousands of views."

"And that's a good thing, right?" Ragnar repeated, with gusto, hoping that emphasis would make it more true.

"You are aware that true Vikings never wore horned helmets? That's not the entire point, but I'm not sure it sent the right message..." He closed his eyes, sipped his tea and sighed once more. "There are positives and negatives to all of this."

"Right-o. Positives," said Ragnar firmly.

"There's been a lot of interest from the general public, and traffic to my website. And it looks like Odinson's Mead could be something of a hit."

"People want to order it?"

"They *are* ordering it. By the crate. If you're able to step up production we may have quite a profitable business model."

"Well, that's bloody wonderful. Well done, man."

"But," said Runesplicer heavily, "the social media campaign has not generated the groundswell of support we hoped to see from the Asatru and wider Pagan community."

"Eh?"

"Other Pagan and Heathen groups in the UK are not inclined to take up your cause as their own."

"They don't want to help us get our ship back?"

Runesplicer shook his head. "In fact, they've gone so far as to distance themselves from you and your family, claiming your cultural practices are a poor interpretation of the key teachings."

"But we did everything tha told us to."

"On top of which, my conversations with the EASS—"

The who?"

"Equality Advisory Support Service – the people who help decide if you've been discriminated against – they think you haven't got a case."

"But tha said we had!"

Runesplicer held up calming hands. "I've got one more tactic. Have you heard of *Street Legal Live*?"

"Is that another one of them social medias?"

"No, it's a television programme. They film in Leeds. It's a sort of legal advice slash quick justice format. Like *Antiques Roadshow* for potential court cases."

"I don't get it."

"I go on, I plead your case with one of their 'judges', and if they think we have a chance, they stump up some cash for us to take it to a real court."

"You think we'll win, like?"

"It's your last best chance of getting your ship back, my friend," said Runesplicer and took a Jammie Dodger from the pack.

59

Some days were difficult, and best aided by a huge chocolate brownie or sausage roll well before lunchtime. Cat's café, next door to the DefCon4 office was, despite the ever-present possibility of a tedious monologue on the subject of theatre, writing and the expressive arts in general, the best place to go for a quick boost of sugars and fats. Cat had already pounced on her prey for that morning: Vance the tattooist from the shop next door. His fried egg sandwich was being delivered with a side order of "Mainstream theatres won't stage my plays because I'm just too avantgarde."

Normally, Sam would leave Cat's poor victims to their ear-bending fate. This time she saw a chance to not only rescue a helpless soul, but follow up on a minor thread of her recent investigations.

"Ah, Cat. Could I have ... what is that? Some sort of pasty?"

"A bean and sausage lattice," said Cat. "If you'll give me a minute, Vance and I were just discussing—"

"Actually, I'm in a bit of a hurry and I needed to ask Vance something myself."

"You do?" said Cat.

"You do?" said Vance. The look of faint horror he'd been wearing hardly lifted. If anything, it deepened.

"I wondered if I could ask you a question."

Vance struggled to chew and swallow the eggy mass in his mouth. "Like what?"

"A professional question."

"You mean, official like?" The man seemed peculiarly edgy. The studs in his brows quivered and rippled.

"Er, yes. Tattoos. You're the man to talk to, right?"

"Oh, just tattoos? That's all? Sure. Fifteen years in the business, man and boy. Interested in a tattoo yourself, is it?" He was visibly calmer now.

Sam smiled. She had no tattoos herself. She had no particular aversion to them, but as they were an expression of personal individuality and it seemed as though everyone had one these days, it often struck her she might express more individuality by not having one. "I don't think I could find one I wanted," she said neutrally.

"Oh, there's a tattoo for everyone," said Vance. "Everyone gets the tattoo they want. Everyone gets the tattoo they deserve."

"Well, that's what I wanted to ask you about. Racist tattoos."

"What?"

"White supremacist tattoos. Fascist tattoos."

"Don't know what you're talking about."

"Exactly. I'm sure a professional such as yourself wouldn't willingly do racist tattoos. The detective constable I spoke to says you guys have some sort of code."

"The police?" said Vance.

"Unless he was mistaken. So I thought, since the vast majority of tattooists would refuse to provide that kind of service, where would one go to get such a tattoo done?"

"Are you getting a racist tattoo, Sam?" asked Cat, twirling the corners of the paper bag with the bean and sausage lattice as she approached.

"Me? No. I'm trying to find a tattooist. Torsten Odinson – don't know if you know him – he—"

There was a scrape of chair. As Sam turned back to Vance he was already halfway to the door.

"Interesting chat and all that," he said, "but I've got a booking." The man had left his fried egg sandwich half-eaten on the plate.

"Oh – okay," said Sam to a closing door.

"Vance did one for me," said Cat.

"A racist tattoo?"

"No, a little one. My spirit familiar." She was reaching for the scooped neckline of her top.

"A cat, by any chance?" said Sam.

"No," said Cat, a little huffily. "My name isn't— I'm not named after a cat." She pulled aside her top to reveal a two-inch long tattoo of an owl. "The owl. Silent. Sees all. Always wise."

Sam thought the image looked surprisingly similar to the logo of Sheffield Wednesday Football Club, but decided telling Cat that would not go down well. Instead, she nodded approvingly and paid for her hot pastry.

Back in the office, she sifted through the day's emails as she munched the crumbly pasty. Sam found a memo from head office that declared it had been blind copied to all staff in the Skegness office.

REMINDER OF DEFCON4 POLICY WITH REGARD TO ALCOHOL

THE STAFF HANDBOOK CLEARLY STATES THAT THE CONSUMPTION OF ALCOHOL DURING WORKING HOURS IS FORBIDDEN. AS ALWAYS, YOUR CONDUCT ON BEHALF OF THE COMPANY FORMS PART OF OUR BRANDING AND THERE IS A RISK OF REPUTATIONAL DAMAGE IF EMPLOYEES ARE FOUND TO BE INTOXICATED WHILE REPRESENTING THE COMPANY.

SAM SHRUGGED and deleted the email. Before she moved on, she saw a notification on the app that assigned tasks to her, so she opened it.

URGENT: DISCIPLINARY PROCESS.

YOU HAVE BEEN NAMED IN A COMPLAINT RECEIVED BY HEAD OFFICE. IT HAS BEEN SUGGESTED THAT YOU AND A COLLEAGUE HAVE BEEN DRUNK AND DISORDERLY AT WORK, AND HAVE BEEN HEARD

SHOUTING ABUSE AT PASSERS-BY FROM THE WINDOW OF YOUR OFFICE.

PLEASE REPORT TO A DISCIPLINARY HEARING WITH YOUR OFFICE MANAGER, TBA. ALL DETAILS OF THIS HEARING MUST BE UPLOADED TO YOUR RECORD IN ORDER TO CLOSE THIS MATTER.

SAM SAT BACK in her chair and considered what this might mean. A complaint levelled at her and Doug was clearly a false one. Someone was attempting to cause trouble in the Skegness office of DefCon4. They knew enough to make the complaint, but they didn't know enough to realise that Doug was a cactus. It might be interesting to speculate on who that might be, but her immediate problem was how to deal with the issue.

Not for the first time, Sam knew there was a correct course of action, and an expedient one. There was no doubt at all that the *correct* thing to do was to phone head office and explain there was no colleague called Doug. She also knew from previous attempts to clear things up about Tba that the message wasn't likely to land well. She had endured several circular conversations which boiled down to the notion that because he (Sam had bridled at the sexism why assume Tba was a 'he'?) was on the computer, then obviously he was a real person. Any logical attempts to point out that Tba was almost certainly not receiving pay were met with stern admonishments about 'data protection', and that it was 'not appropriate to speculate on colleagues' salary details'. Sam had failed in all attempts to report Tba as a non-person, so there was no reason to assume she would be any more successful with Doug.

Sam picked up the letter addressed to Tba. She scanned the code with her app to see what would happen.

PLEASE COMPLETE THE WORKFLOW RECORD SHOWN BELOW AND THEN PRESS COMMIT.

THE RECORD WAS Doug's and the gaps she was being asked to fill were for DISCIPLINARY PROCESSOR and DISCIPLINARY AUTHORISER. Sam stared at the blanks, trying to picture a scenario which didn't store up future trouble. She stared at it for so long that the screen went blank. She hurriedly pressed buttons to make it come back and stared, incredulous, as the record refreshed itself. Her name now appeared as both disciplinary processor and authoriser. She tried to edit the record, but the screen declared she had VIEW ONLY access. When she searched the history of what had just happened, it appeared the record had been updated two minutes ago by the USER SYSTEM.

Sam shrugged, deciding it was now out of her hands. Another notification appeared on her app. Sam had a feeling she knew what this was going to be. She opened it.

URGENT: DISCIPLINARY PROCESS.

. . .

YOUR COLLEAGUE DOUG HAS BEEN NAMED IN A COMPLAINT RECEIVED BY HEAD OFFICE. IT HAS BEEN SUGGESTED THAT DOUG AND A COLLEAGUE HAVE BEEN DRUNK AND DISORDERLY AT WORK, AND HAVE BEEN HEARD SHOUTING ABUSE AT PASSERS-BY FROM THE WINDOW OF YOUR OFFICE.

PLEASE CONDUCT A DISCIPLINARY HEARING WITH DOUG. ALL DETAILS OF THIS HEARING MUST BE UPLOADED TO DOUG'S RECORD IN ORDER TO CLOSE THIS MATTER.

SAM SIGHED and turned to Doug. "I hope you've got a slot in your calendar for later this week. We need to have a chat about your drink problem."

She brushed the accumulated pastry crumbs from her top and set to the genuine work of the day.

60

K iki had not left her apartment once since her return from hospital. It had been days now, although she wasn't sure how many. She was beginning to run out of food, so she needed to do something. Her bruising and scratches were still very visible though. She phoned Phoebe.

"I need you to get some food sent up to me," she said.

"Kiki? Surely you don't—"

"—Do I need to remind you about my injuries?"

"—Fine. Tell me what you want and I'll see what I can do, but you're going to want to come out soon, I'm sure. The film people will be here shortly. Surely you'll want to come out for that?"

"So soon?"

"A few of them are coming to sort out locations and set up facilities. The others will follow afterwards. Exciting isn't it?"

"Nothing I haven't seen before, obviously," said Kiki and hung up. Phoebe tended to forget who she was talking to.

Kiki was dressed as Marguerite again, in the interest of full immersion for her role. She went to the dressing table mirror to check on her outfit. She added more Pan Stik to her face and altered the angle of her paper plate hat.

"Oh, yes," she said to herself. She was very much the image of the Georgian lady. And how like the Scarlet Pimpernel's wife to be trapped at home, with slovenly servants slow to do her bidding, and a wicked interloper, Antoine, waiting to pounce on her and her one true love (in her mind she cast Marvin Applewhite in the role of lord to her lady) away from home.

She penned a letter to Marvin with the stationery set that was still out on the dresser. He had been so kind to her in the short time they'd known one another. She remained hopeful that at some future date the two of them might spend more time together.

MARVIN,

I SO MUCH ENJOYED SPENDING TIME WITH you recently. I find myself distracted with a few personal matters, but I wanted to send you some flirty kisses (see the bottom of this sheet!) with the promise that I should soon find myself with a little more time for socialising. Will you be ready for me?

MUCH AFFECTION

· · ·

Kiki.

SHE APPLIED lipstick and put her lips lightly to the paper. A bit of peachy Pan Stik foundation also came away on the envelope, but that didn't matter. Hopefully Marvin would enjoy her playful tone.

And now, with her letter to her lover written, what was Marguerite Blakeney, wife of the Scarlet Pimpernel to do?

She was torn. She obviously needed to make herself available for filming. But the moment she stepped out of her apartment she made herself a target for the murderous Antoine. She could not allow her guard to drop, or he would strike.

What would Marguerite do? She gave a mysterious smile, winking at her reflection. She whisked purposefully across the room. A woman of action was about to take matters into her own hands. What's more, she was oozing effortless glamour as she did so. If only the cameras were on her now.

She left her apartment and trotted daintily down the main stairs. A few members of the public watched her pass, their mouths hanging open. How often did they get to see something like this? They were getting their money's worth from Candlebroke Hall today! She swept through the grand rooms until she came to the armoury where she spent a few moments making her selection. She needed several options to cover all bases. She helped herself to a sword from the eighteenth century. She lifted it, finding it to be rather heavy. She searched for something lighter, and ended up taking both blades anyway. Then she searched for something she could use in her apartment. Guns were no good to her: she was unlikely to find any ammunition in the display.

She walked the length of the room until she spotted something different.

"Perfect!" she breathed. "A crossbow!"

As she stalked back to her apartments, weighed down with weaponry, she caught a flash of violet silk shirt in the hall. It was Antoine! The villain was here already, and she barely prepared! She stared at him. He stared back, equally surprised. There was no emotion on his face, just a kind of numb shock. It was the first time they had seen one another since his attempt to murder her and his subsequent, much-deserved, accident on the stairs. He didn't look half as dreadful as she felt. Clearly the angels of justice weren't working as hard as they should be.

He raised his hand in greeting. His moustache twitched in an evil grin.

Kiki ran for the stairs and did not stop until she was back in her apartment, a chair wedged under the door handle.

61

Antoine had been stunned to see Kiki in the corridors of Candlebroke Hall. It was her home, of course it was, but the sight of her rooted him to the spot. And what a sight she was! For some reason she had taken to wearing a fusty old dress with swishing skirts, and what looked like a paper plate strapped to her head with a length of gauzy cloth.

He had not seen her since the day she'd tried to kill him with that bookcase and nearly strangling herself with the clothes airer. A murder attempt paid back with karmic retribution. Although she looked in far finer condition than he did. Evidently karma wasn't as powerful as it used to be.

Numbly, automatically, he gave her a small wave and even smaller smile. Kiki's face became a mask of foul hatred and she scuttled off. She appeared to have swords, and possibly even an ancient crossbow, in her arms.

"Good God!" he whispered. The woman had descended into full-blown crazy old baggage mode.

If he was going to stay alive and keep his liberty, he needed to arrange a fatal accident for Kiki sooner rather than later. A small part of him argued he should simply walk away and steer clear of Candlebroke Hall. But he couldn't abandon his dearest Hugh, and he ached at the thought of walking away from the remaining treasures he might still sell on. No, an accident for Kiki was the only course of action.

He stepped out onto the terrace to see where the gardening boys were up to with their wood chipping. They had worked down one side of the huge gardens, cutting back and shredding the unruly border hedges, and now they were working on the hedges closest to the house itself.

"Oh, yes," said Antoine. This was fortuitous. The trailer combined the funnel-fed chipper, and a cage-like compartment that collected the chippings. It was a bulky contraption which one man working alone might just about be able to lug a short distance. Its height was a bit of problem. Antoine could see it would be improbable – nay, unbelievable – for someone to just accidentally fall into it. However, near the house, it would only take a bit of subtle angling to place it below the raised terrace. All a poor soul had to do was take a tumble and – wallop! Bzzz! – instant death.

"You look lost in thought," said Phoebe.

Antoine started in surprise. He was about to rebuke her for startling him when he saw her long mopey face. She might even have been crying as she sat on the stone bench.

There was a spiral bound notepad in her lap and a pencil in her hand, both from the National Heritage gift shop.

Antoine angled his head to look at what she'd written and then crossed out.

~~My position here is untenable~~
    ~~It's not appropriate for me to remain here any longer~~
    ~~I think it's best for everyone if I leave so that~~
    ~~I can't go on with the knowledge that I have failed National Heritage and its millions of supporters~~
    ~~Ich werde nicht um eine Extrawurst haben~~
    Goodbye!!!

THIS LAST WAS FOLLOWED by three exclamation marks, a sure sign that Phoebe, who used punctuation sparingly and appropriately, was currently a woman on the edge. She saw him looking at her words and shamefacedly placed a hand over them.

"Writing a resignation letter is harder than one imagines," she sniffed.

"It's come to that, has it?" he said, imbuing his words with a fake concerned tone.

"Thousands of pounds of antiques – millions, possibly – stolen on my watch and I didn't even notice."

"According to the word of one person, who I hear is a drunk and an incompetent."

"Sam? An alcoholic?"

"Rumours I've heard," he said, smiling inwardly at the fact they were rumours he'd started.

A glimmer of hope sparked in her eyes, but her misery quashed it. "No. No. I've been lax. Unprofessional."

He gave a slow, genial shrug, neither agreeing nor disagreeing. "I, for one, have been glad to have someone of your calibre around," he said, honestly.

His phone buzzed in his pocket. It was Vance. "Excuse me, Phoebe dear."

He moved away before putting the phone to his ear. He pulled it away again almost instantly as Vance squeaked in near hysteria.

Antoine tentatively put it back to his ear. "Stop. Stop it! Vance! Still your chattering mouth! Who has been snooping round? What did she ask you? And what on earth has – sorry? A racist tattoo? – got to do with anything?"

62

Sam looked solemnly across at Doug Junior. Doug stood at his desk, looking perky and bright as always. As a young powder puff cactus, he was good at looking perky and bright. Sam had changed his saucer for the occasion, swapping his usual, jauntily painted one for a more formal plain white. The moment called for formality.

"It's time for our coaching session, Doug," she said. "Now I hope you're prepared to listen. This is important."

She picked him up and placed him in front of her on the desk. "You don't mind if I type as we go?" She opened a document, added the date and a heading saying it was an agreed written record of the required coaching session regarding the allegations of Doug being drunk at work.

"Now Doug, it's right and proper that I ask whether everything's all right with your personal life? You know I have an open door policy, right? You can come to me with anything."

Doug was silent on the matter, but she knew there was a bond of trust between them.

"Want more water? Just ask. Want less water? Just ask. I don't always know what's going on in your world, so this would be a good time to mention anything that might be relevant."

She paused for a moment, in case Doug wanted to speak, but he maintained his cactusy silence.

"So Doug, we've had an allegation that you were drunk on work's time. Do you have any response to that?" Again she paused. "I've not known you to be a drinker. I mean, how old are you anyway? Are you even old enough to drink?"

Doug said nothing. It was a pretty one-sided conversation, but the little cactus was probably nervous, under the circumstances.

"I would say, given all I know about you, that it's highly unlikely you've been drinking on the job. So I'm going to record we have no knowledge of any such incident, and that you're well aware of both company policy and your obligations. Does that sound like a fair summary?" She typed as she spoke. "I should add that your demeanour throughout has been prickly. It seems reasonable, given this baseless accusation. Also it makes me smile, and I'm the only person who will ever read it. Thanks for your time, Doug."

The big job of the day done (well, it was the one with the highest priority rating on her app), Sam considered herself to have had a successful morning. There was a text from Delia asking her to drop in at the shop, and Sam felt sufficiently ahead of herself to go over there.

"Now, is this a chance to show off your latest tie-dyed

bloomers experiment or, by any chance, have you worked out where that stolen glirarium is?" she asked, approaching the counter.

"One, they weren't my bloomers," said Delia. "Two, if you come in with that kind of sass I'm not going to tell you what number three is."

"Sorry. I had to have a difficult conversation with my cactus about his drink problem."

"Er, okay. You can tell me about that later. Number three – the big news!" Delia gave a smug grin. "The gnomework I set has attracted a lot of attention."

"Gnomework?"

"Oh yes. If the maths had as much attention as the gnome puns, we might have reached the answer much sooner, but you know how people are?"

"I have gnome idea," said Sam deadpan.

Delia pointed at her expression. "See this? This is the face of someone who has now heard that joke six times this morning."

Sam laughed. "So what do you have?"

"Check this out." Delia presented a screen to Sam. "This was the homework site where I posted the problem. This contributor was *very* pleased with their efforts. They made a video of themselves whiteboarding the solution. Cup of tea while we watch?"

"Have you got any chocolate hobgnobs?" asked Sam.

"That doesn't even work as a pun, Sam."

"You try to think of a biscuit gnome joke."

"I really don't want to." Delia clicked play. The unseen narrator scribbled some frenzied maths notations on the whiteboard.

"*We have here some known factors, and some estimates that we're going to use. We have been told the windmill is twenty-one metres high, for example. We are using an estimated height of thirty centimetres for the gnome.*"

"I gave them that," said Delia proudly.

"How come?" Sam asked.

"I had one just like it in the shop. It just fitted in the gap between the shelves over there."

"You're such a gnome-it-all."

"Shush and listen!" Delia said.

"*We can estimate the distance to the gnome by assuming that the paving slabs shown in the picture are forty five centimetres wide. We have a cross-reference in several pictures that enables us to estimate the total number of paving slabs between point zero, where the original picture was taken, and the gnome.*"

"Why do we need to estimate the distance to the gnome?" Sam asked.

"It will all make sense in a minute," promised Delia.

It made sense in the way things did when doctors spoke knowledgeably about surgery on TV medical documentaries. Sam didn't entirely follow the thread, but she heard enough phrases like "*similar triangles*" and "*the tan of this angle gives us the unknown distance*" to believe the narrator was a competent mathematician. When the final answer emerged, she felt confident it was correct.

Delia watched the calculations being jotted down. "Heights of towers and distances all worked out. And we didn't even need a theodolite."

"A what?" said Sam.

"You know. A building angle measuring thing. I've got one here ... somewhere..."

By the time Delia had returned with a brass device that looked like a cross between a telescope and a dalek, Sam had double checked her maths.

"So these photos were taken at a distance of a hundred and seventy five metres from the windmill."

"Yes!" Delia grinned and then shrugged. "Give or take."

"You're a regular Sherlock Gnomes," Sam said.

"One more and I'm phoning your dad," said Delia sternly.

"I'm a grown woman. That's no threat."

"Yeah," said Delia. "But if he starts playing this gnome game it will run for weeks and weeks and weeks. Imagine that. Now, consider this your final warning."

Sam looked up the map for Burgh le Marsh on her phone. "Right. If I judge this correctly..."

Delia, tutting, was already going into a storage space under the glass-topped counter. She produced a much-folded and battered Ordnance Survey map of the area, a ball of string, and a pencil. In swift order, she tied the string to the pencil, measured the string against the map scale and a ruler and, with a thumb holding down the string, drew a handy circle on the map.

"Boom," she declared.

The circle covered most of Burgh le Marsh and some of the farmland on the far side of the A158.

"So our gnome and stolen goods are somewhere in that circle," said Sam, doubtfully.

"Better than that," said Delia. "If the calculations are

correct, they should be somewhere along this street here. Or this one."

Sam picked up the map. The treasure, not marked with an X but a curving line, was tantalisingly close. "Time to go on a drive and knock on some doors. Coming?"

Delia began to nod, then her expression faltered. "Bugger. I was going to say Hilde could mind the shop."

"But?"

"She's not here. She had to go home to watch something on TV. A court thing."

"A what?"

"I don't know. I can't come without shutting up shop."

Sam looked around the place. "Well, you are absolutely rushed off your feet."

Delia scowled at her theatrically. "That kind of attitude is no help to the businesswoman of today. However, I might consider closing early if, for example, you'd like to buy this delightful antique theodolite."

"Why would I want that?"

"As a commemorative souvenir of our moment of victory."

Sam rolled her eyes and reached for her purse.

63

Ragnar had permitted a wide-screen LED television to be erected in the mead hall. This was a first, and he made sure to frequently mention it would not become a regular fixture. It was here just so they could all watch Runesplicer take on the authorities, on the Saxon television programme, *Street Legal Live.*

Astrid passed around trays of snacks and drinks. There was a festive mood amongst the Odinsons.

"I still can't believe he's got it all the way to t'court!" said Ogendus, scratching himself as he settled down.

"It's not a proper court, uncle," said Freyella. "It's one they do for the telly. It's popular, though."

"Never 'eard of it," said Yngve.

"Because we don't watch telly," said Hilde.

By the time the judge had dealt with a pair of brothers chasing an unpaid loan, and a woman demanding the return of an expensive wedding present when the happy couple split up, there had been many drinks and snacks consumed, and many opinions shared loudly across the mead hall.

"This Saxon judge talks good sense," declared Sigurd. "Mebbe he'll order them to give us back our boat!"

"It doesn't work like that," said Freyella. "The judge only says if the person has a case to make. And, if they think they would win, they give them cash to fight the case."

"So it's like a quiz show?" said Ogendus.

"He's given that bloke ten grand," said Yngve. "Does that mean we could get ten grand?"

"Shhh," said Astrid. "It's Runesplicer's turn now."

"I wonder what I'd spend ten grand on."

"Shush, boy!"

They all watched in breathless admiration as Runesplicer made their case to the judge. Ragnar was mildly disappointed it wasn't being held in a proper court room, and the supposed judge wasn't wearing one of them silly wigs. But the setting looked serious and sort of authentic anyway.

"You want to bring a case against the Lincolnshire police for indirect discrimination?" said the judge, reading his notes.

"That's right. They have confiscated property that is in fact sacred to the Odinson Viking clan."

"We'll get to that. First of all I must ask: are you a member of this Odinson clan?"

Runesplicer hesitated. *"Yes. I am not a blood relative, but I believe they would consider me one of their own."*

"Very well," said the judge. *"Proceed."*

"Ooh, he's right judge-y, isn't he?" said young Erik.

"The police have confiscated the Viking longship that was

hand built by the Odinsons and is a central part of their way of life," said Runesplicer.

Every Odinson in the mead hall was on the edge of their seat.

"An actual longship? Can we see a picture?" asked the judge.

A picture appeared on screen and there were cheers from the Odinsons. There followed several minutes of cross examination, where it seemed to Ragnar that the judge was exploiting the sensational subject of the longship to make entertaining television. Eventually they got back on topic.

"So, it was confiscated because the wood was stolen?"

"Yes, although that does of course assume one takes a conventional view of what theft—"

"In English courts they very much take a conventional view of theft," said the judge, closing Runesplicer down. *"So, if you're not here to dispute the results of the DNA test carried out on the wood, we can move on. Are you going to dispute those results?"*

"No. No, I'm not."

There was a ripple of dissent around the mead hall.

"Why didn't he say yes?" asked Yngve, outraged.

"There's no point," said Freyella, "Facts is facts."

"So, the ship was confiscated because the wood was stolen," said the judge. *"We have established that much. So tell me about your claim that the Odinson clan, and by extension yourself, have been victims of indirect discrimination."*

"It is based upon the fact, sir, that this is central to the practice of their religion. By removing a core religious artifact, the police have caused them great suffering, which feels like religious persecution. I spent some time with them, documenting their way of life."

Footage was show on screen, highlights of the hours of video Runesplicer had recorded. Gunnolf chopping wood in the compound. Ragnar showing Runesplicer around his palatial caravan. Astrid coming out of the same caravan with trays of hot food and drinks. Torsten tinkering with a car engine. Evenings in the mead hall. In under just a minute of footage, almost every member of the massive family got an opportunity to point and declare, "It's me! It's me! Look! There I am!"

When the home movie ended, Ragnar had to shout at his kin to get them to shut up.

The judge on screen leaned forward, and steepled his fingers. *"Mr Bottley."*

"Who's Mr Bottley?" asked Sigurd.

"It's Runesplicer's real name," hissed someone. "Shh!"

"Mr Bottley," the judge repeated. "I am not fond of this modern predilection for claiming feelings as unassailable facts. It is a fallacy that works well for those in need of therapy. One has feelings that cannot be ascribed to anybody else, this is true. However, when they are paraded in my court, as a naked and frankly amateur attempt to create a verbal Trojan horse, I take a very dim view of it. For those in the audience who do not follow, Mr Bottley has attempted to insert the term 'religious persecution' into the proceedings by labelling it as a feeling. An inexperienced juror might be swayed by such shenanigans. However, judges of all levels would not. Neither you nor any of the other Odinson family have been subject to any religious persecution, and that term is therefore of no value, here or elsewhere. Do you understand me?"

"Yes," said Runesplicer deferential and contrite.

"Now, do you have any further evidence to support the notion of the longship being central to the religious beliefs of this family? In fact, do you have any serious evidence that the Odinsons have religious beliefs, other than a set of loutish preferences for drinking, robbing and 'sticking it to the man'?"

A silence fell upon the mead hall. There were glances between the Odinsons as they tried to remember who had said what (or perhaps more importantly, who had been filmed saying what).

"I ... I do not," said Runesplicer.

"Very well. In which case, I must declare that you have no case against the Lincolnshire police force. And I can confirm there has been no case of indirect discrimination against the Odinsons."

Runesplicer nodded meekly and departed.

"Does that mean I don't get the ten grand?" said Yngve.

"It means they don't reckon we have a chance," said Hilde.

Ragnar turned off the television. "That's it then. T'world says we're not Viking enough to count as proper Vikings."

"Only them bastards in Leeds," Torsten pointed out.

"Folks in Leeds is always stuck up bastards," added Ogendus.

"Only interested in drinking and robbing!" snorted Yngve. "That's slander. We should sue them."

Astrid was taking a tray of snacks for another turn around the room to see who was hungry. "Still," she said, "it was nice to see the ship on the television, wasn't it? Everyone knows we made it. They can't take that away from us."

"Aye," said Ragnar. "We should be proud of our achievements. Right. Hilde. Take the screen down."

There were disappointed groans from many, especially the children.

"I'm not having my mead hall turned into a bloody pub, with football on the big screen every night," said Ragnar. "Whose is it, anyway?"

Ogendus put his hand up. "I borrowed it."

"Borrowed it?"

"House on Gibraltar Road. Door was open. Looked like they had plenty of televisions anyway."

Ragnar stared down at the goblet in his own hand. "Drinking and robbing, eh?" he sighed.

VANCE PATTERSON WAS a man who did not cope well with anxiety and stress. He spent his adult life parading an attitude of inner peace and unflappable calm, but he was able to do that because his life contained little which could send him into a flap. The rent on his shop was low, the rent on his bedsit flat was ever lower, and doing tattoos for holidaymakers and undemanding locals covered all his bills, with enough spare for drinking money, an occasional ounce of weed, and a trip to Glasto or Download every year or so. Vance's world and dreams were small and kept themselves in balance well enough. He didn't need huge reserves of calm or peace to keep his spiritual ship afloat.

"Fuck," he whispered to his empty shop.

Now, the real world was coming at him. And not the regular bits of the real world like bills or children or demanding girlfriends. No, it was the forces of law and order, the bloody cops and the courts. Sam Applewhite had compiled the evidence and...

"Fuck," he repeated.

Karma should have seen him right. Vance had a very specific view of karma. He'd heard people talk as though it was the universe bestowing good fortune and luck on those who had done good deeds. Vance thought this was fine enough, but he took a more mechanical approach. Karma was like ripples in a pool. The more you thrashed and shoved, the bigger the waves became. Vance had always kept his head down, led a neat, private life and, in return, he expected the universe to leave him alone. He'd done nothing to no one, and expected the same treatment in return.

"Oh, fuck."

Antoine had told him to close down all the sales and burn the evidence because Sam had given a list of stolen items to the people who ran Candlebroke, and soon enough the police would be trying to track them down. Then Sam had accosted him in the café – acting all cool and innocent about it – and asked him about the tattoo. She didn't mention Torsten by name, but she didn't have to. The words 'racist tattoo' were enough. She might as well have given him a knowing wink while she said it.

"You're a fucking idiot, Vance," he said and nearly sobbed.

If only he'd checked the tattoo before he'd applied it to Torsten's arm. People came in all the time with pictures and decals and asked, "Can you do that for me?" What if it was badly spelt or horribly tacky? Everyone got the tattoo they deserved, didn't they? If Torsten had found some cool Viking runes on the internet, was it up to Vance to check what they meant? Who cared if it said "Swedish meatballs, one krona each"? Except it bloody hadn't, had it?

He paced his tattoo parlour, a whirl of horrid fears and with no way of excising them. The shop had become his prison cell and he had quickly realised that Vance Patterson was not cut out for prison life.

He had to do something about it.

When he'd phoned Antoine, the man had barely listened to him. Had told him to "Calm the hell down" before hanging up on him. That had not been useful. Calm was not going to achieve anything in this situation. As Antoine had said, they needed to get Sam Applewhite off their backs, permanently. Vance looked up at the ceiling. The offices of DefCon4 were directly above them. A mere foot of plaster and wooden beams separated Vance from his tormentor.

"Burn the evidence," he said.

It was just three words, but they offered immediate clarity and a path out of his nightmare. It made sense. If DefCon4 was no more, if the papers and the computers all went up in flames, there would be no list. Even if there was surviving evidence, the confusion and delay would buy them time.

A plan came to him. He went through to the workspace at the rear of the shop. He had everything he needed here. In the cupboard under the sink was an electric drill. Next to it was a five litre bottle of antiseptic solution he used on his tools, and two metres of clear plastic tubing.

What he had in mind was not only fool-proof, but ingenious.

64

Kiki hauled another cache of weaponry back through the house, making sure she maintained a slightly arrogant untouchable expression. The last thing she wanted was to be delayed by someone who wanted to know where the gift shop was. Creating her defences against the vile Antoine was of the utmost importance.

She heard an ungainly clomping sound on the stairs as she neared the top. It was a horribly familiar sound.

"Kiki," Phoebe called.

Kiki didn't look back. She swept towards her apartment, hoping Phoebe hadn't spotted what she carried in front of her skirts. She sped to the door, hurried through it, and flung her weapons into the bathroom, adding to the pile of swords, maces, crossbows and daggers already there. She pulled the door shut as Phoebe appeared in the apartment doorway.

"Kiki, whatever were you doing? I thought you said you were still ill?"

"I tried to go for a walk, but I didn't feel all that well, so I hurried back." She spat and pulled away a strand of gauze scarf that was stuck to her cheek and lips.

"Oh, yes. You do look awful."

"What?"

"No, I mean your—" Phoebe gestured at her face.

Kiki rushed to her dresser mirror in the bedroom. She put a hand to her cheek and it came away wet with pinkish fluid.

"I think the make up might have infected some of your scratches," Phoebe called after her.

Her face was throbbing slightly, but Kiki had assumed it was just the healing process. She returned to the main room and was surprised to find a tall young woman next to Phoebe.

Phoebe gestured to the elegant creature. "I wanted to introduce you to Imogen from Frightful Symmetry."

"Fearful Symmetry Productions," said the woman, giving a polite incline of her head.

"She's the – location director, is it? – for *The Scarlet Pimpernel*. Imogen, this is Lady Lettuces, or Kiki as her friends call her."

Kiki smiled weakly. "Delighted to meet you. Will you excuse us for one moment, please?"

She pulled Phoebe into the bedroom, which was no distance at all. "What were you thinking, letting the film people see me like this?" she hissed.

Phoebe looked confused. "Sorry, Kiki. I'm not sure it matters, though."

Kiki slammed a hand down on her dressing table. "Not sure it matters! Are you mad?" She pulled open drawers and burrowed through the contents, looking for something – anything! – to fix her face. "Powder. How much powder will it take to remove this shine?"

Phoebe peered at Kiki's face, shaking her head slightly. "It's not a job for powder Kiki. You'll only make it worse."

Kiki ignored her as she found what she was looking for: a tub of loose powder. This was vintage stuff, with a big fluffy puff to pat it on with. No time for that. She grabbed a scarf, draped it across her shoulders to protect her clothes, and tilted her head back. She tipped the powder directly onto her face, making sure it went all over.

"Kiki! Really!"

Kiki coughed and retched as powder went into her mouth and down her throat. She felt awful, but at least the violent retching shook the excess from her face. A quick glance in the mirror showed her face was now perfectly matt, with an even tone. She couldn't see a single wrinkle, which was a bonus. She dabbed on some lipstick and smiled at her reflection.

"Gorgeous," she croaked.

Phoebe started to say something, but Kiki swept past her back into the room. "Apologies Imogen, but Phoebe needed me for a moment. I'm in such constant demand!"

"So I see," said Imogen with a brittle smile.

"Please, tell me more about this production."

"It's a lavish treatment," she said. "Bringing a palette of

jewel tones to the period aesthetic. It's going to be utterly lush. The costume department have outdone themselves. Including the various ball scenes, there will be over seven thousand pieces."

"How delightful!" said Kiki with a clap of her hands. "What outfits will I be wearing, can you give me any clues?"

Imogen frowned in confusion. "Outfits?"

"For me?"

Imogen pulled a phone out of her pocket and tapped the screen. "Sorry, you'll have to forgive me. I don't know what's happening with the extras. I'll—"

"Extras?" Kiki gave a nervous laugh. "Perhaps you misheard my name. I am Kiki Lettuces."

"Uh, huh." Imogen was scrolling on her phone. "Yes – here we are. Do you know if you're in the *peasants at the guillotine* scene or the *villagers perform rural dances while the Pimpernel escapes* scene?"

Kiki shook her head impatiently. "Neither of those. I am Kiki Harris. I'm playing Marguerite."

"Um – no you're not."

"What?"

"There might be some background role that I—"

"You're just a location person! They've come here for me. Me! I'm Kiki Harris. When they were let down by – oh, what's her name? – I agreed to step in."

Imogen pulled a face. Kiki bristled as she thought she saw the shadow of a smirk. "The only thing we were let down by was Castle Howard, near York. Candlebroke will make an adequate stand in."

Kiki could feel herself reeling. If she had a heart attack or a stroke right there and then it would come as no surprise at all.

"Marguerite is to be played by Angel Dibly," Imogen was saying.

"Who the fuck?" whispered Kiki. Her eyebrows shot up, loosening a chunk of the encrusted shell covering her face. It slid from her forehead, over one eye and down her cheek, before slithering down her skirt and plopping onto her foot, where it exploded in a cloud of powder. All eyes were on Kiki's foot.

"Angel is absolutely the up and coming thing. Wonderful young actress."

"I feel certain that you are mistaken," Kiki managed to say.

Phoebe wordlessly pointed at Kiki's foot. Eventually she mouthed *Your face!*

Imogen seemed to be finding it all a bit too much. The corners of her mouth twitched, as if she was working hard not to laugh.

"No," Kiki said, her voice shaking, then rising with anger. "How dare you! How dare you come into my apartment, tell me you've given my part to someone else—!"

"It was never—"

"—And then openly mock me! What kind of a monster does that?"

More pieces of Kiki's face fell off, but she no longer cared. She shoved the two women out of her door, slammed it shut, then collapsed onto the floor behind it. Tears washed more powder down onto her outfit as she howled with impotent rage.

. . .

SAM APPLEWHITE WAS out of the office. Vance had seen her leave earlier. He'd even gone round and pressed the buzzer (with the ready pretext that he wondered if they'd accidentally got his post). The place was empty. He could act with impunity.

With the door to his own shop locked, and the metal roller shutters down, he stood on a step ladder and pushed aside one of the polystyrene tiles in his shop's suspended ceiling. He poked his head into the cavity and drilled through plywood floorboards and into the office space above. It was loud, but there was no one who would hear or notice.

Brushing aside the ancient dust that had fallen on his face, he looked up and saw a small circle of daylight. "Perfect."

Now to pump in the accelerant. His five litre bottle of tool prep solution was alcohol-based and, the label clearly stated, highly flammable. The stout container had a heavy-duty pump nozzle. With a bit of huffing and effort, he was able to force one end of the plastic tubing over it. The tube was, however, only two metres long. Vance had to balance the bottle on the ladder's top step so he could feed the tube's other end through the hole and into the DefCon4 office.

He could just picture it poking out through the carpet, like a translucent worm emerging from its hole. The image provoked an unexpected giggle. He thought it might have been the alcohol fumes, but he hadn't even started pumping yet.

He set to it. A dozen powerful pumps and he could see

the solution rising up through the tube and into the space above. He pumped vigorously. The worm would be vomiting glob after glob of liquid across the carpet. The harder he pumped, the further it would fly. Some of it trickled back down the outside of the pipe, but it was a fraction of the stuff going in.

This was arson, he thought. He'd never committed arson before. He was all in favour of breaking some laws, but this was a big one. It was inspired, though. A fire started from within DefCon4's offices, but where no one had even gone inside. Oh, this would baffle any police or fire investigators. They would have to put it down to natural causes, or whatever.

He was very pleased with himself. Antoine would have to accept Vance had done the right thing.

After emptying half the bottle he decided it was enough. He withdrew the tube, putting it and the bottle safely to one side, by the counter. He looked for his lighter, remembering to wash his hands before using it. It would be foolish in the extreme to set fire to his own hands. He returned to the ladder.

There were droplets intermittently falling through the hole. That was just gravity. Unavoidable. Some splashed on the steps of the ladder, but he just made sure to step over them and kept his hands clean.

He held the lighter up and struck a flame.

What he needed to do was time it so when he put the flame to the hole there wasn't a droplet coming through. He watched their rhythm. *Drip. Drip. Drip.* He prepared to strike. *Drip. Drip.* He pushed the lighter up to the edge of the hole and it caught instantly. He snatched back his hand. There was rush of wind through the hole. From below, all he could see was an orange circle of flame.

A drop of burning liquid fell, a mote of fire. Vance ducked aside. It passed his face but smeared on the arm of his long-sleeved T-shirt. There was line of fire and a split second later, pain.

Vance hissed and tried to slap it out with the palm of his hand. He almost succeeded.

Another burning droplet fell onto the top level of the step ladder.

"Shit!"

He stepped down hurriedly. His foot slipped on a wet step. He half-fell, half-jumped to the floor and fell on his back. Another burning blob hit the floor, finding a puddle of spilled solution. It burst into yellow flame.

And Vance's arm was on fire.

Patting his arm violently, he ran for the back room where there would be a fire extinguisher, a towel, something...

His foot slipped again. He avoided sitting in the burning liquid on the floor but collided with the counter, kicking over the half-full bottle of alcoholic cleaner.

"No, no, *no.*"

The stuff splashed on his legs, spreading towards the flaming puddle. Frantic, Vance tried to scoop the spreading gloop back towards the counter, away from the fire. He worked his arms like a drowning man, and was sort of winning. The sound of a roaring blaze above and the crackle of the smaller fire before him grew. He knew – though he wouldn't consciously admit it – the fire was already truly out of control.

He needed to get out. He leapt forward toward the front door, unlocked the catch and opened it. The shutters were still down. The remote control was on his keyring, on the counter. He ran back.

He didn't see how his legs set fire. He avoided the burning pool and the hole in the ceiling, but somehow, something, somewhere got him.

There was light, more light than sound. As the flames shot up his legs, before the pain hit, he realised he had never considered just how *fucking fast* fire was.

65

T here had been an initial disagreement over tactics. Knocking on front doors and asking "Are you the one who stole antiques from Candlebroke Hall?" was never going to be a winning approach. Whereas "Do you have a gnome and a view of the windmill in your back garden?" just sounded downright crazy.

After a few weird and awkward conversations which yielded limited results, Sam and Delia evolved a number of different, alternating approaches. Sam's "Hi, I'm taking photographs for Lincolnshire Gnome of the Year Award" swiftly determined which people had gnomes and which did not. Gnome owners, it transpired, were often willing to show off their lawn ornaments including various pottery meerkats, rabbits, wishing wells and the humorous signs which dotted their gardens. Delia's "Hi, I'm doing door-to-door purchases of antiques and knick-knacks" drew deeper conversations, and she ended up buying a credenza, a pottery shire horse, and blown glass animals from various houses on Chapman Avenue and Hall Lane. In fact, one of the glass animals she bought from No. 19, she sold on at No. 25 for a ten pound profit (No. 25 said No. 19 loved glass animals, and it would make a nice birthday present). By the time they reached, No. 47, Delia was doing business of some sort at each and every bungalow they came to.

"This is clearly a new business model for me," she said. "I've made thirty quid in under an hour."

"Some of that is mine," said Sam.

"Eh?"

"Didn't you notice you sold my antique theodolite?" She got out of the car and walked up the next drive. "Besides, I think this is the one."

"How do you know?"

Sam had the photos from the auction website on her phone. "The shape of the tree in the last house's back garden. The view of windmill. We're pretty near to the garden that matches this image."

Delia rang the bell. Sam loitered near the rear corner of the house, where the gap between house and garage made a narrow gateway into the rear garden. As Delia launched into her antiques spiel, which had started out as a convenient lie and was now genuine business patter, Sam looked at the lawn she could see from this angle. Yes. This was very promising.

"Sam, would you listen to this?" said Delia loudly. Sam turned. "Terry here says it's her grandson who deals with the antiques and that. *All* the antiques and that."

Sam smiled at the short, older woman. She must have

been in her eighties, but there was a sharp and wily look in her eye that Sam liked. Sam reckoned she would have been wilful and fun-loving in her youth. "Is that so? Does he have a lot of antiques?"

"He just uses my garage for storage. And why are you two giving each other those looks, like you're up to something and aren't willing to share the joke?"

"Sorry," said Delia, composing herself. "We're both just really excited about antiques."

The woman, Terry, gave them a sceptical look. "Anyways, they're not mine, they're Vance's. So I can't sell you nothing."

"Vance," said Sam. "Not many of them about."

"Could we take a look anyway?" said Delia. "There might be something we're willing to make an offer on."

Another sceptical look: Terry weighing them up as potential thieves. Then she tutted and disappeared to fetch the garage door keys. "Here. Don't mess anything about. He won't like it if you've moved stuff."

Terry stood on her doorstep in her slippers while Sam took the garage key and unlocked the up-and-over door. It stuck a little as it went up, and she had to give it a shove to stop it sliding back down. Then she saw the hoard.

There was a moment of reverential awe.

"That's a set of Georgian glasses," said Delia.

"I think that's a Regency tortoiseshell sewing box," said Sam.

"And those could be the Jasperware urns you were looking for."

"And that—" Sam pointed at a brown pot nested in

bubble wrap in a cardboard box. "That is a glirarium. This is it!"

"Anything of interest?" said Terry.

"Oh, you wouldn't believe," said Sam. "Excuse me. I'm just going to make a phone call."

She stepped into the back garden and phoned Skegness police station. And it was the very same back garden. There was the gnome. There was the view of the white-sailed nineteenth century windmill. The only thing different from the picture were rows of paving slabs stacked alongside the garage wall. Sam touched the edge of the outermost slab with her fingertips.

"A nice man helped me move them," said Terry, standing at an open patio door.

"Ah," said Sam in acknowledgement as DC Camara picked up.

"Hello, Miss Applewhite."

"Or you can be normal and call me Sam."

"Is this a business call?"

"Very much so." She moved further away from the old woman. "I have just found dozens of items missing from Candlebroke Hall in a garage in Burgh le Marsh."

"Stolen items, you're saying?"

She nodded. "Yep. Stolen items. And I think it's Vance who runs the tattoo shop near my office who's behind it. Not sure how or why yet."

"Hang on a minute."

He disappeared from the line. Sam turned. Terry was still watching her.

"Is your grandson Vance the one who has that tattoo shop?" asked Sam.

"Maybe," said Terry with the slow hesitation of someone realising someone else was in a lot of trouble.

"Still there?" said Camara.

"Still here. Yes. Vance the tattooist."

"Right. I'm sending a car over to secure the scene. Touch nothing. I'll be there in fifteen. And then I need to talk to you."

"Oh?"

He made an unhappy humming sound. *"Just don't touch anything."* He hung up.

66

Once she'd picked herself up off the floor where she'd been sobbing and shrieking, Kiki tore off her Marguerite outfit, paper plate hat and all, and stuffed it into a binbag. She might take it to the cleaners. Or then again, maybe she wouldn't. She could not afford to look back. If the world of film had rejected her, then so be it.

"The bitches!"

She had showered in her dismal little shower, scraped all of the caked make-up from her stinging face, and dressed in a black sweater and pair of tan jodhpurs so she could turn her attention to practical matters.

She pulled her hair back into a tight bun and stared at her aged and unlovely face in the mirror. "Forgotten, am I? Imogen Know-Nothing location manager!"

Let nobody say that Kiki Lettuces would weep in a corner, licking her wounds. Oh no! She would ensure her survival was taken care of, then rebound in some way she hadn't yet imagined.

It would be a few days yet before the directors and producers – the real film people! – appeared on set. She would remind them of who Kiki Lettuces really was. Her agent, Barcroft, would soon put them right – or he would be fired. Fired! But for now she needed to attend to matters in hand. And that meant protecting herself against Antoine.

She wasn't sure if he was behind her rejection from the film. It would be difficult for him to achieve, but he was wily, and he knew how to hurt her. He was a master manipulator. He would destroy her dream, then finish her off when she was feeling battered and low. She would need to prepare for that. She would concentrate first on some defences within her apartment, and when she'd done enough to feel properly secure, she would go on the offensive. The two swords might be useful. She put one by her front door and one in her kitchen. Phoebe still hadn't sorted out a peephole, and they were a poor second choice. But it would show any intruders she meant business. She did a couple of practice lunges to get the feel of it.

She fetched the crossbow she had taken from the display in the Winter Hall and laid it out on her table. It was very old. She hadn't absorbed the details from the plaque which accompanied the display, and she definitely wasn't going back to check as that might draw attention to its disappearance. What did matter was that she did not have any of the arrows (or were they called bolts?) which went in it. She looked around her apartment, gathering things that might make passable crossbow bolts and put them in a pile for experimentation. Chopsticks, steak knives and knitting needles were all worth a try.

Yes. Kiki Lettuces, ever-resourceful, was not going to put up with other people's crap anymore.

THE UNIFORMED OFFICERS quickly sealed off the crime scene in Burgh le Marsh. It was amazing how, after weeks of Sam pointing out that goods were missing from Candlebroke Hall, the boys in blue positively leapt into action when the evidence was shoved right under their noses. There were at least four officers on the scene, much to the alarm of the confused and probably innocent Terry. Out came the POLICE LINE – DO NOT CROSS TAPE. Delia had to get pretty forceful with them about not including her car and the antiques it contained.

"No, those are mine. They're from my shop. That. I bought that from number thirty-three just now. Go and ask her."

"The fact that we searched her shop after the initial burglary by Hilde Odinson is going to make her presence here seem like an unbelievable coincidence," DC Camara said to Sam as he led her to his car. "I don't like coincidences."

"We're only here because she worked out where the stolen goods were," said Sam.

"And how did she manage that?"

"Well, it's hard to explain, but it involved a gnome and a windmill and trigonometry."

"That had better not be her testimony when this goes to court."

She got into his luxurious car. A man who was all limbs needed a big car, she guessed. He pulled away smoothly and followed the bungalow-lined residential road round to the main road. He turned towards Skegness.

"I've sent officers to go and detain Vance Patterson. Before we get there, you're going to explain what's going on."

And Sam attempted to do so, from the inventory, to the items found on the internet auction sites (which had now vanished), through to the business with the photograph and the windmill, and some GCSE level maths that was ever so slightly beyond her.

"Vance Patterson is selling top end antiques, including ancient Roman pottery on eBay?" said Camara. "That's moronic. It's a surprise he wasn't caught earlier."

"Well … yes," said Sam, giving him a very meaningful look.

Camara looked momentarily sheepish. "I could point out the modern police force is under enormous pressures and we have to decide where and how we use our very limited resources."

"Is that so?"

"I would also point out I might have been disinclined to take your theories seriously because you seemed to have a bee in your bonnet about proving Hilde Odinson's innocence."

"And now that I have?"

His dark eyebrows crinkled in a frown. "No. I don't believe you have."

"It's Vance who's behind this."

"Vance is a master criminal now, is he?" Camara scoffed. "I think I've met him in passing. The man hasn't got the skillset for burglary – and I'm talking about burglary here, a career which attracts the crappiest human specimens around. If we can tie the goods to Vance, the simplest working hypothesis will be that Hilde was stealing the items to order and Vance was selling them on."

"I've already told you, the timings of the burglar alarms and the distances Hilde would have had to cover would make it impossible to—"

He held up a finger to stop her. She was about to give him an earful for the patronisingly rude gesture, then saw what had grabbed his attention. The traffic going into Skegness on Lincoln Road was at a standstill. Ahead, on the far side of the roundabout, behind a parade of shops, a black plume of smoke was spooling into the cold spring sky.

"That's where Vance's shop is," said Camara.

A fire engine, sirens blazing, came down the centre line of the road. Camara pulled out behind it and followed it round the corner. The *Who Do You Ink You Are?* tattoo shop was ablaze. The front window and door were just a melted hole in front of the pavement. A fire crew already on scene were dousing it with hoses.

The office door to DefCon4 was smashed in and fire fighters moved in and out.

Sam stated the obvious. "My office is on fire."

Camara stopped at the edge of the scene. Firefighters and a policeman were already coming towards the car. Camara stepped out to talk to them. Sam got out, if only to see the conflagration more clearly.

Cat from the café stood among the ring of on-lookers who had been evacuated from the shops and the nearby maisonette flats. She had a soot-streaked face and tears in her eyes. She was also taking selfies, so giving off mixed signals.

Smoke filled the DefCon4 windows. Her office. She hated the place. It was cold in winter and airless in summer. The décor and furnishings were dismal and old. It was a lonely and isolating work environment. She hated it. And yet it pulled at her insides to see it under threat.

"The fire started in the shop, they reckon," said Camara, coming back to her. "A witness claims they heard screaming."

"Vance?"

Camara glanced at the on-going blaze. "I think it will be a long time before we know that. You okay?"

Sam nodded, then thought about the question. She nodded again. "I'm alive. No one else hurt?"

"Apart from possibly Vance?"

She thought some more. "Doug."

"Doug?"

She shook her head and herself. "Sorry. Cactus. Unimportant in the scheme of things. Apparently had a drink problem but I dismissed that as—" She was babbling.

"I said I don't like coincidences," he said.

She looked at the burning shop and unwillingly imagined Vance in there, a body turning to charcoal. "You think this was deliberate?"

Lucas Camara had an angular, chiselled face, like an

Easter Island head with the edges softened by time. His pensive looks were very pensive.

"I swear it's not Hilde," said Sam. "There's something crooked at Candlebroke itself."

"You have mentioned."

"And if you think this is a coincidence, maybe consider that I've recently turned in my full report on what was missing to the National Heritage woman."

That brought a nod from him. "Get in."

"Candlebroke hall?" she asked.

"Of course."

67

Kiki knew if she was to use the fearsome crossbow to defend herself from Antoine then she needed to practise using it. And if she was going to practise using the crossbow, then she would need to go outside. She headed for the ornamental gardens to the south side of the house, where the hedge would obscure what she was doing.

Once in the gardens she tipped the water out of a birdbath so she could use it as a table. She arrayed her makeshift bolts next to the crossbow, deciding that a chopstick would be a good thing to start with. It was sturdy, but not terribly spiky. The mechanism of the crossbow was straightforward. A groove ran down the middle, which was where she would put the chopstick. The trigger was actually a metal paddle on the underside. There was a square metal bracket at the front, but she couldn't work out what that was for. Some sort of medieval sighting mechanism? Then there was a stringy part that she would pull back and catch behind the hooky part which the trigger operated. She wasn't sure if the string was made from leather, but it looked old, and had something wrapped around it which crackled and flaked when it flexed. She grabbed the string and tried to pull it back over the hook. After a few seconds she realised it was going nowhere near the hook. Had the string shrunk? Or did it take a lot more force than she was able to apply?

She lifted the crossbow and stared at it, wondering how she could apply more leverage. If she propped it upright against the birdbath and put a foot on the string, she would be able to put all of her weight onto it. That might work. She rested it on the piece that was shaped to go against a person's shoulder. Then she held the top end, braced against the birdbath, and stepped onto the string. It was getting there! Bits of leather shredded away as it stretched further than it had in years, but it was nearly in place. She bounced lightly on her foot, to get a little more stretch and felt it hook in place. She stepped carefully off and lifted the crossbow onto the birdbath.

She heard an engine start up nearby. The gardeners were hacking back the hedges again, ready for the blasted film company. She'd left a strongly worded voicemail message for Barcroft Leaning before coming outside, demanding that she had a bloody speaking role in this *Scarlet Pimpernel* film, or they could find another bloody stately home to use as their location. She'd been in James sodding Bond! She'd worked with dear Michael Caine, Doug McClure and Christopher fucking Lee. Weren't these millennial morons aware of the star quality she brought to the production?

Even though the sound of the gardening machinery was a reminder of how rudely she'd been snubbed, it was useful to realise the noise would drown out anything she might do. Although, she did need to be certain she wouldn't shoot one of them by mistake. She needed to check who was on the other side of the hedge. She left the crossbow and peered round the end.

It was Antoine, out on the terrace. The big woodchipper thing the gardeners had been using was wheeled round so its funnel mouth was facing the terrace. Antoine was looking at it, pacing and gesturing.

"Bastard," she whispered. There was no question he had murder in mind. She could see with utter clarity how he planned to put her in this machine. How ridiculous! How cartoonishly foolish! But it was certainly big enough.

So, Antoine de Winter was going to try to arrange an unfortunate accident for her, eh? Maybe she should arrange an unfortunate accident for him! A crossbow bolt in the back of the head!

"Oh, officer, I was only practising how to use it. I'm a big fan of historical re-enactment. I didn't realise it would go off like that!"

What else was she to do? She could creep back to the house and make a run for it – but where to? To Marvin Applewhite? She was sure he would put her up for a few days in his bungalow. But then what? Kiki would be alone and penniless, with no pension, no savings, and an evil stage magician and fraudulent psychic squatting in her palatial mansion.

"No. That will not do."

"Kiki! Yoo hoo! Kiki, is that you?" Phoebe was approaching across the lawns, notebook in hand. "It's good to see you out."

Kiki instinctively put the readied crossbow down behind the birdbath, hoping Phoebe wouldn't see it. The annoying girl would only tell her not to play with the exhibits.

"What do you want, Phoebe?" she said.

Phoebe began to raise her notepad, then stared at the collection of substitute crossbow bolts on the birdbath. "Goodness me, what are you doing with these things?"

Kiki lifted the knitting needle closest to her and looked at it as if she had never seen it before. "I was thinking of taking up knitting. I was going to come and ask you which of these things were knitting needles."

"Oh, you are funny! Surely even you know the difference between chopsticks and knitting needles!"

"*Even* me?"

"Do you want me to sort you out with some yarn and get you started?"

"That would be nice." Kiki couldn't think of anything worse.

"Well it's nice to see you out and about. I think your skin might need some attention. It still looks a bit inflamed."

Phoebe raised a hand to Kiki's face, but Kiki slapped it away.

"I'll put some ointment on it," she said stiffly. "Is that everything?"

"Well, no." Phoebe's child-like face took on a clumsily solemn expression. "I needed to tell you there are going to be some changes. In the light of recent irregularities—" She held up her notepad. "I think I've got the wording right, and while I expect there to be a thorough audit when I've gone I —" She stopped, looking down. She'd seen the crossbow. "Kiki, what are you up to?"

"What?" said Kiki innocently, pretending to study a knitting needle.

Phoebe stepped round the birdbath and picked up the cocked but boltless crossbow. "This should be in the house! What have you been doing?" She looked at the makeshift bolts anew. "This is not acceptable." She stuffed her notepad in her fleece pocket and cradled the crossbow in both arms. "This is sixteenth or seventeenth century, Kiki. Possibly used by Ingram Lettuces himself to hunt local game. It's not a toy."

She began to stalk back across the lawn to the steps by the summer drawing room. For a moment, she paused and turned. "Sometimes you are quite impossible, Kiki. No National Heritage employee should have to deal with this. You've probably damaged it." Crossbow held in one arm, she poked the string mechanism. "If it had been loaded too—"

There was a sharp snapping sound. Kiki saw a tiny flock of shapes spin away into the hedge.

"Oh fuck," she breathed.

On top of the crossbow, Phoebe's hand was a bloody, ragged mess. She studied it as if it was some curious thing she had just found. The crossbow string had part-severed, part-mashed her fingers into nothing, but her brain hadn't quite caught up with what was going on.

"Oh, fucking God," said Kiki. "We'll get you some help."

Phoebe looked at Kiki, then looked again at her hand, apparently seeing it properly for the first time. She screamed.

"What the eff!" She turned and ran. "No! No! What the eff!"

Kiki ran after her. What else could she do? Phoebe ran down the back of the house, along the terrace. There was a phone and a first aid kit in the tea rooms, perhaps she was making for there. Phoebe's legs visibly wobbled with shock as she ran. And there was Antoine on the terrace.

He turned at the sound of Phoebe's approach, automatically holding out his hands to catch her. Like a wicket keeper ready for a wild ball. Did Phoebe flinch at the thought of running into him? Kiki couldn't tell, but Phoebe swerved, her wobbling legs going from under her. Antoine turned, perhaps trying to grab her, but doing nothing more than ushering her round as she pitched off the edge of the terrace.

Kiki saw her go. Then the noises stopped. Not just the sound of Phoebe screaming, but also the sound of the woodchipper. Antoine stared at the shredder, dumbstruck. It had stalled: hardly surprising as Phoebe had fallen into it head first. Half a torso and two legs stuck out of the funnel, stiff, jutting like a clothes store mannequin. Bloody pulp dripped gloopily into the chippings cage at the back. Flecks of bobbly fleece and shredded notepaper hung momentarily in the air, a tiny settling snow flurry.

"What did you do?" whispered Kiki.

Antoine looked at her, blood spattered across his chest and face. "What did *you* do?" he whispered back.

68

On the A158 out to Candlebroke, Sam saw an ambulance with blue lights flashing some distance ahead of them.

"You know when you suddenly get a bad feeling about something?" said Camara, nodding at the ambulance.

"Coincidence?" said Sam.

The ambulance slowed at the Candlebroke roundabout and turned down the track towards the stately home.

"Hell and damnation," Camara seethed.

"It could be unrelated," said Sam. "An old dear ate one too many cream teas and exploded, or something."

Even as she said it, Sam felt an unusual fatalism. The antiques trail had led to Vance Patterson, and he had apparently died in a fire before they reached him. And now, as they followed the trail back to Candlebroke, there was an ambulance on the scene.

"And there's a police car," she said, spotting the squad car on the gravel drive in front of the house.

Over to the left, by the public entrance to the house grounds, a loose line of fleece-wearing National Heritage volunteers were herding people out towards the main car park. Camara squeezed his car past and parked up as the paramedics hurried away from the ambulance with their gear.

KIKI'S MIND WAS WHIRLING. The sight of Phoebe's pulped remains made her feel something more than queasy. She had crossed the fields of nausea, into some wild landscape of revulsion and insanity. However, she decided to utilise that feeling. It was a standard acting technique – Stanislavsky or Strasberg, or one of them. She gained precious time for gathering her thoughts by having the paramedics treat her for shock. She was now sitting in the café, draped with a silver blanket and sipping a cup of tea. Antoine's voice boomed nearby. He was talking to the policeman, Camara.

"That poor, damaged girl. If only she'd reached out to someone. Terrible way to go! Can't believe she would do a thing like that."

Kiki stared into her tea, afraid she would give herself away if she glanced over. She had hidden the crossbow. Even while she was having some kind of meltdown, yelling at Antoine and howling with rage and revulsion, a part of her brain had spotted the antique weapon on the floor and knew it would raise questions. She had pushed it underneath some shrubbery a couple of dozen yards down the wildlife path, thinking she might be able to remove it later. That left the chopsticks and knitting needles on the birdbath, but she could explain those away.

"She did say earlier she might have to resign from her position here," said Antoine carefully. "She seemed very upset."

Kiki surreptitiously glanced at Camara. He had his notepad and phone in front of him and was looking down. She saw Antoine trying to see what the detective was looking at, but Camara sat diagonally across from him and did not offer any further insights.

Kiki sipped her tea and dared to hope that she and Antoine might not be implicated. Of course, Antoine had been the one with the murderous woodchipper, so it was clearly more his fault than anybody's. But her mind was in no doubt: if his back was against the wall, he would take her down with him.

"She was aware that a number of antiques had gone missing from the house," said Camara.

"Goodness gracious!" said Antoine. "Surely Phoebe wasn't responsible for stealing antiques from her employer?"

Kiki wondered if Camara could see Antoine's transparent attempts to plant ideas. It was the same technique she'd seen him use as a psychic entertainer. He was such a hack.

Camara was nodding along as he consulted his notes.

Kiki saw an opportunity to help cement the idea in place. She stood up shakily and walked over. "This is simply dreadful. To think she would often come and ask me about some of the pieces in the house. Are you saying that all along she was doing it so she could sell them off to the highest bidder?"

"I'm not sure we should leap to any conclusions—" began Camara, but Kiki was already groaning dramatically, leaning heavily on the back of a chair. Use your emotions, she told herself. Use the energy.

"I feel terrible. Does this mean I have aided and abetted a criminal?" She opened her eyes as wide as she could, but the still healing injuries on her face were no doubt spoiling her attempt to portray a dewy-faced innocent.

Camara started to answer, but bit down on whatever his reply was going to be. "We need to investigate further. Please continue to make yourselves available."

SAM STOOD by Camara's car as fresh police vehicles arrived. The paramedics left an hour after they'd arrived. They were empty handed, which Sam took to be a good sign or an astonishingly bad one. Bored and curious, she strolled round the side of the house, following the general traffic of police officers. only to be halted by a uniformed officer she didn't recognise. With the scene at Burgh le Marsh, the fire in the town centre and now this, the police must be pulling in officers from Boston and Lincoln.

"Can't come this way," he said, simply.

Sam glimpsed a line of police tape, and a white tent set up over one end of the terrace. Figures in white scene of crime outfits milled around. Looked like 'astonishingly bad' was a fair assessment.

Sam went back to the car, checked in with Delia, who

had managed to protect her boot full of knickknacks from being seized by the police, then phoned her dad. She didn't tell him the details. She had no details to share and suspected he would simply worry. Instead, she focussed on small talk. He told her about the Spanish tortilla and patatas bravas he was making for dinner. The mundanity of domestic chores was a comfort.

It was only then it occurred to her she ought to tell her employers about the fire. She almost balked at the idea. Labyrinthine automated phone systems were bad enough at the best of times, but attempting to report something as catastrophic as an office fire was a deeply unpleasant challenge. It took her forty minutes to get someone – anyone! – to record that the Skegness DefCon4 office had burned down, rather than being rebuffed and told to report it through the appropriate management systems.

Camara eventually returned to the front of the house. "You're still here," he said, apparently surprised.

"You brought me here," she replied.

"I did. Yes."

"And?" said Sam, jerking her head towards the scene on the opposite side of the house.

"Phoebe Chiddingfold. She, er…"

"What happened to her?"

"An accident with a woodchipper."

"One of those big…?" Sam made a sort of funnel shape with her hands.

Camara nodded.

"An accident accident?" Sam asked.

"Investigations are ongoing." Camara hesitated for a

moment, then took out his phone. He swiped to a photo and showed it to Sam. It was a scrap of paper, torn on all sides, seemingly laid on or stuck to an orange metal surface.

There were words, ...*can't go on with the knowledge that I have failed National H*—, written by hand and crossed out.

Sam couldn't help but notice the dark red smear on the metal at the bottom of the picture.

"Did Phoebe ever strike you as ... troubled?" asked Camara.

Sam thought on it. "Troubled as in out of her depth? Yes. Troubled mentally? I don't think that kind of thing was in her lexicon. She was more of a 'Toodle pip, let's all go to the gymkhana' type. She was worried about the inventory, though." She looked at Camara and tried to read his expression. "You think she killed herself?"

"Investigations are ongoing."

"And she was the one stealing the antiques?"

Camara didn't respond. Out of the people working at Candlebroke Hall, Phoebe had not registered as a possible suspect. The woman had seemed too naïve, too enthused by history for history's sake.

"I'm going to be here a while," Camara said. "I could get an officer to drive you home..."

"I can phone Delia," said Sam and added, "Do you like Spanish food?"

"Why?"

"My dad's cooking tonight."

He laughed, almost silently, entirely humourlessly. "I'm going to be here a *long* time. And there might be a lengthy conversation with an inspector or even a superintendent in my near future."

"But will you eventually be eating food today?"

"Undoubtedly."

"Okay," she said. "You have my number." She turned and walked towards the long driveway leading back to the main road and phoned Delia.

69

Throughout the day, Hilde noticed that a good many of her relatives were acting strangely. Clandestine whisperings and little gatherings made her pause as she walked towards her workshop. Something was going on. She followed Hermod and Gunnolf, who were carrying a flipchart stand towards the mead hall. She hung back slightly at the entrance and saw Ragnar standing with a marker pen, eagerly awaiting the flipchart.

"Champion. Let's get some of these ideas down." He held the pen up. "So far, we've got *steal a helicopter with a big harness*. That's a good 'un."

"Drones!"

"Robots!"

"Huskies!"

The ideas were coming thick and fast from the rest of the group.

Hilde realised Astrid was standing beside her with a covered tray.

"Mormor, are they planning to steal back the ship?" Hilde asked.

Astrid frowned. "Your Farfar said he was just having a chat with some of the lads. They planning something stupid?"

"It's not so much they're planning something stupid, but planning to do it in a stupid way."

"Then it's a good job you and I are here," said Astrid. "Sounds as though they might need some oversight from a more ... practical person."

Astrid interrupted the meeting with the irresistible lure of freshly baked scones. While everyone was distracted, Hilde sidled up to Ragnar. "You need my help."

"Aye," he nodded. "Tha's got a good grasp on these things. We wanted to keep you out of trouble though, what with them thievin' charges hangin' over you an' all."

"Who built the ship, Farfar?" Hilde demanded, taking the pen off him.

Ragnar made a grumbling noise of acknowledgement and stepped away. "Hilde will help put finishing touches on our plan," he announced to the room.

Hilde pointed at the flipchart. "Who here knows how to fly a helicopter?" She scanned the blank faces of the audience.

A voice piped up from the doorway. It was Freyella. "Perhaps they are still in the brainstorming phase? Getting ideas down without judgement."

Hilde shook her head. "A stupid idea is a stupid idea,

Freyella. I'm just going to pop a couple of others on here so we can think about them. For starters, I'm going to add that we do exactly the same as we did last time, when it worked."

There was a grumbling sound from the audience.

"It'll bring back bad memories," said Ragnar. "Why not try summat new?"

"Most people would like to try something new in a way that didn't put them in jail," said Hilde. "Do we have any more ideas?"

Freyella sat down next to Ragnar. "We should do a risk analysis. It might be that the most sensible course of action is simply to build a new ship. It's something we have proven we can do."

"Blooming nonsense!" Ragnar yelled. "Saxons took our ship, and they'll blooming well give it back!"

Astrid had given out all of her scones so she sat down next to Ragnar and put a placatory hand on his arm. "Don't shout at Freyella. She's trying to help."

Hilde looked around the room at the expressions of disappointment. She realised why the meeting had been held secretly, in an effort to avoid reasonable suggestions such as risk assessments and repeating their successful efforts with the low loader. There was a craving for adventure and mischief running through the Odinsons, like lettering in a stick of Skegness rock. Ragnar was the worst of them, of course, but Hilde could see it in all of their eyes.

"Right, I have an idea," she declared. She turned over onto a fresh page and drew a vertical line straight down the middle. "Here on the left, we will list ideas for stealing and transporting the ship. We will grade each idea by its likelihood of success. On the right we will list some ideas for creating a distraction so the ship-stealing crew can carry on their business undetected."

Her unspoken hint was that she masterminded the stealing part, while the rest indulged themselves in whatever reckless nonsense they fancied in the name of creating a distraction.

Ragnar gave a slow nod. "Aye, I reckon that'll work."

"You'll definitely need a distraction," said Freyella. "I heard there's a film crew coming on site at Candlebroke Hall. Loads of people will be around."

"A film crew eh?" said Ragnar. "Problem or opportunity? Let's think on that, eh?"

70

Kiki had applied a face mask in an attempt to counter the ravages her skin had suffered in recent days. Phoebe's shocking accident had caused such emotional upset Kiki felt sure it had slowed the healing process. But there was little that couldn't be fixed with Turkish clay, enriched with algae, so she slathered it on generously and lay down to relax her expression. The smell of it took her right back to her heyday. She used this stuff all the time. She had been known for her radiant complexion, so took great care of her skin. It was important to allow the facial muscles to settle into a mellow position as the mud tightened everything up. She'd always had the idea she might fix a scowl into place if she wasn't careful.

The police had taken Phoebe's body away, mostly in bags. Things at Candlebroke had returned to something like normal in the day and night which followed. Many of the volunteers had not turned up to work because of the shock.

The house was in organisational disarray, and the police said they would have further questions, but all that aside, Candlebroke was finding some sort of new normality.

Kiki's mind strayed to the Scarlet Pimpernel production which was, she assumed, still going ahead. Perhaps she would take them up on their offer to work as an extra. It would be good to be part of something, even if she wasn't the leading lady. Once her face was on screen again, they would realise she still had that indefinable something; that star quality. She resolved to cultivate them in every way she could.

The mask tightened on her skin as the mud dried out. In the past it had always felt like a wholesome, restorative kind of discomfort, this time it was accompanied by sharp pains from the scratches and marks on her face. As though the wounds were being pulled further open. She would power through it.

"Beauty knows no pain," she growled. Then she remembered her rule about a benign and relaxed expression. She tried to remember what a relaxed face felt like, but her features would only form into something like Munch's *The Scream*. She could stand it no longer. She went to the bathroom and splashed warm water onto her face. As she rinsed the mask off, the muddy water swirled into the sink, red with blood. That was discouraging. She splashed cold water onto the clean skin and patted her face with a soft dry towel. A glance in the mirror told her the mask had not helped. The tiny scratches and cuts were newly livid and bleeding. Specks of Turkish clay were embedded in each wound, making her look as though she had tattooed herself in the style of a cracked eggshell. She could not heal like that! What if those dark lines were etched onto her face forever? She used a fingernail to try and dig out the mud remnants. It was very painful, and not all that successful.

There was a knock on her door. She dabbed her face on a towel now smeared with quite a bit of blood and went to answer.

"Who is it?" she called. She experienced a moment of anger that Phoebe still hadn't installed her spyhole, then remembered.

"It's Antoine."

She paused, wondering what he wanted, and how safe it would be to answer the door.

"Don't worry, Kiki. I want to make sure our, ah, thinking is aligned with regard to Phoebe's passing."

She opened the door a crack and peered out.

He held up his hands, palms up. It was body language intended to convey he meant no harm, but Kiki knew not to be fooled by Antoine's mastery of persuasion. Still, what else could she do but talk to him? They shared a highly incriminating secret. They would need to be sure they gave the same story to anyone who asked.

"Come inside."

Antoine stood watching Kiki as she put the kettle on. "Your face looks a little ... uncomfortable. Should you perhaps—?"

"My face is not what we need to be talking about right now!" she snapped.

"No. Of course not. Phoebe is perhaps the topic *du jour*."

Kiki raised her eyebrows. It was meant to speak volumes

about the real unspoken topic of conversation: namely them both preparing deadly traps for the other. Unfortunately it pulled her face into further agony and she cried out with the pain of it.

"Are you sure you're all r—?"

"Phoebe then!" She clamped her lips together to ensure that her range of expressions was limited.

Antoine breathed a long sigh. "It rather appears we may have fallen on our feet. If the police continue to run with the idea that she killed herself in remorse at stealing antiques, it lets us off the hook for theft and murder."

"Manslaughter."

"Whatever. It is very fortunate. We must do everything in our power to help keep it as the only credible idea."

Kiki nodded. "We need to stay close to that policeman, monitor his investigation."

"Yes we do," agreed Antoine. "Look out for anything that undermines us and nip it in the bud."

It was good to be co-conspirators again, rather than trying to kill each other. Kiki smiled at Antoine, or rather she started to smile, then the pain made her grunt. "Let's take care of all the events in the house. We want them to go without a hitch. Also we will need access to Phoebe's records."

"That is a good idea. We can monitor the investigation, as well as minimising the ripples in the pond caused by Phoebe's demise."

As Kiki showed Antoine to the door she found herself wondering about ripples in the pond. When she died, she wanted there to be ripples, goddammit! Not swept under the carpet as an inconvenience. She was different to Phoebe, though. Phoebe had been such a practical girl, she would surely have wanted it this way.

THE FILM CREW began to arrive in dribs and drabs over the following days.

Antoine watched the first lorries trundle down the driveway and, as they neared, stepped out to meet them. A tall young thing in wellies got out of the lead range rover and walked over to Antoine.

"You with the house?" she said.

"Only tangentially," said Antoine. "More of an enthusiastic observer."

The tall young thing made a peeved noise and looked at her tablet. "I'm the location director. Is Phoebe Chiddingfold around?"

"No longer with us," said Antoine, "but I can point you in the right direction."

The location director brought up something on her tablet screen. It was a plan of Candelbroke, with side and rear gardens dominated by multi-coloured boxes.

"We know where to go, assuming the areas have been cleared as agreed," she said. "We've got—" she looked along the line of vehicles "—power and drainage. Toilets. Prefabs. Washrooms. Kitchens. Always good to get the basics down."

"Let's take a look, my dear," said Antoine, gesturing to the side of the house.

"No one told me about Phoebe," said the location manager as they walked.

"It was quite sudden," said Antoine.

"Left under a cloud?" Her tone had shifted from peeved to slightly concerned.

Left *in* a cloud, more like, he thought. A fine red mist. He was tempted to say, "She simply went to pieces", but such a clever pun might look suspicious if the woman found out what had actually happened.

"People come and people go," he waxed emptily. "But good old Candlebroke remains."

Ten minutes later he left her and the crew to set up trailers and tents, and returned to the house. Kiki was watching from the Summer Room. She had recovered some of her poise in the intervening days. Phoebe's death had created a perverse peace between the two of them. Kiki's attempt to murder him with a bookcase, and her propensity thereafter to carry a crossbow had not been forgotten, but like enemy sailors sharing a life raft, they now clung together for mutual survival. Kiki glared from her position behind the French windows. The lines of her injuries were like red bootlaces glued to the wrinkles in her face.

"You have a face like a wet weekend in Clacton, *ma cherie*," said Antoine stepping through.

"That's her," said Kiki.

"Hm?"

She tapped the glass irritably. "Imogen something. The location director. Said some very rude things to me when I was at a low ebb."

Antoine thought the woman had been nothing but professional, but he knew the benefit of maintaining social bonds in adversity. "Perhaps let me deal with her."

"Oh, I can deal with her," Kiki seethed.

"I can perhaps be more tactful."

"Are you saying I lack tact?"

"We each have our strengths, and I am going to rely on yours. We have a house to run, fears to allay, and a unified front to present."

"She's still a bitch."

"Remember, we're not making waves," he said.

71

L ucas Camara met Sam outside the offices of DefCon4. The door was boarded up, as were two of the upstairs windows. The third window was grey with smoke stains. The *Who Do You Ink You Are?* tattoo parlour below was similarly boarded up.

"I'd show you around," said Sam, "but I'm not allowed back in until the structure has been secured."

"Must be disheartening," said Camara.

"It was a crappy office," said Sam. "Convincing head office to release funds to redecorate will be a major task."

"Positively Herculean, I'm sure."

"Want to come see the convalescing survivor?"

"Huh?"

She took him into Cat's Café. The place had been forced to close for a couple of days while it was confirmed the fire had not caused any structural problems. Sam ordered coffees and directed Camara to the table in the window. She rotated the saucer in the window where Doug Junior stood. He was discoloured on one side, where the heat of the fire had dried his flesh, but Sam thought (or at least hoped) he would pull through.

"Have you met Doug before, Lucas?"

"I don't believe I have."

"Best colleague I've ever had."

"Ouch. Doesn't say much about the rest."

Cat brought the coffees over and, after the minimum of pleasantries, began to monologue about the one woman show, *The Terrible Persistence of Fire*, she was currently 'workshopping and experientially developing'.

"Not now, Cat," said Sam, and the woman retreated. Sam grinned sheepishly. "I'm playing the 'still shocked and emotionally raw' card. Gives me licence to be blunt."

"Some people don't need a licence. Does she talk about herself all the time?"

"She doesn't mean to be a bore."

"Well, she makes decent coffee," said Camara, sipping. "So: facts. The body is Vance Patterson. There were dental records, luckily. Also, there were the remains of his studs." Camara ran a long finger over his eyebrow. "It's him and, yes, he started the fire."

"Jeez," said Sam softly.

"We doubt it was suicide. It appears the fire started in the ceiling cavity above his shop, below your office. He was trying to set fire to your office from within his shop."

"But that's ... stupid?"

"Yes, I believe you've met people before. So, I need to ask—"

"What he might have against me? Nothing. I assumed he got wind of my investigations into Candlebroke."

"Investigations?" said Camara archly.

"The inventory. The counting of the silver and the art. He knew somehow. Maybe someone told him." She didn't want to say Phoebe's name. She still found it hard to comprehend. She frowned.

"Yes?" said Camara.

"He was weird."

"Weird how? Weird, like everyday people are weird? Specifically weird?"

Sam tried to recall the exact scene. "I was in here, chatting to him. I asked him about racist tattoos and who might do them?"

"Because of what I told you about Torsten?"

"Right. And he couldn't get out of here fast enough. It was like—" A thought occurred to her, a belated one. As it dropped into place, she laughed softly.

"Like he had done it," she and Camara said together.

They looked at each other, each juggling the thought. Then Sam realised they were just looking at each other, hands clasped on their cups, staring across the table. She coughed and looked away.

"Racist tattoos tend not to lead to arson," said Camara.

"True." Yet there was something there. A line from Candlebroke Hall, to Hilde Odinson's antics, to Torsten, to the racist tattoo, to Vance, and back to Candlebroke Hall via Phoebe.

"I need to see that inventory," said Camara. "If Phoebe's

death is declared a suicide then the fraud squad boys will want to investigate."

"Do people commit suicide by woodchipper?"

Camara straightened in his seat. "I could do that thing where I tell you I've seen things in this line of work that you wouldn't believe. Try to sound all macho and mysterious. But I'd probably come across as a bit of a twat."

"Uh-huh," said Sam.

Camara shrugged. With his gawky frame, he looked like a vulture flexing its folded wings. "Suicide by woodchipper is entirely feasible."

"Nice line of work you're in," she said.

He touched the base of Doug's saucer and rotated the cactus a quarter turn. "Least no one tried to burn my office down."

72

Kiki counted the National Heritage volunteers present for the day. There were enough to man the ticket booth and the tea room, but few to act as attendants and guides within the house. The visitors would have to manage without being told which baronet had redecorated this room, or which tribespeople the Lettuces had stolen that particular artefact from.

Kiki checked the wall planner in Phoebe's office for the events of the day. There were two workshops booked in. One was *Leaf Printing Fun* and the other *Herbal Wellbeing For Beginners*. Kiki looked around the office for anything that might show more detail. There were some folders on a shelf labelled SIGN-UP FORMS FOR WORKSHOPS. She leafed through and found the folders contained the consent forms for activities. The course details were printed at the top of each form, and both workshops were happening in a couple of hours' time. They were taking place in the kitchen and scullery rooms, and would not encroach on the filmmaking. A visit to the kitchen garden would be fine, as it was surrounded by walls and nowhere near the film set.

"Uh-oh." Kiki was about to snap shut the folder when she saw the leaf printing course was meant to be run by Phoebe herself. How had she missed this? She looked at the other course and saw someone named Nigel Bottley was due to run it. There was a phone number next to Nigel's name. She rang it, hoping Nigel worked for some sort of agency that could provide a leaf printing expert.

"Hello, Enchanted Glade. How can I help you?"

"Can I speak to Mr Bottley?" Kiki asked.

"Speaking."

"Ah. I'm from Candlebroke Hall. You're running a herbal workshop here?"

"Yes, that's right. Two p.m."

"I have, erm, a bit of a scheduling problem. Do you have anyone who could run a leaf printing workshop?"

Nigel gave a gentle chuckle. *"Sorry, that's not my area of expertise."*

"What? How hard can it be to print with leaves? Just send someone!"

"There is nobody but me. I run workshops on the afternoons when my shop's shut."

"Well, what am I supposed to do about the leaf printing?" said Kiki.

"Can't you do it? You said yourself it can't be that hard."

Kiki ended the call and huffed with frustration. Well, that was bloody useless. She'd have to deal with the leaf workshop when she came to it. It was like Bottley said. It couldn't be that difficult.

"Lady Lettuces!" The first assistant director from the film set was coming towards her down the corridor.

Having appointed herself official liaison with the film people, Kiki had quickly learned that the first assistant director, a woman called Saffron with a ready smile and a loud voice, was the person who made things run smoothly on set. Unlike the impertinent location manager, the first AD was a delightful professional.

"Just wanted to check in with you before tomorrow's first day of filming," said Saffron.

'Check in'? The woman was both courteous and refreshingly modern. Back in Kiki's heyday, everyone behind the camera was a man. From the cinematographer down to the runners. Even most of the hair and make-up team were delightful gay old boys. Kiki wasn't a hundred percent sure how she felt about all these women on the production side of things. She was all for equality for women – of course she was – yet somehow she felt that women in the more practical roles took the shine away from the women in front of the camera. Scullery maids and princesses did not belong side by side. Saffron was a delight nonetheless.

"And how can I help you, dear?" said Kiki.

Saffron rattled through various items, and Kiki was happy to make notes of random details tossed her way. She was surprised at the emphasis on food, given the film people had brought their own catering, along with vehicles and trailers that looked as though an entire village had been set up in the grounds.

She checked her list for outstanding tasks.

- *Café to have area roped-off from public for informal discussions and relaxing*
- *Assume uptick in café sales will be approx: daily snacks and sandwiches for 75 (ensure vegan + gluten free options)*
- *Get extra help in café to make food deliveries to set*
- *Mention filming to visitors, but advise they are not to enter the gardens or any rooms as per the displayed schedule*
- *Watching garden scenes from the terrace is recommended for visitors*
- *Need to keep a check-in/check-out log of any furniture or smalls moved out of the house for the production*

"THAT'S ALL SIMPLY MARVELLOUS," said Kiki.

"No, we should be thanking you," said Saffron. "Don't think we don't know who you are. *Humanoids of the Deep* was on Netflix the other night, and I have to say your performance is one of the things that still stands up to critical scrutiny."

Kiki laughed because it was charming and true.

"And I've had a word with the director," said Saffron. "We'd be delighted if we could have you as part of a scene tomorrow."

"Crowd scene?" said Kiki, not wishing to get her hopes up.

"An, er, intimate crowd scene. The principal actors will be on location for the garden party scene and we'd like you in the mix, as it were."

"Oh, right," said Kiki brightly, not wanting to sound too grateful for this morsel of a role. "Me? In shot."

Saffron looked at her face and Kiki could almost feel her eyes tracing the lines of her injuries. But it was a fleeting thing.

"You. In shot. A treat for the discerning viewer. An Easter egg for the connoisseur."

Such a small thing was enough to put a spring in Kiki's step. It was with positively wild abandon that she decided there and then to run the leaf workshop by herself.

She found some paints and paper in the store room near to the scullery. She laid out the workshop space in the old stable block with classroom table clusters and put sheets of paper at every seat. It was almost time for her group to arrive. She opened up the folder to check the attendance list again. Twenty names! She fervently hoped there were some no-shows.

Her attendees started to trickle into the room just as she discovered a folder containing leaf prints done by a previous class. She pulled out a couple of examples and blu-tacked them onto the wall at the front.

"Welcome, welcome everybody!" she trilled as they took seats. It appeared to be a fairly even split of grandchildren and grandparents – the easily bored and the eager to please.

"Today we will be printing with leaves. I hope you're all looking forward to it as much as I am!"

"Can you stamp my Passport to Fun?" asked a woman.

"Your what?"

"It's the loyalty programme. When I get ten acorn stamps in my passport I can have a free workshop."

Several of the others held up their passports. It seemed popular.

"I see. I will find the stamp while you're all doing your work. Thank you for reminding me. Now, are you all prepared to walk the grounds and gather some leaves?"

There was much enthusiastic nodding, and Kiki felt oddly pleased with herself. With a bit of luck, half of the time would be spent on a gentle ramble in the gardens and then they could all come and daub paint around until home time.

They all trouped out into the garden. Kiki realised they were hot on the heels of the other group, those seeking herbal wellbeing. She hoped the best printing leaves were not also useful for the herbalists, or there might be trouble.

The leader, who was presumably Nigel Bottley, spoke loudly to his group. "Over here, we have that staple of the kitchen garden, the wonderful rosemary. We might use an infusion of its leaves as a hair rinse."

Kiki noticed several of her own students were watching him with interest. She couldn't allow them to get distracted. She made sure to project her voice as she addressed them. "Over here we have leaves that will make a very interesting print. I like to think they are a good example of a typical leaf shape." She trailed a hand through the shrubbery, waving everyone over.

"Don't we want something with a stronger vein structure?" asked a young woman from the back.

"Very good, you're all learning fast. Follow this young lady and find me some good veiny leaves."

Back in the stable workshop with bags full of leaves, Kiki tried to inject some of Phoebe's trademark nonsensical twittering as she instructed her class. "Very good, you all have a nice pile of leaves. You will see the paints on the desk in front of you, so I urge you to get creative and just have fun. Remember, there is no right or wrong way to do this. It's about learning through doing and immersing yourselves. We can all learn to be mindful, a pastime like this will really help."

Kiki was satisfied with her Phoebe performance. If there were award ceremonies for such things, she would be looking forward to the plaudits.

She walked around the class, checking on progress and making encouraging noises. There were a great many paint-covered leaves strewn around the place, a testament to the industry of her students. Some of them had created pages and pages of leafy splodges while others had taken great care with each placement of a leafy splodge. Kiki found herself on the cusp of passing judgement several times, but remembered she was supposed to be channelling Phoebe and just made appreciative and encouraging sounds instead.

"Goodness me, it's almost time for you all to leave!" she declared. "I do hope you'll be taking your masterpieces home with you, so your loved ones can admire them." She remembered the cross-selling and upselling that Phoebe was so keen on. "Don't forget you can get a discount in the café if you've been on one of our workshops. You will want to sample our award-winning pastries."

One of them had to spoil her mood by reminding her about the stupid acorn stamp. She offered to sign the square in lieu of a stamp, but she could tell they did not like this departure from protocol.

They took most of the paper with them, so the tidying mostly consisted of gathering painted leaves. They were biodegradable so she simply scooped them up and threw them out into the garden.

73

The big day had arrived.

Ragnar had invited everyone for a breakfast send-off in the mead hall. It would serve a dual purpose. Firstly, he could make sure everyone was well-fed for the upcoming rigours of the day. Secondly, he could make a rousing speech that might just help concentrate their minds.

He looked around with pride. A hearty breakfast made for happy Vikings. He grunted at the thought. It was a good line. He might add that to his book.

He raised both hands to indicate he intended to speak. "Let's mark the start of this day with a breakfast feast. Mebbe we can end it with a feast of celebration to mark the return of our ship."

There was a roar of approval.

"Our goal is clear," continued Ragnar. "The ship must be brought home. In case tha has questions during the day, there's a chain of command. Even lawless heathens need discipline for summat like this – so pay attention! The team removing the ship will take their lead from Hilde. The team in charge of creating a distraction will take their lead from Torsten. Understood? We have a runner here for urgent messages between the two teams." He laid a hand on Freyella's shoulder. She beamed round at the room.

Astrid, who had been slicing bread on Ragnar's other side, frowned at this. "Freyella is a bit young to be involved in such things."

"The girl's right nippy on her toes," said Ragnar. "Besides, she was keen to be a part of it. She'll be safe enough. Everyone here has a role to play in today's effort. Trucks, look outs, the distraction team. Bees. Where's Bjorn?"

Uncle Bjorn, beekeeper and producer of the finest mead-making honey, was ushered forward. The bearded chap was nearly two decades younger than Ragnar, but carried himself like an old man. Maybe a quiet life among the hives had brought on a sedentary slowness.

Bjorn held up three small boxes, each suspended on a leather thong. "I've popped the three queens into these boxes and loaded their hives onto the truck. I need at least two volunteers to wear bee beards."

Ragnar smiled at the reaction from the rest of his family. He knew Bjorn had something up his sleeve, but they had only vaguely discussed the distraction bees might cause. Bjorn was taking it to another level.

"What's a bee beard?" asked Yngve. "I mean, I know what it sounds like, but surely that's not right?"

Bjorn cupped a hand to his ear. The prematurely aged man was also hard of hearing. Yngve repeated the question.

Bjorn slapped himself at the open collar of his shirt where a few greying chest hairs curled. "I'll show you. I suspend the queen around here, and the bees from that queen's colony will swarm to be with her. They'll cover my throat and mouth like a beard. Brilliant eh?"

Yngve put a hand to his face, horrified. "Bees all over your face? But they'll go in tha mouth and up tha nose! They'll go down tha shirt and—" He broke off with a shudder and made a brief keening noise.

Bjorn slapped him on the shoulder and leaned in to whisper. "You do up the top button and keep yer mouth closed. Them's only bees, lad. If you keep calm, they'll settle down."

Yngve buried his face in his hands and shook his head, his bandana flapping.

Ragnar looked across the rest of the group and saw faces that reflected a similar lack of enthusiasm for the idea.

"Come on, Odinsons!" he roared. "Who is man enough for this challenge?"

"I'll do it!" said Freyella. She met his eye with a steady, challenging gaze.

"Tha's the runner," said Ragnar firmly. "Tha can't do both."

"I'll be runner!" said a voice.

Ragnar looked up. "Who said that?"

Hands shot into the air from nearly everybody.

"Me!" called young Kalf.

"No, me!" called young Erik.

Uncle Bjorn smiled at the crowd and raised a hand for silence. "That's settled then. Freyella, Ragnar and I will have bee beards."

"Wha—?" Ragnar had not seen this coming.

"But first!" Bjorn called, "we must tell the bees. It is customary, as you know, to keep the bees informed of major events in the household. We must therefore take a moment to tell them of their key role in returning our beloved ship to us."

"But, wai—"

Bjorn silenced Ragnar with a hand and walked to the hives on the trailer outside, murmuring quietly to the bees. The group all listened, but apart from the rising and falling of Bjorn's tone, they could not make out what he was saying.

Ragnar looked at the rest of the group, and the relief on their faces, now they were not going to be faced with wearing a bee beard. He looked down at Freyella and locked eyes with her. He straightened his shoulders and fastened the top button on his shirt.

SAM CAME into the kitchen for breakfast, just as her dad was saying, "Then that's decided. I'll see you later. Bye." He hung up the phone and returned his attentions to the scrambled eggs on the hob.

"Making enough for two?" said Sam.

"I always make too much," he said. "Clear a couple of spaces."

Sam moved the clutter on the kitchen counter so they could sit down and eat. There was the usual post. Sam eyed it for any bills. Letters in ominous brown envelopes and occasionally threatening red ink had been a common feature in the house since her return to Skegness more than a year ago. Their frequency seemed to have declined, but she suspected this was due to her dad squirrelling away any such post before she got chance to see it, rather than any financial restraint. There was a scattering of tiny cogs underneath the post.

"I'm finding these things everywhere."

Marvin looked over from his pot stirring. "I'm still practising the old wristwatch restoration trick." He looked at his pot. "Maybe I could develop an egg unscrambling trick."

"Might be easier to build a time machine."

"But that's the charm," he said, serving up. "The fact that time travel is impossible makes it all the more magical. The improbability of it dazzles."

"Dazzles, right," she said and tucked into eggs on toast.

Fire damage meant she had no office to go to for work. The DefCon4 tasks were slowly piling up on her phone app while she had no base to operate from. She had never valued the office, but without it she lacked focus and impetus. She was in no hurry to leave the house.

Marvin milled pepper onto his eggs "I might show Kiki the watch trick later. You think she'd like it?"

"You going courting?" she said.

"Courting?"

"A-wooing. I'm sure you've used both those terms when I'm meeting a man."

"She did send me a rather flirtatious letter," he said.

"I'm not sure I want to know." She played with her rubbery eggs. "You're going to Candlebroke?"

"This morning. I suggested popping round for a chat. Apparently, there's a big film production using the terrace and lawns. Some period drama. I worried I might get in the way, but Kiki practically insisted."

Sam smiled. "You can be her groupie."

"I've had groupies in my time. Seems only right to do my fair share of groupie-ing."

Sam recalled some peculiar letters from female fans at the height of his fame. She recalled that his assistant, Linda, received far more. Sam had a vague recollection, from her mid-childhood, of Linda telling her she kept some and burned others. Young Sam had never thought to ask what criteria Linda used for determining which were saved.

"I can give you a lift," said Sam.

"Oh, don't put yourself out. I was going to get a taxi."

"I need an excuse to go there myself. I left some paperwork in Phoebe's office—"

"Poor girl," said Marvin automatically.

"Yes. It's unbelievable," she agreed. She put a forkful of egg in her mouth and chewed thoughtfully. Yes, even after the shock of her death had passed, it was still very unbelievable.

74

The Odinson clan split in two at the driveway entrance to Candlebroke Hall. Ragnar, Uncle Bjorn, Torsten and Freyella jumped down from the lead vehicle. Bjorn's bee hives were lifted down and hefted onto sack trucks.

"We wait for your signal," said Hilde. "Then we move the ship."

Ragnar nodded tersely and his group moved stealthily off through the grass towards the house, pulling the bee hives behind them. Hilde watched them go. The Odinsons did a good impression of being an experienced heist team, able to follow a complex plan. Hilde felt a mild concern that impression was all it was.

Yngve put the low loader into gear and drove on towards the house.

"Loop round the back and park far out of sight," Hilde told him.

"I know what I'm doing, lass," he said in a surly manner. "We've done this thrice now."

He wasn't wrong. Once to steal the wood, once to return the ship, and now to steal it back. "Just keep tha distance, uncle."

Yngve slid the vehicle onto one of the rough tracks which cut through the old deer park and circled the ornamental lawns at front and rear. There were at least three articulated lorries, and a throng of other vehicles parked outside the house. This film malarkey was ideal cover. What was one more truck among dozens?

As they rattled on through mud and gravel, Hilde looked back for sight of her Farfar, but he was lost among the grass and trees. However, she did see another vehicle coming along the driveway towards the house. Normally it wouldn't have held her attention for more than a split second, but the dinky three-wheeled van was a distinctive sight, and it usually presaged grief of some sort.

Sam Applewhite was at Candlebroke. Hilde grunted. The woman was nice enough for a Saxon, her heart in almost the right place. As long as she didn't get wind of their plans and try to interfere, everything would turn out right.

She looked at Uncle Yngve and her other relatives bouncing in the cab as the low loader rumbled along the track. Sam was not going to be their main barrier to success.

THE DAY HAD ARRIVED at Candlebroke Hall.

The film crew had been setting up over the course of a number of days, but like a circus decamping in a field, none of it seemed real or significant until the Big Top was erected and the clowns in costume.

Kiki went downstairs in a simple but elegant combination of beige trousers, white blouse and her no-nonsense leatherette jacket. She thought of it as her 'Charlie's Angels' outfit, showing she was ready to leap into action when needed – but could also head off to wardrobe whenever they called. First assistant director Saffron approached her along the main gallery.

"Ah, Kiki. Just the woman."

Yes, thought Kiki, enjoying the buzz of on-set excitement she hadn't felt in years. She was indeed just the woman. The woman of the hour. The *belle du jour*.

"They're about to film one of the fight scenes. The risk assessment we did with Phoebe says we should check in with you before we start."

Kiki nodded wisely, all the while wondering what Phoebe had planned to do. Probably just wanted to watch. "I will absolutely be there."

"And Sebastian, the director, has confirmed that, due to the light conditions, we're going to switch things round and do your scene straight after lunch."

"My scene," said Kiki in a calm and professional tone, while inside a little voice was screaming *"My scene! My scene!"* and jumping about with excitement.

Lines or no lines, she told herself a character part was just what she needed, and that it would be an amazing opportunity. "And I'm to play one of Marguerite's close friends. Her inner coterie."

"A family member perhaps?" said Saffron brightly. "A

maiden aunt, perhaps. As soon as you've approved the risk assessment, we'll get you over to wardrobe and make up."

At the words 'make up', Saffron's eyes involuntarily glanced at Kiki's face.

"I'm a damaged old hag," said Kiki, not sure if she was trying to make a joke of it. "Make up will need a bloody trowel and cement."

"You are an actress," said Saffron. "Your face communicates emotion. Every little ... nuance. You're beautiful, Lady Lettuces."

It was possibly the kindest thing anyone had said to her in days. Catching her off guard, it was almost enough to make her cry. And she instantly knew she would swap that kindness and her *nuanced* fucking beauty for one single extra day of her youth.

"You are too kind," she managed to say. "Let's take a look at that risk assessment, shall we?"

Saffron accompanied her out onto the breezy terrace and began explaining at length that the rear of Candlebroke would double for both Sir Percy Blakeney's home, Blake House, and the Chateau Rodiere, where the villainous Citizen Chauvelin was about to kill a despised rival in an unfair pistol duel. While tables and chairs and pavilion tents were being set up for the later garden party scene, the duel was taking place by the old stable block.

Camera units and lighting rigs were set up, and a handful of actors were taking instructions from an assistant and a serious looking fellow in hi-vis orange holding a flintlock pistol. Kiki was sure she had seen the young dark-haired actor playing Chauvelin before. Had she seen him play a murderer on an ITV drama?

Saffron rattled through the risk assessment and the serious looking gun technician spoke, but Kiki didn't really take any of it in. She was just soaking up, breathing in, the atmosphere of the movie world once more. The runners, the lighting, the swarm of technical bods, the frisson of immortal celluloid moments about to be made.

"What is that on Chauvelin's groin?" shouted a baseball cap wearing man, evidently the director Sebastian.

A five pointed leaf had straddled the actor's crotch area, looking for all the world like a hand grasping for his manhood. The actor peeled it away, revealing a sticky red paint print.

"Why has Chauvelin got a painted leaf on his balls?" asked the director.

Wardrobe swarmed and there was general commotion. Kiki just kept quiet.

HILDE HOPPED down from the low loader. Yngve had parked up beyond the cedars at the far side of the pond. The twins, Gunnolf and Hermod, parked their muscle truck behind that. Trees and the contours of the land all but hid them from the house. Just as well, as neither of the vehicles blended in.

The twins sauntered over, thumbs tucked in belts. They had both come in linen tunics and leather trousers. With their tattoos, beards, and hammer pendants they were every inch the heavy metal Viking warrior. They had both wanted to wear their seax knives sheathed at their waist, but Hilde lectured them about carrying offensive weapons, and they had removed them with some reluctance. The plan was to leave the low loader within easy reach, but out of sight, until they were ready to lift the ship into place on the truck bed.

"Right. Let's get our ship," said Sigurd.

"Wait," said Hilde. "We make sure the ship's ready to go, then we wait for Torsten to come over from the other group. We can't go and get the ship until we know everyone's attention is elsewhere."

The men gave a variety of begrudging nods or mock salutes. They generally weren't of a mind to take orders from a young woman, but Hilde spoke with authority. Years of experience had taught them where there was a choice of actions, wise men watched what Hilde Odinson did. The dozen or so Odinsons moved forward through the lightly wooded gardens towards their ship. The grounds by the house were much busier than on their last visit. The film crew had set up a massive encampment. It looked as if a small village had brought itself to Candlebroke.

"Sweet lookin' trailer there," said Sigurd.

"Reckon that would make a champion recording studio," said young Cousin Erik, who was the lead singer of the Viking Metal trio, *Meat-Heads*.

"We're not here for stealing," said Hilde.

"No harm in a little light raidin'," said Yngve.

Their beautiful longship, *Sandraker*, designed by Hilde, built and crewed by all of them, stood at the top of a rise overlooking the formal lawns and the house.

"What's that all round it?"

As they got closer, Hilde saw that the *Sandraker* was

hemmed in by mounds of earth, with a few bits of shrubbery planted here and there.

"Why've they bloomin' done that?" asked Hermod.

"They buried it," said Yngve.

"Who buries ships?" said Gunnolf.

"Actually, lots of chiefs got buried in their ships," said Sigurd. "Like that one at Sutton Hoo."

"Sutton who?" said Ogendus.

"That's the one."

"It's going to tek ages to shift that lot," said Gunnolf.

"Did we bring shovels at all?" said Hilde, knowing full well they hadn't.

"We ain't using our hands," said Hermod.

"But I bet they got spades and that down by the 'ouse," said Erik. "Big garden. Stands to reason."

"Time for a little light raidin'," said Yngve, grinning.

They all lifted their heads at the sound of sharp crack from the film set. A puff of white smoke rose into the air.

"Were that an explosion?" said Gunnolf.

"It wunt a *proper* explosion," said Hermod.

Hilde knew what Hermod's idea of a proper explosion was.

"Meks you wonder what they've got over there that can blow things up," said Gunnolf slowly.

"Aye," said Hermod. "Be handy for shifting soil, that."

Hilde grimaced and then huffed. "No explosives. If we're going to excavate the ship then we're doing it properly. Yngve, Erik – go check out those buildings over there by that herb garden bit. Hermod, Gunnolf – go round to those sheds down there. Do not get seen. I'm going to go down to Ragnar and tell him we're a bit delayed."

"And what about the rest of us?" said Sigurd.

Hilde was explicit. "Stay here. Do nothing. Shift some of the soil with your hands if you fancy. But no going off, and no getting clever ideas."

There were harrumphs and grumps, but the men complied.

75

Marvin eventually located Kiki in a wardrobe trailer, being trussed up in a long corseted dress. It gave Kiki a startlingly proud cleavage that Marvin did his best not to stare at.

"Ah, you found me!" said Kiki. "Come in, come in. You get by security okay?"

Marvin nodded agreeably. "Sam flashed her ID at the clipboard warriors and gave some blag about burglar alarms and inventories."

"Sam? Your daughter's here?" She made to look past him.

"Oh, doing something in the house," he said dismissively. "Got some documents to collect or something."

"I see."

One of the dressers said, "You're done. Ready to go. Join the seats by make up and go in when called."

Kiki swished her skirts and eyed Marvin. "What do you think?"

"Well, Miss Harris, I sure do say you look as purdy as a picture." He gave her an idiot grin. "Not sure why I slipped into Wild West speechifying there. This is a Georgian era thing, isn't it?"

"The Scarlet Pimpernel," she said, taking his hand so he could help her step down from the trailer, skirts rustling.

"Ah, gay blades and derring-do."

"Very much so," she said. "Though I'll leave the sword fighting and derring-do to others."

"You look every bit the lady of the manor," said Marvin.

"As I am."

"As you are."

He escorted her over to the make up trailer and the awnings outside where seats had been left for cast and crew. He looked at the organised chaos of a film set in action. His own experiences of entertainment were much more confined to the world of theatre and the near-totalitarian culture of late twentieth century TV production. He found himself able to guess what half of the people might be doing, but the rest... He blew out his cheeks.

"It's like the circus has come to town," he said.

"I know," said Kiki and she had a child-like wonder on her face.

"It's nice to see you happy again."

Her expression faltered for a moment. "Why wouldn't I be? Lights, camera, action. And one of my favourite men at my side."

. . .

HILDE APPROACHED the film set cautiously. She needed to locate her Farfar and the others. There was no point in them setting off their bee distraction if the ship team weren't ready to move *Sandraker*. Although there were official looking types with clipboards and walkie-talkies on the set, they seemed to be clustered on the far side, by the house. The gardens were left unguarded and free. As Hermod and Gunnolf drifted off in their search for spades, Hilde passed through the outskirts of the trailer village, heading towards some undefined point where she imagined her grandfather and the others might be.

The film set was like a complex machine, with many intricate pieces, each with a specific job to do. There were people, lorries, caravans and tents involved. Some parts were easily identified, others less so.

She passed a Saxon man looking over the open panel of a trailer-mounted generator. The engine started, rumbled, sputtered and stopped. A general haze of smoke hung over it. He went to twist something inside, hissed and pulled away. Sucking his thumb angrily, he saw Hilde.

"What are you doing?" he said.

Hilde momentarily panicked, then pointed. "It's probably the carburettor," she said.

"What?"

"Honda engine, isn't it?"

The man gave her a blank look. "All I know is the output fluctuates and then the engine cuts out."

She nodded. "You overloading it?"

He jerked at thumb at the big trailer behind him. "AV unit. Same as usual."

"Here, let me look." She had places to be, but an ingrained part of Hilde couldn't just walk on by while an idiot male tinkered amateurishly with a quality engine.

"CAN YOU SMELL THAT?" said Hermod.

Gunnolf sniffed. "Fireworks?"

"Like fireworks," agreed Hermod.

They looked around. The sheds they'd been directed to were effectively derelict, taken over by weeds and wood rot. Of shovels and other excavating gear, there was no sign.

"Explosives?" said Gunnolf.

"Hilde said no explosives."

"I heard that she'd prefer it if we got shovels. No sign of shovels, but..." He sniffed again.

In short order, Hermod and Gunnolf had found a compound dedicated to props and wardrobe. There was a table arrayed with pistols. There was even a small cannon nearby.

"Explosives," whispered Gunnolf, automatically looking round to see who was watching.

YNGVE ODINSON and young Erik crept across the lawns to the promising looking buildings along one side of the gardens. There was clearly a walled off area and some buildings within. Erik was not an expert on stately homes, but he reckoned maybe, in the olden days, this was where the rich people kept their slaves. Or maybe their toilets. He wasn't sure.

A gap in the wall was filled with a chain link fence. There was a locked gate and a series of insistent signs.

ACCESS FORBIDDEN.
AUTHORISED PERSONNEL ONLY.
NOT OPEN TO THE PUBLIC.

"BINGO," said Yngve.

"Eh?" said Erik.

"That's a good sign."

"I've seen better."

"A good sign that there's something worth having inside," said Yngve. "The more they tell thee to keep out, the bigger the prize within. Stands to reason."

"Tha reckons there's shovels inside?"

"Or summat worth 'avin'." He sniffed sharply. "That's the smell of loot."

Erik sniffed. It didn't smell like loot. It smelled sort of earthy. A bit like a farm. A lot like that fox den they'd found under one of the caravans last summer. A mix of meaty, dungy, furry musk.

"Is tha sure?" he said, wondering what on earth they'd keep in a caged off area.

"Sure as eggs is eggs." Yngve slipped his lock picks out from under his bandana and set to work.

· · ·

"THIS IS YOUR PROBLEM," said Hilde. "The water-cooling is all well and good, but with this model they've put the cooling system over the top, which leads to condensation here, and then you get water in the carburettor..."

The trailer man realised something was expected of him. "I just do the AV. I've lost all monitoring and they're due to film the garden party scene next."

Hilde whipped a screwdriver from her belt bag and had some of the internal plastic covers off in moments. She needed to check that fuel was getting where it was needed first of all. Methodical practical work like this was Hilde's bread and butter. She'd catch up with her family when she'd made this beautiful machine work again.

"Cup of tea?" asked the man.

"Eh?" said Hilde. "You've got no power."

"I can go and get one from catering."

"Milk, no sugar, then," said Hilde without looking up.

HERMOD AND GUNNOLF carried a blue plastic drum apiece back to the *Sandraker*. Hermod was pleased not only with their sneaky lifting of the several pounds of gunpowder from the whatever-it-was-called trailer, but was also glad to see the family had stayed well-hidden and out of sight.

"What's that then?" said a rustling bush that sounded a lot like Ogendus.

"Black powder, ain't it?" said Gunnolf.

Another bush sprouted Sigurd's head. "I thought tha were looking for shovels."

"Found this," said Hermod.

"And what did Torsten say? Are they doing their distraction thing?"

"Din't see him," said Gunnolf. "But we're gonna go get more of this."

"I don't reckon we should be blasting the ship out," said Sigurd. There were grumbles of agreement from other hidden spots among the foliage.

"Tha's just being a wuss," said Hermod. The grumbles of agreement were louder this time.

"We should dig it out or..." The bush sprouted a pointing hand. "Reckon there's a mobile crane down there, among the lorries an' that."

"Aye, and tha's welcome to look then," said Gunnolf. They dropped the tubs by the plant covered mounds of earth and jogged back down to the film set.

They entered the shanty town of trailers, portacabins and marquees. Remembering exactly where the props and explosives were was not as simple as it should have been. As they entered a likely looking area, a blonde Saxon woman waved sternly at them.

"Background artists?" she said.

"What?" said Hermod.

"Who put you in those?" She gestured at their attire. "We're not even doing Parisian street scenes at this location."

"This?" said Gunnolf, tugging at his tunic. "Listen, love—"

The woman looked like she had been slapped. She rebounded with a tightly controlled voice of fury. "Do not ever 'love' me again, or you are off this production, buster! Now, you're background artists, aren't you?"

Hermod and Gunnolf were gobsmacked. They weren't used to Saxon women talking to them so sternly. Oh, they got a sharp word off Mormor Astrid and the other womenfolk at home, but Saxon women usually ignored them, even crossing the road to avoid them. Both were momentarily struck dumb.

"Do you have speaking roles?" the woman said slowly.

"I don't—" Hermod managed.

"No, of course you don't," she said. "Come on, there's no time to lose!" She ushered them up the steps of a trailer and closed the door behind them.

They were in something like a cross between a hairdresser's salon and the backstage of a theatre. There were mirrors, lights and tables, with all manner of tools and products and things on hooks and racks. It was, to a Viking outsider, a mesmerising sight.

"Juju," the stern Saxon said to one of the women in the trailer. "I don't know what's gone wrong here, but I need you to work on this pair. Twin footmen, they need to match perfectly. Get them in breeches, powdered wigs and so on. No idea what the agency were thinking. No offence guys, you have the twin thing for sure, but we need to smooth those rough edges off a little." The stern Saxon woman went to the door. "You've got thirty minutes, tops. They're needed for the garden party arrival scene."

Hermod glanced across at Gunnolf with a shrug and sat down in the seat, as indicated by Juju. Moments later, the two of them were draped in towels and lathered up for a shave.

76

Awning or no awning, waiting outside to be called into make up while wearing a dress with a sweepingly low neckline was cold. It was barely springtime and the sun was in hiding. Kiki had goosebumps on her elevated bosom.

Marvin offered her his jacket. Then she asked if he would do her the favour of popping back to wardrobe and seeing if he could find the leatherette jacket she'd left in one of their storage tubs. He practically leapt into action. Marvin might be a little old for her tastes but he had three qualities she admired: he had money (well, some), he was famous (well, almost) and he was keen.

He'd barely gone when a make up woman called her in.

"We have been mad rushed off our feet, dear," she said, steering Kiki into a chair before an illuminated mirror.

The act of simply sliding into a make up chair on set was enough to give Kiki goosebumps. More goosebumps.

"Oh, you look cold, dear," said the make up artist, giving Kiki's shoulders a rub. "Don't know how they think they're going to shoot a classy period drama if all the women have frozen boobsicles. Now, let's take a look at you..."

While the woman gathered together make up tools, Kiki glanced at the two men in the next seats along. One had shaving foam slathered around his jaw. The other had the pink fresh complexion of the freshly shaved. To Kiki's eyes, the pair of them appeared to be something akin to terrified.

"Oh, we're a regular barbershop here today," sighed the make up artist.

"What roles do you two have?" Kiki asked. It was always good to make small talk with other artistes, even the extras.

"We're twins," one managed to mumble.

"Aye. Footman twins," said the other.

"You *will* be," said the woman descending on the lathered up one with her razorblade.

Terrified, Kiki thought.

RAGNAR and his crew huddled in a copse near to the film crew, while Bjorn fussed around his hives like the loving bee father that he was.

"Yer'll need to listen to Uncle Bjorn. He's in charge of t'bees, right?"

"You've already said that," said Freyella.

"You have," agreed Torsten.

Maybe he had, but Ragnar was nervous. He could not afford to show he was nervous about the idea of a bee beard. Not only was he the patriarch, with the whole family looking to him as a role model, he was sure the bees would sense if he was not calm. He glanced at Freyella, who looked happy at the idea of bees buzzing around her head as they sought their queen.

Bjorn came over and held up the queens in their boxes. "One each. Are we ready?"

Ragnar nodded, then added, "I wonder if I should carry mine on my arm or summat? If I need to tell folks what to do, I'll need my mouth, won't I?"

"I suppose so," said Bjorn, waggling a finger in his ear thoughtfully. "You can wear them like a sleeve. Or mebbe like a sword?"

"A mighty sword, aye!" Ragnar was pleased at that idea.

"I'll tie it onto your wrist. Can't have you dropping my lovely queen."

Ragnar would have preferred to have an option to drop the queen, but he wasn't going to say so.

"So, the three of us will walk amongst the film people," said Ragnar loudly. "Then the bees will start to arrive."

"Aye. Torsten will release the bees. Then, once he's given the signal to the others to take our ship, he'll come back over with the smoker. Yes, Torsten?"

Torsten was looking around in the manner of someone trying to remember which thing was the smoker.

It was a good plan, Ragnar told himself. A solid plan. Distract everyone with a swarm of bees. Get the ship on the low-loader. Fade away like nothing had happened. Everyone knew their crucial part and would enact it precisely. Ragnar was sure of that. He was mostly sure of that.

77

M arvin felt an unusual sensation as he walked through the trailer village of the film set. Passing different people – this one carrying cables, this one carrying a reflective photographer's umbrella, this one carrying a bundle of fancy lace tablecloths – he had the unshakeable excitement and nerves of being backstage without permission.

There was something magical about the world of entertainment. It was not one of the things that had initially attracted Marvin to a life on stage, but it had given him energy throughout his career. There was a world of trades – from the technical, to the practical, to the downright esoteric. It was a society in its own right, with as many mysteries and fraternities as the more mundane reality outside.

And, in this one, Marvin was an outsider, an excited trespasser.

He knocked politely on the open wardrobe trailer door. Inside a woman looked across.

"Yes?"

"I've come to collect Lady Lettuces' coat," he said. "She's cold."

The woman gave him a disinterested look, waved at a stack of translucent plastic storage boxes and said, "Go for it", before returning to the jacket she was repairing.

Brown leatherette jacket, Kiki had said. Marvin scanned the boxes until he saw one with a sticker saying *K Harris*. He prised off the lid, found the caramel-coloured coat, and lifted it out. An envelope fell from the pocket as he did so. He picked it up automatically.

"I've got it," he said to the wardrobe woman. She didn't seem to care.

He stepped out of the caravan and, about to tuck the envelope back into the coat pocket, glimpsed the front.

Open in the Event of my Death, it read.

It was an odd and dramatic address to find on an envelope, but Marvin was a great respecter of privacy. Yet, as he turned it over, he saw the envelope wasn't sealed. There were several sheets of folded writing paper inside.

Even as he was slipping it out to have a quick peek, his brain was concocting his excuses. *"Oh, Kiki, it all fell out and I was just putting it back..."*

He read the first line and had to stop to read it again.

I, Lady Kiki Lettuces, and Mr Antoine de Winter, have removed and sold on hundreds of items from Candlebroke Hall.

"Oh, Kiki."

· · ·

THE DOOR to Phoebe's office was locked. Sam wasn't surprised. She wouldn't have been surprised if there'd been official police crime scene tape over it, either. Camara had promised the fraud squad would be looking into the peculiar and ultimately tragic events at Candlebroke Hall, but Sam had not heard anything further on the matter.

The interior of the house felt deathly silent. This was partly due to the total lack of visitors, but was made all the more apparent by the muffled sound of the film crew activity at the rear of the house. Glimpses through rear windows revealed busy folks about their work, interspersed with men and women in eighteenth century costume.

As Sam walked through the central halls, she made sure to stay away from the rearmost rooms, in case she accidentally appeared in shot of whatever was going on and caused some Hollywood type to have a fit of rage. The act of walking, alone and in silence, allowed her thoughts to tumble and turn.

In one sense, a very practical sense, the crooked business at Candlebroke was settled. An antiques racket – fraud or embezzlement or simple theft – had been uncovered. The supposed conspirators, Phoebe and Vance, were dead, and the bulk of the missing items found in Vance's grandma's garage. But the loose ends, particularly Hilde's inexplicable and frankly impossible involvement, remained unresolved. And then there were tangential elements: Torsten and his tattoos and Ragnar's own drinking horn, that seemed like they belonged, but had no meaningful place.

Sam came to the foot of a staircase and, on a whim, climbed them.

"Lay it out in order," she said to herself.

There was Candlebroke Hall, a treasure trove belonging to National Heritage. There was lonely former actress, Kiki. There was Phoebe, the National Heritage manager. And, circling the house, like a turd-eating fly, was the disgraced magician turned psychic, Antoine de Winter.

There had been thefts, going on for months or possibly years, the stolen items passing through Vance Patterson's hands on the way to black market buyers. Vance the tattooist.

Then there was Torsten, who had a racist tattoo and somehow managed to get hold of a beautiful aurochs horn to give to Ragnar. Had Torsten bought it from Vance?

"No. Maybe it was compensation," she said.

Torsten had been given a racist tattoo, but the boy was too sweet and stupid to have requested such a thing on purpose. He'd likely picked the Nordic design without scrutinising it too closely. Vance had inked him with it, too stupid or lazy to question its meaning. And, in a roundabout way, it had landed Torsten in court on an assault charge. If he'd not known what it was, he would certainly have been angry when he found out. Angry enough to try to extract some sort of vengeance from the tattooist?

"Vance gave him the horn as compensation."

And all was well, until Freyella and the other little Odinsons had gone on a school trip to see the History of Drink. Freyella had seen one just like it. Had she told Torsten the value of the item he now possessed? And had one of them told Hilde?

And had Hilde – out of jealousy, out of greed? – decided to steal the bejewelled horn from Candlebroke in a burglary that was simultaneously idiotic and genius, requiring Olympic levels of athleticism to fit in with the timings of the burglar alarm and the police arrest—?

That's where it all fell apart.

Hilde's motivations were, at the least, entirely out of character. She wasn't jealous of Torsten; there was nothing to be jealous of. Material wealth and social status meant nothing to her. Give her tools to use and place to work, and she was master of her own world. And there weren't two aurochs horns on the Candlebroke inventory. The item was effectively unique. But Vance had given one to Torsten and Freyella had seen another. If Vance hadn't got the original one from Candlebroke, then where had he got it from?

"None of it makes sense."

Sam found herself standing in an upstairs gallery and facing one of the many wall displays of arms and armour found around the house. There was a gauntlet pinned to the wall. Next to it was a shield bearing the Lettuces coat of arms. There was a dark shadow on the light green felt, the perfect outline of an absent sword and the wire hooks that had held it in place. As visual metaphors went, it was compelling.

"Yeah, I'm missing something," she agreed.

"Is this eighteenth century?" said a voice.

There was a woman in a hi-vis tabard in a doorway, holding a wooden chair.

Sam nodded. "Eighteenth century joined oak Derbyshire chair," she recited from her inventory. "Note the hand-turned bobbin and the applied beadwork."

"Er – thanks."

As the woman went to leave, Sam followed her. "I assume you're not just a super-confident burglar," she said.

The woman tilted her head. "Needed for the scene outside. Light's not right for the early garden party scene, so we're doing the second bit first. All sorts out in the edit, but we need an extra chair."

The woman headed down the stairs. "Just make sure you put it back when you're done," Sam called after her. "Everything needs to go back where it was."

Sam wandered on. She briefly stood in an upstairs room and looked out at the movie town laid out below. She guessed her dad was down there somewhere, doing his best to woo Kiki with magically restored watch tricks, or maybe just having a good old natter with someone who had as many showbiz anecdotes as he did.

How the brain worked was a constant mystery to Sam. People were irrational creatures, each following trains of logic that no one else would follow. That's how a young Odinson woman ended up charged for a burglary she couldn't have committed. That's how an idiot tattooist managed to set himself on fire while trying to carry out an act of arson. Even Sam's own brain defied understanding – because one moment she was standing there wondering where her dad might be, and the next the problem of the impossible burglary resolved itself automatically in her mind.

"Bloody hell," she said to no one and ran for the stairs. She flew down them in a stumbling run, over-taking the movie woman with the chair.

"You all right?" the woman called after her.

"The History of Drink!" Sam shouted back and kept on running.

IN KIKI'S OPINION, the make up woman, Juju, was a miracle worker. She didn't lie to Kiki about how obvious and unsightly the wounds on her face and neck were. She described the situation as fact and then set about remedying it.

"Camouflage and fixing are the way to go."

She dressed the worst of the cheek wounds with a fine gauze, then set to with her pot of magic camouflage.

"Ideal for tattoo covering too," she said as she worked. "I had to do Shia LaBouef front and back for his last film. Nearly used the whole tub."

When she was finished, Kiki was stunned. The wounds were gone. And half her wrinkles too.

"Don't want to overdo," said Juju. "Don't want to end up looking like a plastic surgery nightmare." She took out a clear spray. "Now to fix it. We don't want your cover sliding three inches by mid-afternoon."

A few squirts of the tightening spray and Kiki was good to go. And my, oh my, she thought, ready to weep, she did look good. She was no preening starlet, but a mature and regal looking actress in her prime. With a Georgian wig from the woman working on the two shaven and powdered twins, Kiki was ready to step outside for her public to see.

"Break a leg," she tittered giddily to the twins and went outside.

There was Marvin, coming towards her. He had her coat

over one arm and something in his other hand. It was a heavy envelope. Had her Academy Award nomination come through already? she joked to herself, before recognising it.

There was an uncertainty in Marvin's expression. "Got your coat, madame," he said, holding it out.

Kiki snatched the envelope. She'd forgotten about putting it in this coat pocket for safekeeping. "Did you look at it?"

He hesitated. "It's a surprising thing to see on an envelope."

"Did you read it?"

"It just fell out of the pocket. I wouldn't normally pry." He tried to offer her the coat. "Kiki, are you in some kind of trouble?"

She could have laughed at that. Some kind of trouble? If she thought about it, she was in every kind of trouble – theft, fraud, and something that was somewhere between reckless endangerment and murder. What she didn't want to do was think about this today. Today was her special day, Kiki Harris was treading the boards once more.

"It's nothing," she said. "A little joke. A work of fiction."

"If you're in trouble and you need help..." He said it with such damned earnestness, Kiki could have slapped him. There were times in any woman's life when she wanted a knight in shining armour to come riding by. He was not the knight she needed, and this was definitely not the time.

"Come with me," she said and headed towards the house.

78

"Stranger's coming!" hissed someone.

The hissed warning went up and down the bushes and trees by *Sandraker*, to the extent that any approaching stranger might have thought the undergrowth was conspiring against them.

The stranger turned out to be Torsten. Sigurd popped up and waved him over.

"Where's Hilde?" asked Torsten.

"Gone to find shovels," said Sigurd, gesturing at the banked earth around the ship. "We din't bring any ourselves."

"I saw a crane down among the film folk's vehicles that'd lift that out," said Torsten.

"Aye. I was reckoning to go get it."

"Maybe you should." Torsten kicked the blue plastic tubs stored at one end of the ship. "What's this, then?"

"Black powder. Hermod said we could blast the ship out, but I reckon—"

"Good idea," said Torsten. "Very good idea." The lad grinned at the tubs of explosive.

"And what does Ragnar say?" asked Sigurd.

"Eh?"

"Did he send you? Are they ready to start distracting folk?"

"Oh, aye," said Torsten, distracted. "Ten minutes, he said."

"Right then, we best be ready."

"Go get that crane if you fancy. I might begin laying out these charges. Any of you lot got fuses?" he called to the bushes in general.

Sigurd huffed. Inexpertly planted explosives led to trouble. He'd have thought every Bonfire Night, and the burnt out shell of Ogendus's old caravan would have been testament to that. Still, he reasoned to himself as he jogged towards the film set and the mobile crane, planting the tubs of black powder around the ship would keep them busy and out of trouble for a while. It's not like they were going to blow up the ship while his back was turned, was it?

THE WALK through Candlebroke Hall and up two flights of stairs was wearying in a full Georgian gown, with its restrictive undergarments, but Kiki wasn't sure where else to take Marvin. The journey to her quarters gave her enough time to cook up a half-baked plan.

"Kiki," said Marvin, somewhat out of puff himself after

the short march. "Can you explain? I don't rightly understand."

She had the door unlocked and told him to go in. "Sit there." She pointed at one of the two dining chairs.

Marvin silently complied.

Kiki flung her arms wide at the battered furniture, the damp wallpaper, the dusty and rotting coving. "I apologise for the state of the place, but as you can see, it's a shithole."

"This is your place?" he said, surprised.

"This tiny corner is all I have. Hellish, isn't it?" She squeezed past him to get to the kitchen and came back with her sturdy roll of duct tape. "The pipework is so poor, I have to tape it to stop it leaking everywhere. And most of my water comes from the most disgusting roof tank." She pointed at the hatch leading to the roof. "The indignities I have suffered."

"This is far from ideal," Marvin agreed and began to rise.

"Sit," she said. He sat.

"You have no idea what a woman has to do to maintain her position in life." She went to her bedroom and pulled the crossbow that had maimed Phoebe from under her bed. She bought it back through into the main room.

Marvin frowned at it. "An original antique?"

"Sixteenth century, I think Phoebe said." Shortly before slicing off half her fingers and diving head-first into a shredder, she didn't add.

Kiki put a foot in the metal stirrup at the front of the crossbow and hauled back the string until it snagged into place. She inspected the stinging red line the string had made across her hands. But that was the point, wasn't it? Success came at the cost of suffering.

"Are you all right?" said Marvin. "Those things can be dangerous."

"Mmmm," Kiki nodded in agreement. She took a crossbow bolt off the table by the door. "And I've actually found the proper arrow things to go in it this time." She slotted one into the groove and aimed it at Marvin.

"Bloody hell, Kiki," he said, flinching. "Point that thing somewhere else."

Keeping the crossbow aimed with one wavering hand, Kiki scrabbled for the roll of tape and tossed it to Marvin. "Tape your legs to the chair legs."

"What?"

"And your arm to the arm."

His frown was profound and puzzled. Kiki sighed, irritated.

"Marvin, you're a great guy, but I'm having a tough day. And it's an important day. For me. I look—" She found the nearest mirror. "I look a million dollars, and I really don't want anything to spoil this magical moment."

"You want me to tie myself up?" he said, perplexed.

"And I'll be checking it," she said. "I know you're Mr Marvellous. I can't have you ruining things by escaping with magic tricks."

"I don't understand," said Marvin.

Kiki wasn't going to debate the point. "Tape. Chair. Crossbow. Do it, Marvin. My audience is waiting for me."

79

H ermod and Gunnolf couldn't keep the stunned looks off their faces. They were clean shaven for the first time since puberty. Hermod scrambled to the mirror to take a look, but he had no time to register how soft and fleshy his bare face was before he was pushed back down into his seat so that powder could be applied to his face. He could see Gunnolf suffering similar indignities in the other chair. The blonde woman reappeared with a pair of outfits and hung them near the door. They were pale blue frock coats, with braiding and embroidery. The silver buttons down the front reminded Hermod of custom alloys. The woman gave a nod to Juju.

"You might need to do their legs as well. Not sure how thick the silk stockings will be."

"What was that about my legs? No!" Hermod wriggled.

"We'll see. You might be all right," soothed the make up woman. "Now, let's get these wigs on, shall we?"

Ten minutes later, the pair of them were outside, with a cold breeze on their bare faces.

"So we're footmen, aye?" asked Hermod. He looked at his brother's outfit. It was an eye-catching look, although not one that would go down well back home. They looked like a cross between those posh court lawyers who wore the wigs and ballet dancers in their tights.

A tall woman came over to collect them. "Twin footmen?"

Hermod and Gunnolf just stared at her.

"Matching footmen were all the rage back in the day," she said. "The pair of you look fantastic."

"We do, don't we?" murmured Hermod, turning this way and that.

"With me!" She led them through the set.

"Did footmen have guns?" Gunnolf whispered to Hermod. They needed to circle back round to the weapons and the explosives.

"You're thinking of the duelling scene," said the tall woman as though he might be talking to her. "We've done with that for today."

"We need to go and, er..." Hermod waved in the direction of things they needed to do. There were other Odinsons waiting on them to blast the ship free.

"No time," said the tall woman. "You're due on set in two minutes. Step lively."

When she'd realised the generator was more than a two minute job, Hilde knew she should have left the man to it.

But she couldn't let a technical problem go, and such a seemingly simple one at that.

"Here's your cuppa," said the man, putting a white mug on top of the generator.

Hilde let it stand. She was almost done. She'd discovered the generator's air inlet and filter were blocked. She scraped off some of the tacky debris. It looked like leaf fragments covered in some kind of crusted dried mess, almost like paint. Painted leaves? She picked off the worst of it from the filter and the inlet slots. She fastened everything back together and started the generator. It fired up first time and chugged amiably.

She picked up the cup of tea and took a sip. It was time to go and get some shovels. It wasn't like her useless family were going to find any without her.

"Nice job," said the man.

"All part of the service," she said.

"Don't suppose you're any good with electrical wiring?" he asked.

"Of course," she said, simply and honestly.

He gestured to his trailer. "One of the light fixtures in here is causing a problem."

Hilde didn't look at her watch to gauge the time, because she didn't own a watch. She looked at the sky and puffed her cheeks and shrugged. Surely, someone in her family would have found shovels by now. They could manage without her for ten minutes.

"Sure. Show me," she said.

. . .

IN SAM'S EXPERIENCE, National Heritage volunteers at Candlebroke emerged from the woodwork when you weren't looking to either rebuke you for the perfectly innocent thing you were doing, or to launch into an unwanted lecture on the history of the room you stood in.

Now, when she wanted one, there wasn't one to be found and she had to go out to the tea-rooms near the stable block to find one. A trio of volunteers in their branded fleeces worked to serve the queue of mostly movie people needing hot beverages and generously proportioned cakes to get them through the day. Sam ran to the head of the queue.

"Tell me," she said to the bespectacled woman guarding the glass-covered cake stands, "The History of Drink."

"There is a queue, you know," said the woman.

Sam shook her head. "Official business. There was an exhibition on the History of Drink. When was it?"

The woman looked at her blankly.

A taller grey-haired volunteer, with the bearing of a former librarian or teacher, or possibly high-class dominatrix, looked over sternly. "It was before your time, Julie."

"Good!" said Sam, realising her fervour to confirm the new theory made her sound more than a little manic. "When was it?"

The ex-librarian looked up and tried to recall. "Not sure."

"If it was before – Julie, is it? – when did Julie start?"

"I've been here two years now," said Julie.

"I just want a cheese scone and a latte," said the man Sam had pushed in front of.

"And the History of Drink exhibition was before Julie came?" said Sam, ignoring him.

"Oh, definitely," said a third volunteer. "Cos Gordon was here then. Remember him, Sue? All hands, he was."

"I can get my own scone," said the waiting customer, reaching for the cake stand. Julie snapped at his finger with cake handling tongs.

"Two years ago," said Sam, spinning away. "Christ!" She was halfway to the door before remembering to throw a "Thank you!" back at the women.

She hurried across the courtyard and back into the house, reslotting her thoughts into order. Through to the Summer room where Hilde had first broken in, and where one of the bottom panes of the French windows was still a temporary piece of board.

In Sam's original understanding, Vance had received the jewelled horn from his inside man at Candlebroke around the time Torsten had got his tattoo from Vance. Torsten had then got into a fight over it and ended up paying the price in court. Angry, he'd gone to Vance to have it out with him, and Vance had placated him by giving him the horn. Freyella's school trip had gone to Candlebroke where she'd seen a similar one on display. She'd told Torsten and Hilde. And Hilde, for inexplicable reasons, had decided to steal the second one herself. Then, maddest of all, Hilde had snuck to the house in the middle of the night, broke in through this door and, while the alarm was ringing, managed to sneak through a darkened house, go into the cellar, break through the store room door, find the other horn, and get out and run half a mile or so back up the driveway in the short time it took the police to arrive at the scene.

That other nonsense Antoine had tried to feed her about a break in at a different window was just lies. And irrelevant lies at that. None of it had previously made sense because she had put the facts in the order that had seemed to make the most sense.

But it was the wrong order. Like a movie filmed out of sequence, like one of her dad's stupid tricks. It looked impossible when seen in the wrong order.

In reality, the school trip to Candlebroke had been two years ago. Sam hadn't previously thought to ask when. The horn had then been stolen and passed to Vance some time after that. When Torsten had come to Vance, seeking vengeance, the horn Vance had given him – a priceless horn to stave off a savage beating, or whatever Torsten had come to mete out – that horn was the same one Freyella had seen on her school trip. There had only ever been one horn, which meant—

"Hilde wasn't stealing it. She was putting it back," Sam said out loud to the empty room.

There was a motivation which made sense. Or at least made sense in the mind of an Odinson. The moment Hilde heard what Freyella had to say, she realised what trouble Torsten could have found himself in. He'd only just finished the last of his community payback for the assault charge. He was known to the police. Being in receipt of stolen goods, possibly charged with burglary, Torsten would end up with a significant prison sentence. So what was Hilde to do? She wouldn't hand it in to the police and explain the truth.

Odinsons had no trust in the police, and certainly no sense of civic duty.

So, instead – crazy stupid genius plausible – Hilde took it on herself to break into Candlebroke Hall and put it back. She'd hiked over to the house and, thoroughly prepared with her toolkit, broken in at this door. But the alarm went off at once. Hilde, scared, decided to abandon the job. She didn't even set a single foot inside the house. With tools and horn, she set off home again, only to get caught by the police fifteen minutes later.

"She's innocent," she said.

Well, innocence was a relative term. Possibly guilty of handling stolen property, concealing a crime, criminal damage and going equipped for theft. All serious offences. But of the crime of burglary and of the theft of the horn in particular, Hilde was innocent. As she'd said all along.

"Who's innocent?"

Sam turned. Antoine de Winter leaned in the doorway, arms crossed in front of a shimmering silk shirt.

"Sorry?" said Sam.

"You said 'she's innocent'," he smiled. "I'm just curious who is innocent of what?"

"Just thinking out loud."

"Weren't you just. You ought to watch that. You never know what you might end up saying."

80

Hermod stood at the side of the horse-drawn carriage which had been brought round the side of the house. He kept his back straight as a rod, the crown of his head pushing upwards, as he'd been instructed. He stole a glance over at Gunnolf who was doing the same on the other side of the door.

"We're gonna be in a film!" he hissed. "Look at us!"

"Aye, I know!" said Gunnolf.

They both stared straight ahead. They had been told that being still as statues was their role in this scene: the decorative footmen on display as their rich employer descended from her carriage.

That wealthy employer was some young fit bird and her husband. They were chatting away while they waited for things to start. They just had to sit there. They didn't have a tough job like staring straight ahead.

Hermod thought he and Gunnolf were doing a brilliant

job of staring straight ahead. In fact, they were brilliant footmen all round. Maybe if they did a good job they could do it again, as a sideline. Footmen were probably in demand somewhere, especially trained ones, which they obviously now were.

The first assistant director, Saffron, who had given them their 'staring straight ahead no matter what' instructions, was now herding an old woman in a big posh frock into the midst of some other women in big posh frocks.

"We've been ready for five minutes," Saffron said.

"I was just sorting out something inside," the old woman replied.

"Positions?" someone important shouted.

Hermod didn't know what that meant but he just kept quiet and stared straight ahead.

KIKI STOOD on her position as directed by Saffron, among a half dozen similarly dressed women. She was undoubtedly the oldest among them. The most experienced. She nodded to those nearest to her.

"Did I see you at rehearsals?" whispered one woman under a towering wig to her left.

"Last minute casting," she whispered back. "I'm Kiki Harris."

The waif-like woman in a much saner wig and more elegant dress at the front of the coterie turned and gave her a warm smile. "Kiki," she said and took hold of Kiki's hand for a brief shake. "I'm Angel. We love your house."

There were general 'Ah's of understanding, and friendly nods.

The camera units were set up close by. It was a universal cliché, observable at any time in cinema history, but the cameras were smaller than they used to be. On an outdoor production, Kiki would have expected to see huge camera units on dolly tracks, but there appeared to be only one of those. Otherwise they were using Steadicams.

The director, Sebastian, chatted with a colleague while Saffron recapped where the group of ladies were walking from and to.

"Across to that point there where Lord Grenville will meet you and the Vicomte as they walk over from their carriage. Chauvelin comes in from that side. Lines. Scene."

Kiki paid close attention. It might be a part with no lines. She might have a man tied up in her apartment. But right now she was a professional actress.

SIGURD FOUND the mobile crane that they'd seen from afar. It was truck-mounted and, by the looks of the lifting frame and straps, it had been used to unload film units and those portaloos lined up by the wall. He climbed into the cab. This would be perfect for the job of hoisting the *Sandraker* from the soil. The keys were in the ignition.

"Reckon they just wants someone to nick it," he said.

He turned the ignition. The engine sputtered and struggled and refused to fire.

He tried turning it over again.

. . .

"Blake House party, scene five, take one," said the assistant cameraman, holding up the digital clapperboard to camera.

Director Sebastian gave a last glance around and called, "Action."

The gaggle of women moved down the lawn towards the carriage, shadowed by the Steadicam guy. Keeping her best side presented, Kiki maintained a position that ensured she was never blocked from camera by another woman.

They covered the short distance to the actors by the carriage. The pompously dressed, ruddy faced man playing Lord Grenville stepped forward as the young couple disembarked from the carriage.

"And now allow me, Comtesse, to introduce to you—"

There was the distant reverberating sound of an engine misfiring.

"Cut!"

"Someone find out who that was and give them a clip round the ear!" shouted Saffron. "Positions."

Lord Grenville smiled genially and stepped away. The women moved back up the lawn to the edge of the terrace to resume their positions.

Ragnar and Freyella moved slowly through the film set with Bjorn leading the way. They'd gone from the copse and into the village of caravans and trailers. As they moved onward, Ragnar caught a glimpse of tables and food and old carriages.

"They filming a wedding or a party or somesuch?" Ragnar said.

"Mm hmm," nodded Freyella, her lips firmly shut.

"Oh, bees on the way are they?" Ragnar said. As soon as he'd said it he heard the buzz as a bee zipped past his ears. He too clamped his lips shut, even though the bees were not aiming for his face. He held his arm out to the side, watching for the arriving bees, trying to focus on remaining calm.

Ragnar's eyes met Freyella's and he inclined his head slightly, indicating they should move around, slowly of course, to make sure that the dispersal of the bees had maximum impact. They rounded the side of the house and moved onto the periphery of the actual set. There were a great many people walking around in oldy-timey costumes. There were chairs, tables and decorative tent things arranged for a summer party. Ragnar was surprised to see all this set up just for a film. Part of him had assumed filming movies was all just trickery and props, but this was a garden party big enough for the Queen.

As he looked at the nearest cake on a table, a handful of bees flew straight for it and began to circle. He supposed they might be debating whether to stop for a nibble before continuing the search for their queen. They decided against it and joined the growing swarm buzzing about them.

81

Antoine stroked the surface of a polished table, even though it was behind the red sash barrier and one of the 'Do not touch' exhibits in the Summer Room. "I still don't understand what you're doing here, Sam," he said.

"The inventory," she said.

"But it's done, isn't it?" He gave her a sly, sidelong look. "Done and dusted and tied up with a bow, surely?"

"I've just got to pick up some documents. Stuff I left behind in the office."

"Oh?" he said and twitched his heavy moustache. "The office that's this way, you mean?" He turned, tilting his shoulders to indicate she should walk with him, and led the way back towards the central halls of the house. Their footsteps on the tiles sounded louder than ever.

"I enjoyed our date, you know," he said.

"The dinner," she said, correcting him. "Yes, it was

definitely in the top something-or-other of all the dinners I've had."

"You think it was a disaster," he said and laughed loudly. "We sparred. We argued. Sparks flew."

"Words were said," she agreed.

"Probing each other's defences. Each with our own ulterior motive."

"You had an ulterior motive."

Even though he was barely an inch or two taller than her, he contrived to somehow look down at her. A peculiar look. She decided he resembled a department store Santa with a practised but imperfect 'And what would you like for Christmas, little girl?' expression.

"I'm very much a people person," he said. "I read people. Like books. That's how I've made my living. I wanted to know you."

"Didn't realise I was worth knowing."

"Oh, my petite kitten. Even people with less depth than a pamphlet are worth reading."

They reached Phoebe's office. Antoine tried the handle. It was still locked.

He clicked his fingers. "Of course it's locked," he said theatrically. "Phoebe's dead."

"Um – yeah."

"Poor mad greedy Phoebe. Stole all the valuables. Caused no end of confusion and then, pausing only to dash off a suicide note, did a swan dive into that mincing machine thing." He said it with a sprinkle of glee. "Phoebe is dead. Your job here is done. And yet..." He leaned against the carved door frame and faced Sam. "I know why you're really here."

The silence around them seemed to bloom. They were at the heart of the house. Alone. Just the two of them. It was not a good feeling.

"You can be honest," he said. "You are open to me. Naked."

"What?"

"The attraction is obvious."

Laughter burst out from her like bubbles released from the deep ocean. The man was relentlessly self-deluding. He had no idea he was utterly resistible. "I don't fancy you," she said.

"Don't hide behind laughter. Search your feelings. You know it to be true."

She took a step back just to make the point. "Antoine. I am not attracted to you."

"I overwhelm you."

His cologne might overwhelm her. His taste in shirts was bedazzling. But she wasn't going to tell him that. "You're not my type," she said, which was a cop-out line.

"Your father probably spoke badly of me. He still blames me."

"Blames you? You're just not my type, Tony. Okay?"

"I am every type. I'm a hypnotic chameleon."

"Wow. Look, you're just too old for me."

He frowned, an actual dent in his over-confidence. "Old?" He straightened up and puffed out his chest, immediately wincing at a pain in his back. He held up a hand. "That's not old age," he said hurriedly. "I hurt myself."

"Right, the..." Sam's words trailed off. What had he said in Phoebe's office all those days ago? Helping an old lady move some paving slabs. She thought of Vance's grandma, Terry, and her mention of the nice man who'd helped her move the slabs.

How easy would it be for Terry to identify Antoine in a line-up? And if Phoebe hadn't committed the crime, hadn't committed suicide ... then there were thefts and a death yet to be explained.

All these thoughts passed through Sam in a single moment of sudden comprehension.

Antoine's expression shifted. However good his people-reading actually was, her surprise must have been obvious. She felt rising panic and backed away one step. He stepped forward in turn.

"I think I just..." she began.

"Is there something I need to...?"

"I'm just going..."

"You don't look like..."

It spiralled wordlessly to a fight or flight situation.

Sam ran. And Antoine de Winter ran after her.

82

Sigurd had barely got the engine of the crane truck turned over when there was a loud thump on the door and a woman stepped up to look in the open window.

"What the hell are you doing?" she demanded.

"Well, I'm just—" said Sigurd, who had learned from experience that simply starting the beginnings of a reasonable sentence could often be enough.

"We're shooting a bloody film!" snapped the woman. "You can't be doing this here."

"Fair enough," said Sigurd. "Should I move it?"

The woman blinked. "Of course, you should bloody move it. Get it out of the way."

"Right-o," said Sigurd. He put the crane into reverse and looked at her. "Tha's on my running board, mate."

The woman gave him an irritated look and stepped down. Sigurd turned out towards the track.

He looked in the wing mirror to see if anyone was running after him. "Well, she told me to move it, din't she?" he said to himself. "Stands to reason it's not stealing."

THE SECOND TAKE of the party scene got as far as Lord Grenville saying, "And now allow me, Comtesse, to introduce to you, Lady Blakeney, who honours us with her friendship. You and she will have much to say—" when a halt was called again due to a brightly painted blue leaf on the floor being in shot.

The women went back up to the terrace, the offending leaf was removed, and they started again.

A pink leaf was spotted this time.

Director Sebastian yelled at someone. A tiny army of runners and film folk scoured the grounds for painted leaves. There was some debate over whether they should clear all the fallen leaves from the area, or just search for painted ones.

It was another pink leaf which interrupted the third take. There was further argument over whether this was the same pink leaf.

"I recall when we were filming *Star Crash* we had to do one scene thirty-seven times – mostly because the horses wouldn't behave," Kiki said to the younger actresses as they resumed positions for the fourth time. "We look back on it and laugh now."

When a yellow leaf flew up and splatted against the side of the carriage on the fourth take, Kiki suppressed a scream.

. . .

Antoine caught up with Sam Applewhite at the foot of the grand staircase. He grabbed her shoulder, half-managed to snag her collar and then, in desperation, stuck a foot out and tripped her. She sprawled against the bottom step. She rolled over and stared at him with a wildness that was equal parts fear and anger.

"Get away from me!" she said.

"I don't know why you're running," he said, as confused by his own behaviour as hers.

"I will scream."

He laughed at that. "What? And why?" He looked round. "And who would come?"

Sam appeared to consider that question. When she spoke again she was quieter and more measured. "Did you kill Phoebe?"

Antoine had to laugh again. "Are you crazy? You think I push people into gardening machinery?"

"She didn't steal anything from Candlebroke Hall."

"The police think so," he said, instantly regretting it. Tone was everything in conversation, and even to his own ears that had sounded like a criminal boast.

"Are you going to kill me too?"

"I said I didn't kill her." He sighed and looked to the heavens for solace.

Sam pushed herself up, practically jumping, and hurried up the stairs, using hands and feet like an energetic toddler.

"Wait!" Antoine shouted. She didn't. He had no choice but to give chase.

. . .

HERMOD AND GUNNOLF watched the posh women in frocks walk off again for yet another take.

"This is smashing, innit?" said Hermod, talking out of the corner of his mouth while he stood ramrod still.

"I know!" agreed Gunnolf from the corner of his mouth. "Din't think being in the movies would be like this."

"Who'd a thought they'd do bits of it again and again. I thought they'd do the whole thing in one go, like at the pantomime."

"I love the pantomime."

"Wait till we tell mum we've been in the movies."

"At this rate we'll never be finished," said the crusty red-faced man who was being the posh lord. "Places."

The bloke in the baseball cap shouted "Action!" and the women walked once more. They hadn't got ten feet when one of the young ones made a squeaking noise and flapped her arms.

"Bee!" she shouted. One of the others turned to rebuke her, immediately yelping herself as a pair of bees buzzed her.

"Cut!"

Hermod chuckled. "Brilliant."

"And we ain't fucked up once," said Gunnolf proudly. "We're dead good at this."

83

U p to the first floor and halfway along the main corridor, Sam slowed to look back and saw Antoine was a considerable way behind her. He wasn't doughy, but he didn't look the type to do much cardio. She was faster than him, for now. Still moving, she used up precious seconds feeling in her jacket pocket for her phone.

"Sam!" Antoine shouted.

"I'm calling the police!" she shouted back. She swiped to her keypad and hit 999.

"Wait!"

From the corner of her eye Sam saw Antoine wrestling with something. He was ripping a spear-like weapon from its display housing on the wall (fifteenth century spontoon with modern replacement shaft, her inventory-taker's mind added). Once it was freed, he hefted it like an Olympic javelin.

"Emergency service operator, what service do you require?" said the voice on the line.

"Police," Sam whispered.

Antoine hurled the spear. Sam could see it was a poor throw even before it left his hand, and it was that judgement which nearly killed her. She should have run. His throw was too high, but the spear wobbled in a weird manner and came down unexpectedly close to her shoulder. As it clattered to the floor the spell was broken. Sam shouted in alarm and ran again.

"Police! Candlebroke Hall! He's trying to kill me!"

"I didn't kill her!" Antoine yelled.

She looked back and saw him wrench a sword from the same display and come charging after her.

TAKE SEVEN, and bees were now a major problem.

"Can someone do something about the bees!" someone shouted, but it seemed no one considered it their job. There were set people, and general dogsbodies, and blokes whose job it was to lug things about, but no one had bee-herding on their job description.

"On *Humanoids of the Deep*, sandflies were a huge problem," Kiki said conversationally. "But film was expensive. Dear Roger wasn't one for splashing the cash. So we just had to push on through."

"These are your bees, aren't they?" said one of the young actresses.

"I beg your pardon?" said Kiki.

"This is your place. Your bees."

"I didn't invite them onto the set!"

"Ladies," said leading actress Angel gently.

The technical crew were ready.

"Action!" called the director.

They walked down towards the carriage. There were still bees, but the actresses maintained their composure and walked on. They reached the carriage. The French aristocrats stepped down. Lord Grenville stepped in.

"And now allow me, Comtesse, to introduce you to Lady Marguerite Blakeney, who honours us with her friendship. You and she will have much to say to one another. Every French noble is welcome here. An enemy of my enemy is my friend—"

"Cut!" shouted the director.

"What now?" Kiki snapped.

"One of the footmen is mouthing along with Lord bloody Grenville."

"I weren't!" said one of the footmen hotly.

"I might have been," said the other. "We've heard nothing but them words all day."

Over by the garden party chairs and tables, a man yelped, flapped his wig about him and accidentally kicked over a table of cakes.

"Bee! Bee!" he shouted.

"Back to positions!" growled Saffron.

SAM REBOUNDED off a door frame and as she stumbled into a room, fumbled her phone back to her ear.

"Are you still there?" said the operator.

"Yeah," said Sam.

She looked about, trying to retrieve her mental map of the place. The King James drawing room on the first floor. There were three exits from the room: back the way she'd come through the ante room to the long gallery, a door to the billiards room and the apartments beyond, and a narrow door to the servants' stairs.

"How long until the police get here?" she gasped, hurrying to the servants' stairs.

"They're on their way. Can you tell me what happened?"

At the door to the stairs, Sam nearly ran headlong into Antoine's blade. She yelped.

He held the sword high and shouted, "Stop running!"

Sam tripped backwards, managed to turn the fall into a skidding, twisting turn, and fled back the other way.

With an animalistic roar, Antoine ran, swinging his weapon. It hacked a wedge out of a floorboard. Sam ran on into the billiards room, skirting the antique snooker table which dominated the room, and made for the rack to grab a snooker cue. She grabbed at one, for a moment battling to release it (how stupid it would have been to die from a blow to the back while failing to free a snooker cue), then swung the long cue round in an arc that nearly cracked Antoine across the head.

He ducked back, hair in disarray, a crazy, disbelieving look on his face. "Mad bitch!" he exclaimed, sounding more offended than anything else.

He retaliated with powerful sword swings. Sam's dad had used stage fencing for a few of the more extravagant shows he'd performed. It was a bitter relief to see Antoine had no such training. His attacks were all tree-chopping whacks. Sam held out her cue to fend them off; a blow hacked it in half. The next jarred it from her hands completely.

"Why are you being like this?" he said.

She ran round the table and out of the door before he could circle back. She sprinted along the long gallery once more. He was heavy-footed and older, but he had power in his stride. He would be on her soon.

She literally leapt to drag a kite shield down from its position on the gallery wall. She turned, deflecting one sword blow with the shield held in both hands, then managed to slide her arm into the straps and deflect another.

In that moment, on the cusp of being hacked to death, Sam contemplated the value of plate armour. She also realised, somewhere along the way, she had dropped her phone.

SIGURD STOPPED the mobile crane by the *Sandraker*.

"Folks'll see thee," said Ogendus as Sigurd stepped down.

Sigurd looked down toward the film set. There was a lot of movement, but nothing focused on their activities with the Viking ship. "We'll be fine. Right, let's get the low loader into position and put some straps around our ship. Where's Yngve?"

"Him and young Erik went looking for shovels down in them buildings with the cages."

"I'll move the low loader," said Ogendus and went off to do that.

"I thought we were using the explosives," said Torsten.

"And blow a hole in the bottom of our ship?" said Sigurd. "If tha wants to do something useful, take a force of men and take position by the topiary in case someone tries to stop us."

"Toe-who?"

"The funny-shaped bushes, lad," said Sigurd. "Go armed, go quiet, and keep a look out."

"Don't reckon there's much glory in invading some bushes," Torsten muttered.

"That one looks like a bunny," said Cousin Harbard.

"I thought it was more like a bird," said Torsten.

"Well, go an' bloody see, eh?" said Sigurd, hauling the lifting straps over to their ship.

THERE WERE shouts among the film folk as upended furniture was righted, actors were shuffled from one place to another, and folks waved boards and stuff to try to clear the pervasive cloud of bees. Despite the chaos, it was inevitable someone would eventually spot the two men and a girl with bee beards, wandering among them.

"Oh, my God," yelled one man, stumbling back from the trio. "What the hell?"

"Don't alarm them," said Bjorn calmly. "They mean us no harm."

That might be true, but Ragnar felt far from safe. His arm, from the elbow down, was a ball of bees. That it felt practically weightless was disturbing. Tiny legs and flickering wings all hanging off him like they didn't have a care in the world. He wished he'd worn a tunic with tighter cuffs. He could feel them wriggling up his wrist and lower arm.

"What the fuck happened?" exclaimed a woman.

Freyella had a beard reaching from her nose to her thighs, like one of the Snow White's dwarfs. And she seemed to be having a whale of a time. She was definitely a brave one, but this was possibly too much. If someone agitated the bees and set them to stinging, Ragnar would have hell to pay.

Those film folk nearest were all surprised to the point of idiocy.

"You need help?" said one.

Another came towards them with a long coat, apparently to beat away the bees.

"Don't tha bloody dare!" said Ragnar. "Go get help. Proper help."

84

People learned how to behave from what they saw in TV and films.

It was something Marvin had told Sam when she was a girl. He said in real life people only fell down when shot because that's what they'd seen on the telly. Whether the shot/falling thing was true or not, it was clear Antoine had learned his sword fighting basics from the silver screen. In real life, the object of sword fighting was to hit the soft squishy bits of your opponent, but now Sam had a shield in her hands, Antoine targeted that. With a decent lunge, he might have run her through, but he was intent on hacking at the shield, with a real possibility of him breaking her forearm.

Sam gauged the rhythm of his attacks. In a lull between beats, she shoved at him. With the sword pinned against his body, Antoine stumbled back and fell. Sam discarded the shield and ran. She didn't have a plan beyond hoping he might grow tired, or come to his bloody senses.

"Take ten," said the assistant cameraman.

Kiki wiped any irritation from her face. Multiple takes were not uncommon. She told her fellow actors about the thirty takes they had to do for a scene on *Fall of the Eagles,* because one of the young American actors kept fluffing his lines. Few of the selfish little girls seemed interested in her fascinating anecdotes. Still, Kiki had never seen so many retakes for a scene where no one had yet managed to say a complete line. It was, in truth, infuriating. The Georgian shoes she was wearing made her feet ache, and she feared the significant make up she'd had applied to her face would slip eventually. She growled in frustration. She had entered into this on the promise she'd be immortalised on film one last time.

"Let's do this," she whispered to herself.

"Ignore the bees. Ignore all distractions," said Sebastian and called action.

The women walked down to the carriage. Bees whipped around Kiki's head. She was sure at least a couple of them had got stuck in her wig. She ignored them, keeping her hands fixed in a ladylike pose.

Five steps from the carriage there was a crash from somewhere on the set. Kiki kept her eyes straight ahead, as did the others. They could fix that in post-production.

At the carriage, the twin footmen stood smartly to

attention. If one had his lips pressed into bloodless white lines then so be it. Kiki didn't look.

Lord Grenville stepped forward into shot to introduce the comte and comtesse.

"And now allow me—" he began. There was another crash and a distant yelp. "—to introduce you to Lady Marguerite Blakeney, who honours us with—"

"Cut!" shouted the director.

The lead actress, Angel, groaned.

"You have got to be kidding me," said Kiki.

"What the hell is that in my shot?" Sebastian pointed up the lawns. Kiki saw an unnatural silhouette among the distant trees. Some sort of crane? "You can barely see it," she said. "Let's just do this thing."

"Positions!" called Saffron, utterly ignoring her. "Duncan, go see what that is and move it."

As they walked back, Kiki said to whoever would listen, "One can be too much of a perfectionist. In my day, film-making was a warts and all process."

"In your day, in your day," muttered one of the women. Kiki wasn't sure who.

"Cinéma verité and all that," she sniffed.

This drew a scoffing laugh, definitely from Angel Dibly.

"Something to add, young lady?" said Kiki.

The lead actress swatted a bee away. "You seem to have a lot of opinions, Kiki, given—" she pulled a face "—the size of your role."

"There are no small roles, dear," Kiki said automatically.

Over by the trailer village, behind the cameras, people

were running and waving their arms frantically. Nearby, a man in a Georgian frock coat flailed at a bee (real or imagined), whirled and fell against a table. He managed to stop the table tipping, but a plate of cream cakes and sandwiches slid onto the floor, missing the ladies' skirts by inches.

"Jesus!" hissed Angel.

"Get over yourself," said Kiki, picking up the plate and the mishappen mound now on it. "It's just food. We all have to get our hands dirty in this business."

Set folk were coming over to clean up. The frock coated gent was apologising profusely.

There was a shout from elsewhere. Another painted leaf had been found in shot.

Kiki leaned towards Angel. "A word of advice from someone who's been there. Just because you're in the bloom of youth and wafer thin doesn't mean you're a star. And it doesn't mean you're indispensable."

A wardrobe assistant began fussing over garments to check none had been spattered with food.

Angel leaned back towards Kiki. "And a word of advice for someone I've never heard of, not once, and who has only been permitted to appear in this thing because we're using her fucking insect-infested house, and the first AD feels sorry for you because you're a sad and lonely old baggage: shut the fuck up and just be glad you're allowed to be involved."

There were shouts from the bushes down by the long pond. Half a dozen men wearing rough clothing and waving axes leapt out of the topiary at the security men advancing towards them. The security men yelled and ran for it. The wild Viking raiders gave chase. Kiki had lost the energy to be surprised.

What she did have was a plate full of creamy, cakey, mushed up mess in her hand. She shoved it in Angel Dibly's face.

"Have you seen this?"

Hilde snapped the cover back onto the light fixture and turned to the AV man. He sat in his AV suite at the end of the trailer, looking at the feeds from multiple cameras around the site. Hilde watched the action on the screens.

"Is this part of the movie?" she asked.

He looked at his notes. "It's the arrival at the garden party scene, or should be. Not sure why there's now a food fight and all that running around."

Hilde peered at a screen showing a pair of beautifully groomed footmen in powdered wigs and dressy outfits. They stared into the middle distance like flabby faced soldiers, stock still while chaos unfolded around them.

"And I've really no idea who these guys with the axes and shields are," said the AV man.

Hilde looked at the Viking raiding party coming across the lawns to join in the melee. She was about to say it was time for her to be on her way, when another sight drew her attention.

"Oh, and the police have arrived," said the AV man.

85

S am took the stairs up, ducked through a doorway, and realised she had come to an effective dead end. The uppermost rooms in the south wing were a cul-de-sac of bedrooms and private rooms. She couldn't hear Antoine following her, but wasn't going to gamble on that. Now was probably the time to hole up somewhere and wait for the police to arrive.

She tried a door, but it was locked. So were the second and third.

Now she could hear Antoine's clodding footsteps. "Sam!"

The fourth door opened and she slipped through. There was no key in this side of the lock, but there was a bolt, up high. She threw it across and stepped back.

She was in a small, cluttered living room type space, with textured wallpaper that had been painted over so many times the peeling pieces were a centimetre thick. There was a semi-circular dining table shoved up against a window.

There was a battered and slightly mildewed sofa less than four feet away from a small television. There was also her dad, taped to a dining chair by his wrists and ankles.

"Thank goodness you found me," he said.

"Dad?"

The door to the apartment rattled. Kiki's apartment. Of course it was, she realised.

"Open this door, Sam," called Antoine.

Sam crouched by her dad and tried to pull apart the tape bonds, but the material was unyielding.

"I've got a pocketknife somewhere," said Marvin.

Sam went past him to the tiny kitchenette, found a serrated steak knife, and went back to cut the tape.

"Open this now!" shouted Antoine and began to barge at the door.

"Antoine was stealing the antiques," Sam said as she sawed through one wrist bond.

"They were both at it," said Marvin.

"What?"

"Kiki too." With his free hand he pointed to the dining table, then took the knife from Sam so he could cut the rest himself.

On the table was a folded handwritten letter next to an envelope. Next to that a loaded antique crossbow. The bolt was a foot-long spike of iron-tipped oak.

"What the hell happened?" asked Sam.

"Kiki caught me reading her confession," said Marvin. "They're in it together. Have been for a long time."

The bashing at the door paused a second and was replaced by something harder and louder.

"Antoine's got a sword," said Sam.

"Is he mad?"

Sam nodded. "Desperate." She reconsidered. "And mad. I phoned the police." She raised her voice. "The police are on their way, Antoine!"

The hacking sword blade didn't stop, but was joined by a bitter and frantic swearing.

"We can defend ourselves," said Marvin, standing up now he was freed.

Sam looked at the steak knife in his hand.

"I meant with that," he said, gesturing at the crossbow.

Sam touched it up warily. "It might take someone's eye out."

"That's sort of the point, dear."

"I mean it might take *my* eye out. Thing's ancient."

Marvin cast about. "There's a way out to the roof."

"Where?"

He pointed to a wooden hatch in the ceiling.

A sword blow shook the door and a splinter of painted wood flew out across the room. They'd need to do something before Antoine hacked his way through.

"Let's take a look," said Sam.

THE FOOD FIGHT and Torsten's raid (which was as much about yelling and running about as it was actual axe-waving) occupied many of the cast and crew members. The bees had served their purpose.

Ragnar nodded towards the track by the side of the house, and the blue flashing lights. "Ey up. Looks like the coppers are here. Let's see what they mek of a young girl and a couple of older men, just out fer a walk with their bees. No crime there, aye? Reckon that'll confusticate them a bit while our lads get the ship on the low loader."

Bjorn gave Ragnar a cheery thumbs up to the plan.

"Freyella, lead the way," said her Farfar. "Two blokes with bee beards is alarming, but they'll have bloody kittens when they see you."

Freyella was enjoying being in the eye of the storm. At first it had been alarming to have the bees all over her face, but now they were near to their queen, they seemed content. They swirled and danced across her skin, and from time to time they got in the way of her nostrils, but Uncle Bjorn had shown her how to move them gently away.

Freyella saw the same reaction on the face of every person she came across. They would stare at her, as their brains tried to understand what they were looking at, then they would understand that here was a young girl wearing a beard of bees. They looked horror-stricken, worried for themselves, and to varying degrees for her as well. She wanted to tell them she was fine, but it was best if she kept her mouth shut, for obvious reasons.

As a police car came round the big house, Freyella walked to meet it. She stood in front of it on the grass. She stared through the windscreen as two police officers talked to each other and pointed at her, clearly mirroring the same reaction she had now seen many times. They were reluctant to get out from the safety of their vehicle, but they did anyway, hanging back behind their doors.

"Are you all right?" one of them asked.

Freyella shook her head. The longer she could occupy the policemen, the longer her family had to make their escape.

"Just stay calm," the policeman said to her.

Freyella wanted to roll her eyes, but didn't. She watched as he made a call on his radio, asking for assistance with "a situation". It wasn't easy to catch his muttered attempts to describe exactly what that was, but Freyella heard the phrase "one false move and she's dead" and was pleased.

A dark car stopped behind the police vehicle and that lanky Saxon detective got out. Once he got over the surprise of seeing Freyella and her bee beard, his eyes narrowed and he looked up at the house.

As Hilde ran across the set, she ducked through the food fight. Georgian ladies and gentlemen were hurling cakes and sandwiches at the Viking raiders and each other. The more ambitious had moved onto the crockery, and Hilde watched as a dish of bright red jam cartwheeled through the air, leaving a splatter formation that despoiled a great many outfits. An older lady in a powdered wig smashed a plate of pastries into a younger woman's face.

"I'm a star, bitch!" she was screaming. "Christopher Lee said I was magnetic. Roger Moore! He gave me a wink and he doesn't hand out many of those!"

The deranged woman grabbed a plate of scones and started hurling them at the film crew who were trying to intervene.

Hilde ran down to the horse-drawn carriage, and the two

footmen who were still standing perfectly still. "Hermod? Gunnolf?"

Hermod seemed to exert great willpower in an attempt to not to turn to her.

"Look at me!" she said.

"We can't," whispered Gunnolf between still lips. "We're in the movie."

Hilde slapped his face.

"Ow!" he winced. "We're in a scene! We can't move!"

"Look around you, idiots! Your scene is done."

"He hasn't said cut yet."

"Weren't you supposed to be doing a job?"

"All in hand," said Hermod. He felt around in his breeches for the lighter.

86

Ogendus backed the low loader into position near to the longship. Sigurd was confident it was close enough for the crane to lift it clear of the soil mounds hemming it in, and place it on the back.

"We'll soon have thee home, *Sandraker!*" he called cheerily.

Sigurd beckoned the family present to join him around the ship. "We need to rock the ship so that we can get the straps under it."

"We should have shovels for this," said Kalf.

"We not going to set off the explosives?" asked Horik.

"Tha carried it to the sea for its launch," said Sigurd, "so this should be no problem. Now into position and ... up!"

The longship failed to move. Sigurd could see the faces of everyone trying to lift it. They were straining madly, but it was having no effect.

"Mebbe it's nailed down," said Horik."

"Mebbe there's something inside," suggested Ogendus. He swung himself aboard and lifted the panel hatches. "Sigurd!" he called in a strangled yell.

Sigurd scrabbled aboard. He saw that every nook and cranny was packed with boxes. Ogendus pulled one out to look inside. It was substantial, made to click shut and be weatherproof. When he opened it, Sigurd saw it was packed with porcelain figurines, each packaged carefully in bubble wrap. Ogendus tried another, and found beautifully mounted curio cabinets, at least six of them. They were the type of thing that an oldy timey Saxon bloke might have arrayed on the walls of his study. The top one contained a display of those shiny round crystal things, each with a beautifully handwritten label. The next one down had fossils. "These're from the blummin' hall," he breathed, understanding at last.

Ogendus called down to their relatives. "The *Sandraker's* full of treasure!"

"It's a raid!" yelled someone.

"A raid!" came another shout.

"We've done a raid! The *Sandraker's* first raid!"

"We still need to get it safely home!" shouted Ogendus.

"Which means we'll need to lift the ship!" Sigurd pointed out. "So put your backs into it."

Raiding treasure was a fine motivator. The Odinsons worked together, rocking the ship in its foundations just enough for a strap to be slid up it fore and aft.

Sigurd went back to the crane to retrieve the radio controller. It seemed fairly self-explanatory. There were three knobs. The leftmost one swung the boom, and the right hand one controlled the up and down motion. He took up the strain on the straps under the longship. It creaked and sagged, but held firm as he raised it.

A HAND GRABBED Ragnar's arm, a bold move considering it was only two feet away from his other arm, which was covered in bees. It was Hilde.

"What's going on?" she said.

Ragnar waved a bee arm at the police. "We were just discussing our bee predicament with these fine officers of the law."

Detective Camara looked like a man who had been given a basket of serpents for his birthday. His face couldn't decide between shock, confusion, or annoyance.

"What *is* going on?" he said.

"Is Freyella all right?" said Hilde, seeing the young girl nearly covered with her share of insects.

"Don't you worry yoursen," said Ragnar. "That's why Torsten's got the smoker. It subdues the bees."

Hilde looked across the confusion of the film set to where Ragnar was pointing. "Torsten?" she asked.

"Aye."

"Torsten – who is carrying what I am *utterly certain* is a nail gun?"

Ragnar squinted at the chaos on the back lawns and groaned when he realised she was right.

"We are going to have words about this in a bit," said Camara.

"Aye, all in good time."

"Now, have any of you seen Sam Applewhite?"

"Why are you looking for Sam?" asked Hilde.

SAM all but pushed Marvin up the steps and through the hatch onto the roof. The opening was a good ten feet from the edge, but with no railing or high parapet to stop them falling, and a stiff breeze coming in from the direction of the coast, Sam instinctively kept low.

A big stately home had a big roof, but the size of it was still a surprise. Its patched up, felted and tarred surface was long enough to play football on – if you could avoid the domed grid of skylights near the centre of the roof, and also the weird patio garden someone had built. Sam clocked the potted plants and the deck chair, and the peculiar gibbet-style washing line. It hardly fitted in with stately home aesthetic.

She realised she ought to shut the hatch behind them. As she pushed it down, a sword blade wedged in the gap to stop it shutting completely. She stood on the hatch. The sword waggled and Antonine grunted. Marvin dithered, bending to grasp the blade and wrench it from Antoine, before wisely deciding that grabbing a sharp sword wasn't a great idea. He stepped back and tried to stamp on the blade, which was probably no better.

HERMOD AND GUNNOLF jogged back towards the longship, which was not necessarily easy in weird tights and chunky buckled shoes.

"I was enjoying being in a film," complained Gunnolf.

"Aye, but Ragnar wants his ship, so…"

Someone had found a crane and *Sandraker* had been lifted a few inches. There were a few of their kin around the low loader nearby.

"Standin' around like clueless chickens," said Hermod. "Let's get that fuse lit."

They bent to the trail of fuses.

"How long d'ya reckon they burn for?" said Gunnolf.

Hermod shrugged. "If we run away fast then maybe it dunt matter?"

Kalf and Horik were vigorously waving at them from the bushes.

"Yeah, yeah, we're on it," Gunnolf shouted.

The fuse fizzed. Hermod and Gunnolf pegged it for the cover of the bushes.

WHILE SAM FOUGHT to keep the hatch closed, Marvin came at it with a folding deckchair.

Frazzled with adrenaline, she wondered if he simply planned to sit on the hatch. He brought it down to the level of the waggling blade, then pushed the deckchair shut. It gripped the sword like a mouse in a trap.

He rotated it in his hand. With effort, and the physics of levers of his side, he twisted it from Antoine's grip. There was swearing from below. Marvin yanked the folded chair and sword through the gap and Sam stood squarely on the hatch.

"Get that plant pot!" she said, pointing.

Marvin looked at the heavy, soil-filled planter. "With my back? At my age?"

She dragged him onto the hatch and went to fetch it herself. It was bloody heavy, but once in place on the hatch, it was never going to be shifted from beneath.

Chest heaving, Sam looked about.

The height and size of the roof meant, from here, there was no view of the immediate grounds. The flat landscape of south Lincolnshire spread in all directions. That way, fields. That way, woods and yet more fields. That way, a line of road and the smudgy grey suggestion of sea in the distance.

"Have you got your phone?" she said.

Marvin shook his head, also breathless. "Downstairs. What about yours?"

"Dropped it."

He took several deep breaths. "Well, we're a right pair, aren't we?" Marvin looked at the hatch. "Was he actually trying to kill us?"

Sam nodded. "And he killed Phoebe, I guess."

"And I thought I couldn't hate him more than I did."

She gave her dad a look. "You never fully explained why you had an issue with him." She didn't wait for an answer, but moved crabwise to the nearest edge of the roof to look down.

Her heart somersaulted in joyful relief at the sight of three police vehicles directly below. What exactly was going on was less clear. There were film people and ... others shouting and waving. Was that a food fight at the edge of the film set?

Sam waved her arms. "Hey! Hey! Up here!"

She couldn't make out any of the police among the figures below, and the noise everyone was generating was too loud to shout over. Maybe she could drop something on them to get their attention. Nothing too heavy, obviously. She didn't want to kill anyone.

Maybe she could just throw down some of the gravel pieces that had come free from the roof. She scooped up a light handful.

"Er, Sam," said Marvin.

"Hang on, dad, I'm—"

"Sam!"

She looked round. Antoine was approaching alongside the great domed skylight.

He waved the crossbow from Kiki's apartment in both hands and shouted something, but the wind took it.

"What?" Sam shouted back. She looked to the hatch, wondering how quickly she could move the plant pot, lift the hatch, and get her dad down. Not quickly enough.

She bent to pull the sword from the deckchair and cast the gravel behind her, over the edge of the roof.

"I *said* did you think there was only one way onto the roof?" Antoine shouted.

He rounded the skylight and stopped twenty feet from Sam and Marvin. The business end of the crossbow wavered between them. Sam looked at the fat little bolt in the groove and tried not to imagine what it would be like to be shot in the chest by the thing.

"I just wanted to talk!" said Antoine, irritated.

"Really?" said Sam. "It didn't feel like that. You chased me."

"You ran!"

"You won't get away with this," said Marvin, clearly getting his lines from the Scooby Doo playbook.

"With what?" squeaked Antoine, indignation strangling his voice. "I did not kill her! She fell! She ran and tripped and fell!"

"And all the valuables you stole?" said Sam.

"It wasn't me!" The crossbow wobbled dangerously as he momentarily freed one hand to push his wind-tossed hair out of his eyes. "I'm not the crook here."

Marvin scowled. "Kiki confessed. She wrote it all down."

Antoine's face became a hard mask for a moment. He pushed his tongue between teeth and lips as he thought this over. "Well, that's just inconvenient, isn't it? I can't go to prison. What will Hugh do without me?"

Antoine raised the crossbow to sight along the bolt groove. There were two of them and one bolt, but Sam still didn't like those odds. She'd brought a sword to a crossbow fight, and that was not a good thing.

87

S lowly but steadily, and much to Sigurd's delight, *Sandraker* was clear of the ground and holding firm. He used the controls to lift it clear of the earth mounds, before working out how to swing the boom around towards the low loader.

"Nice and slow."

It was going to be tricky to bring it to rest exactly on the supports, but Sigurd knew it was lined up correctly. All he needed to do was take it steady and lower the boom really carefully.

At that moment there was the *whump* of an explosion. There was noise, a hail of dirt, and the mobile crane was tilting, then tipping...

THE THUNDEROUS SOUND caused Kiki to pause in the victorious cake pummelling she was giving the young actress beneath her. Her dress was torn, her make up gouged by fingernails and it was possible, in the melee, she had accidentally moved from one jumped-up pubescent starlet to another but – by God! – she was having fun.

She looked up and saw the distant end of the lawns had disappeared in a mushroom cloud of brown loamy dirt.

Lucas Camara would later swear he felt the explosion before he heard it. There was an ear-smacking crack of thunder, and a fat pillar of dirt was flung high into the air. He had seen controlled demolitions of World War Two ordnance out in the Wash as part of his job, and he knew a bloody big explosion when he saw one.

"Hell's biscuits!" he shouted. Everyone was probably too deafened to hear him.

From her vantage point on top of Candlebroke Hall, Sam saw the explosion as a fountain plume of dirt. A huge, unappetising chocolate fountain. The boom was incredible, startling.

Antoine was distracted. The crossbow was pointed elsewhere.

She ran at him, casting aside the sword. There was no point trying to engage him in a fight. She needed to get the crossbow off him.

Antoine saw her coming, but she was close enough. She grabbed his arm, forced it and the crossbow up, then barged him backward. He stumbled. She stumbled with him.

Together they stepped onto the hard, smooth surface of the skylight.

Antoine was complaining in the aggrieved tones of a man convinced the situation was simply unfair. They turned and waltzed together, neither wanting to pull back and give the other an advantage. His mistake was keeping hold of the crossbow. Despite the momentum she had, he was stronger. He could wrestle her away, if only he let go.

Glass creaked under their feet.

"Just get..." Antoine grunted.

Marvin was shouting to Sam, a dreadful, fearful plea.

The crossbow was trapped between them, pressed between their faces and pointing straight up. Sam realised the long trigger lever was just in front of her chin. She shifted position and hit it with the flat of her hand.

The crossbow twanged and the force shook them apart. The bolt vanished upward. They stumbled away from each other, still standing on glass. Antoine stared at her, wide-eyed. He put a hand to the glistening circular wound where the tip of his nose had once been.

"Ow!" he said, a pained whisper. "Why did you do that?"

Sam blinked. "You were trying to kill us!"

Antoine touched his nose and winced sharply. "You might have inferred that..."

"What?"

"Inferred it."

"You're a piece of work, Tony Winters," said Marvin bitterly.

Antoine turned to him. "Hey. Now listen, Marvin—"

Sam only heard the briefest, whistling whoosh. Antoine

twitched. Sam couldn't work out what she was seeing. As if Antoine had suddenly grown a tiny, blood-red goatee. A spike of dripping red hung from under his chin. His mouth hung half open. Behind his perfect white teeth there was a length of bolt running through his mouth, top to bottom. She saw the tail end of the flights poking from the top of his skull.

He stayed upright for several seconds. Then one leg went and he fell heavily onto the skylight. Sam shuffled quickly back, belatedly aware the glass or frame might give way under the weight.

Antoine de Winter slid sluggishly down the sloped pane. His eyes were wide open, but there was no life behind them anymore.

Sam looked at the sky. What goes up...

Marvin put his hands on her shoulders. She instantly grabbed him and held him tight.

SIGURD STUMBLED from the crane cab and looked around. Soil covered everything for yards. The *Sandraker* looked as though it had been dusted with cocoa. Remarkably, it had not been smashed by the falling crane, but it had collapsed onto the back of Yngve's low loader.

Sigurd went to look, along with a dozen other shellshocked Odinsons. The ship was not sitting safely on its cradle, but was not too far off. If he rounded up the clan he was confident they could lift it into place and secure it for transport.

He brushed off the worst of the soil and took a few

wobbly steps, then paused. His hearing was off because of the blast. Everything sounded as if he was underwater, muted and a bit alien, but surely that was the wailing of sirens? He backtracked to the low loader. They'd come this far. It would be heart-breaking if the police spoiled their plan at the last minute.

He unfastened the harness to release the longship from the crane. Silently the equally stunned Kalf and Horik helped him. He made to climb into the low loader's cab, but Ogendus was already there.

"Police are here!" Ogendus yelled in the manner of a man who was suddenly and profoundly deaf. "We need to go!"

"We need to secure it more!" Sigurd shouted back.

"What?"

"We need to secure it!"

Ogendus grinned. "Like a charm!" he agreed and put the low loader into gear.

Sigurd scrambled to the wobbling *Sandraker,* along the side of the low loader, as Ogendus hauled the ship towards the rough tracks leading to the exit. Family members scrambled to get on board before it left them behind.

Yngve and Erik appeared from somewhere. Their eyes were wild and their clothes were shredded.

"Bloody big cat they've got down in them buildings," grumbled Erik.

As the low loader rumbled down the uneven track, *Sandraker* swung and lurched from side to side. Odinson men, mindful of being crushed between planks of seasoned stolen oak, jumped off. Sigurd watched with despair as he pressed his back against the cab.

"Ogendus! Stop!" he yelled, but Ogendus was deaf and on an escape mission. The truck turned onto the gravel that led to the road. Sigurd had an unbroken view from the rear of the truck, presumably one much better than Ogendus. His heart sank when one of the three police cars turned around on the grass and followed them out of the grounds. Sigurd thumped on the cab to attract Ogendus's attention, but it was a futile effort.

The police car started its siren and flashed its lights, in a clear attempt to pull them over. Ogendus must have finally spotted the police car. His response was to floor the accelerator.

"Chuffin' hell!" Sigurd yelled.

He had to brace himself firmly against the rear of the cab, watching in dismay as the long ship bucked and swayed. This was surely far worse than the beautiful ship had experienced at sea.

88

The self-important juvenile actress, Angel, had squirmed away from Kiki, but it no longer mattered. The bitch had crawled away with her wig ripped off, her dress torn, and her face covered in equal amounts of jam, cream and mud. The job was done, and Kiki had made her point. She wasn't entirely sure what that point was, but if she just gave herself a moment to sit down and collect herself, she was sure it would come to her.

She found a chair, righted it, and sat on the lawn next to a table where, against all probability, there was still a plate of unmolested petit fours. A bee was picking over a glazed éclair. Kiki let the bee be and selected a tartlet.

Around her, bedlam still reigned. The set was in disarray. The horses, unshackled from the carriage, had wandered off to nibble grass. Up by the trees there was now a crater and a circle of earth where that hideously out of place ship had once stood. Someone had blown it up. Good for them.

The film set was not exactly ruined – a localised food fight and the appearance of some men dressed as Vikings had not laid waste to it all – but Kiki was experienced enough to know it would take the best part of a day to put right. At least the bees had mostly gone, along with the mysterious Viking men.

There was a tickle at her scalp. Kiki put a hand to her temple and it came away with blood on her fingertips. She must have clonked her head at some point. That possibly explained why she was feeling a little tired and not thinking straight.

She looked round for the cameras. It would be a shame if they had not caught her magnificent performance. Scripted or not, it should have been captured. And she knew, just *knew*, that if the director watched the rushes, he'd immediately recast Kiki as Marguerite. The role demanded a woman of substance. A *lady* of substance.

She spotted the cameras, although there was no sign of the director, or that lovely first AD Saffron. She did however see Detective Constable Camara coming towards her, his long dark coat a contrast against the white tablecloths and shambolic gaiety of the garden party. He held a plastic evidence bag with a letter and envelope inside.

Kiki could also see Marvin Applewhite and his daughter on the terrace, arms about each other's shoulders. A family, albeit a small one. Kiki was struck by how lovely that looked.

"Lady Kiki Lettuces," said the detective, "I am arresting you on suspicion of theft, selling stolen goods and the murder of Phoebe Chiddingfold. You do not have to say anything, but it may harm your defence if you do not mention when questioned something you later rely on in court. Anything you do say may be given in evidence."

Kiki nodded. The bit about Phoebe was a surprise, but she was sure it would all get sorted out. "You'll have to forgive me, officer. I've had a rather tiring day. I think I might need to go and have a lie down."

"We can arrange that," he said and made a call on his phone, asking someone to bring the paramedics over.

SAM AND MARVIN were required at the station to give statements. It was understandable, given there was a dead psychic on the roof with a bolt in his skull. The day had taken its toll on the pair of them and they were silent as they walked round the house to where her van was parked.

"What are you thinking, dad?" she said eventually.

Marvin hummed. "Pea and broad bean shakshuka."

"What?"

"You mean for dinner, right?"

"I meant generally."

He thought. "Pea and broad bean shakshuka. We've got a lot of eggs in and I do like Moroccan spices. I cooked a massive shakshuka for brunch once for Stu Francis and Duncan Norvelle when we were doing summer season in Blackpool. Not that we called it brunch in them days. It was just breakfast for people who've got up late."

Sam shook her head. "You're unbelievable, sometimes."

"Only sometimes?" he said, pretending to be disappointed.

Camara finally came round to meet them. "Follow me

straight to the station and I'll get one of the team to take an initial statement," he said. "Then we'll call you in for further statements as necessary."

"Further statements?" said Marvin.

"This is going to take a while to unpick."

Sam and Marvin followed Camara's car down the driveway to the Candlebroke roundabout on the A158. The roundabout had undergone a recent and dramatic renovation. It had previously featured a colourful display of annual bedding plants. Now it featured a Viking longship. There were heavy tire tracks gouged into the grass along the edge of the roundabout, as though a very large vehicle had tried to swerve round it at speed and failed.

Police officers were directing traffic around the scene. Camara got out of his car up ahead. Sam hopped out of the Piaggio Ape to follow him.

Sam imagined the *Sandraker* had been on the back of a long vehicle, probably Yngve Odinson's low loader. It had slid sideways and the load had been shed onto the roundabout. The *Sandraker's* dragonhead prow faced back towards Candlebroke Hall. If anything, it looked quite pleased with itself. Of the low loader and possible thieves there was no sign.

Camara put a hand over his face and groaned.

"I think it looks quite good there," said Sam.

Camara shot her a look, and not a happy one.

"Just saying," she said.

"Well, it's got to go."

"Oh aye?" said Ragnar Odinson, emerging from nowhere.

"This is your doing," said Camara.

"Me?" The grey-bearded Odinson put an innocent hand on his chest. "I was just out walking me bees. You saw me. An' I reckon that ship's staying there."

"Be sensible, Ragnar."

Ragnar crossed the road and pointed to a sign lodged on the roundabout. Sam peered at it. There was a rough cartoon caricature of a bearded figure who might just be Ragnar.

THIS ROUNDABOUT IS PROUDLY SPONSORED BY ODINSON MEAD — FROM THE CLAN THAT CARES!

"It's my island, Saxon," said Ragnar.

Camara gave a wry look. "Just because you have a sign doesn't mean it's legit, Ragnar."

"Me an' my traffic island reckons otherwise."

Camara sighed wearily.

Sam put a comforting hand on his arm. "Do you like Moroccan food?"

"What?"

"My dad's cooking tonight."

Camara shook his head "This – whatever the hell this is – is going to take a long time to sort out."

"But will you be eating food today?" she said. "Eventually."

He looked at the mess before him. "Eventually."

"Then you know where we live."

She went back to her van and her dad and left the detective to his work.

AFTERWORD

Many thanks for reading book three in the Sam Applewhite series.

We're grateful to all of the readers who continue to support our work and help us to keep writing.

If you can find the time to share your thoughts in a review, it not only helps us, but it helps other readers too.

We're very busy writing new books, so if you want to keep up to date with our work, you could subscribe to our newsletter. Sign up at www.pigeonparkpress.com

Heide and Iain

ABOUT THE AUTHORS

Heide lives in North Warwickshire with her husband and a fluctuating mix of offspring and animals.

Iain lives in South Birmingham with his wife and a fluctuating mix of offspring and animals.

They aren't sure how many novels they've written together since 2011 but it's a surprisingly large number.

ALSO BY HEIDE GOODY AND IAIN GRANT

Clovenhoof

Getting fired can ruin a day...

...especially when you were the Prince of Hell.

Will Satan survive in English suburbia?

Corporate life can be a soul draining experience, especially when the industry is Hell, and you're Lucifer. It isn't all torture and brimstone, though, for the Prince of Darkness, he's got an unhappy Board of Directors.

The numbers look bad.

They want him out.

Then came the corporate coup.

Banished to mortal earth as Jeremy Clovenhoof, Lucifer is going through a mid-immortality crisis of biblical proportion. Maybe if he just tries to blend in, it won't be so bad.

He's wrong.

If it isn't the murder, cannibalism, and armed robbery of everyday life in Birmingham, it's the fact that his heavy metal band isn't getting the respect it deserves, that's dampening his mood.

And the archangel Michael constantly snooping on him, doesn't help.

If you enjoy clever writing, then you'll adore this satirical tour de force, because a good laugh can make you have sympathy for the devil.

Get it now.

Clovenhoof

Oddjobs

It's the end of the world as we know it, but someone still needs to do the paperwork.

Incomprehensible horrors from beyond are going to devour our world but that's no excuse to get all emotional about it. Morag Murray works for the secret government organisation responsible for making sure the apocalypse goes as smoothly and as quietly as possible.

In her first week on the job, Morag has to hunt down a man-eating starfish, solve a supernatural murder and, if she's got time, prevent her own inevitable death.

The first book in a new comedy series by the creators of 'Clovenhoof', Oddjobs is a sideswipe at the world of work and a fantastical adventure featuring amphibian wannabe gangstas, mad old cat ladies, ancient gods, apocalyptic scrabble, fish porn, telepathic curry and, possibly, the end of the world before the weekend.

Oddjobs

A Spell in the Country

Jenny doesn't know what they'll do when they find out she's a wicked witch.

She can't help being a wicked witch. It's in her blood.

She's supposed to plot dark deeds with her foul-mouthed imp familiar, Jizzimus. Instead, she's rescued a girl, Kay, from a terrible fate. To keep her safe they have signed up for a college course in an English country mansion. Jizzimus is not impressed.

The mansion is not the safe haven they thought it would be. They say they want to turn good witches into *great* witches, but witches are going missing, there are far more ghosts round here than there ought to be and there is something huge and terrible in the woods.

If Jenny thought that messing up her witchcraft coursework and getting distracted by the handsome gardener was going to be the worst of her problems, she's dead wrong.

With new witch friends, sexy mind-controller Caroline and soft-hearted herbalist Dee, Jenny's determined to get to the bottom of this mystery. It turns out that at Effie Fray's training college you have to learn fast or die trying.

You'll love this fun-loving witch academy book because sometimes it needs friends to show us how to be a better version of ourselves.

A Spell in the Country

Printed in Great Britain
by Amazon